Andrew Linn
Cambridge 1991

Scandinavian Language Contacts

Edited by
P. STURE URELAND and IAIN CLARKSON
University of Mannheim

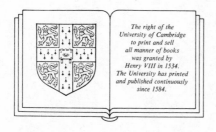

The right of the
University of Cambridge
to print and sell
all manner of books
was granted by
Henry VIII in 1534.
The University has printed
and published continuously
since 1584.

CAMBRIDGE UNIVERSITY PRESS

Cambridge
London   New York   New Rochelle
Melbourne   Sydney

Published by the Press Syndicate of the University of Cambridge
The Pitt Building, Trumpington Street, Cambridge CB2 1RP
32 East 57th Street, New York, NY 10022, USA
296 Beaconsfield Parade, Middle Park, Melbourne 3206, Australia

First published 1984

Printed in Great Britain by
The University Press, Cambridge

Library of Congress catalogue card number: 83–18871

British Library cataloguing in publication data
Scandinavian language contacts.
1. Scandinavian languages
I. Ureland, P. Sture II. Clarkson, Iain
439'.5   PD 1545

ISBN 0521 25685 2

UP

Contents

1 Introduction

P. STURE URELAND AND IAIN CLARKSON

The articles contained in this volume describe Scandinavia and its languages in the past and the present. Here Scandinavia is treated as a linguistic and cultural unit, and the language contacts within this area are treated according to the geographical direction of contact with other non-Scandinavian languages: in the north, in the east, in the west, and in the south.

The basic tenets in most of the articles of the book are: (a) that the essence of every language is the way in which it varies from a geographical point of view in its development through time and its social use; (b) that this variation is the result of a whole series of factors of which language contact between bilingual or bilectal individuals (due to natural or literary bilingualism) is the major one.[1] Thus variation and change in language are caused by bilingual speakers everywhere that we can register social upheavals due to (1) *conquest* (e.g. the British Isles and Normandy in the Middle Ages), (2) *settlement* (Iceland, northern Scandinavia, Finland, Russia, and the Baltic States), (3) *trade* (the Varangian settlements in the Ladoga, Novgorod and Kiev areas during the Viking Age or the Low German colonies in the cities of the Hanseatic League), and last but not least (4) *literary bilingualism* as a result of learning, religion, the law, scholarship – the use of (Medieval) Latin as the language of the church, the administration, and the legal system. In our century this learned influence has even been reinforced by the coining of a Greek–Latin nomenclature for technical innovations. As far as the continental Scandinavian languages are concerned the role of German (in particular Middle Low German in the Middle Ages (1100–1500) and New High German after the Reformation in the 16th, 17th and 19th centuries), French (in the 18th and 19th centuries) and English (in the 19th and 20th centuries) must also be considered in an overall treatment of language change and development in Scandinavia since 1100 AD. Specific cases of the fundamental influence which other European languages had upon the Scandinavian languages are discussed in the articles published in this volume.

1 Language contact as an impetus to linguistic change

The role of language contact in causing linguistic change is not unknown in the history of linguistics. However, the genetic-evolutional view of change dominated the field in the past century and still prevails in most modern introductory books on historical linguistics. The spectacular success of the evolutionists in the Neogrammarian camp as well as the consolidation of the synchronic structuralist and generative paradigms in this century has made research on language contact a peripheral activity. The search for inherently conditioned evolutional laws – *Lautgesetze* – was the preoccupation of the majority of German scholars and of those working within the German tradition of historical linguistics. Also, the search for synchronic systematism in structural and generative grammars gave little or no space to the study of linguistic change caused by languages in contact.

This statement may be an overgeneralization as far as some of the leading Indogermanists (e.g. Whitney 1881, Windisch 1897, Wackernagel 1904, Pisani 1974: 17, Tovar 1976 and 1977), Germanists (Paul 1886: 390),[2] Slavists (Miklosich 1861) Celtologists (Pokorny 1927–30), and Romanists (Ascoli 1887, Sandfeld 1930, 1938 and Schuchardt 1882–3, 1891, 1909, 1914) are concerned. For them language mixture and borrowing were equally important factors in the development of languages.[3]

Since the year 1887 when Ascoli coined the term *substratum* for a specific type of language contact, many more dimensions of language contact have come to light.[4] In the past few decades especially linguists and ethnologists have focused more and more on the bi- or multilingual individual: the focus of linguistic change is no longer exclusively on the linguistic systems themselves but rather on the bilingual speakers. This change of perspective occurred after the publication of two monographs on bilingualism that described the bilingual situation and linguistic changes in Switzerland and in the Scandinavian settlements of the United States (Weinreich 1953 and Haugen 1953 respectively).

What is important in these two works is the emphasis on the powerful effect which interlinguistic contacts exert upon the competence of bilingual speakers.

2   External and internal language contacts in Scandinavia

Language contact in Scandinavia is the main topic of this volume. Specialists from particular fields (Nordic, Germanic, Slavic, and Finno-Ugric studies) have been invited to write articles on the rich spectrum of language contact in Scandinavia. The Scandinavian languages are an excellent object of study in the field of languages in contact. Although Scandinavia is geographically on the fringe of Europe, innovations from the west, south, east or north have entered the Scandinavian languages at various periods in different ways throughout their history.

Two major directions of contact are involved here: contacts within Scandinavia proper and external contacts with non-Scandinavian languages from outside this area. The emphasis in this book is on external contacts, i.e., Scandinavian in contact with languages outside Scandinavia. Since 1000 AD some of the Scandinavian languages – Danish, Norwegian, and Swedish – have undergone dramatic changes due to foreign influence, whereas the Insular Scandinavian languages (Faroese and Icelandic) have preserved more of an Old Norse typology after their immigration to the Atlantic Isles. This is probably due more to a specific socio-cultural development than to their relative geographical isolation in the west. In spite of the differences between the Scandinavian languages and dialects within the vast area of northern Europe we will treat Scandinavia as a linguistic and cultural unit where Scandinavian is spoken or has been spoken earlier.

According to the interests and expertise of the contributors certain geographical areas within Scandinavia proper and outside have been chosen where Scandinavian language contacts have taken place or where traces of bilingual processes in the past are still visible in the languages spoken in these areas. Examples are the North Germanic dialects spoken south of the Danish–German border (see the article by Bent Søndergaard),[5] or in the north the linguistic fusion of Norwegian and Russian – *Russenorsk* – (see the article by Ingvild Broch and Ernst Håkon Jahr), in the east the possible remnants of North Germanic syntax in the North Russian dialects (see Baldur Panzer's article), or in the west the development of the Faroese language (see Björn Hagström's article) and the development of the Swedish language in America (see Sture Ureland's article).

3 Inner drift and external forces of change

There is an implicit claim hidden in the title of the present volume: Throughout their history the Scandinavian languages have been subjected to varying degrees of change through contact – direct or indirect – with their neighbours in the west, south, east, and north. The significance of an internal trend of development due to inner drift, which Scandinavian shares with other western languages, is not denied here. However, none of the Scandinavian languages have existed in a state of isolation, not even the most remote mountain dialects in the Norwegian *fjord* landscape, in the vast Swedish forest area, on the stormy Faroe Isles, or on the volcanic West Islands south of Iceland. Without considering the contact with other dialects or with languages which have a more important communicative role it is not possible to describe adequately any of the present-day dialects or standard languages spoken in Scandinavia. If we view the Scandinavian languages from a panchronic and pandialectal point of view the external forces of linguistic change seem overwhelming. It is the lack of contact-linguistic information from the past which forces the historical linguist to treat prehistorical language change as a biological process. This genetic–evolutional perspective of linguistic change is abundantly represented in all handbooks on Scandinavian philology – a heritage of the historical–biological view in the linguistics of the past century.

The contact linguistic perspective, on the other hand, draws more on the ethnic–social view. However, the important role which it plays in the development of a given language has certainly not been acknowledged, since the processes of contact in bi- and multilingual areas cannot easily be formalized in categorical development schemata. A *tertium quid* arises through the process of contact, so that in the interferences or transferences the seed of a new linguistic form or of a new linguistic variety can be detected. It is only a question of social, political or cultural acceptance, whether this or that interference or transference structure in the speech of bilinguals will be accepted as an innovation by the native speakers or rejected as an alien element in the linguistic system.

4 Earlier and present research on language contact in Scandinavia

The present volume deals with the Scandinavian languages from a Pan-Scandinavian and contact linguistic point of view. This is, however, not the first occasion in the history of Scandinavian philology and linguistics that scholars have dealt with the linguistic and cultural convergences between Scandinavia and other European areas. But these scholars have mostly been interested in selected areas of Scandinavia, not in Scandinavia as an entity. A number of philological meetings with aims which differed in accordance with the interests of the organizers took place in the fifties and sixties. Beside this conference activity, some individual scholars with contact linguistic orientation should also be mentioned. These locally oriented contact linguistic activities can be summarized as follows:

(a) Four Viking Conferences on *Norse–Celtic Contacts* from 1950 to 1961. The proceedings of these conferences are now available (cf. Simpson (ed.) 1954, Falck (ed.) 1955, Eldjárn (ed.) 1958, and Small (ed.) 1965).

(b) *Celtic–Norse* research as published in the *Proceedings of the International Congress of Celtic Studies* (papers by Jackson and Sommerfelt) ed. by Brian O'Cuiv 1962.

(c) *Scando–Slavic* relations as described in *Varangian Problems* 1970, The Eastern Connections of Nordic Peoples in the Viking Period and Early Middle Ages (ed. by Rahbek Schmidt *et al.*). (For a summary of this research see Söderlind 1978 and Söderlind's and Lägreid's articles in this volume.)

(d) North-Germanic and Finno-Ugric contacts have been treated in two recent symposia and one Festschrift: *Nordskandinaviens historia i tvärvetenskaplig belysning* ed. by Baudou and Dahlstedt (1980) and *Cultural Contacts in the Arctic Area* ed. by Nylund and Wande (1979); *Språkhistoria och språkkontakt i Finland och Nord-Skandinavien* ed. by Dahlstedt *et al.* (1982).

However, linguistic and cultural contacts between the Lapps, the Finns and the North Germanic population have also been described in a considerable number of monographs and articles since the past century: *Lappish–North Germanic*: Thomsen 1967 (1870); Qvigstad 1893; Wiklund 1892, 1914; Nesheim 1953, 1958, 1964 and Sköld 1961; Hansegård 1967 and 1971; Ruong 1982; Korhonen 1974 and 1982, and Dahlstedt 1982. *Lappish–Finnish–(North Germanic)*: Qvigstad 1883; Äimä 1908; Itkonen 1941 and 1966; Nesheim 1967; Hansegård 1968 and 1977; Loman 1974 and 1975; Jaakkola 1973; Korhonen 1982 and Dahlstedt 1982; Aikio and Lindgren 1982 and Jernsletten 1982. Laurén and Strömman 1981; Allardt and Starck 1981 and Woivaldin 1981 deal with the sociolinguistic situation of the Swedes in Finland and on the Åland Islands. Korhonen's article in this volume is thus a further contribution to the description of the Lappish–North Germanic, and the Finnish–Lappish language contacts.

(e) The *Pan-Scandinavia contributions* to contact linguistics will also be mentioned: Haugen and Markey's 1972 State of the Art report *The Scandinavian Languages: Fifty Years of Linguistic Research* contains a lot of scattered information on Scandinavian contact linguistics as does Haugen's monumental work *The Scandinavian Languages* 1976 (cf. also Ureland 1980 and Braunmüller 1982 on syntactic change in Scandinavian). From a language-cultivating point of view books and surveys of the Scandinavian languages have been written, which are concerned with the social and political future of the Nordic languages (cf. Dahlstedt 1974; Molde (ed.) 1974; Sigurd (ed.) 1977 and Loman 1982. Munske's article in the present volume on the

French transferences in Scandinavian phonology can also be seen in the Pan-Scandinavian context.

(f) Recent conferences held within Scandinavia on minorities and bilingualism should not be forgotten in this context: *Grannspråk och minoritetsspråk* 1975; *The First, Second, and Third Nordic Conferences on Bilingualism*, the proceedings of which were edited by Skutnabb-Kangas 1977, Stedje and Trampe 1979, and Ejerhed and Henrysson 1981. *The Symposium on Mutual Language Understanding in the Nordic Countries*, proceedings, edited by Elert 1981, treated the problem of semi-communication between the Scandinavian peoples. Outside Scandinavia proper, papers on Scandinavian language contacts have also been presented at various conferences and symposia: seven papers on Scandinavian language contacts were published in the proceedings of the First Symposium entitled *Contact+Confli(c)t* in Brussels which were edited by P. H. Nelde and published in 1980 (cf. Braunmüller 1980, Haugen 1980, Hyldgaard-Jensen 1980, Koller 1980, Søndergaard 1980, Ureland 1980). At the Second Symposium entitled *Contact+Confli(c)t* in Brussels in 1982 and also edited by P. Nelde 1983, three other papers were presented on Scandinavian language contacts (cf. Laurén and Strömman 1983, Rischel 1983, de Vries 1983). After the *Glasgow Minority Conference* in 1980 six articles were published which deal with Scandinavian minority languages and problems: Haugen 1981, Keskitalo 1981, Oftedal 1981, Poulsen 1981, Reuter 1981, Søndergaard 1981. At the 5th Symposium on *Language Contact in Europe* held in Mannheim in 1982 E. H. Jahr presented a paper on 'Language Contact in Northern Norway'. In Tokyo, at the 13th International Congress of Linguists a Work Group on Language Contact in Europe was organized, in which Jahr and Ureland presented aspects of Scandinavian contacts to be presented in this volume and elsewhere (cf. P. Nelde, P. S. Ureland and I. Clarkson (eds.) forthcoming).

(g) In the past few years a number of *projects on multilingual or bilingual problems and conflicts* – mainly those of migrant workers in Scandinavia – have been launched, of which only a few can be enumerated here: The *Sprins*-group in Gothenburg is dealing with the linguistic development of the children of guest workers in Sweden (cf. Tingbjörn 1982). Another group in the same city is dealing with *Second Language Acquisition by Adult Immigrants* (cf. Allwood, Strömqvist and Voionmaa 1981–6), which is an extension of a pan-European *Research Project of the European Science Foundation on the Migration Workers of Europe* which is based in Strasbourg (cf. Perdue (ed.) 1982).

The interest in ethnic, bilingual and bilectal perspectives is spreading in Scandinavia at the present time: A *Research Programme on Urbanization and Language Change* is being planned by quite a few institutes of linguistics and Nordic languages in Denmark, Norway, Finland, and Sweden (see *Nordic Linguistic Bulletin* Vol. 6 (1982), No. 2–3: 35–50 for further details). This extensive research by nine different Scandinavian institutes will hopefully be supported by research councils for the humanities in each of the four Scandinavian countries so as to create an interesting cooperative project on contact linguistic research in Scandinavia.

(h) Some recent monographs and articles on language contact, bilingualism and general problems of contact linguistics which are characteristic of the recently awakened interest in ethnicity in Scandinavia should also be mentioned here: Els Oksaar's early writings on bilingualism have inspired many of the ethnolinguistically oriented projects enumerated in section (g) above (cf. Oksaar 1966, 1972, 1976, and 1982). Skutnabb-Kangas 1981 has drawn extensively on Oksaar's writings and given an extensive account of the dilemma of bilingualism in Scandinavia, in particular that of Finland. Tingbjörn and Andersson 1981 describe the difficulties of the children of the migrant workers in the Swedish school system. Rönmark and Wikström 1980 describe, from the viewpoint of educational science, the bilingual situation in Torneå Valley. Raag 1982 treats the Swedish interferences in the lexicon of Estonian bilingual speakers living in Sweden. Johansson 1973, 1975 and 1977 has dealt extensively with the educational problems of the Swedish Lapps from pedagogical and sociolinguistic points of view. Finally, Broch and Jahr 1981 is a Norwegian version of their article on Russo-Norwegian which appears here in English. Olsen 1981 and Rischel 1983 describe the ethnolinguistic situation of the Greenlanders.

The list of contact linguistic monographs which deal with minorities, bilingualism and migrant workers in Scandinavia is by no means complete here. It has only been possible to give a cross-section of publications which exemplify the general trend towards an ethnically oriented type of research which Scandinavian linguistics seems to be undergoing at the present time. The contact linguistic impulses from abroad have in the past few years been so numerous as to diminish the former formal linguistic dominance among Scandinavian linguists.

5   A programme for Scandinavian contact linguistics

This volume is therefore to be seen as a contribution to the research on contact linguistics in Scandinavia. Our aim is to stimulate other scholars in the field of Scandinavian studies to adopt a more ethnic and socially oriented approach to the development of the Scandinavian languages and dialects rather than the overly theoretical emphasis of contemporary approaches which are principally concerned with one-dimensional systemic theory construction. Linguistic variation and change are the essence of every language. Any theory formation which disregards this fact is doomed to sterility, because it does not account for the essential feature of a given language: variation. In a natural language this variation is created by a whole set of factors and here language contact between bilingual individuals is seen as the major cause of language change. The contact between two languages or between two or more varieties of the same language within one and the same individual must be seen from an ethnic–social viewpoint. The cultural and social aspects of language contact play a large role in that they give us an explanation of why this variant gained the upper-hand in the rise of a standard language or why that variant became obsolete. The processes involved in the establishment of royal and ecclesiastic bureaucracies in Scandinavia must be studied in detail in order to understand what models of written and spoken forms arose due to foreign or native models. The formation of the Scandinavian writing systems from the runes in the 3rd century AD to the first Old Norse manuscripts of the 12th century cannot be understood unless the foreign prototypes are studied and compared. This statement refers not just to the writing but also to the lexicon and the syntax of all Old Scandinavian texts. The documentation and compilation of the oldest law texts of the 12th, 13th and 14th centuries were inspired by Roman law. Similarly the rise of religious literature is to be seen in the framework of christianization through Latin and the beginnings of Scandinavian national literatures in an international West-European framework. As far as Scandinavia is concerned, the models and ideals created on the basis of Latin and Middle Low German texts were decisive for linguistic development. It is this type of learned bilingualism which first put its stamp on all Scandinavian languages. Later on, with the arrival of Middle Low German tradesmen and artisans in the continental Scandinavian areas, longer or shorter periods of natural bilingualism in all the important trading centres of the Hansa (Bergen, Visby, Stockholm, etc.) must be assumed. (See Seip 1915–18, and 1919; Brattegard 1945; Wessén 1954; Törnqvist 1977 and Elmevik 1979 for references on the Low German, Dutch and Scandinavian contacts during the Middle Ages.)

New horizons and new viewpoints will be the result, if all fields of Scandinavian linguistics are concentrated in a historical, synchronic, and ethnic–social approach. The goal is to solve the multifaceted problem of language change which is due to contacts between languages in specific areas during periods of known bilingualism (natural or learned). The present volume on Scandinavian contact linguistics is only the beginning of such a large-scale undertaking. Only when linguists from all branches of the discipline are willing to cooperate with each other in the new framework will it be possible to carry through this project successfully.[6]

6 The language contact approach to Scandinavian variation and change

6.1 In the north

The contributions to the present volume on Scandinavian language contact are presented in a geographical order: north, east, west, and south. Not only the geographical perspectives of the direction of language contact are involved here, but the different chronological order of contact in the history of the Scandinavian languages is also implied: the present, the past *and* the future. In accordance with the geographical plan the first section of the book is headed North Scandinavia. In the first article Ingvild Broch and Håkon Jahr describe the pidgin language *Russenorsk* which developed in northern Norway towards the end of the 18th century as a result of contacts between Russian merchants and Norwegian fishermen and continued in use until the beginning of this century. The background to the development of this pidgin is the Pomor trade – Russian merchants sailed west along the coast in the spring, traded grain for fish with the Norwegian fishermen during the summer months and returned to Russia in the autumn. The fact that its use was largely limited to the summer months is the reason why *Russenorsk*, which is one of the few genuine pidgin languages recorded in Europe, did not become creolized, despite being in use over a period of 140 years, but remained relatively simple in its structure.

Russian and Norwegian were the main languages from which *Russenorsk* was developed but Lappish, Finnish, Swedish and a number of western European languages – English, Low German/Dutch and even French – were also represented. Broch and Jahr give the fullest linguistic description yet available of *Russenorsk* and present a detailed account of the fascinating historical background to this little-known episode in the linguistic history of Europe.

6.2   In the east

The borderline between trade and conquest was never clearly drawn in the distant past when other conditions of commerce and standards of behaviour prevailed. The Scandinavians or the Vikings in Russia are the topic of two articles written by Annelies Lägreid and Stefan Söderlind. Lägreid accepts the *Roþs*-hypothesis suggested in the past century by the Dane Thomsen (1877) as the most convincing explanation of the ethnic terms *Russia* and *Russian*. This claims that these terms derive from an old Swedish prefixal element meaning 'oarsmen or sailors living in the Province of *Roslagen*', situated north-east of Stockholm on the Baltic coast. Söderlind rejects this established hypothesis and derives the ethnic terms *Rossía* and *russkij* from the Proto-Slavic term for Goths in Russia in the 5th century – **Rus'*, a feminine singular collective form derived from the Proto-Slavic adjective **rusu* 'red' – which meant 'the Red-Blond People'. This term was adopted by bilingual Goths and changed in accordance with their phonological system into **Rauþs* [roːþs]. By suggesting two different stems, one Proto-Slavic with a *u*-vowel (**Rus'*) and one germanized Gothic with an *o*-vowel (**Rauþs*), Söderlind explains the occurrence of Middle Greek (*Rhōs*), Estonian (*Roots*), and Finnish (*Ruotsi*). (The difference in the meaning of the latter two words (Sweden) is also explained.) The consequences of Söderlind's Red-Blond-People hypothesis for a possible reassessment of the rise of the kingdom of the Rus' are still to be investigated and evaluated in the light of all historical and archaeological research carried out lately both by Soviet and Scandinavian scholars.

Lägreid attaches more importance to the latest archaeological discoveries, details of which were published in the *Norwegian Archaeological Review* in the 1970s (*inter alia* by Avdusin, Bulkin, Kleijn, and Lebedev). The investigations of the Leningrad and Moscow archaeologists have cast a new light on the old controversy between Normanists and anti-Normanists. Söderlind's article consists of a summary of past research and a synthesis of the Normanist and anti-Normanist hypotheses: It was neither the Slavs nor the Varangians who founded the East Slavic Kingdom, but the Goths.

Baldur Panzer's article in the volume is also to be seen as a contribution along the lines of the contact linguistic development outlined above, with reference to the Russian dialects, although Panzer's conclusions on the inner cause of the rise of the post-positive particles and the possessive perfect in the North Russian dialects are not clearly in favour of contact linguistic processes. He examines the evidence as to whether these structures were developed as a result of internal development or whether they were the result of interference processes. In the case of the post-positive article Panzer concludes that the crucial question remains unresolved as to whether the development of an article or a quasi-article from a demonstrative represents a phenomenon which is typologically a parallel to the Germanic or Romance languages or whether interference occurred as a result of language contact over an extended period. He concludes that this is not impossible but equally that it is impossible to find conclusive historical or dialect-geographical evidence to prove it.[7]

Panzer also examines the development of the possessive perfect in North Germanic and North Russian with a brief look at Latin, the Romance and West Germanic languages. On considering the question of whether there is a historical connection in the sense of language contact and a loan relationship or whether these forms were the result of parallel but independent development, Panzer concludes that the hypothesis of parallel development within Russian seems more likely to him since it is not quite possible to link the possessive perfect to the oldest period of Russian during which a Germanic influence is most probable. After his examination of these two phenomena it seems to him that the theoretical question of how borrowings are to be distinguished from genuine parallel developments still remains unresolved. However, the reader is struck by the correlation in the geographical distribution on the maps presented of the two structures around the areas formerly ruled by the city of Novgorod and the (North) Germanic settlements in these areas. Are the two structures treated here not to be seen as products of 'Germanic–Slavic contacts from the earliest period' or were they brought about by 'the later Germanic influence during the Hanseatic League'? Although Panzer does not regard the evidence as sufficiently conclusive to permit a definite positive answer to the two questions, the reader is free to make his choice between the two alternatives: parallel development or interference.

A further chapter also focuses on the contacts in the east (and north) of the Scandinavian Peninsula: Olavi Korhonen's article on the migrations of the Lapps and the Finns in the Baltic States, in Finland, and northern Sweden. He deals with the geographical spread of five lexical items which are used as terms in navigation in Finnish, Estonian, Swedish, Lappish, and Russian. The spread of these terms around the gulfs of Finland and Bothnia is seen as a result of cultural contacts during the Viking Age and the late Middle Ages. The most interesting of the five terms is the term for a (rowing) boat: Finnish *haapio* 'a boat hollowed out of an aspen tree trunk', Estonian *haabjas*, East and North Swedish *håp/hap*. Ethnographical material and historical sources are drawn on to illuminate the important role of the aspen dug-out in Finnish culture. Judging from the shape of the boat its origin must be eastern i.e. the inner areas of Russia. How far west and north was the aspen dug-out used? In what period did it spread from its eastern area of origin into the Baltic States (Estonia and Latvia), Finland and northern Sweden? Who were the people who brought it to these far-off places? Two even more important questions are asked in this context: Why did people who used the aspen dug-out migrate into the areas around the Gulf of Bothnia? What activities brought them so far?

By using a dialect-geographical method combined with ethnographical information Korhonen asserts that the distribution of the boat term *haapio* in the areas just mentioned corresponds well to the travelling patterns which are known to have been prevalent during the Viking Age and the late Middle Ages.[8] It is known that the Vikings travelled extensively through the Gulf of Finland and up the River Neva into Lake Ladoga. A route via the River Dvina further south was also available for entering the Russian river system. The participation of the Finns in these expeditions in the east and the north still remains an unwritten page in the history of the Varangians. However, the spread of the soft dug-out as evidenced by the spread of the Finnish terms into Estonia, Latvia, Finland and around the Gulf of Bothnia into Northern Sweden – into the North Swedish and Lappish dialects – gives us new perspectives on the Viking period in the east and the later Finnish migrations during the late Middle Ages.

Korhonen considers the *Cwenas* mentioned in the *Anglo-Saxon Chronicle* to have been Finns and the boats which Ottar mentions as being used in the attacks on Norse settlements in the north to have been some sort of dug-outs. They were light and could be easily carried between the lakes and rivers, and even across mountains. In the light of this information we should, according to Korhonen, study the activities of the Rus' in Russia, who must also have been dependent upon this type of boat for travelling between Novgorod and Constantinople.

6.3   In the west

After this description of eastern migrations and settlement we turn to the west, to the Faroe Isles in the Atlantic, the language of which is also a product of trade and settlement by Norwegian Vikings and Danish merchants. After the Nordic Union in 1380 the Faroes became a part of the Dano-Norwegian Kingdom. From this period on the bilingual situation arose, as the people were Norwegian-speaking but the language of the administration was Danish. The Reformation resulted in a linguistic catastrophe for Norway and the Faroes since no bible translation became available for the development of a national standard language in Norway and the Faroes. The foundation for bilingualism was laid in the Faroes during this period. West-Nordic Faroese and East-Nordic Danish were by now so different that Danish clergymen and officials could not understand the language spoken in the Faroes.

Björn Hagström discusses the consequences of the lack of a national language in the Faroes, especially for the development of the technical vocabulary in all official domains. The Danish influence finally grew so strong that it threatened to ruin the Faroese language. However, unlike most Island Celtic languages and the Scandinavian dialects – the Norn – of the Orkneys and Shetland, Faroese survived as a living language and has succeeded in establishing a written norm.[9] It has developed into the language of local administration, the church, the primary school, the newspapers, and the radio. In his detailed article Hagström gives us ample evidence of the success of language cultivation and language planning in a bilingual community. Language contact as found in the Faroes tells us a lot about how the negative effects of bilingualism can be overcome when intelligent and effective measures are taken by interested members of a speech-community and where the will to maintain the native language is the most decisive factor in its survival.

6.4   In the south

If we turn to the southern part of the Scandinavian area, to Schleswig, we find two ethnic groups which can be said to have been forced into a bi- or multilingual situation: the South Jutlandish and North Frisian minorities south of the Danish–German border.

Bent Søndergaard examines the problems of interference in the dialects spoken in Schleswig. Schleswig is an area where five Germanic varieties coexist: Low German, North Frisian, Southern Jutlandish, High German, and Standard Danish. In his study of the effects of Danish–German–Frisian multilingualism he concentrates on the problems of interference by German on the Danish dialects spoken in Schleswig. On the basis of considerable documentation he presents a picture of extremely widespread lexical interference and – to a lesser degree – of phonological and morphological interference between German and Danish. He also finds evidence of lexical and syntactic interference from Danish on German.

Nils-Erik Larsen takes a different approach to the consequences of multi- and bilingualism in his statistical investigation of language death in Rodenäs, a North Frisian community on the Danish–German border. His study is conceived within the new theoretical concept of contact linguistics. He examines the statistical data which he presents in relation to the quantitative and the qualitative aspects of language death. His aim is to describe the language shifts which are taking place between the five language varieties spoken in the area (Standard German, Low German, Standard Danish, South Jutlandish and North Frisian) and to predict the likely trends in language shifts in the future. Using data from a survey carried out in Rodenäs, Larsen presents statistics on the diminishing number of dialect speakers in relation to different age groups in the population and concludes that from a quantitative point of view the dialects are threatened by language death. The parallel deterioration in the quality of the spoken dialect is apparent in the steadily increasing proportion of dialect speakers who are unable to speak their dialect fluently, the 'semi-speakers', a phenomenon which has also been observed among the Scottish Gaelic speakers of East Sutherland by Dorian 1973 and 1981. Larsen does not present explicit examples of the deterioration of the quality of the spoken language but concludes on purely statistical grounds that a progressive deterioration is taking place in these varieties which is likely to lead to language death in the foreseeable future.[10]

6.5   Pan Scandinavian

A completely different factor – that of literary or learned bilingualism – is the topic of an article by Horst Munske on the transferences of nasal vowels in the graphemics and phonology of Germanic languages, with emphasis on the Scandinavian languages (Swedish, Norwegian, and Danish). He analyses the processes by which the French loan words with nasal vowels are integrated phonologically and graphemically into the Germanic languages. The French nasal vowels are an excellent topic for describing the superstratum effect of learned bilingualism in specific Germanic languages. He elaborates the grapho-phonemic correspondence rules which underlie the spelling of French nasal vowels in 190 French lexemes, that is: how they are pronounced and spelled in the West Germanic (German, English, and Dutch) and the Scandinavian languages, e.g. French *pardon* occurs spoken as German [par'duːn] or [par'doŋ], as English [paːdn], but as Swedish [par'dʉːn], or [par'doŋ]; French *alliance* is spelled as German *Allianz*, Dutch *alliantie*, and Norwegian and Swedish *allians*. The language-cultivating factor is dominant in many transference processes so that a national spelling of the French nasal vowel is often preferred (especially in Norwegian and Swedish, whereas Danish more often keeps the French spelling). Munske's article is Pan-Scandinavian in its scope and is an important contribution to the complex task of describing the effects of literary or learned bilingualism on the standardized varieties of the Scandinavian and other European languages.

6.6   Transatlantic

The last contribution to the volume is a chapter by Sture Ureland which deals with how the language of the Swedish immigrants in Texas, Kansas, and Illinois has been changed by contact with American English. The main topic of the article is the nature of interference in American Swedish. It is concerned with the question whether the interferences or transferences documented in Ureland's tape-recordings follow a certain pattern, an ordered selection of lexical items and grammatical constructions, or whether such interferences and transferences are to be seen as accidental processes in the speech of bilingual American Swedes. Here data of created americanisms found in Vilhelm Moberg's immigration novels are systematically compared with authentic data documented in field work on American Swedish. By comparing his own data of interferences and transferences in the speech of American Swedes recorded in the 1960s and 1970s with those of other investigators of American–Swedish bilingualism (Hasselmo and Hedblom), Ureland arrives at the conclusion that the hypothesis of 'a scale of adoptability' as suggested by Haugen in the 1950s and later elaborated into a hypothesis of 'a communicative norm' (cf. Haugen 1977) is inadequate for describing the processes of interference, integration, and transference in such bilingual communities as the Scandinavian settlements in North America.

Notes

1 The contact between two varieties (dialects or sociolects) of the same language, which causes changes in the speech of bilectal individuals (bilectalism), is also meant here. For the purposes of our discussion 'language contact' has been used in the wider sense.
2 In the first edition of *Prinzipien der Sprachgeschichte* (1880) by H. Paul there is no chapter on 'Sprachmischung'. It was only after Paul had read Schuchardt's works on creole languages (1882–3) and Schuchardt's book *Slawo-Deutsches und Slawo-Italienisches* (1884) that he was forced to include the chapter on the mixing of languages in the second edition of 1886 (cf. pp. 390–403).
3 See for instance the following quotation from Schuchardt which reflects a view of the growth of European languages. It is completely different from that of the

established Neogrammarian or structuralist paradigms but corresponds closely to the conception of growth and change underlying the articles of the present volume:

Mischung durchsetzt überhaupt alle Sprachentwicklung; sie tritt ein zwischen Einzelsprachen (= Idiolects/S.U.), zwischen nahen Mundarten, zwischen verwandten und selbst zwischen ganz unverwandten Sprachen. Ob von Mischung oder von Entlehnung, Nachahmung, fremden Einfluss die Rede ist, immer habenwir wesensgleiche Erscheinungen vor uns. (cf. Schuchardt 1928: 193).

4 In Romance studies the contact perspective has an even longer history. Since the late Middle Ages Spanish and Italian scholars have occupied themselves with the question of the origin of Romance languages – the *Corruption hypothesis* according to which Spanish, Italian, and French are corrupted products of the mixture of Basque, Celtic, Arabic, Germanic on the one hand, and of Latin on the other, e.g. Juan de Mena, Juan de Lucena (15th c.), Flavio Biondo, Leonardo Bruni (15th c.), Juan de Valdes (16th c.), B. Aldrete (17th c.) and Mayáns i Siscár (18th c.) (see Kontzi (ed.) 1978: 3 and 1982: 3–4 and Schmitt 1982: 40–5 for further details on the rise of the Romance languages).

5 For more details on Danish–German language contacts and bilingualism in Schleswig see Wilts 1978, Hyldgaard-Jensen 1980, Søndergaard 1980 and 1981. See also Skautrup 1947: 296–301; 1953: 117–27; and 1968: 41–7.

6 Such a research undertaking involving cooperation between contact linguists from various fields is already a fact on the European continent. As a result of a number of symposia and conferences hundreds of articles on the consequences of language contact in Europe have been published. Two coordinating centres of this research are the Linguistic Circle of Mannheim and the Research Centre on Multilingualism in Brussels (cf. the publications in the series on *Language Contact in Europe* ed. S. Ureland 1978, 1979, 1980, 1981 and 1982 and on *Contact and Confli(c)t* ed. P. Nelde 1980 and 1983).

7 In two articles on morphosyntactic and syntactic parallels between Swedish, Finnish, Latvian, and Russian, which also take account of data from Runic Swedish and Old Russian it was assumed that a prehistoric *Sprachbund* existed around the Baltic (cf. Ureland 1978, 1980). The bilingual or multilingual Varangians or *Rus'* acted as distributors of particular shared features in phrase structure and the lexicon of the Old Scandinavian, Slavic, and Baltic dialects.

8 Dahlstedt (1982) has published an article on the geographical spread of the Finnish/Lappish term for 'reindeer cow' from northern Finnish dialects into the Lappish and North-Swedish dialects. This spread of a lexical item (Sw. *vaja* Lappish *váža* Finnish *vaadin*) is a beautiful example of how cultural contacts in the north created linguistic adaptation and integration through migrating bilinguals or multilinguals. Dahlstedt's investigation lends support to Korhonen's claims of extensive spread of lexical items in space through migrations and bilingual or multilingual speakers.

9 For more details on the contacts between Insular Norse, Insular Celtic (Gaelic and Irish) and English (Scots) see the bibliography in Werner 1964; for an orientation on the present-day ethnolinguistic situation of the 'small' languages in the extreme west (Faroese, Gaelic, Welsh, Breton and Irish) see Greene 1981.

10 For more references on the Danish–German–Frisian contacts see the bibliography compiled by Søndergaard (ed.) 1980. See also Fink (ed.) 1979 and Karker 1981 for more details on the present-day ethnolinguistic situation in South Schleswig.

Bibliography

Aikio, M. and A.-R. Lindgren, 1982: Den finske minoriteten i Nord–Noreg. In Bull and Jetne (eds.) 1982: 118–33.

Äimä, F., 1908: Lappalaisia lainasanoja suomen murteissa. In *Suomalais-Ugrilaisen Seuran Aikakauslehti* 25: 3–64. Helsinki.

Allardt, E. and C. Starck 1981: *Språkgränser och samhällsstruktur. Finlandssvenskarna i ett jämförande perspektiv.* Lund.

Allwood, J., S. Strömqvist and K. Voionmaa, 1981–6: The Ecology of Adult Language Acquisition – Second Language Acquisition by Adult Immigrants. A Research Project of the European Science Foundation Centre of the Swedish Group: Dept. of Linguistics. Univ. of Gothenburg. *Nordic Linguistic Bulletin* 6 (1): 17–38.

Ascoli, G. I. 1887: *Sprachwissenschaftliche Briefe. Übersetzt von B. Güterboek.* Leipzig.

Baudou, E. and K. H. Dahlstedt (eds.), 1980: *Nordskandinaviens historia i tvärvetenskaplig belysning.* Acta Universitatis Umensis. Umeå Studies in the Humanities 24. Umeå.

Brattegard, O. 1945: *Die Mittelniederdeutsche Geschäftssprache des hansischen Kaufmanns zu Bergen.* Vol. 1: *Die Sprache der Blütezeit.* Vol. 2: *Der Ausklang des Niederdeutschen.* Skrifter fra Norges Handelshøyskole. Bergen.

Braunmüller, K. 1980: Formen der Mehrsprachigkeit in Skandinavien. In Nelde (ed.) 1980: 319–24.
   1982: *Syntaxtypologische Studien zum Germanischen.* Tübingen.

Broch, I. and E. H. Jahr, 1981: *Russenorsk – Et Pidginspråk i Norge.* Tromsø-Studier i språkvitenskap 3. Oslo.

Bull, T. and K. Jetne (eds.), 1982: *Nordnorsk. Språkarv og språkforhold.* Oslo.

Dahlstedt, K.-H. 1974: Den nordiska språkgemenskapen. In Molde (ed.) 1974: 171–87.
   1982: Ord för 'Renko' i nordsvenska dialekter. In Dahlstedt, *et al.* (eds.) 1982: 21–66.

Dahlstedt, K.-H., Å. Hansson and S. Sahlman-Karlsson (eds.) 1982: Språkhistoria och Språkkontakt i Finland och Nord-Skandinavien. Studier tillägnade Tryggve Sköld den 2 November 1982. *Acta Regiae Societatis Skytteanae,* 26. Umeå.

Dorian, N. 1973: Grammatical Change in a Dying Dialect. *Language* 49: 413–38.
   1981: *Language Death.* Philadelphia.

Ejerhed, E. and I. Henrysson (eds.) 1981: *Tvåspråkighet. Föredrag från tredje Nordiska Tvåspråkighetssymposiet,* 4–5 June 1980. Acta Universitatis Umensis. 36. Umeå.

Eldjárn, K. (ed.) 1958: *Þriðji Víkingafundur.* Third Viking Congress. Árbók Háskóla Íslands. Reykjavík.

Elert, C.-C. (ed.) 1981: *Internordisk språkförståelse.* Umeå Studies in the Humanities 33. Umeå.

Elmevik, L. 1979: Svenskt och lågtyskt: Kring ett tvåspråkighetsproblem. In Stedje and Trampe (eds.) 1979: 226–39.

Falck, K. (ed.) 1955: Second Viking Congress. Bergen. *Universitetet i Bergen Årsbok* (1955). Hist.-antikvarisk rekke 1: 1–143.

Fink, T. (ed.) 1979: *Mødet mellem sprogene i det dansk–tyske graenseområde.* Aabenraa.

Forskningsprogrammet urbanisiering och språkförändring i Norden 1982. *Nordic Linguistic Bulletin* 6 (2): 36–50.

Grannspråk och minoritetsspråk i Norden. 1975. Nordiskt språkseminarium 4–6 April, 1975. Hanaholmens kulturcentrum. Esbo, Finland, ed. Nordiska Rådet. Stockholm.

Greene, David, 1981: Neo-Celtic and Faroese. In Haugen, McClure and Thomson (eds.) 1981: 1–9.

Hansegård, Nils Erik, 1967: *Recent Finnish Loanwords in Jukkasjärvi Lappish.* Acta Universitatis Upsaliensis. Studia Uralica et Altaica Upsaliensia 3. Uppsala.

1968: *Tvåspråkighet eller halvspråkighet.* Stockholm.

1971: *Finnish Loanwords in Jukkasjärvi Lappish Classified according to their Meaning.* Supplement to Recent Finnish Loanwords in Jukkasjärvi Lappish by the same author. Acta Universitatis Upsaliensis 6. Uppsala.

1977: Loman och halvspråkigheten. *Invandrare och minoriteter* 2: 36–51.

Haugen, E. 1953: *The Norwegian Language in America*, Vols. 1–2. Philadelphia.

1976: *The Scandinavian Languages.* London.

1977: Norm and Deviation in Bilingual Communities. In P. A. Hornby (ed.) 1977: *Bilingualism.* New York, pp. 91–102.

1980: Language Problems and Language Planning: the Scandinavian Model. In Nelde (ed.) 1980: 151–7.

1981: Language Fragmentation in Scandinavia: Revolt of the Minorities. In Haugen, McClure and Thomson (eds.) 1981: 100–19.

Haugen, E. and T. Markey, 1972: *The Scandinavian Languages: Fifty Years of Linguistic Research.* The Hague.

Haugen, E., J. D. McClure and D. S. Thomson (eds.) 1981: *Minority Languages Today.* Edinburgh.

Hyldgaard-Jensen, K. 1980: Die Begegnung des Dänischen und des Deutschen in Schleswig. In Nelde (ed.) 1980: 237–41.

Itkonen, E. 1941: Lappalaista merkitsevistä nimityksistä ja niiden historiallisesta taustasta. *Virittäjä* 1941: 67–93. Helsinki.

1966: Lappalaisten esihistoria kielitieteen valossa. *Tietolipas* 20: 85–131. Helsinki.

Jaakkola, M. 1973: *Språkgränsen. En studie i tvåspråkighetens sociologi.* Stockholm.

Jackson, K. 1962: The Celtic Languages during the Viking Period. In Brian O'Cuîv (ed.) 1962: 3–11.

Jahr, E. H. 1982: Language Contact in Northern Norway. In Ureland (ed.) 1982: 307–20.

Jernsletten, N. 1982: Språket i samiske samfunn. In Bull and Jetne (eds.) 1982: 101–17.

Johansson, H. 1973: Sameundervisning – Samernas önskemål och behov i skolfrågor. Part 1. Pedagogical Reports No. 30 (1973) University and Teacher Training College in Umeå.

1975: *Samerna och Sameundervisningen i Sverige.* Umeå.

1977: *Samerna och Sameundervisningen i Sverige.* Umeå University. Umeå

Karker, A. 1981: Om tysk og dansk sprog i Sønderjylland. *Språk i Norden*, pp. 20–8.

Keskitalo, A. I. 1981: The Status of the Sámi Language. In Haugen, McClure and Thomson (eds.) 1981: 152–69.

Koller, W. 1980: Zum Sprachverhalten von in Norwegen lebenden Schweden und von in der Deutschschweiz lebenden Deutschen. In Nelde (ed.) 1980: 487–92.

Kontzi, Reinhold (ed.) 1978: *Zur Entstehung der romanischen Sprachen.* Darmstadt.

(ed.) 1982: *Substrate und Superstrate in den romanischen Sprachen.* Darmstadt.

Korhonen, Olavi, 1974: Den samiska språkvårdens problem. In Molde (ed.) 1974: 211–29.

1982: *Samisk-finska båttermer och ortnamnselement och deras slaviska bakgrund.* Umeå University. Umeå.

Laurén, C. and S. Strömman 1981: The Functioning of the Two National Languages in a Minor Enterprise in the Province of Vasa, Finland. *Journal of Multilingual and Multicultural Development* 2 (1): 53–63.

1983: Aims and Methods of an Investigation into Bilingualism in some Minor Firms in Vasa, Finland. In Nelde (ed.) 1983: 311–17.

Loman, B. 1974: Till frågan om tvåspråkighet och halvspråkighet i Tornedalen. In Loman (ed.) *Barnspråk i klassamhälle*, pp. 43–79. Lund.

1975: Halvspråkighet eller pappegojsvenska. In: *Invandrare och minoriteter* 4: 27–8.

1982: Idéer och motiveringar i nordisk språkplanering under de senaste hundra åren. *Språk i Norden* 45–76. Stockholm.

Miklosich, F. 1861: Die slavischen Elemente im Rumunischen. In: *Denkschriften der Phil.-Hist. Kl. der kaiserlichen Akademie der Wiss.* 12: 1–70.

Molde, B. (ed.) 1974: *Språkvårdsstudier.* Stockholm.

1974: De nordiska språkens ställing, nuläge, framtidsperspektiv. In Molde (ed.) 1974: 189–209.

Nelde, P. (ed.) 1980: *Sprachkontakt und Sprachkonflikt.* Wiesbaden.

(ed.) 1983: Proceedings of the Symposium 'Contact + Confli(c)t II', June 2–5 1982, Brussels. Vol. 1: *Current Trends in Contact Linguistics*; Vol. 2: *Theory, Methods, and Models of Contact Linguists*; Vol. 3: *Comparability of Language Contacts*; Vol. 4: *Multilingualism.* Bonn.

Nelde, P., P. S. Ureland and Iain Clarkson (eds.) forthc.: *Language Contact in Europe. Proceedings of the Work Group held at the 13th International Congress of Linguists in Tokyo, 29 Aug.–3 Sept. 1982.* Ann Arbor.

Nesheim, A. 1953: Noen nordiske ord- og kulturlån hos samene. *Studia Septentrionalia* 5: 123–48. Oslo.

1958: Samisk og nordisk – felleskap og kulturkontakt. *By og Bygd* 11: 1–18. Oslo.

1964: The Lapps, Fur and Skin Terminology and its Historical Background. *Studia Ethnographica Upsaliensia.* 21: 199–218. Uppsala.

1967: Eastern and Western Elements in Lapp Culture. *Lapps and Norsemen in Olden Times*, pp. 104–68. Oslo.

Nylund, E. and E. Wande (eds.) 1979: *Proceedings of the Symposium on Cultural Contacts in the Arctic Area*, 6–8 June, 1977. Fenno–Ugrica Suecana 2. Uppsala.

O'Cuiv, B. (ed.) 1962: *Proceedings of the First International Congress of Celtic Studies.* Dublin.

Oftedal, M. 1981: Is Nynorsk a Minority Language? In Haugen, McClure and Thomson (eds.) 1981: 120–9.

Oksaar, E. 1966: Tvåspråkigheten och invandrarna. In D. Schwarz (ed.) 1966: *Svenska minoriteter.* 68–87. Stockholm.

1972: Bilingualism. In T. Sebeok (ed.) 1972: *Current Trends in Linguistics.* Vol. 9: *Linguistics in Western Europe*, pp. 476–511. The Hague.

1976: Interference and Bilingual Interaction. In G. Nickel (ed.), *Proceedings of the 4th International Conference of Applied Linguistics* 2: 101–11. Stuttgart.

1982: Language–Integration–Identity. Sociocultural Problems of New Minorities. In *Cultural Identity and Structural Marginalization of Migrant Workers*, ed. European Science Foundation. Strasbourg.

Olsen, C. 1981: Sproglovgivning och sprogudvikling i Grønland. *Språk i Norden*, pp. 34–41.

Paul, H. 1880: *Prinzipien der Sprachgeschichte.* Halle/Saale. 1st edn (2nd edn, 1886).

Perdue, C. (ed.) 1982: *Second Language Acquisition by Adult Immigrants – A Field Manual.* European Science Foundation. Strasbourg.

Pisani, V. 1974: *Indogermanisch und Europa.* München.

Pokorny, J. 1927–30: Das nicht-indogermanische Substrat im Irischen. In: *Zeitschrift für Celtische Philologie*, 16 (1927): 93–144, 231–66, 362–94; *Zeitschrift für Celtische Philologie*, 18 (1930): 233–48.

Poulsen, J. H. 1981: The Faroese Language Situation. In Haugen, McClure and Thomson (eds.) 1981: 144–51.

Qvigstad, J. K. 1883: Beiträge zur Vergleichung des verwandten Wortvorrathes der lappischen und der finnischen Sprache. *Acta Societatis Scientarum Fennicae* 12: 114–246. Helsinki.

1893: *Nordische Lehnwörter im Lappischen*. Kristiania.

Raag, R. 1982: *Lexical Characteristics in Swedish Estonian*. Acta Universitatis Upsaliensis. Studia Uralica et Altaica. Stockholm.

Rahbek Schmidt, K. *et al.* (eds.) 1970: See *Varangian Problems*.

Reuter, M. 1981: The Status of Swedish in Finland in Theory and Practice. In Haugen, McClure and Thomson (eds.) 1981: 130–7.

Rischel, J. 1983: Language Policy and Language Survival in the North-Atlantic Parts of Denmark. In Nelde (ed.) 1983: 203–12.

Rönmark, Walter and Joel Wikström, 1980: *Tvåspråkighet i Tornedalen*. Umeå.

Ruong, I. 1982: *Samerna i historien och nutiden*. (4th edn.) Stockholm.

Sandfeld, K. 1930: *Linguistique Balcanique. Problèmes et Résultats*. Paris.

1938: Problèmes d'interférences linguistiques. In: *Actes du Quatrième Congrès International de Linguistique*. Copenhagen 1936, pp. 59–61.

Schmitt, C. 1982: Die Ausbildung der romanischen Sprachen – Zur Bedeutung von Varietät und Stratum für die Sprachgenese. In Ureland (ed.) 1982: 39–61.

Schuchardt, H. 1882–3: *Kreolische Studien I–IV. Sitzungsberichte der Wiener Akademie der Wissenschaften*. Vols. 101, 102, 103, 105. Wien. (For a detailed bibliography see Spitzer (ed.) 1928 (2nd ed.): 22–3.)

1884: *Slawo-Deutsches und Slawo-Italienisches*. Graz. (Re-edited as a photolithogr. reproduction of the German original by Dietrich Gerhardt 1971. München).

1891: Beiträge zur Kenntnis des englischen Kreolisch: das Indo-Englische. *Englische Studien* 15: 286–305.

1909: Die Lingua Franca. *Zeitschrift für Romanische Philologie* 33: 441–61.

1914: Die Sprache der Saramaccaneger in Surinam. *Verhandelingen der koniklijke Akademie van Wetenschappen*. 16: 4.

1928: Sprachwissenschaft. In Leo Spitzer (ed.) *Hugo Schuchardt-Brevier. Ein Vademecum der allgemeinen Sprachwissenschaft* (1928): 189–204. 2nd edn. Darmstadt.

Seip, D. A. 1915–19: *Låneordsstudier*, Vols. 1 and 2. Kristiania.

Sigurd, B. (ed.) 1977: *De nordiska språkens framtid*. Stockholm.

Simpson, W. D. (ed.) 1954: The 1st Viking Congress. Lerwick, July 1950. Aberdeen University Studies No. 132. Edinburgh/London.

Skautrup, P. 1947, 1953, 1968: *Det danske sprogs historie*. Vol. 2 (Section on South Jutland on pp. 296–301); Vol. 3 (Section on South Jutland with detailed maps on pp. 117–27); Vol. 4 (Section on South Jutland with maps on pp. 41–7). Copenhagen.

Sköld, T. 1961: *Die Kriterien der urnordischen Lehnwörter im Lappischen*. Vol. 1. Uppsala.

Skutnabb-Kangas, T. (ed.) 1977: *Papers from the First Nordic Conference on Bilingualism, Hanasaari, Espoo, Finland*. Meddelanden från Institutionen för nordisk filologi. Helsingfors Universitet, Serie B, Nr 2. Helsinki.

1981: *Tvåspråkighet*. Lund.

Small, A. (ed.) 1965: *The Fourth Viking Congress*, York 1961.

Söderlind, S. 1978: *Rusernas rike, Till frågan om det östslaviska rikets uppkomst*. Stockholm. ·

Sommerfeldt, Alf, 1962: The Norse Influence on Irish and Scottish Gaelic. In Brian O'Cuiv (ed.) 1962: 73–7.

Søndergaard, B. (ed.) 1980: *Preliminary Research into Danish German Bilingualism –
A Bibliography.* Danmarks paedagogiske bibliothek. Copenhagen.
1980: Vom Sprachenkampf zur sprachlichen Koexistenz im deutsch-dänischen
Grenzraum. In Nelde (ed.)1980: 297–305.
1981: The Fight for Survival. Danish as a Living Minority Language South of the
German Border. In Haugen, McClure and Thomson (eds.) 1981: 138–43.
Spitzer, L., (ed.) 1928 (1978): *Hugo Schuchardt-Brevier. Ein Vademecum der allge-
meinen Sprachwissenschaft.* Darmstadt.
Språk i Norden. 1981: Stockholm.
Språk i Norden. 1982: Stockholm.
Stedje, A. and P. af Trampe (eds.) 1979: *Tvåspråkighet. Föredrag vid det andra
tvåspråkighetssymposiet,* 18–19 May 1978. Stockholm.
Thomsen, V. 1877: *The Relations between Ancient Russia, Scandinavia and the Origin
of the Russian State.* Oxford/London.
1967 (1870): *On the Influence of Germanic Languages on Finnic and Lapp.* Blooming-
ton. (Photolithogr. reprod. of the German trans. from Danish. Halle 1870.)
Tingbjörn, G. 1982: SPRINS-Gruppen. In *Nordic Linguistic Bulletin* 6 (1): 39–47.
Tingbjörn, G. and A.-B. Andersson, 1981: *Invandrarbarnen och tvåspråkigheten.*
Lund.
Törnqvist, N. 1977: *Das niederdeutsche und niederländische Lehngut im schwedischen
Wortschatz.* Neumünster.
Tovar, A. 1976: Indogermanisch, Keltisch und Keltiberisch. In K. H. Schmidt (ed.),
Indogermanisch und Keltisch. Kolloquium der Indogermanischen Gesellschaft in
Bonn. Wiesbaden, pp. 44–65.
1977: Krahes alteuropäische Hydronymie und die westindogermanischen Sprachen.
Sitzungsberichte der Heidelberger Akademie der Wissenschaften. Phil.-Hist.-Klasse.
Heidelberg, pp. 1–42.
Ureland, P. S. 1977: Some Comparative Aspects of Pronominal Cliticization. In G.
Drachmann (ed.) 1977. *Salzburger Beiträge zur Linguistik.* Akten der 2. Salz-
burger Frühjahrstagung für Linguistik. Tübingen, pp. 301–19.
1978: Typological, Diachronic, and Areal Linguistic Perspectives of North Germanic Syntax. In J. Weinstock (ed.) 1978: *The Nordic Languages and Modern
Linguistics* 3: 116–41. Austin, Texas.
1979: Prehistoric Bilingualism and Pidginization as Forces of Linguistic Change.
The Journal of Indo-European Studies 7: 77–104.
1980: Language Contact in Scandinavia as an Impetus to Language Change. In
Nelde (ed.) 1980: 441–51.
(ed.) 1978: *Sprachkontakte im Nordseegebiet.* Akten des 1. Symposions über
Sprachkontakt in Europa. Tübingen.
(ed.) 1979: *Dialekte und Standardsprachen in mehrsprachigen Gebieten Europas.*
Akten des 2. Symposions über Sprachkontakt in Europa. Tübingen: Niemeyer.
(ed.) 1980: *Sprachvariation und Sprachwandel. Probleme der Inter und Intralinguistik.*
Akten des 3. Symposions über Sprachkontakt in Europa. Tübingen.
(ed.) 1981: *Kulturelle und sprachliche Minderheiten in Europa.* Akten des 4. Symposions über Sprachkontakt in Europa. Tübingen.
(ed.) 1982: *Die Leistung der Strataforschung und der Kreolistik – Typologische Aspekte
der Sprachkontakte.* Akten des 5. Symposions über Sprachkontakt in Europa.
Tübingen.
Varangian Problems, 1970: The Eastern Connections of Nordic Peoples in the Viking
Period and Early Middle Ages. Ed. K. Rahbek Schmidt *et al. Scando–Slavica.*
Suppl. I, Copenhagen.
de Vries, John, 1983: The Swedish–Finnish Mobility Project: Opportunities for
Language Contact Research. In Nelde (ed.) 1983: 359–75.

Wackernagel, J. 1904: Sprachtausch und Sprachmischung. In: *Göttinger Gelehrte Nachrichten*, pp. 90–113.

Weinreich, U. 1953: *Languages in Contact*. New York/The Hague.

Werner, O. 1964: Die Erforschung des Inselnordischen. In: *Zeitschrift für Mundartforschung*. Beihefte N.F. 6 (Festschrift für W. Mitzka 1964): 459–519.

Wessén, E. 1954: *Om det tyska inflytandet på svenskt språk under medeltiden*. Stockholm.

Whitney, W. D. 1881: On Mixture in Language. *Transactions of the American Philological Association* 12: 1–26.

Wiklund, K. B. 1892: Die nordischen Lehnwörter in den russischlappischen Dialekten. *Journal de la Société Finno-Ougrienne* 10: 146–206. Helsinki.

1914: Urnordiska ortnamn i södra lappmarkerna. *Namn och Bygd* 2: 105–20.

Wilts, O. 1978: Dänisch, Nordfriesisch, Hoch- und Niederdeutsch in Schleswig-Holstein. In Ureland (ed.) 1978: 149–66.

Windisch, E. 1897: Zur Theorie der Mischsprachen und Lehnwörter. *Verhandlungen der Sächsischen Gesellschaft der Wissenschaften* 49: 101–26.

Woivaldin, Folke, 1981: Språksituationen på Åland. *Språk i Norden*, pp. 16–20.

I *North Scandinavia*

2 Russenorsk: a new look at the Russo-Norwegian pidgin in Northern Norway*

INGVILD BROCH AND ERNST HÅKON JAHR

1   Introduction

Russenorsk (RN) is the pidgin or trade jargon which was used in northern Norway (Finnmark and Troms) by Russian merchants and Norwegian fishermen during the Pomor trade. The Norwegians traded their fish for Russian flour, grain, birch bark, hemp, wood planks etc.

In several ways RN is different from other pidgins which are based on European languages. The most important is the fact that there was no significant social difference between the users of the pidgin, and hence no social distinction between the two major languages on which RN was based, Norwegian and Russian. This feature of RN is in sharp contrast to, for example, English- or French-based pidgins, where the social difference between users is reflected in the fact that the European base language dominates the pidgin language in a way which is not comparable with the relationship between Norwegian and Russian in RN.

Another interesting feature of RN is the long period of time that elapsed from the earliest evidence we have of the existence of RN until its extinction with the First World War and the Russian Revolution in 1917. We will show that the period from the first definitely attested occurrence of a RN word until the last text of substantial length was written, encompasses 141 years. A pidgin language rarely becomes this old without being creolized; i.e. it expands functionally and grammatically until it becomes a mother tongue and fulfils all the functions required of a natural language.

The main reason why RN could exist over such an unusually long period of time without being expanded functionally, but more or less maintain a minimum of grammar and vocabulary, is that RN was used in connection with the seasonal trade during the summer months. This circumstance is another special feature of RN compared to other pidgins, and is the reason why RN was not developed any further as a pidgin language and why it could remain so simple structurally despite its extensive use over such a long time. However, we will later argue that RN was used also *between* trade seasons, and that the texts indicate that RN could have developed functionally and grammatically if contact between the Norwegians and Russians had been intensified and further expanded.

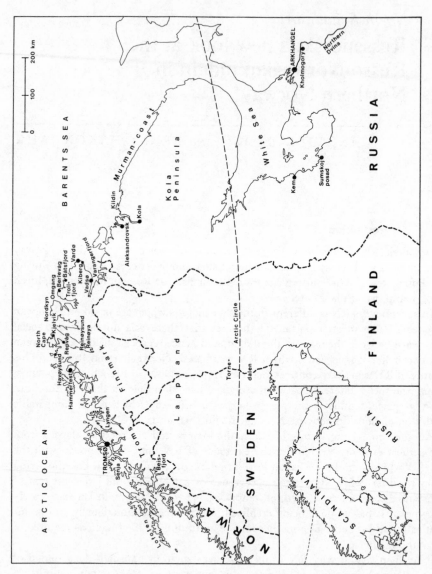

Map 1: Northern Scandinavia and the Kola Peninsula.

2   The Pomor trade

2.1   The 16th and 17th centuries

The Russian trade in northern Norway had a long tradition, even though its extent
has varied over the centuries. In 1516 a treaty between Grand Duke Vasilij Ivanovič
and King Christian II guaranteed completely open trade between the kingdom of
Denmark and Norway and Russia (Johnsen 1923: 225). But towards the end of
the 16th century the opportunities for trade in northern Norway were restricted:
the Finnmark trade was controlled by the merchants in Bergen, and it was forbidden
to trade with 'another man's debtor' (Brox 1954: 518). Violation of this law was
severely punished, and it appears that the Russian trade declined during the 17th
century. However, it increased again the following century.

The legality of this trade also varied, but as long as the Russians had a grain
surplus and needed fish, and vice versa for the Norwegians, bartering continued,
even when it was illegal. The Norwegians cut timber and hay, and gathered moss
in the areas where Russian and Norwegian territory overlapped (the Common
Districts), and in east Finnmark both Russians and Norwegians fished side by side.
From the middle of the 18th century more and more Russians came to Finnmark
to fish (Johnsen 1923: 219).

Earlier the Russians only had small boats, but after studying navigation in
Holland, Peter I encouraged shipbuilding in his country. As a result larger boats
were also built in the White Sea and these new vessels set out on longer journeys.

2.2   Contacts and attempts at trading in the 18th century

As has often been mentioned, Amtmann[1] Sommerfeldt writes in his description
of Finnmark that the Russians first came to the county in 1742, whereas in Major
P. Schnitler's border-control records we find that Russians travelling from Archangel
to Vardø arrived three years earlier (Ytreberg 1940–2: 482). The legal records
(*Justisprotokollene*) from Finnmark[2] show that there had been earlier attempts to
trade: in the *Justisprotokollene for Finnmark* (No. 31, fol. 133 Vardø *ting*, August
11, 1714) we can read that the Russian merchant Olachse Olachsevitz, from the
town of Summa 300 km from Archangel, was accused of trading illegally. (Sumskoj
posad was later a starting point for the Pomor trade.)

In 1717 and 1715 the records from Vadsø *alm. ting* mention that a man was
sentenced who was originally accused of calling a woman *ryssehore* (Russian's
whore) (Justisprotokoll for Finnmark No. 31, fol. 150 and fol. 234). A word like
this shows that there must have been close contact between Russians and
Norwegians.

The sale of Russian goods in Troms was first reported in 1725. In the same year
the cargo of a Russian boat was confiscated in Tromsø, but released the following
year. Ytreberg (1940–2: 483–4) does not believe that this was the first time a Russian
trade vessel had come to Troms, and supports his view with descriptions of
decedent estates (for instance from Lyngen in Troms 1724) where various Russian
articles are listed.

Those who represented the monopoly watched the increase in the Russian trade with uneasiness, and complained to the authorities. But in reality nothing concrete was ever done to bring an end to this trade. And in a letter from *Rentekammeret* (The Exchequer) in Copenhagen to Amtmann Hagerup in Finnmark in 1764 it was stated as a fact that 'nothing could be done to keep the Russians from selling necessary meal to the populace' (Ytreberg 1940–2: 493). But duty on the goods had to be paid to the local tax collectors, and after 1765 court witnesses were interrogated concerning Russian skippers, vessels, merchandise, and to some extent prices, and this makes it possible for us to follow the development of the Russian trade.

In 1770 a merchant's clerk in Vardø wrote to his employer in Bergen: 'Not only do the Russians repress the inhabitants with their fishing, but they even dare to go around to the fishing villages to barter for and buy fish, which they acquire much more easily than we do, being willing to pay twice the price we have stipulated' (Helland 1905: 777). But the Russian traders were generally popular (Johnsen 1923: 225); we even have some instances where Norwegians refused to help the local police arrest Russians accused of illegal trading (Justisprotokoll for Øst-Finnmark 1817–30, fol. 14–5, Vadsø *ekstrarett* 11 June 1818). However, it was more usual that the Russian fishermen quarrelled with the inhabitants. The total number of Russian fishermen varied greatly from year to year. According to Amtmann Fjeldstad there were 1,300 Russian fishermen in Finnmark in 1774. At that time only 300 Norwegian families lived there (Helland 1905: 787).

Towards the end of the 18th century the legal records include several examples of indictments for illegal trading: e.g. at Omgang on July 9, 1773 two fishermen from Trollfjord were charged with selling fish to the Russians. They had traded the fish for bread, and justified this by claiming they lacked salt (to preserve the fish) (Justisprotokoll for Finnmark No. 42, fol. 151). And on 23 June 1783 it is reported from Gulholmen (Omgang) that merchant Christian Hvistendahl had travelled between Nordkyn and Berlevåg and met a Russian fisherman who admitted buying 550 kg of cod from Norwegian fishermen. The merchant confiscated the fish and placed it in a shanty, before travelling on. But skipper Ivanevits took the fish back on board and sailed to Russia after the merchant had gone (Justisprotokoll for Finnmark No. 44, fol. 184). In addition, it was quite usual for Norwegian merchants to report the Russians for illegal trading. And both Norwegians and Russians were sentenced for illicit trading.

That relations during the 18th century were more extensive than was previously realized can also be deduced from finds made in the wreck of the St Varlamii from Kholmogory (Grannes and Lillehammer 1980). The St Varlamii sank outside Kvitsøy near Stavanger on the south west coast of Norway *en route* from Archangel to St Petersburg during the summer of 1792. Correspondence with the shipowner was found on the captain's body, which shows that the ship's crew was going to take part in the cod fishing in Lofoten, then take the fish to St Petersburg and sell it there. The detailed description of how they planned to go about it shows that this was not an isolated incident. For instance, they were to contact a certain person who would provide them with the necessary equipment and arrange for some Norwegians to go with them – it was illegal for foreigners to fish in Lofoten. They were also going to arrange to buy Spanish salt so they would have enough for the next year's fishing. According to the papers, one of the crew, Grigorij Martinov, was boatswain and interpreter. The ship owner, Sergej Kulakov, who had connections in Norway, having been there several times, sent a letter written in Danish to the Amtmann in Stavanger after the shipwreck.[3]

2.3 Trade and friendship pacts: 1782, 1818

Relations between Denmark–Norway and Russia improved towards the end of the 18th century. In 1782 a trade and friendship pact was signed; in 1787 trade in Finnmark began, and Troms and Senja were incorporated under Finnmark. In the county of Troms the Russians were only allowed to trade in the town of Tromsø, whereas in Finnmark they could trade at small towns and trading-centres. Duty-free export of all kinds of goods from Finnmark and duty-free import of everything but liquor was permitted. Eventually opportunities for trading were further extended: after 1796 the Russians were allowed to deal directly with the Finnmark fishermen – at first only for raw fish during *makketida*, between 15 July and 15 August ('the maggot-season' – when it was difficult for the fishermen to find other markets for their catch); later the period was extended several times, and permission was given to trade in commodities other than raw fish. After 1818 the Russians were also allowed into the trading-centres in Troms (Brox 1954: 521–2).

Journeys were long. The log book of the farmer Vadaev from Kem, which according to Tatjana Alimova (1976) dates back to the end of the 18th century or beginning of the 19th century, shows that Vadaev sailed from Kem on 1 June, arrived at Archangel on 13 June, and stayed there until 6 July. On 29 July he passed Kildin, and had fair wind all the way to Vardø. He estimates the distance Archangel–Vardø at 1,124 km. But Vardø was not his destination; from there he sailed to Kjelvik and then to Havøysund, where he stayed two days. On 13 August Vadaev wrote: 'Sailed into Reinøysund to trade. Stayed there eighteen days.' The distance from Vardø to Reinøyene is 644 km according to Vadaev; hence the whole journey was approximately 1,770 km. He did not make any entries concerning the return voyage; nor does he mention what commodities he dealt in (Alimova 1976: 390–1).

During the Napoleonic Wars grain exports from Russia were forbidden, but this had no effect on the trade in the north. During the early 19th century the supply of Russian meal was so good that it was sold south to Nordland, Trondheim, and in one case to Copenhagen. Trade possibilities were extended to permit trade by barter in Troms too, and the trade period was extended several times. Finally it applied from 15 June to 30 September (Brox 1954: 527).

2.4 The legal Pomor trade by barter in the 19th century

It is this trade in kind which is called the Pomor trade. The White Sea coast is called *Pomor'e* in Russian; those who live there and along the Murman coast are accordingly called *Pomors*. The inhabitants of Kola on the Murman coast, and of Kem and Sumskoj posad by the White Sea were the first to have the privilege of trading Russian meal for Norwegian fish – that was in 1810. After 1837–8 all Pomors were given permission to barter (Bernštam 1978: 115). The Pomors were competent boatbuilders and generally built their own boats. It was usual for them to have a small farm as well, but most of the grain sold in northern Norway came to the White Sea area, from the Vologda and Vjatsk districts along the northern Dvina. Besides rye-flour, and a little wheat-flour and grain, the Russians also brought other provisions with them, especially lumber, rope, linen and birch bark. They traded mostly for fish – fresh fish which they salted directly in their holds, and ready-salted fish, but also salt, hides, grindstones, etc. The Russians bought fish at a time when it was difficult to sell it in Norway. Nor were they too fussy about the quality. Northern Norway lacked meal; the Archangel district needed fish, and fish was an important source of food for the Russians, particularly because of their long fasts. The fishing on the Murman coast was not as good as on the Norwegian coast, nor did the season last as long – the fish went out to sea in July, and it was both safer and more profitable to go to Norway than to follow the fish out to the ocean. Much of the fish bought by the Pomors in Norway was sold on the autumn market in Archangel (Finstad 1910).

The Russian traders were popular in northern Norway because they distributed candied fruit and Russian nuts to the children and served tea from their samovars (and something stronger!) after the bartering was over. Some of the Norwegians who traded with the same Russian skipper year after year were invited on board, especially if the skipper was accompanied by his wife. (e.g. Korneliussen 1968: 365).

After a while the trade attained a substantial scale. In 1872 the Russians delivered 14,500 sacks of flour each weighing 144 kg, in 1900 almost twice as much. If this amount is divided by the population of Finnmark and Troms, this is about 40 kg per person (Hanssen 1978: 83). In 1881, 470 vessels from the White Sea, with a total crew of 2,287 men, sailed to Vadsø, Vardø, Hammerfest and Tromsø. They exported from this area goods worth 708,532 rubles, and imported goods to the value of 754,931 rubles (Bucharov 1883: 19–20). Around the turn of the century, 600,000 *pud* (about 98,400 (metric) tons) of salted fish was exported yearly from northern Norway to the Archangel district (Helland 1899: 459). The total value of exports from the harbours in northern Norway to northern Russia in 1898 was 2.4 million Norwegian crowns, while goods were imported to the value of 1.3 million (Helland 1905: 778).

Several sources claim that the Russian grain prevented starvation in northern Norway during the famine years at the beginning of the 19th century. Eriksen (1971a: 132) says that Norwegian expansion and activity in Finnmark during the 19th century would have been unthinkable without the Pomor trade. From their point of view the Russians emphasize the importance of this trade for the development of industry in the Archangel area (Bucharov 1883, Bernštam 1978).

Many Russians worked during the summer in the warehouses in Finnmark, e.g. 71 Russians worked for different merchants in Vardø in the summer of 1909 (*Murman* No. 11, April 1909). It was not only the fishermen and merchants who dealt with the Russian skippers, but also women and children. The women washed and mended their clothes for them (Eriksen 1971b: 71), and the small boys fished and traded for candied fruit and rusk (Eriksen 1971b: 17).

After the steamboat connection between Archangel and Vardø opened in 1875, the merchants sent merchandise back and forth with the steamers. At first these ships were only in service during the summer season, but in 1905 a winter route was established between Vardø and Aleksandrovsk (now Poljarnyj) on the Kola Peninsula, when the White Sea was frozen.

The Russian fishermen stayed mostly on the Varanger Peninsula. Because of disagreements with the Norwegians, fishing was regulated in 1830, with the result that the Russians were permitted to fish 10 km from shore between Kiberg and Nordkyn. The Russians had permanent boathouses there, and often left a man behind to look after things during the winter, or paid a Norwegian to keep an eye on them. The Russian fishermen also bartered, and sometimes they left their boats in Norway during the winter and went home by land or on the steamer.

2.5   Dictionaries, textbooks and newspapers

This extensive contact between the Russians and Norwegians resulted in the printing of several dictionaries and textbooks, and also of Russian newspapers.

Norsk–Russisk Ordbog og Parleur (Norwegian–Russian Dictionary and Phrase-Book) published by A. Hansen, Bergen 1862, was intended for 'merchants and fishermen who come to Finnmark, and also with anyone who wishes to be easily understood in Russian' (Hansen 1862: 3). It is not especially extensive, containing 300 words and numerals, and nearly ten pages of conversation between a 'Russian and a Norwegian concerning fishing and business-affairs'.

This book is special because it contains one example of the RN pronoun *moja* (Lunden 1978a: 5).

Kortfattet norsk–russisk Haandbog samt Tabel til Udregning af Melkvantum ved Russehandel (Short Norwegian–Russian manual, with Tables for Calculation of Grain Quantities in the Russian Trade) was published by Urdal, who was a publisher in Tromsø, in 1899, 2nd edition in 1900. The foreword includes the following: 'The intention of this little book is to help fishermen and others who come into contact with Russian fishbuyers to learn the most essential words and expressions concerning this trade and fishing.' The book comprises about 500 words, two pages of numerals, some common sentences and nearly 20 pages of calculating-tables.

In Russia, A. Koškin published *Russko–norvežskij slovar'* (Russian–Norwegian Dictionary) in Archangel in 1912. Koškin had lived in Vardø for six years as Russian vice-consul, and received financial support from the governor of the Archangel region to work on the book. In the foreword he writes: 'Since this dictionary's main goal is to support our Pomors in their constant relations with our neighbouring country, my book should be used as a handbook.' This book contains 27,500 words and has pronunciation rules worked out by Olaf Broch. Koškin also says that his book is the first Russian aid to learning Norwegian, but in the newspaper *Murman* 1907–9 we find advertisements for a short *Russko–norvežskij slovar'*. However we have not been able to discover anything more about this book.

Russian newspapers were printed in Vardø during the summer; *Murman* appeared with a total of 15 issues in 1907–9, and a newspaper called *Pomor* is also mentioned

(Frette 1959: 8). These papers were intended for the Pomors and gave information about the political conditions at home and abroad, especially in Norway. *Murman* at least had a definite socialist inclination.

2.6   New restrictions and the end of the Pomor trade

Around the turn of the century, the trade changed character from being basically a barter-trade to becoming increasingly a cash-trade; and while exports of fish increased, imports of grain decreased.

In 1905 the Norwegian Parliament passed a law forbidding the Russians to sell their wares directly to the inhabitants of Finnmark; all trade had to go through commercial channels, but the barter-trade continued nevertheless.

While fish imports to Archangel increased after 1908, the number of vessels engaged in the Pomor trade decreased. The richest Pomor skippers, partially supported by well-established merchants in Archangel, took over the trade (Eriksen 1971a: 68).

Russian sources claim that the Pomor trade was in decline by the beginning of the 20th century, because the Norwegians had started trading with western Europe and America (Bernštam 1978: 116).

The First World War and the Russian Revolution in 1917 put an end to trade relations between the Norwegians and Russians.

2.7   The Russians remembered

Vilfred Dybos in his article (1959) describes the barter-trade in Vardø at the turn of the century: The fisherman, Erik Barstad, sails into the harbour and goes alongside skipper Korkonosov's craft. Korkonosov appears on deck immediately, greets Barstad and inquires about his family before letting the conversation turn to trading matters. Barstad explains that he has haddock, cod, some catfish, and small halibut. Korkonosov offers 1 *pud* (= 18 kg) of rye-flour for 2 *pud* of haddock, catfish and halibut; and flour for cod, weight for weight. Barstad does not consider this good enough. He wants the same arrangement for catfish and halibut as for cod, and he does not want rye-flour, but grain and wheat-flour. Korkonosov looks around but does not see any other fishing boats. They agree upon half and half rye- and wheat-flour for the fish-weight the fisherman had suggested. The conversation has been conducted in RN.

The door in the boat's rail is opened, the gutting starts, after which the fish is thrown up on the other boat. Barstad goes onboard to check on the weighing. After the fish is weighed, it is split along the back in Russian fashion and thrown unwashed into the hold for salting. Barstad receives his flour and some plank cuttings. Then he follows the skipper into the cabin for a little vodka, and dry-cake and nuts for his wife and crew. When Barstad goes ashore, he is encouraged to return with more fish.

The long contact is still not forgotten in Troms and Finnmark. Older people often relate their memories of the Russians. In South Varanger they had a saying that went: 'When the fog comes over [the mountain] Domen, the Russians are on

the way' (Eriksen 1971b: 86, see also Grøttland 1978: 28) – this was a sign that
the ice had broken on the White Sea.

A teacher, Johan Stålsett, remembers the last Pomor trade he experienced, in
Vadsø: They had traded their fish for flour, planks, and a bundle of birch bark, and
were drinking tea with skipper Korniloff, who was in a good mood. Then another
Russian boat came with a letter, the mobilization order. 'We feel that this is the
last good-bye. Farewell dear Korniloff, your sons and men, and thank you for honest
trade and good friendship for many long years!' (Hanssen 1978: 85).

3 Earlier linguistic descriptions

The first linguistic description of RN was published by the Norwegian phonetician
and slavist Olaf Broch (1867–1961) in 1927.[4] He had collected material about RN
for several years, and received most of his information from the outstanding lappol-
ogist Just Knud Qvigstad (1853–1957) in Tromsø. In his article Broch described
mainly phonetic, morphological and lexical features of RN. The syntax and the
sociolinguistic aspects of RN were hardly mentioned. On the other hand, the
origins of various RN features – word forms, and vowel and consonant usage – are
thoroughly discussed.

In 1930 Broch published the RN texts which were known then, and which he
had used as a basis for the description in 1927. The material consisted of a total of
13 texts, mostly dialogues and wordlists, but there is a lot of repetition from text
to text. Nevertheless, this material is our main source of information on RN as
the texts which have appeared later are few and short in comparison.

In 1965 RN was discussed and compared with other auxiliary languages of the
same type elsewhere in the world for the first time. Günter Neumann (1965)
compared RN with various other pidgins and demonstrated considerable con-
formity in the structures.

In an unpublished paper, *Russenorsk: A study in language adaptivity* (1973), the
American anthropologist James A. Fox claims that the Lappish and Finnish (or
Kvensk)[5] influence on RN has been neglected to a large extent in earlier descriptions.
He argues that many users on the Norwegian side must have been Lapps or Finns.
Fox also presents a hypothesis on the origins of RN, which he believes to have
developed from an international, north European vocabulary. Fox's theory is that
RN existed primarily as a core vocabulary which was grammatically deployed
according to the RN user's primary grammar – whether this was Russian, Norwegian, Lappish or Finnish. Consequently RN would be a sublanguage for each
user, grammatically subordinate to the user's primary grammar (mother tongue),
but with a common vocabulary. The similarities between RN and other pidgins
(see Neumann 1965) are described by Fox as surface phenomena which can better
be explained by an adaptivity theory based on universals of 'markedness', 'indexi-
cality', and 'motivation' (Fox 1973: 72).

A synopsis of Broch's results regarding RN, and his sources and texts, are given
in Siri Sverdrup Lunden: *Russenorsk Revisited* (Lunden 1978a). In addition this
work presents information about sources and texts which have been found since
Broch published his description. Lunden claims that it was only during the second

half of the 19th century that RN acquired a more stable norm, partly because some RN texts were printed then. She assumes that these texts would have the effect of standardizing future use of RN. This hypothesis is strongly refuted by Gyda Dahm Rinnan, who claims that these randomly printed texts could under no circumstances have brought about a standardization of RN to the degree Lunden suggests (Rinnan 1980). It is difficult not to agree with Rinnan, and we will later also argue that the structural and stable units of RN were established much earlier than the second part of the 19th century. Thus the first printed RN texts are not a significant factor in this connection.

Lunden 1978b presents interesting hypotheses on the development and origins of certain aspects of RN, especially the personal pronouns *moja* and *tvoja*. It appears that these pronouns can also be found in the same form in the Sino-Russian pidgin of Kjachta – on the border between Russia and China (Neumann 1966). The form *moja* is relatively easy to explain according to the phonotactical rules of this language. Lunden believes that Russian merchants might have introduced *moja* and *tvoja* from Kjachta into RN. The connecting point must then be mid-Russia and the contact between the merchants who traded eastward to China and those who traded northwestward to Norway. The hypothesis is interesting and, for the time being, perhaps the most plausible explanation of the origins of these pronouns in RN (see, however, 4.2.3). Lunden (1978b) also discusses the possibility of a connection between a possible Russo-English pidgin in Moscow and RN during the 17th century, a thought which was first presented by Robert A. Hall Jr. as an explanation for the English words in RN (Hall 1966: 13).

In a short article, Ronald E. Peterson (1980) bases his description of RN exclusively on Broch 1927 and 1930. Therefore he does not contribute anything new to the study of RN.

RN has been mentioned fairly often in international linguistic literature, usually with reference to the German edition of Broch 1927a.[6] We also find frequent references to RN in the literature which deals with trade jargons and pidgin and creole languages.

4   A linguistic description of RN

The RN texts which are available today consist of single words and isolated sentences, various wordlists of different lengths, and conversations in the form of dialogues. The text material Olaf Broch published (Broch 1930) includes 357 different words (Fox 1973: 60). Later new words were collected from different sources, so that we now have some 390 different words in the collection of RN material. However, about 50% of them are *hapax legomena*, i.e. words which appear only once in the texts. This means that the vocabulary of RN consisted of a core of 150–200 words – a not unusual number of words for a pidgin of this kind.

Most of the texts were collected from the Norwegian side, and the longer texts were handed on by Norwegian merchants and customs officials. In view of the fact that the fishing population was the primary user of RN, this is unfortunate, as the texts are then often a result of how the informants thought RN was used, or of how they had heard it used by the fishermen and Russians. In some cases we can assume that the informants were genuine RN users (e.g. Broch 1930: 132–5). It appears, however, that the majority of the texts, including the most important ones, show very little variation. This can be regarded as evidence that most of the texts are fairly reliable, so that we need not sort out the more dependable ones.

Only a few of the texts come from the Russian side. This naturally gives the texts a certain lopsidedness: they are more coloured by Norwegian than corresponding texts from the Russian side would have been. Unfortunately we have no texts from the Lappish side. And since there is no doubt that many of the RN users were Lapps (see Fox (1973: 12–17) for a discussion and documentation of this), this is particularly regrettable. The only text we have from the Finnish side (Paulaharju 1928 (1973: 231)) consists of just five small expressions which differ somewhat from the other RN forms we find. We must assume that many of the *Kvens* were also active users of RN, so here too the existence of some more texts would have been most helpful.

The following account of the grammar of RN is therefore chiefly based on the Broch texts (Broch 1930). All examples given are from Broch (where other texts are used, the individual source is named).[7]

4.1   Phonology

Today it is difficult to determine the pronunciation of RN; we are working from written texts, most of which were written down by Norwegians. The spelling of individual words can vary from text to text, and we can establish that the pronunciation of RN has varied, depending on the language and dialectal background of the individual speaker. Broch 1927a has a detailed discussion of the different sounds; both Broch and Qvigstad have also tried where possible to specify pronunciation. But rather than search for explanations – e.g. the phonetic reason why a RN word has the final sound -*a* where we would expect -*o* (from North Russian) – as Broch 1927a does, one must see the whole language structure as a system. Then we observe a certain tendency toward systematization, e.g. that nouns and adjectives often end in -*a*.

4.1.1. *Consonants.* In RN, as in pidgins generally, phonemes which occur in only one of the base languages easily disappear. In RN this applies to Norw. [h] > RN [g], e.g. RN *gav* or *gaf* < Norw. *hav* (sea), *galanna* < Norw. (dial.) *halvanna* (one and a half); but *har* (have), *han* (he, him), *hal* (half) from Norw. do occur in RN. Also Russ. [χ] > RN [k]: *klæba* < Russ. *chleb* (bread), *oreka* < Russ. *orech* (nut) etc. The Russ. affricate [tʃ] is reproduced partly as [ç], partly as [tʃ], e.g. RN *kjai* [ç] and *tsjai* [tʃ] < Russ. *čaj* (tea). Because Norwegian cannot have an initial *mn*-combination the Russ. *mnogo li* > RN *nogoli, nogli* (many); we also find *mangeli* (many) < Norw. *mange* + Russ. *li* (interrogative particle).·

Even though both languages have the phoneme [ʃ], verbal forms from Russ. 2nd pers. sing. which end in -*š'*, are consistently used with -*s* forms, as in *kupisli* < Russ. *kupiš'li* (buy), *vros* < Russ. *vrëš'* (lie) etc.

It is impossible to establish whether the spelling -*sk*- reflects the pronunciation [ʃ] or [sk]. Probably both realizations occurred. According to Broch (1927a: 216) the fact that a Russian source has *kanske* indicates that the pronunciation in the word *kanskje* 'maybe' was with [-sk-]. Such a pronunciation is widespread in Finnmark (and in Lappish, which has borrowed the word in the form *gánske*). However, the example that Broch mentions does not provide sufficient evidence to determine the pronunciation in RN. In the Russian text to which Broch refers, the word occurs in the expression *kanske bra*, which is translated *det er bra* (it is good). Then in this case *kanske* must derive from the Norwegian word *ganske* (hence 'ganske bra' = 'pretty good') and not from *kanskje*, which does not fit the translation. Needless to say, the pronunciation of the relevant sequence in *ganske* must have been [-sk-]. The alternation between voiced and voiceless consonant is not specific to this word; there is a general tendency for words containing a voiced or voiceless plosive to develop parallel forms, e.g. *gav–gaf* (sea), *stoka–stoga* (storm), *basiba–spasiba* (thanks), *kak–gak* (when, how), *presentom–bresentom* (give), *strasvi–drasvi* (hello).

When Norwegians imitate Lapps who speak Norwegian, they often use the confusion of voiced and voiceless consonants to characterize the language. Here it should be mentioned that the Lappish plosives do not have the same distribution as their Norwegian counterparts. We know that the Lapps traded with the Russians (Paine 1957: 52), but we do not have any recorded use of RN by the Lapps. It is tempting to assume that the RN numerals we find in Broch (1930: 131) have made their way into RN via Lappish. Cases in point are *tva* < Russ. *dva*, *tvenatsit* < Russ. *dvenadcat'* (12), *tvatsit* < Russ. *dvadcat'* (20). The variants *stoka*, *stoga* etc. can be explained as a result of the fact that Norwegians tend to pronounce voiceless plosives as voiced. The voiceless plosives have less aspiration in Russian than in Norwegian, and hence we can assume that the Norwegians perceived them as voiced (cf. also RN *damosna* < Russ. *tamožnja*, duty or customs).

As Russian does not have voiced plosives or fricatives in final position, a change like *gav* > *gaf* (< Norw. *hav*, sea) is typical of a Russian speaker and will quickly be picked up by a Norwegian who is trying to conform to the way other people speak.

Russ. [z] and [ʒ] become unvoiced [s] in RN, e.g. *snai* < Russ. *znaj* (from *znat'*, to know), RN *damosna* < Russ. *tamožnja* (duty or customs). This is connected with the fact that most of the texts were written down by Norwegians. In the few Russian texts we know (Jakovlevič in Broch 1930, and Prišvin 1908) there are examples of [z], such as *prezentom* (give). While Norwegians say *prinsipal* (captain), Russians say *printsipal* (with [ts]), each in accordance with the pronunciation in their own language.

4.1.2. *Vowels.* The special Russian vowel [i], transliterated *y*, which is half-closed, central unrounded, is not represented in the Russian examples of RN texts. Hans Blom (1862: 32) writes about this vowel: 'The *i*-sound in question varies between i, y and partly u; the last when it is carelessly pronounced, and in the mixture of Norwegian, English (maybe also Dutch) and distorted Russian, which is used for some of the more indispensable expressions, under the name of RN.' In Broch's texts there are few words where the Russian original has [i]; only *vudra* < Russ.

vydra (otterskin); *Kodi reisa* and *Ko di reisa* (Where are you going?) where *kodi* <
Russ. *kudy*. In *Moia skasi* Broch interprets *skasi* as Norw. *ska(l)si* (shall say) (Broch
1930: 131), but it could just as well have come (or as a parallel) from Russ. *skaži*
(2nd pers. sing. imperative of *skazat'* – to say) where *-i* in Russian would have been
pronounced [i̇]. The Russian word for fish *ryba* [ri̇ba] does not occur in Broch's
material. Paulaharju (1928 (1973: 231)) has *ryjpa*, while Dybos (1959) uses
ryjba, ryjbak (fisherman). However, Dybos calls RN 'The now forgotten Pomor-
language', and it is obvious that his text is strongly influenced by his knowledge
of Russian. Therefore it cannot be used as a basis for a phonetic description of
RN.

New Norwegian vowels which do not exist in Russian are also sometimes changed:
/y/ is rendered as *y, ju, i* e.g. *lygom–ljugom–ligom* (to tell a lie); *dyr–djur* (expensive)
(cf. Broch 1927a: 251–2); for /ø/ Prišvin (1908) writes *ju* in the word *s'jul'* < Norw.
sjøl (-self). And while the Norwegians used the sound [ʉ] in e.g. *russmann* (Russian),
the Russians would pronounce [u] in accordance with their language.

4.2 Morphology

The morphology of RN is very simple. This is to be expected – pidgins in general
have little inflection and few, if any, conjugation categories. Categories such as
gender, number, case, tense, aspect, etc., which in Norwegian and Russian are
expressed morphologically, are almost non-existent in RN. The lexemes are as a
rule uninflectable and unchangeable, and the elements of meaning which are expressed morphologically in Norwegian and Russian must be expressed in another
way in RN, if they are expressed at all. As a rule the correct interpretation of an
expression will depend considerably upon the context. This is also an important
feature of the sharply reduced languages, of which RN is an example. Nevertheless
it is possible to say something about the morphology of RN, notably about how the
differences between the parts of speech are marked.

4.2.1. *Nouns.* The nouns in RN have a strong tendency to be marked by a final
-a, e.g.:

damosna	(customs office)
groppa	(grain)
klæba	(bread)
mokka	(meal or flour)
klokka (but also *klokk*)	(time, clock)
balduska	(halibut)
silka	(herring)
saika	(coalfish)
fiska	(fish)
penga	(money)

For some words *-ka* can perhaps be considered to be a noun marker, not only *-a*, see
above *balduska, silka, saika*. Other examples are *platka* (scarf), *futteralika* (towel),
etc. In these words the suffix *-ka* has two different origins: partly the Russ. fem.
diminutive suffix; partly masc. gen. as in RN *platka* (Russ. *platok*, gen. *platka*).

A certain number of nouns taken over from Russian end in -*i*:

RN		Russian
sukkari	(wheat rusk)	*suchar*, pl. *suchari*
kruski	(mug, cup)	*kružka*, pl. *kružki*
svedski	(candle)	*sveča*, pl. *sveči*
spitski	(matches)	*spički*
djengi	(money)	*den'gi*
treski and also *treska*	(cod)	*treska*

Nouns from Norwegian with only one syllable often retain this form in RN:

RN		Norwegian
vin, but also *vina*	(wine)[8]	*vin*
skip	(ship)	*skip*
ven	(friend)	*venn*
fisk, but also *fiska*	(fish)	*fisk*
gaf	(sea)	*hav*
mann	(man)	*mann*
pris	(price)	*pris*
glass	(glass)	*glass*

Likewise from Russian: *ras* (year, time) < *raz*, *tsjai* (tea) < *čaj*.

Nevertheless only -*a* aspires to be a general noun marking suffix. The nouns have no inflection, but – as we have seen from the examples – we can have doublets such as *fisk/fiska*, *dag/daga*, *vin/vina*, etc., without being able to show any systematic variation here.

Broch (1927a) discusses where the *a*-suffix could have originated, and he emphasizes that this ending often gives words 'a foreign sound' (1927a: 227) to Norwegian ears. In this connection he points out the exaggerated use of -*a* when Norwegians try to speak Swedish. It is not impossible that the *a*-suffix could have come to RN from Swedish, e.g. via *Borgarmålet* (see below pp. 51–2). Other possibilities include -*a* coming from Russ. fem. nominative or Russ. masc./neut. genitive – a natural form to use in connection with merchandise (partitive genitive). Two other reasonable possibilities, not mentioned by Broch, are the ending -*a* in the indefinite form of weak fem. nouns, an ending which is frequently used in northern Norway, or the *a*-ending in the sing. definite form of all fem. nouns in Norwegian.

Ove Lorentz has pointed out (personal communication) that this may also be due to Lappish influence. In Lappish, lexical morphemes are not normally monosyllables. In this language, monosyllabic loan words are usually made disyllabic by adding a final -*a*:

Norw. *bil* (car) > Lappish *biila*
Norw. *penn* (pen) > Lappish *peanna*
Norw. *stat* (state) > Lappish *stáhta*

It is quite plausible that this word-formation rule in Lappish is the origin of the tendency for RN nouns to acquire the word-final marker -*a*. This tendency must at least have been reinforced by the Lappish affixation process. It is difficult to decide whether one of these possibilities is more reasonable than the other. The ending -*ka*, however, can most reasonably be classified as coming from Russian. And the -*i* ending in several of the nouns likewise comes from Russian plural nominative/accusative. (The Russian words corresponding to RN *sukkari*, *spitski*, *djengi* are normally used in the plural.)

4.2.2. *Adjectives and adverbs.* The RN adjectives taken over from Russian end to a large extent in *-a*, e.g. *bela* (white), *bolsa* (big), *dobra* (good), *mala* (small), *malenka* (small), *stara* (old), *tsjorna* (black, dark), but this suffix is far from universal. *Korosjo* (good), with the stress on the last syllable, keeps the *-o* from the Russ. neuter form, while *dobro–dobra* (good) exhibits parallel forms.

The adjectives are not inflected: *bela mokka* (fem.) (white flour), *mala jonka* (masc.) (small boy), *fol maga* (masc.) (full stomach), *fol skip* (neutr.) (full ship). The adverbs also show a tendency towards an *-a* suffix, often with parallel forms: *mere–mera* (more), *litt–lite–lita* (little).

4.2.3. *Pronouns.* The *-a* suffix seems also to have spread in the pronouns. There are parallel forms *nokke* and *nokka* (some), *eta–etta–ette* (this). A possible explanation of the typical RN pronouns for 'I' and 'you' *moja* and *tvoja* (1 and 2 person singular personal and possessive) might be the expansion of the suffix *-a* in RN generally, supported by the use of the possessive feminine *moja, tvoja* in connection with the frequently used nouns *fiska* (fish), *groppa* (grain), *mokka* (flour).

4.2.4. *Verbs.* RN shows no copula, and has no verb for 'to have'. Even though the Norwegian RN users occasionally employ the Norwegian verb for 'to have' it is most usual to express this with the aid of the preposition phrase *på + pronoun/noun.* Verbs in RN have no inflection, and are as a rule marked with a suffix, *-om*, added to the verb root.

betalom	(pay)
drikkom	(drink)
lygom	(lie)
kastom	(throw)
slipom	(sleep)
skaffom	(eat)
robotom	(work)
reisom	(go, travel)
vegom	(weigh)
kralom	(steal)

However, a great number of verbs are not marked with this suffix; in this case the verbs have a form which is derived from different inflection categories in the base language:

bestil	(do)	Norw. imperative	*bestill*
ligge ne	(lie down, be)	Norw. infinitive	*ligge ned*
veit	(know)	Norw. present tense	*veit*
kom	(come, become)	Norw. preteritum	*kom*
plati	(pay)	Russ. imperative sing.	*plati*
pisat	(write)	Russ. infinitive	*pisat'*
vros	(lie)	Russ. 2nd pers. sing. present	*vrěš'*
stoit	(cost)	Russ. 3rd pers. sing. present	*stoit*
propal	(sink)	Russ. masc. sing. preteritum	*propal*
sprek	(say)	Low German imperative	*sprek*

Lunden (1978a: 16) has dealt with the verbs we find in the corpus with the verb marker *-om*. She has found that most of the verbs with this suffix are of non-Russian origin. There are only five verbs which are exceptions: *kopom* (buy), *robotom* (work), *smotrom* (see), *kralom* (steal), *podjom* (come). (Here we must add that the first four of these verbs occur frequently in the corpus: the total number of occurrences of -*om* verbs is thus more characterized by Russian than we would expect when only five of the verbs in the -*om* group are derived from Russian.) Lunden has also established that over 50% of the occurrences of $V + om$ are found in expressions beginning with *davai* or *værsego* (please), that is, in obvious hortative expressions. This seems to support Broch's view (Broch 1927a: 249) that the suffix -*om* has its origins in the Swedish hortative form, e.g. in *sjungom* (= let's sing).

Other explanations of the origins of the -*om* suffix have also been suggested. O.H. (1891: 140) claims, for example, that the suffix comes from Latin. More plausible is Daa's (1870: 162) suggestion that the suffix could have been derived from Russian, a hypothesis supported by Neumann (1965: 228) and Fox (1973: 53). Broch (1927a: 248-9), on the other hand, rejects the hypothesis of a Russian origin because of the recorded pronunciation of the suffix. In the texts it is claimed, at least from the Norwegian side, that the suffix was pronounced [um]and not [om], as Broch believes we would expect if Russian origin were correct.

Broch touches on the possibility of a Norwegian origin, via the preposition *om*, used post-positionally, as in the parallel expressions *stann-opp*, *ligge-ne* and *sitte-ne(d)*, but rejects the idea immediately. 'Man findet keine Spur einer solchen Verbindung' (We find no evidence of such a connection), he claims (1927a: 249). Lunden (1978a: 16) discusses this in depth with reference to the frequently used expression *trok(k) om trok(k)* (= ware for ware), and she believes that the preposition *om* could have played a role here: we also find *trokkom trok*, meaning 'let us trade'. Lunden refers to the French 'troc pour troc' as a better explanation for this expression than Broch's hypothesis about the verb 'troquer', and points out that we have parallels in Norwegian such as *pø om pø* from French 'peu à peu' alongside the expression *smått om senn* (slowly but surely). Lunden is obviously right in suggesting that the preposition *om* can have played a part in the development of *trok om trok* > *trokkom trok*. And it is perhaps not impossible either that the suffix -*om* expanded as a general verb marker from this, in view of the frequent occurrence of the expression *trok om trok*. However, we believe that Broch was right concerning the etymology of the *trok om trok* expression. The verb *troquer*, which Broch claims is the origin of *trok om trok*, occurs very early. In a letter from Amtmann Sidelmann in Finnmark in 1725 we find the expression 'troquere drikkevarer mod fisk' (trade liquor for fish), and in a letter from 1759 we find 'Troquering imod andre (. . .) Vahre' (trading for other wares). (Indkomne Breve fra Finmark 1695-1740 og 1750. Rentekammeret. Riksarkivet i Oslo.) Regardless of its origin, the suffix -*om* in RN has achieved a general verb-marking function, even though it is not used in all the verbs.

4.2.5. *Prepositions, conjunctions and numerals.* In principle only the preposition *på* is used in RN. This preposition is used to express all dependence relationships. However, we do find a few examples of the use of other prepositions:

(1)   *kak tvoja betalom for seika?*   What do you pay for coalfish?
       (what you pay for coalfish?)

(2)   *grot stoka na gaf*   heavy storm at sea
       (heavy storm on sea)

(3)   *moja vil kopum* hos *tvoja*   I will buy from you
        (I will buy at you)

På is found in both Norwegian and Russian (= *po*); *for* and *hos* are Norwegian, while *na* is Russian. We find several conjunctions.[9] *Og, i, ja, jes* are coordinating conjunctions. But we find only one which is subordinating, viz: *kak*:

(4)   *moja smotrom* kak *ju pisat*   I see that (how) you write
        (I see that you write)
(5)   kak *ju vina trinke, Kristus got vre*   When (if) you drink wine, Christ will be
        (when you wine drink, Christ very angry) very angry

Kak is from the Russian, where it has an extensive use. *Og* is Norwegian, *i* Russian; both mean 'and'. In Russian the word *da* (= yes) is frequently used in colloquial speech as a coordinating conjunction, particularly. It is interesting to note that in RN the Norwegian and English affirmatives *ja, jes* carry this function.

Numerals were important in RN, as is to be expected with all trade-jargons, and it appears that RN users could normally count in each other's languages (Broch 1927a: 236). We assume that this was an insurance against the use of wrong numbers and prices, either for the weight of fish or the weight or price of other goods.

4.3   Word formation

RN shows different word-forming mechanisms: there are examples of suffixes, compounding and reduplication.

4.3.1. *Suffixes*. As described above, RN had developed two general suffixes. The suffix *-a* is used to form nouns (see 4.2.1) and also – although less consistently – adjectives and adverbs (see 4.2.2). The general suffix *-om* is used to form verbs (see 4.2.4).

There is also a special suffix, *-mann*, used to designate persons of different nationality, or of different ethnic or social groups: *russmann* (Russian), *filmann* (Lapp), *kukmann* (merchant). This special suffix is attested in the earliest RN word we have found (i.e. *Rusmand* = Russian, in 1785; see p. 49).

4.3.2. *Compounding*. Forming new words by combining two nouns is very common in Norwegian. In RN we find compounds like *jemmreisa* 'home travel', taken directly from Norwegian (Norw. *hjemreise* < *hjem* = home, and *reise* = travel (noun)). But we also find some genuine RN compounds of this sort, showing that this word formation rule was productive in RN, e.g. *kuasjorta* 'cow-shirt' = cow-hide, *kuasalt* 'cow-salt' = salted meat, *russmannjunka* = Russian boy, and *morradag* 'tomorrow-day' = tomorrow. This type of word formation occurs in other pidgins as well (cf. Todd 1974: 56–7). When we find compounding as a way of forming new words in RN, we can consider this a general pidgin-feature manifested in RN, a feature which is indeed supported by similar ones in Norwegian.

4.3.3. *Reduplication*. The texts provide one example of word formation by re-duplication: *morra-morradag* (= day after tomorrow) formed from Norwegian (*i*)*morra* (= tomorrow) and *dag* (= day). While compounding is common in

Norwegian word formation, reduplication is not. However, word formation by reduplication is a common pidgin trait (cf. Todd 1974: 19–20, 55–6), which we also find frequently in child language.

4.4   Syntax

Broch 1927a has only a few comments to make on the syntax of RN. It is obvious that he regards RN as being almost without syntactic rules, e.g. a remark such as 'die jeder Regelung trotzende Freiheit in der Ausdrucksweise des RN' (the freedom of ways of expression in RN which defies any attempt to set up rules) (1927a: 231).

The syntax of RN is far from being without rules, but the syntactical possibilities are quite restricted. The largest variety seems to have developed in interrogative sentences, which is not unexpected considering that RN was used to ask questions about prices and barter for merchandise.

4.4.1. *Conjunction and subordination.* In RN sentences are generally combined paratactically without embedding or subordination. However, sentences can be coordinated by means of juxtaposition; the coordination may be indicated overtly by *så* (so, and, then):

(6)	*moja på anner skip nåkka vin drikkom, så*	I drank some wine on another ship, then
	moja nåkka lite pjan, så . . . etc.	I got a little drunk, then . . . etc.
	(I on other ship some wine drink, so I	
	some little drunk, so . . . etc.)	

In other cases we find the conjunctions *i, ja, jes*:

(7)	*principal grot pjan i på kåna kludi, ja*	The captain was very drunk and beat
	kanske på vater kastom	his wife, and maybe he'll throw her in
	(skipper very drunk and on wife beat,	the water
	yes, maybe on water throw)	

In some cases it is difficult to decide whether we have coordination or subordination:

(8)	*moja smotrom ju kralom*	I saw you steal
	(I see you steal)	
(9)	*moja smotrom junka kralom tros*	I saw the boy steal the hawser
	(I see boy steal hawser)	

The most likely interpretation is that the second sentence is embedded in the first in 8 and in 9; see sentence 10, where the embedding is clear:

| (10) | *moja smotrom kak ju pisat* | I saw that you were writing |
| | (I see that you write) | |

Similar comments apply to the following sentences:

(11)	*kak ju vil skaffom ja drikke te, davaj på*	If you want to eat and drink tea, then
	sjib tvoja ligge ne jes på slipom	come on board and lie down to sleep
	(If you will eat and drink tea, please on	
	ship your lie down and (on) sleep)	
(12)	*kak ju vina trinke, Kristus grot vre*	If you drink wine, Christ will be very
	(If you wine drink, Christ very angry)	angry
(13)	*Kristus grot vrei, tvoja ljugom*	Christ will be very angry, if you lie
	(Christ very angry, you lie)	

(14)   *moja ska si: ju grot lygom*   I must say you lie a lot
         (I shall say: you much lie)

(15)   *Gilbert, gammel go ven, sprek på moja:*   My good old friend Gilbert told me that
         tvoja grot rik   you are very rich
         (Gilbert, old good friend, says on me:
         you very rich)

4.4.2. *Main clauses.* We find declarative, interrogative and imperative/hortative
main clauses in RN. It is reasonable to assume that sentence intonation was often
used to signal the syntactic status of the sentence.

Declarative sentences were presumably marked by falling sentence-intonation.
Examples of declarative sentences are given above.

Interrogative sentences constitute the most heterogeneous group in RN. Five
different ways of forming them can be distinguished:

By using the question word *kak* (more rarely: *kor, koda, kodi, kori*):

(16) a.   *kak tvoja levom?*   How are you?
          (how you live?)

   b.   *kak pris på tvoja?*   What is your price?
          (what price on you?)

   c.   *kor ju stannom på gammel ras?*   Where did you stay last year?
          (where you stay on old time?)

   d.   *koda tvoja stannop*   Where are you staying?
          (where you stay?)

   e.   *kodi reisa?*   When are you leaving?
          (when leave?)

   f.   *kori vaskom?*   Where shall we wash/paint?
          (where wash/paint?)

The Norwegian equivalents of the above sentences normally have inversion of the
subject and verb: *wh- V. Subj.* instead of *Subj. V.* as in declarative sentences.
The fact that RN interrogatives do not exhibit inversion has previously been
explained as a syntactical simplification (e.g. Fox 1973: 55). However, here RN
follows the pattern set by Russian, which has SV order in questions beginning with
a *wh*-word when the subject is a pronoun. This is also the normal word order in
northern Norwegian dialects:

(17)   *kor du va i går?*   (Where you were yesterday?)

In most Norwegian dialects this question is serialized as:

(18)   *hvor/kor var du i går?*   (Where were you yesterday?)

In other words the lack of inversion in such sentences in RN is a result of transference by RN users from their native tongues. There is no need to interpret it as
part of a general syntactic simplification.

By intonation. Rising intonation is another criterion which can mark an interrogative sentence:

(19)   *tvoja fisk kopom?*   Will you buy fish?
         (you fish buy?)

   b.   *ju på morradag på moja treski njem?*   Will you fetch cod for me tomorrow?
         (you on tomorrow on me cod fetch?)

In interrogative sentences containing a modal verb, we find that RN corresponds to northern Norwegian dialects, and Norwegian generally:

(20)   *vil ju på moja stova på morradag*   Will you eat at my place tomorrow?
        skaffom?
        (will you on my house on tomorrow eat?)

By the suffix -*li*, which can be suffixed to different word classes:[10]

(21) a.   *mangoli år tvoja?*   How old are you?
           (many years you?)
     b.   *nogoli dag tvoja reisa?*   How many days did you travel?
           (many days you travel?)
     c.   *kak vara ju prodatli?*   What kinds of goods are you selling?
           (what goods you sell?)

By starting a sentence with the word *kanske*. This type is particularly common among the Russian RN-users.

(22) a.   *kanske lite tjai drikkom?*   Do you want to have some tea?
           (maybe little tea drink?)
     b.   *kanske tvoja vil glass tjai?*   Do you want a glass of tea?
           (maybe you will glass tea?)
     c.   *kanske litt på skaffom?*   Do you want to have something to eat?
           (maybe little on eat?)

Besides marking interrogation, this word was used so frequently that it almost became just a polite phrase without any concrete meaning.

Imperative sentences begin by directly naming the person one is speaking to:

(23) a.   *burman zakrepiko trosa lite gran'*   Fisherman, tighten the hawser a little!
           nemožko!
           (fisherman tighten hawser little some-
           thing little!)
     b.   *junga grebi moja po lan'!*   Boy, row me ashore!
           (boy row me on shore!)
     c.   *burman kom fiska!*   Fisherman, bring your fish!
           (fisherman come fish!)

A more *hortative* function is found in sentences which begin with *værsego* or *davaj* (please). The subject is usually not expressed:

(24) a.   *værsågo på skib kastom!*   Please, throw (the fish) on board the
           (please on ship throw!)   ship!
     b.   *vešagu fiska prezentom!*   Please, give me some fish!
           (please fish give!)
     c.   *værsego ju på moja skib vaskom!*   Please, wash/paint my ship!
           (please you on my ship wash/paint!)
     d.   *davaj på moja kopom!*   Trade with me!
           (please on me buy!)
     e.   *davaj på fiska dragom!*   Let's fish!
           (let's on fish haul!)

Note that in sentences where the listener is addressed directly, the verb is placed in second position, whereas the verb is normally placed in final position in sentences beginning with *værsego/davaj*.

4.4.3. *Dependent clauses, embedding.* We find very few examples of dependent or embedded clauses in the corpus, but we shall mention those which exist. There is one example of a dependent noun-clause:

(25)	*moja smottrom kak ju pisat*	I saw that (how) you were writing

The word *kak* (how) is used as a subordinating conjunction, and it is the only word to have this function in RN. We find a few conditional clauses:

(26) a.	*kak ju vil skaffom ja drikke te, davaj på*	If you want to eat and drink tea, (then)
	sjib tvoja ligge ne jes på slipom	come on board and lie down to sleep
	(if you will eat and drink tea, please on	
	ship you(r) lie down and on sleep)	
b.	*kak ju vina trinke, Kristus grot vre*	If you drink wine, Christ will be very
	(if you wine drink, Christ very angry)	angry

It is also possible that we have a conditional embedding in:

c.	*Kristus grot vrei, tvoja ljugom*	Christ will be very angry if you lie
	(Christ very angry, you lie)	

Even though we find very few examples of dependent clauses in the texts, there can be no doubt that the hypothesis that RN has no subordination on the sentence level is false (Slobin 1977: 201). It is not unreasonable to assume that the small size of the corpus is the reason for the rarity of dependent clauses attested. Once the word *kak* was introduced as a general conjunction, RN had clearly developed the grammatical apparatus necessary to mark subordination. Both Norwegian and Russian have a wide choice of conjunctions for marking various types of embedding and subordination. In RN this is simplified in such a way that *kak* is used on the sentence-level (macro-level) in the same way as the preposition *på* is used on the syntagma-level (micro-level).

4.4.4. *Word order.* Normal Norwegian word order in main clauses is SV(O). Norwegian has the verb-second constraint. Sentence adverbials are placed after the finite verb, but before an object. Other adverbials are normally placed in final position. By topicalization of either an object or an adverbial, we get inversion of the subject and verb, e.g. Adv. VS(O).

Because of the morphological structure of Russian, with six cases, personal endings in the present/future tense, and gender endings in the past tense, the word order is less strict than in Norwegian. The normal word order in Russian is SV(O). Sentence adverbials are usually placed before the finite verb. By topicalization of long adverbials we normally get inversion of the subject and verb.

Sentences which consist of a subject and verb have the order SV in RN:

(27) a.	*tvoja sprek*	You say/said
	(you say)	
b.	*moja slipom*	I sleep/slept
	(I sleep)	
c.	*tvoja lygom*	You lie/lied
	(you lie)	

Sentences which contain a subject, verb and direct object normally have the serial order SVO:

(28) a. *tvoja kopom oreka?*   Will you buy nuts?
         (you buy nuts)
     b. *moja kopom fiska*   I will buy some fish
         (I buy fish)
     c. *tvoja vegom fiska*   You must weigh the fish
         (you weigh fish)
     d. *tvoja kralom tros*   You have stolen the hawser
         (you steal hawser)
     e. *tvoja har konna?*   Have you got a wife?
         (you have wife?)

The texts show very few exceptions to this, but we do also find SOV order:

     f. *tvoja fisk kopom?*   Will you buy some fish?
         (you fish buy?)

In sentences containing an adverbial, the verb usually occurs in final position:

(29) a. *Moja tri vekkel stannom*   I stayed three weeks
         (I three week stay)
     b. *værsego ju på moja skib vaskom*   Will you wash/paint my ship?
         (please you on my ship wash/paint)
     c. *moja ette ort perevoj ras på Norge stan-*   I stay in Norway for the first time this
         nom   year
         (I this year first time on Norway stay)
     d. *moja tvoja på vater kasstom*   I shall throw you in the water
         (I you on water throw)
     e. *moja på anner skip nåkka vin drikkom* I drank some wine on another ship
         (I on other ship some wine drink)
     f. *han ikke sandfærdig sprek*   He is not speaking the truth
         (he not truthful speak)
     g. *moja på stova på Kristus sprek stannom* I was in church
         (I on house on Christ speak stay)

This placing of the verb is impossible in Norwegian. In Russian, however, it is possible if the sentence contains no object. In RN we also find these exceptions to the pattern in 29 a–g:

     h. *junga grebi moja po lan'*   Sailor, row me ashore
         (boy row me on shore)
     i. *kak tvoja betalom for seika?*   What do you pay for coalfish?
         (what you pay for coalfish?)
     j. *moja på ju bresentom bånbån*   I will give you a sweet
         (I on you give sweet)
     k. *ja robotom domo*   I work at home
         (I work home)

The negation-adverb (*ikke, njet*) is virtually restricted to second position:

(30) a. *etta njet dobra*   This is not good
         (this not good)
     b. *moja njet vros*   I don't lie
         (I not lie)
     c. *på den dag ikke russefolk arbei*   On that day Russians do not work
         (on that day not Russians work)
     d. *moja njet skaffom govedina på den vekkel* I do not eat meat that week
         (I not eat meat on that week)

The following examples are exceptional:

e. *mangoli år moja njet smotrom tvoja*   I have not seen you for many years
    (many years I not see you)
f. *den pris moja ikke betalom*   I will not pay that price
    (that price I not pay)

In the VP of a sentence, the verb (V), object (O) and adverbial (A) can be placed freely in relation to one another, even though there is a tendency for the verb to come in final position if it co-occurs with an adverbial. The existing possibilities can be shown as follows:

(31) a. V O A *(moja njet) skaffom govedina på*   (I do not) eat meat that week
         den vikkel
         ((I not) eat meat on that week)
     b. O V A *treska kopom på den dag*   buy cod that day
         (cod buy on that day)
     c. A V O *på ju bresentom bånbån*   give you sweet
         (on you give sweet)
     d. A O V *på moja skib kjai drikkom*   drink tea on my ship
         (on my ship tea drink)
     e. O A V *tvoja på vater kasstom*   throw you in the water
         (you on water throw)

For the last possible combination (V A O), there is not a great deal of evidence in the corpus. It is not inconceivable that the following sentences can be subsumed under this category:

f. V A O *(Gilbert, gammel go ven) sprek på*   (my good, old friend Gilbert) told me
    moja: tvoja grot rik   that you are very rich
    ((Gilbert, old good friend) say
    on me: you very rich)
g. *(moja) skasi på ju, kak ju*   (I) shall tell you, if you . . .
    ((I) shall say on you, if you . . .)

In addition to the six possible combinations listed above, we also find sentences with two VP-adverbials after another. In this case the verb is placed in final position as usual:

(32)   *ju på morradag på moja treski njem*   Will you fetch cod from me tomorrow
       (you on tomorrow on me cod fetch)

Our material contains several examples of topicalization. However, the direct object cannot be moved to initial position, because there is no morphological difference between subject and object. A topicalized object would be interpreted as the subject, and accordingly the active part in the sentence. Adverbials, on the other hand, can be topicalized:

(33) a. *på den dag ikke russefolk arbei*   On that day Russians do not work
         (on that day not Russians work)
     b. *mangoli år moja njet smotrom tvoja*   I have not seen you for many years
         (many years I not see you)

4.4.5. *Noun phrases.* An NP usually consists of only one noun, but it can also include an adjective:

(34) a. *gammel ras*   (last year; lit. old time)
     b. *grot storm*   (heavy storm)

Article, modifier and head are attested in:

   c.   *den gammel uri*   (that old catfish)

Otherwise we find combinations with pronouns:

(35)	a.	*moja kantor*	(my office)
	b.	*ander kantor*	(another office)
	c.	*kak sort fiska*	(what kind of fish)
	d.	*nåkka vin*	(some wine)

The following NP is very complicated:

(36)	a.	*stova på Kristus spræk*	(church; lit. house on Christ speak)

found in the sentence:

	b.	*moja på stova på Kristus spræk stannom*	(I was in church; lit. I in house on Christ speak stay)

4.4.6. *Adjective phrases (predicatives).* The predicate can consist of a predicative alone. RN has no overt copula, a common trait in many pidgins, and also in Russian.

An adjective phrase in predicative position can consist of several elements, even though the texts do not have many examples of this:

(37)	a.	tvoja *grot rik*	You (are) very rich
	b.	Kristus *grot vre*	Christ (is) very angry
	c.	moja *nokka lite pjan*	I (am) a little drunk; (lit. some little drunk)
	d.	ju *dovolna pjan*	You (are) rather drunk

4.4.7. *Adverbials.* The adverbials in RN consist partly of adverbs, partly of prepositional phrases and partly of the Norwegian negation word *ikke* or the Russian *njet*.

(38)	a.	ja robotom *domo*	I work at home
	b.	moja tvoja *på vater* kasstom	I shall throw you in the water
	c.	han *ikke* sanfærdi sprek	He is not speaking the truth
	d.	moja *njet* vros	I don't lie

4.4.8. *Case relations.* Case relations are generally expressed by means of the preposition *på* (*po*). Slobin (1977: 200 and 1979: 45) claims that the combination noun+noun expresses a possessive relationship in which the first noun is the possessor, the second the person or object possessed. But the only examples in the corpus to which this could apply are *kuasjorta* (cowhide) and *kuasalt* (salted meat), which must rather be analysed as two compound words. However, a possessive relationship in RN is expressed by a pronoun preceding the noun, or by a prepositional phrase:

(39)	a.	*kor ju stova*	(Where is your house?)
	b.	*på moja stova*	(in my house)
	c.	*kak posjivat tvoja madam?* (Dybos)	(How is your wife?)
	d.	*mangoli klokka på ju?*	(What time do you have?)

Expressing a possessive relationship by a prepositional phrase is normal in Norwegian.

In other words the preposition *på* can be used to express all the dependent relationships in a sentence, even a possessive relationship. We can divide the use of *på* into the following semantic categories:

(40) a. possessive: *klokka på ju*   (your watch)
    b. local: *mala penge på lomma*   (little money in the pocket)
    c.   *principal på sjib?*   (Is the captain on board the ship?)
    d. temporal: *på morradag*   (tomorrow)
    e.   *på gammel ras*   (last year)
    f. directional: *moja tvoja på vater kasstom* (I will throw you in the water)
    g.   *nogoli dag tvoja reisa på*   (How many days did you travel from
             Arkangel otsuda?   Archangel (to get) here?)
    h.   *på Arkangel reisom*   (go to Archangel)

4.4.9. *Tense and aspect.* Both Norwegian and Russian express tense by a verb form, whereas only the verbs in Russian show number, gender, and aspect. In RN the latter categories are not normally expressed by the verb. However, in some instances the present tense form of the Norwegian modal auxiliaries *skulle* and *ville*, together with the base of the lexical verb, refers to pure future or volition + future:

(41) a. *vil ju på moja stova på morradag skaffom?*   Will you eat at my place tomorrow?
       (will you on my house on tomorrow eat?)
    b. *tvoja skal bli kammerat på moja på anner*   You shall be my friend next year
       år
       (you shall be friend on me on other year)
    c. *moja vil spræk på principal*   I want to speak to the captain
       (I will speak on captain)
    d. *moja vil snakka på tvoja*   I want to talk to you
       (I will speak on you)
    e. *moja vil kopum hos tvoja*   I want to trade with you
       (I will buy at you)

We do not find any examples of number inflection in RN. However, it has been suggested that RN did develop a way in which to express aspect. Fox (1973: 57–60) claims that the construction *på* + V could possibly be used to distinguish between finite and non-finite verbs, and that aspectual conditions could be indicated in this way. As far as we can see, the texts do not lend support to such a view. First, it is unclear what Fox means by 'finite' and 'non-finite' verbs; secondly, it is difficult to posit common grammatical-semantic components for the 18 occurrences we have of the construction in question:

(42) a. *værsågo, lita klæba på presentom*   (Please, give me some bread)
    b. *kanske litt på skaffom?*   (Perhaps you want something to eat?)
    c. *davaj på skrivom*   (Let me write)
    d. *no tvåja på kastom visit treska* (Now you can throw the cod on board
                         and weigh it)
    e. *davaj på skib tvåja ligene jes på slipom* (Let us have a rest on your ship)
    f. *grot på slipom*   (Sleep much/heavily)
       (*strasvi, junka. Principal på skib?*) (Hello, boy, is the captain on board)
    g. *-jes, på skaffom*   (Yes, he is eating)
  (h.) *-jes, på slipom*   (Yes, he is sleeping)
    i. *davai påproberom*   (Let us try)

    j.   davai *påsmotrom* på skib   (Let us have a look at the boat)
    k.   *podjom*   (Come here)
    l.   moja *poslagom* po tvoja   (I shall hit you)

In addition to these examples, which are taken from Broch 1930, we can quote the following ones from Lunden 1978a:

    m.   russemann dårlig mann, grot skade på   (The Russian bad man, you have done
           tvoja, *påschlagom*   much damage, I shall beat you)
    n.   nå gaima kanskje trovva *på presentom*   (Now perhaps my namesake will give me
                                        some firewood)
    o.   tvoja *po-rejza?*   (Are you leaving?)

Finally, there are two examples in Dybos (1959) and one in Mikkelsen (1978: 87):

    p.   prinsipal *på slipom?*   (Is the captain asleep?)
    q.   gå *på slipom*   (Lie down and go to sleep)
    r.   Reise på Rosland! På slagom! På slagom!   (Go to Russia! To fight! To fight!)

A problem which Fox also mentions explicitly, is whether the *på*-element here should be analysed as a verbal prefix or as an independent grammatical element. As we can see, the corpus contains examples of both these constructions. In most of the examples it would be possible to say that *på* + V indicates future time. However, such an analysis does not account for (g) and (h). As Fox notes, there appears to be no common aspectual feature. He contends that (h) is 'limited durative', that (a) 'appears to be perfective' and that several of the other examples are 'purposive'. If it were the case that *på* + V expressed aspectual content, then we would have to assume that it was something *common* at least, so that a feature [± aspect] could be used in the description. But since we cannot have a verb that does not express any aspectual relationships on the content-level, this analysis is inadequate. Therefore we have to reject Fox's analysis, and conclude instead that the construction *på* + V and V alone can be used interchangeably.

4.4.10. *Verbs with existential meaning.* Some verbs (*ligge ne, slipom, stannom, stannop*) can convey existential meaning:

(43)   a.   *Altsamma på salt ligge ne* (or *slipom*)   Everything has been salted
            (everything on salt lie down (or sleep))
        b.   *værsego på moja skib ligge ned tjai drik-*   Come on board my ship and have some
            kom   tea
            (please on my ship lie down tea drink)
        c.   *Kor ju stannom på gammel ras?*   Where did you stay last year?
            (where you stay on old time?)
        d.   *Kor ju ligga ned på gammel dag?*   Where were you yesterday?
            (where you lie down on old day?)
        e.   *Ja på madam Klerck tri daga ligene*   I stayed three days at Madam Klerck's
            (I on Madam Klerck three days lie down)
        f.   *nogli ras på gav ju stannom (spaserom)?*   How many days did you stay at sea?
            (many times on sea you stay (walk)?)
        g.   *moja tri vekel stannom*   I stayed three weeks
            (I three weeks stay)
        h.   *moja, jes, på Besfjur liggné*   Yes, I was at Besfjord
            (I, yes, on Besfjord lie down)
        i.   *koda tvoja stannop?*   Where did you stay?
            (where you stay?)

4.5 Semantic expansion, circumlocution

It is usual in pidgin languages to find quite drastic semantic expansion of certain terms. In addition to this, new terms are often formed by rewriting previously known words and terms. One example in RN is the existential meaning of the verbs *ligge ne*, *stann op*, *slipom* (lit. lie down, stand up, sleep); another example is afforded by the verb *vaskom*:

(44) a. *lille junka på kjerka* vaskom   (baptize)
      (little boy on church wash)
   b. *i kahyt* vaskom   (paint, wash)
      (in cabin wash)

The most quoted examples, however, are *kuasjorta* for 'hide' and *kuasalt* for 'salted meat' (here, the Russian *govedina* (beef) is also used). Besides the word *kjerka* (church), the very complicated circumlocution *stova på Kristus spræk* (house on Christ speak) is also found. Another example is the expression *gammel ras* (old time) used for 'last year'.

4.6 Lexicon

The RN corpus consists of approximately 390 words, half of which are *hapax legomena*. As has been mentioned earlier, the vocabulary of RN derives from several languages:

Dutch/Low German		English		French		Swedish	
grot	(big)	*jes*	(yes, and)	*trokk*	(goods)	*kukmann*	(merchant)
krank	(ill)	*better*	(better)	*trokkom*	(barter)		
sprek	(speak)	*slipom*	(sleep)			*Finnish*	
junka	(boy, fellow)	*ju*	(you)			*pojka*	(boy)
njem	(take)	*verrigod*	(very good)			*gaima*	(namesake)
pakkhaüs	(storehouse)					(could also be from	
vater	(water)					Lappish)	
vat	(what)						

International nautical jargon
skaffom   (eat)

Lappish
jossa   (haddock)
tiksa   (haddock)
balda   (halibut)
saika (?) (coalfish)

However, Russian and Norwegian are definitely the main sources. Fox estimates that appr. 47% of the vocabulary stems from Norwegian, 39% from Russian (Fox 1973: 62).

In the case of words derived from English, Dutch or Low German, we generally find parallel forms stemming from one of the two base languages, e.g. *drinkom*, *trinkom* besides *drikkom* (drink) from Norwegian; *grot* besides *bolsa* (big) from Russian. A typical feature of the lexicon of RN is the many doublets. This is especially striking in the case of the adjectives. Their number is small, but most of them have parallel forms: *stara–gammel* (old), *bolsa–grot* (big), *mala–malenka–lite–lita* (small, little), *bra–good–dobra–dobro–korosjo* (good, well), *dorgli–dorogli–dyr–djur* (expensive).[11] The adjectives mostly stem from Norwegian and Russian; the only exceptions are *grot* (big) from Low German, a word that is frequently used, *krank*, *kranke* (ill) also from Low German, and *verrigod* from English. While *full* in Norwegian means both 'intoxicated' and 'filled', RN *fol* means 'filled'. For 'drunk' RN uses the originally Russian *pjan* (Russ. masc. adj. short form *pjan* = drunk).

While verbs, nouns etc. tend to have parallel forms in RN, grammatical words exhibit the opposite tendency. Thus *på* occurs in a number of functions; and the RN *wh*-words cover a much broader range of questions than the same words do in their base language. The part of the lexicon that covers the bartering goods does not usually show parallel forms. This is obviously a field where precision was necessary. Nonetheless, the names of the various species of fish present a more complex picture (cf. also p. 52). As regards the concept 'fish', the Broch corpus has only *fisk/fiska*.[12] Some fish names occur frequently in the texts. We shall now take a closer look at these names:

treska, *treski* (cod, from Russ. *treska*) and *subadtka*, *sobaka* (lumpfish, from Russ. *zubatka*) are very common.[13] *Saika* (coalfish, from Russ. *saida* or Lappish *sáidi*) also has the form *seika*, which is possibly derived from Norw. *sei*+the common suffix *-ka*. Halibut and haddock have many names in RN: *paltus*, *paltuska*, *baltuska*, *paltasina*, *baldasina* (halibut) come from Russian *paltus*, *paltasina*, while the form *balda* may be connected with Lappish *bálddis*. *Piksa*, *piksja* (haddock) is derived from Russ. *pikša*, while *tiksa*, *tiksja*[14] may go back to Lappish *diksu*. Reusch (1895) has the form *jossa* besides *tiksa*. It is likely that this form is related to Lappish *juksu*, which together with *diksu*, is the Lappish designation for 'haddock'. The processed fish is referred to as *laberdan*, *runtovva–runtofki* and *råskerka*. The last two words are also listed in Podvysockij's dictionary of the Archangel dialect (1885: 149–50). He points out that the words are corruptions of *rundfisk* and *rotskjær* (the Norw. forms), and that they are used in Kola. In fact, these words are borrowings from RN.

The goods that the Russians brought to Norway also took their RN names from Russian, e.g. *mokka* (flour), *groppa* (grain), *beresta* (birch bark), *masla* (butter), *spidits* (matches), from Russ. *muka*, *krupa*, *beresta*, *maslo* – gen. *masla*, *spički* – gen. *spiček*.

5   Origins, development and use of RN

RN is first referred to between 1812 and 1814. Baron F. W. Wedel Jarlsberg (1787–1863) was Amtmann in Finnmark in this period. He wrote several memoranda about the county. These notes were published in the sixth volume of the magazine *Illustreret Familielæsning* in 1887. F. W. Wedel Jarlsberg writes here, after first having commented on Norwegian, Lappish and *Kvensk*: 'A fourth language is also spoken in Finnmark; put together from Norwegian, Russian, Dutch, German, Lappish and maybe "Kvensk". One could call it the Trade Language

(*Handelssproget*), because it is used by traders in order for them to understand each other. However, it is only used when dealing with Russians' (Jarlsberg 1887: 152).

We see that Wedel Jarlsberg calls RN a 'language', but according to him this language was only used during trade with the Russians.

Wedel Jarlsberg's reference to RN is the earliest we have found. Olaf Broch found his first example of RN in Lund 1842. Lunden (1978a) was able to move this further back still to 1827, taken from Blom 1830. In our material, however, RN words occur as early as 1785 and 1807.

A lawsuit in 1785 provides us with the RN word for a 'Russian': *russmann*, spelt 'Rusmand'. This word is listed in Reusch (1895: 47, cf. Brun 1878: 82) along with words for Lapp (*filmann*), Norwegian farmer and fisherman (*burmann*), mountain Lapp (*olenamann*, literally 'reindeerman'), and merchant (*kukmann*). It is obvious that the suffix -*mann* is used to designate both nationality and different occupational groups. In the lawsuit in 1785, one of the witnesses is called 'Rusmand Gregorius Pettersøn Breche'.

Usually in the legal records Russians are called 'Rus(s)' or 'Rys(s)', and this is the only time the RN word for a Russian is used (Justisprotokoll for Finnmark No. 44, fol. 242, Hammerfest gjesterett 1 April 1785).

In the legal records for Finnmark for 1807 we have found a new occurrence of a RN word. A Russian fisherman is quoted directly as shouting 'Biønemad' and 'Krallum': 'the first word is in Danish [i.e. Norwegian] a rude term of abuse towards the Danes [i.e. the Norwegians]. The second word has the same meaning as to steal or to commit theft, as the witness explained.' (Justisprotokoll for Finnmark No. 48, fol. 28, Vardø ekstrarett 27 November 1807.) *Krallum* (< Russ. *krast'*, pret. *kral-*, = to steal) later occurs several times in the RN corpus, and we see the first occurrence of the verbal marker in RN, here spelt -*um*. The other word, *Biønemad* (= Russ. *ebëna mat'* < *ëbat'* = 'fuck', and *mat'* = mother) does not appear in any later RN text, but is a common and very vulgar insult.[15]

The words *Rusmand* from 1785, and *Krallum* from 1807 are the first definite occurrences of RN we have found. More doubtful is an expression from a lawsuit in 1760, where the Russian Jan (Ivan) Foederovitz had accused the hired hand Urias Larsen because the latter had assaulted him (lit. injured his health) ('Denne skal have læderet ham paa sin helsen') (Justisprotokoll for Finnmark No. 41, p. 543, Kjelvik ting, 21 July 1760). The interesting point here is the use of the preposition *på* (on) in '*paa* sin helsen' (on his health). It is possible that we have here the first example of the general preposition *på* which is used in RN. However, *på* is not an unexpected preposition in this case, e.g. the expression 'ta skade *på* helsa' ('injure one's health'). Therefore we do not venture to consider this to be a reliable example of the *på*-use in RN. Another consideration which makes the example unreliable is the fact that the Russian had an interpreter along with him before the court, and we cannot be sure whether he really expressed himself in this way or not. However, in 1764 in Vadsø in a lawsuit against ten Russian fishermen accused of drunken fighting, it was possible for them to express themselves without the aid of a translator, so they were obviously able to make themselves understood in a common language. (Justisprotokoll for Finnmark No. 41b, pp. 1166–9, Vadsø ting 24 June 1764).

In view of these findings, we must assume that RN developed during the second half of the 18th century, and that by the early 19th century it was developed to the extent that we find it in the later texts.

After Wedel Jarlsberg, Blom 1830 is the next person to report on RN, and he claims RN was incomprehensible to those who had not learned it. Blom describes RN as 'a kind of Norwegian which is spoken and understood by those who are accustomed to dealing with the Russians' (Blom 1830: 298). We also find a very short sample of RN here. Still, this sample shows that several of the characteristic features of RN have developed: the use of *på* to express dependence, and the use of *ligge ne(r)* in its existential meaning: 'Tre Daga paa Christensen ligge ner og otte Daga paa Mad. Kildahl ligge ner.' (Three days on Christensen lie down and eight days on Mrs Kildahl lie down, i.e. I spent three days at Christensen's and eight days at Mrs Kildahl's.) Note that all the words in the quoted sentence are Norwegian. The reasons why we can say that this is RN are the use of *på* and the expression *ligge ner* meaning 'to be'.

We have four different and independent reports of RN dating from around 1840. Rode (1842) refers to RN in his records from Finnmark 1826–34, when he served there as a priest. Lund (1842) describes a journey to Finnmark in 1841, Lönnrot (1842) a journey to Kola in 1842, and Siljeström (1842) a journey to Finnmark in 1838. Lund 1842 and Lönnrot 1842 are dealt with in Broch 1927, but we discovered Rode 1842 and Siljeström 1842. In the latter we find the first occurrence of the expression *Kuaskjorta* (Siljeström writes *koskjorta* (Siljeström 1842: 13)) meaning 'cowhide', an expression later used to exemplify – and perhaps ridicule – the RN way of speaking. Far from being ridiculous, this expression is a good example of how it is possible to develop the vocabulary with compound words, where the root-words are already known. This way of expanding vocabulary is usual in Norwegian too.

Together Lund, Lönnrot and Siljeström give examples of all the characteristic features of RN which we know from later sources, with the exception of the personal pronouns *moja* and *tvoja* (*moja* is first recorded in Hansen 1862: 31, *tvoja* in Brun 1878).

Early in the 19th century RN spread to the most important trading centres in Finnmark and Troms. Up to 1842 the use of RN is reported in the following areas: Wedel Jarlsberg and Rode just mention Finnmark in general; Blom (1830) mentions Tromsø; Siljeström (1842) refers to RN in Hammerfest; Lund (1842), in Repvåg (in the Porsangerfjord) and Tromsø, while Lönnrot (1842) mentions Kola. The area in which RN use is reported up to 1842 spans the distance from Kola, (Russia) in the east to Tromsø (Norway) in the west, a stretch of coastline about 740 km long.

For RN to have been spread this far it must have achieved a certain degree of solidity. It is difficult to believe that the language could have attained so great a circulation if it contained an endless number of varieties. From Wedel Jarlsberg's and Blom's reports we see that RN was regarded as an existing 'language', and the anonymous author of an article in the journal *Skilling-Magazin* (1855: 231) writes that RN 'has until now, been the ordinarily used language between the Norwegians and Russians'. This must mean that as early as in 1855 RN was considered to be a language which had been in use for a long period of time. Therefore it can hardly be correct (as Lunden 1978a: 14 writes) that RN was not circulating in its fully developed form until the end of the 19th century. We must assume that RN was a fully developed contact vernacular early in the 19th century for use in transactions between the Russians and Norwegians.

As mentioned earlier, Fox 1973 claims that RN was developed by the 'grammaticalization' of an international Northern European base-vocabulary, that is, that a grammatical structure was superimposed on an existing vocabulary. The main argument for his hypothesis is that no report or trace exists of any earlier pidgin in this area from which RN's grammatical structure could have originated. Regardless of whether any earlier pidgin existed or not, Fox's hypothesis of a grammaticalization of the base-vocabulary which he claims existed, can barely stand up to close examination. Fox has not produced convincing evidence or arguments that such a vocabulary existed. He thinks this vocabulary was brought northwards by, among others, soldiers at the Vardøhus fortress, and that there existed in Scandinavia at the time a Scandinavian–European soldier's slang ('a soldier's cant') which contained most of this vocabulary.[16]

We think we can progress beyond Fox's theory. One reason for this is that we have found evidence of a pidgin in the northern area previous to RN. Pehr Högström (1747) reports on a Swedish–Lappish auxiliary language which the Lapps called 'Borgarmålet'. Högström's examples of this vernacular show obvious pidgin attributes: the verbs appear in only one form (imperative) and the nouns show no inflection. We also see a tendency towards expanded use of the preposition *uti* ('out in' (e.g. the garden)), but it is difficult to say whether or not this use can be compared to the use of *på* in RN. Högström (1747: 76–7) writes as follows:

Lastly I wish to say, that while there are different peoples in Lappland who trade with each other, Swedes, Lapps, Finlanders, Danes [= Norwegians], and Russians, all of whom have their own languages, they still have a common language, *lingua communi*, which they use regularly and all understand. In Lule–Lappland Lappish is used, which Finlanders and Swedes can somehow manage to understand. In Tornedalen and Kemi-Lappland, Finnish is the generally accepted language, which everyone (Swedes, Lapps, Russians, and others) understands so well that they can manage to communicate.

In the southern parts of Lappland a large proportion of the Lapps understand Swedish, and a large proportion of Swedes understand Lappish. But in some places nearly everyone can express themselves in the language they call *Borgarmålet*. I do not know why some members of the *Borgerskap*[17] in the market towns who trade with the Lapps and have dealings with them annually at their usual places of business, have started to use a language which is distinct from both Swedish and Lappish.

We see that *Borgarmålet* is directly connected to the trade between Lapps and Swedish merchants. We cannot share Högström's astonishment at the fact that merchants started using this auxiliary language: even if a number of Lapps spoke Swedish, and some of the merchants spoke Lappish, it was surely more usual that they did *not* know the other language and therefore needed a common vernacular. Högström gives five sentences as examples of *Borgarmålet*:

(45)   *Du stick uti mäg din skin, så ja sätt uti däg min bränwin.*
      (You give me your leatherware, then I give you liquor in return.)

(46)   *Du släpp din räf uti min våm, så få du din bak den pelsomesak.*
        (You give this turnip to my stomach, then I give you this fur in return.)
(47)   *Den Lapman kast sin renost bak i den borgar.*
        (The Lapp gives the reindeer cheese to the *borgar*.)
(48)   *Som du wara rätt stin.*
        (You are very expensive.)
(49)   *Hur sit din heit?*
        (What are you called?)

The Lapps claimed they had learned this from the *Borgerskap*, but according to Högström they were fully aware that this was not Swedish. When asked whether they spoke Swedish, they answered that they could only speak *Borgarmålet*, or 'that which they had learned from the *Borgerskap*' (Högström 1747: 77).

There is not much in Högström's examples which directly reminds one of RN. The vocabulary is predominantly Swedish, while the syntax is predominantly Lappish (Ruong 1980: 33). But *lapman* for 'Lapp' is formed in the same way as its equivalent in RN (*filmann*). We saw above that the first definite occurrence of a RN word was formed in exactly this way. (That is, *Rusmand* for 'Russian', from 1785 (see p. 49).) Compared with Swedish and Lappish the simplifications in Högström's examples further show that this must have been a pidgin of the same kind as RN. It is therefore incorrect that no pidgins existed in the area previous to the development of RN. What remains to be discussed is whether this earlier pidgin had any influence on the development of RN. Lönnrot (1842: 325) claims that *Borgarmålet* 'in all probability' is a dialect of the *kakspreck* (= RN) he describes.

In an earlier paper (Broch and Jahr 1980) we claimed that there is a possibility that RN took over the grammatical structure of an earlier pidgin from this area, and that RN emerged by relexification, which then affected the substance of the Lappish, Finnish and Swedish words. It has also been claimed (Broch 1928) that there were several time-levels in RN, and that Lappish must have contributed to a larger degree to the earlier vocabulary of RN than it is now possible to establish on the basis of the available texts. Fish names in RN (cf. 4.6) show several interesting doublets which can be used as an indication of possible relexification. Broch (1927a: 257) comments on this as follows:

Namen der für Zubereitung und Handel wichtigeren Seefische, von den Norwegern gegeben, wurden in früheren, zum Teil sogar sehr alten Zeiten von den Lappen des Eismeerufers aufgenommen. Die später hinkommenden Russen haben die betreffenden Namen nicht von den Norwegern erhalten, sondern zuerst, und zwar wohl bevor sie mit den Norwegern in direkte Handelsbeziehungen traten, von den Lappen. Aus der so entstandenen russ. Nomenklatur hat die späte Schöpfung des RN seine Fischnamen bekommen; in neuester Zeit waren aber die jetzigen norw. Namensformen im Begriff, in das RN einzudringen.[18]

What Broch describes could be an example of relexification of part of the RN vocabulary. It is not improbable that other parts of the vocabulary might have undergone the same process.

The contact between Lapps and Russians is also reflected in some Russian loan words in Finnmark–Lappish. Nesheim (1947) mentions a total of ten words which he claims are borrowed directly from Russian into Lappish. These words show what kind of goods the Lapps mainly got from the Russians. The Lappish word *rássa* = time (once, twice, etc.) corresponds directly to *ras* in RN (< Russ. *raz*), in the expression *på gammel ras* = earlier; while the Lappish word *gásak* = Russian sailor (this special meaning attested in Polmak) < Russ. *kazak* corresponds to *soi(k)a* in RN (Eriksen 1971b) < Russ. *zuëk*, gen. *zujka* = young Russian sailor. Another word which Nesheim believes shows direct contact between the Lapps and Russians is *roagga* = Russian sack, with or without flour in it (< Russ. *rogoža* = bast sack). The word for 'Russian sack' occurs in RN as *kul moki* (< Russ. *kul' moki* = grain sack) and in Bergh (1950: 135) as *matta* (< Norw. *matte*).

Also worth mentioning is the fact that the Lapps are known for being generally skilled in languages. It was not unusual for Lapps to speak two or three languages (Lappish/Norwegian/Finnish). In Finnmark we often find Lapps mentioned as interpreters in lawsuits in which Russians were involved.

From our point of view it is even more interesting that the Lapps have shown a large degree of linguistic creativity in developing secret languages to use among themselves to prevent others from understanding their conversation. Qvigstad (1909) gives several examples of such jargon.

Thus there is reason to believe that the Lapps played a far greater role in the formation of RN than the few Lappish elements in the later RN texts could reveal.

Lönnrot (1842: 325) claims that RN (which he calls *kakspreck*) 'contains the basic elements not only of the Russian and Norwegian languages, but also of Finnish and Lappish'. And Siljeström (1842: 13) refers not only to an auxiliary language of Norwegian and Russian, but also to vernaculars of Norwegian and Lappish, and Norwegian and *Kvensk*:

The merchant usually understands somewhat the three different languages needed to deal with Russians, Lapps, and Kvens, and the latter on their part usually understand a certain amount of Norwegian, so that the trade jargon is composed of a kind of gibberish ('rotvälska') of the latter language, and of one of the three former.

It is only to be expected that we will find several such mixed languages in the area. But eventually it was RN that proved to be the most important vernacular, and it was this jargon which acquired a certain structural solidity, in contrast to the other varieties which remained improvised solutions to the problem of the communication barrier. This does not discount the fact that RN could have borrowed and developed structures and grammatical elements from some of these varieties, which later disappeared.

As mentioned above, there is not very much in Högström's examples of *Borgarmålet* which corresponds directly to RN; however, it is worth mentioning that the features of RN which were earlier assumed to have Swedish origins are precisely the ones which affect the grammatical structure: the verbal marker -*om* and the noun marker -*a*. It it is true that these grammatical markers originally came from Swedish, then it is not inconceivable that they entered RN via an earlier auxiliary language of which Swedish was one of the base-languages.

Tatjana Alimova (1976) has come across a small hand-written phrase book in the collection of manuscripts at the Puškinskij Dom in Leningrad. She claims that this Russian–Swedish phrase book was used by Pomors from Vytegra when they traded with Norwegians. In all, it contains three pages of words and twenty sentences dealing with trade. The texts are in Russian and in a somewhat corrupt Swedish. One of the 'Swedish' sentences reads:

> Kukmaned ferer mjuke pengar' (the merchant has much money)

We find the word kukmaned particularly interesting: this is the very word used in RN (the final d must be due to a slip of the pen). This word is an important and frequently used word in RN; if it was taken over from Swedish, e.g. via a Russian–Swedish phrase book, then it is not unreasonable to assume that other Swedish features may have made their way into RN in a similar manner.

Today, it is of course difficult to determine whether RN was based on earlier pidgins, and whether it adopted features from these possible pidgins as well as from primitive phrase books of the type mentioned above. Nevertheless, we contend that Högström's report on Borgarmålet and the Russian–Swedish phrase book shed new light on the origin and development of RN.

The descriptions of RN from the 19th century vary with regard to the degree to which the language was judged to be solid and permanent. Since RN was usually compared to natural, fully-developed languages, the descriptions were often rather depreciatory. Lund (1842: 62) calls RN 'the most constructionless mode of communication imaginable'. Daa (1870: 162) calls RN dette Kragemaal (literally 'this crow-language'), but he 'admits' that he has 'only heard a few words of this RN. All of these contained ridiculous misunderstandings, still they were understood by both nations.' A.W.S. Brun (1878: 82) characterizes RN as 'a hodgepodge' and a 'Sjakersprog' = derog. 'barter-language'. O.H. (1891: 140) calls RN 'a curious crow-language' which is 'neither fish nor fowl', but otherwise he gives a fairly good description of the language. Helland (1905: 781) refers to RN as 'this hodgepodge', and describes it as 'an idiotic mixture of certain Norwegian, Russian and English words'.[19]

But other descriptions, or rather reports, were more positive, and RN is here accorded the same status as the other languages in the area. The one who goes furthest in this respect is Reusch (1895: 47) who compares RN with the kind of pidgin English we find in the Chinese ports. He writes that pidgin English is a 'fully usable language, developed from a mixture of Chinese and English, in which people can manage perfectly in regular day-to-day communication'. Reusch claims that such a language also exists in Finnmark, namely RN, which he describes as follows: 'It is not a simple mixture of the two languages [Norwegian and Russian] which each individual makes up as best he can when he needs it, but it is really a fixed idiom [en fæstnet taleform].'

This is the most exact description we have from a contemporary observer of what kind of language variety we are dealing with here. The fact that Reusch compares RN with pidgin English makes it difficult to dismiss his evaluation. Broch (1927), who does not spend much time comparing RN and other pidgins, discusses Reusch's opinion that RN was 'a fixed idiom', but does not agree. Broch claims that RN 'trotz gewisser steter Redeweisen bei weitem nicht in die Reihe normalisierter "Sprachen" hinaufgelangt, sondern doch eine halbwegs amorphe Masse geblieben ist, innerhalb deren der größte Spielraum für subjektive und augenblicksbestimmte Bildungen übrig war. Gewisse eigentümliche grammatische Kristallisationen kommen jedoch in Spuren vor' (1927a: 221).[20]

Since Broch chooses to compare RN to natural, fully developed languages, his conclusions are bound to be of this kind. But this comparison is unilluminating – Reusch's comparison of RN and pidgin English is far superior since he is then comparing similar phenomena. (The first to compare RN and other pidgins in detail was, as mentioned above, Günter Neumann 1965.)

In *Skilling-Magazin* (1855: 231) it is claimed that RN has 'until now', that is 1855, 'been the usual means of communication between the two nations, but in recent years, most of the Norwegian merchants in Finnmark have begun to use Russian. The result is that these people now mostly use the latter language [i.e. Russian] in their communications with the Russians.' From this we can assume that there was a turning-point in the history of RN around 1850. Before 1850 RN was commonly used by Norwegians, both fishermen and merchants, in dealing with the Russians. After 1850 it was mostly fishermen who used RN, while the merchants learned Russian. It is striking that the available reports and evaluations of RN on the whole are more positive before 1850 than after. The reason for this is possibly that as long as the merchants used – and had to use – RN, the pidgin was socially accepted by the local upper class as a language equal to other languages. But when the merchants started learning Russian, and RN as a result was limited to the common fishermen, the use of RN was likewise devalued socially. This in turn also influenced its status as a language as such. Without doubt there is a great difference in attitude from the time Wedel Jarlsberg (in 1812–14) describes RN as the fourth language in Finnmark and calls it 'Handelssproget' (the Trade Language), until Helland (1905: 781) dismisses RN as 'this hodgepodge' and 'an idiotic mixture of certain Norwegian, Russian and English words'.

It is important to emphasize the role children must have played in the transmission of RN from generation to generation. Odd Gustav Eriksen's interviews in 1968 and 1970 with people who had participated in the Russian trade indicate that children had active contact with the Russians, and also that language contact was easy for them.[21]

Children learn languages quickly and with facility, and it strengthens the claim that RN was a 'fixed idiom' (Reusch 1895: 47) that the children's role seems to have been significant in passing on (knowledge of) RN from generation to generation. However, one has to remember that RN, as all pidgins, stood in a continuum between Norwegian and Russian: the salient grammatical elements constituted the language as RN and nothing else, but otherwise each user would vary as far as he was able to in the direction of the other language, especially in vocabulary. There were surely Norwegian children who learned Russian well enough not to need RN, and others who did not learn RN at all. But the fact that the children had so much contact with the Russians means that *at least* RN was passed on.

The fisherman Gothard Eriksen from Kiberg (b. 1892) told Odd Gustav Eriksen (1971b: 109) that it was not difficult to speak with the Russians, 'Because we knew a little, and they knew a little as did most of the others.' Gothard Eriksen personally knew neither Russian nor RN, but claimed that 'the old ones all knew Russian'.

Russian must here mean RN, and *the old ones* must have been people born before 1860. This tallies with what we should expect. The Pomor trade reached its absolute peak during the last half of the 19th century, and RN must have been most widespread at this time. When Gothard Eriksen claims that it was 'Russian' the older fishermen knew, we must assume that this is an expression for the often-mentioned phenomenon that RN users believed they spoke the others' language. The first time we find this mentioned is in Lund 1842 and Rode 1842, but later this special situation is reported nearly every time RN is referred to. Most people appear to accept this assertion, and the interview with Gothard Eriksen above seems also to point in this direction.[22]

Fox (1973), however, contests this view. He points out that RN was referred to by several different names; apart from 'Russenorsk', 'moja-på-tvoja'–language and 'kakspreck'.[23] These names indicate, says Fox, that the users were fully aware that RN represented a specific language variety separate from Russian and Norwegian.

It is difficult to prove this today, at least when one tries to argue, as Fox does, against the consensus of opinion that has been passed on. However, several circumstances lend support to the opinion that RN-users really believed they spoke the others' language, or at least that the Norwegian users of RN believed they spoke Russian. First, we can take the question of the name of the language, to which Fox chooses to attach decisive importance. Of the transmitted names for RN, 'moja-på-tvoja'-language was surely the most common among the Norwegian fishermen. We must remember that we are here concerned with people who had very little schooling; many of them were probably illiterate. Therefore it is likely that they interpreted the name 'moja-på-tvoja'–language as something like 'Russian, as we speak it'. Furthermore, this viewpoint may be traced back to the fact that RN was learned by the Norwegians while they were children, probably chiefly from Russians who spoke RN to them in order to make themselves understood. The children consequently thought that the Russians really spoke this way – even among themselves – and not just to the Norwegian children and the Norwegian fishermen.

Lunden 1978a is also critical of the transmitted opinion that RN users believed that they were speaking the others' language. She quotes the answers a number of informants gave in a questionnaire about what sort of language they used in the trade with the Russians, and finds that 'the informants who can still remember RN have a markedly more humble attitude to their knowledge of Russian than that described by the learned travellers of the 19th century' (Lunden 1978a: 9). But Lunden adds that this can be taken as 'a product of our age, when people have realized that RN was not real Russian' (p. 10). This is obviously an important objection and since other informants give information pointing in another direction (see Gothard Eriksen above), we can hardly draw definite conclusions from what people tell us today about opinions they had such a long time ago. Nor is it a valid argument against the transmitted opinion to point, as Lunden (1978a: 10) does, to the verb *pjolske*, which some informants used to mean speaking the language in which they communicated with the Russians. Lunden seems to think that since they had their own verb for speaking RN, they also must have believed that RN was a separate language, or at least a variety clearly distinct from Norwegian or Russian. But the verb *pjolske* is not restricted in meaning to speaking RN. In northern Norway it is generally used meaning to speak a mixed language, or rather to speak a language one does not know, but attempts to speak.[24] This means that we cannot use the existence of the verb *pjolske* to argue that RN-users were fully aware they spoke RN, and nothing else.

Thus, today it is difficult to arrive at any definite conclusion about this hypothesis. The only thing we can say is that nearly all the earlier descriptions and reports of RN repeat the prevailing opinion, but that lately some doubts have been raised about the validity of this hypothesis (Fox 1973, Lunden 1978a). However, Adler (1977) is of the opinion that it is this phenomenon which makes RN especially interesting. He writes (p. 40):

What is especially interesting in the case of Russenorsk is the fact that both parties concerned were firmly convinced that they were speaking the other language. The reason for this may be that the Norwegians had never visited Russia and the Russians never entered Norway proper but stayed for short periods of time only in the borderland of that country. It may be also assumed that a certain prestige was attached to thinking that one could speak the other language properly, and this the more so because the two languages have very little in common although they are both of Indo-European origin. It is a kind of auto-suggestion which is pleasing to those who are subject to it, and it did not matter that the grammar of Russenorsk was very simplified because the ordinary people who spoke it were not interested in the peculiarities of each language and had not the mental apparatus to become aware of them.

The primary functional area of RN was the trade between Norwegian fishermen and Russian buyers of fish, in particular when they bargained about prices and weight. There is clear evidence of this in the texts, where the names of fish and other merchandise are particularly well developed. But many Russians also stayed in Norway during the winter, partly to take odd jobs, partly to get a head start on the next year's trading. Only after the ice had broken could the Russian boats from Kola set out for Norway, and an early departure was important (Eriksen 1971a: 27). Therefore it is not correct to claim that RN was used exclusively during a few summer months each year – as often has been done, citing Broch (1927a).

Consequently RN must also have been used in communication about other subjects than those which directly dealt with the trade. For example, we know that the fishermen in Finnmark often played ball with the Russians (Steen 1961: 60, Gamst 1967: 45, Bjørgan 1969: 137 and Westrheim 1979: 277) without this having been recorded in the RN texts. On the other hand we find in the texts words and expressions related to feasting and drinking, and also religion. In Bang 1873, the author mentions a 'gibberish of Norwegian, Lappish and Russian' (Bang 1873: 198). Presumably, Bang has RN in mind. The language in question was used by a Russian guide talking about conditions along the Russian–Norwegian border. All this indicates that RN was on its way to becoming something more than just an auxiliary language associated exclusively with trade.

All the factors discussed above must carry weight when we consider the question of stability in RN. Was the language nothing more than an amorphous mass characterized by temporary linguistic expedients, or can we assume that it had a stable grammatical structure in addition to a fixed vocabulary? The vocabulary comprises quite a few doublets, particularly words from Russian and Norwegian. This condition *can* be interpreted as instability: each speaker used as many words as he knew of the other language and otherwise made use of Norwegian and Russian words respectively. But the condition can also be explained by the relexification hypothesis that we have put forward (Broch and Jahr 1980): in a relexification period it is natural to find a large number of word doublets. The objection might be raised that in the case of RN the relexification process appears to coincide with the entire period for which there is evidence of RN. Perhaps this is not so strange. It has been pointed out as an important feature of RN that the two base-languages, Norwegian and Russian, were of equal social status and in this RN differed from other pidgins with a basis in the languages of colonial powers such as English, French or Spanish. It is therefore not surprising that Norwegian and Russian words more or less competed with each other, resulting in the many doublets we find in the texts.

The relexification hypothesis implies that the grammatical structure was to a large extent transferred from one or more earlier pidgins in the area. If this is correct, then this structure must have been relatively stable and uniform. Such a view is supported by the considerable degree of uniformity throughout the lifetime of RN, all the way from the first reports to the last known text. The role of children in transmitting RN from one generation to the next points in the same direction, as does the fact that RN was not merely a seasonal jargon, as has often been claimed.

It is important here to emphasize that RN – like any other language – had to be learned. The interviews that Odd Gustav Eriksen conducted in 1968 and 1970 with older people who had experienced the Russian trade towards the end of the 19th century and at the beginning of the 20th (Eriksen 1971b) show clearly that the language problem often was burdensome.

Thus, around the turn of the century there was still a need for RN in communication between Norwegians and Russians. But the closer we get to the First World War, the more cash-trade took over, and as a result the barter-trade became less extensive. On both sides the big merchants were responsible for an increasingly larger part of the activities, and these merchants often understood the language of their trading partner: hence the need for RN declined. In this way, the basis for RN, the barter-trade between the Norwegian fishermen and Russian buyers of fish, became steadily more limited, even though it is clear from Eriksen (1971b) that the barter-trade also continued until the last Russians disappeared from northern Norway after the Russian Revolution in 1917. However, it is doubtful whether the barter-trade was so extensive and important towards the end that it alone could have ensured continued use of RN. We must therefore agree with John E. Reinecke (1938: 112) when he claims that RN would have disappeared regardless of the First World War and its results. The need to continue using the language became too slight.

The history of RN can then be summarised as follows: The jargon was developed during the last half of the 18th century and emerged as an adequate auxiliary language in the first decades of the 19th century. Until the middle of the 19th century RN was used on the Norwegian side by both fishermen and Norwegian merchants, and the use of RN was socially accepted at all levels of society. From about 1850 the merchants increasingly started to learn Russian as a result of longer stays with business connections in, for example, Archangel. Thus, the use of RN was eventually limited to the common fishermen on the Norwegian side, and RN was not viewed as favourably as previously as a result of the upper class being able to compare RN to Russian proper. The social evaluation of RN in this way approached the level characterizing most of the pidgins in the world. After the turn of the century the socio-economic conditions for RN gradually disappeared as a result of new regulations, the decline of the barter-trade in favour of the cash-trade, and the big merchants gaining increasing control over the trading contacts. Presumably ability to speak RN became less extensive as a result of the disappearance, during the last few decades of the Russian trade, of the communicative situations in which it would have been used.

Notes

* This work was financially supported by the University of Tromsø, School of Languages and Literature, and by The Norwegian Research Council for Science and the Humanities. Stud. philol. Bente Martinussen worked on the project as research assistant and stud. philol. Ann Vølstad made a first draft of the translation from Norwegian into English. We thank Professor Leiv Egil Breivik for his contribution to the second draft English translation. The final English version was prepared by Iain Clarkson. The map was drawn by Liv Larssen.

1 *Amtmann* – the Government's chief administrative officer of a county.
2 All legal records referred to in this article are kept in the 'Statsarkivkontoret i Tromsø'.
3 The name Kulakov is mentioned in the legal records of Finnmark several times: a skipper Kulakov, who might be Sergej Kulakov, appears twice in 1785. (Justis-protokoll for Finnmark No. 44, fol. 241–3, Hammerfest gjesterett 1 April 1785, and fol. 271–2, Vardø gjeste og politirett 21 June 1785).
4 The first linguist to make reference to RN was Ragnvald Iversen (1913: 3). However, the reference is very brief and only says that RN had not affected the local dialect of Senja in any way. RN did, however, affect the dialects of northern Norway. Several words from RN have entered these dialects and are in daily use (Broch and Jahr 1981: 88–90).
5 The term *Kvensk* is commonly used for the Finnish dialect spoken in northern Norway by Finnish immigrants and their descendants.
6 We will briefly indicate what these references have been mainly used to illustrate.
   The Norwegian linguist Alf Sommerfelt was the first to refer to RN after Broch had published his description in 1927, and in this case as an example of a mixed language which served as a lingua franca (Sommerfelt 1929). Later Sommerfelt made several references to RN in his works (1948, 1954, 1960). In Uriel Weinreich's famous book, *Languages in Contact*, published in 1953, we find a reference to RN as proof that in 'the highly hybridized makeshift trade languages, most obligatory categories expressed by bound morphemes are well known to be abandoned' (Weinreich 1953 (1970: 43)).
   In Roman Jakobson's article 'Why "mama" and "papa"?' (1959), 'moja på tvoja' as a name for RN used by RN users themselves – presented by Broch (1927a: 220) as 'I (speak) in your (way)' – is compared to a motherese word which, to be successful – that is, accepted by the child – has to 'meet the infant's linguistic requirements and thus follow the general line of any interlanguage' (Jakobson 1959 (1971: 539)).

Dan I. Slobin (1977, 1979) uses RN as an example of an extreme minimum language as regards grammatical constructions, and compares RN to the language use of two to three year olds (Slobin 1977: 200f, 209, 211). The grammatical elements found in RN comprise the absolute minimum a language needs to be processable, claims Slobin. In an interesting survey he lists a total of eight rules which in his view gives an exhaustive description of the grammatical structure of RN (Slobin 1979: 43–6). But there are a number of exceptions to these rules. Slobin has simplified RN to a point beyond reality, in order to be able to use it as an example of an absolute minimum language.

7 A slight problem is the placing of the text material which we find in Maksimov 1859. Maksimov claims that he is reproducing Norwegian, but the language here has both pure Norwegian traits and clear RN features beside the obvious German elements. We have suggested earlier that the difference between the Maksimov text and most of the other texts reflects a different degree of relexification (Broch and Jahr 1980), but other explanations are also possible. On the basis of the Maksimov text Lunden (1978a: 13) believes that during the 1850s at least two varieties of RN existed, which were later combined. But this is hardly a plausible explanation. RN was developed 50 years earlier, and it is unlikely that two different variants of RN could have existed at such a late date. It is probably more reasonable, as Lunden has also proposed, that the Maksimov text should be regarded as 'just about a simplified German, "pidgin-German" with some Norwegian words' (Lunden 1979: 23). At any rate it is difficult to consider the text material Maksimov presents on the level of other texts, which are definitely RN texts.

8 Here the word *vin* comes from Norwegian, while *vina* is probably the Russ. gen. (Russ. *vino*, gen. *vina*).

9 Hence Slobin's claim (1977: 201) that RN had no conjunctions is incorrect.

10 In Russian the interrogative particle *-li* is only used in interrogative sentences. This is not the case in RN: *Etta dorogli* (this is expensive) (Russ.: *Eto dorogo*). Note also that in contrast to Russian RN can have both a question word and *-li* in the same sentence: *kak vara ju prodatli?* (What kind of goods are you selling?) (Russ.: *Kakie tovary ty prodaeš'?*).

11 *Djur* does not look like a Norwegian form, but is probably influenced by the Russian way of rendering the sound [y]. (Cf. also the spelling *mjuke* for Swedish *mycket* (Alimova 1976: 392) p. 54.)

12 The short Paulaharju text (1928 (1973: 231)) differs somewhat from the main corpus. Paulaharju has *ryjpa* (Russ. *ryba*, fish). Dybos (1959) also uses *ryby* as a doublet to *fisk*.

13 Broch (1927a: 255) says that he has not found the word *sobaka* (Russ. dog) mentioned in connection with fish names in Russian, but he supposes that the word could be a description of the catfish's head and teeth (compare another English name for catfish: wolf fish). It is, however, more likely that the RN form *sobaka* represents a phonetic simplification of the Russian *zubatka*: the Norwegian RN texts do not have voiced *s*. The consonant group *-tk-* has also been simplified. This explanation of RN *sobaka* is also supported by the spelling *subaka* in Eidnes (1973: 114).

14 Eidnes (1973: 114) has *teska* with metathesis.

15 It is interesting to note that this expression was also known in other places outside Russia during the 18th century. For example we find the same expression in the Swedish poet and composer Carl Michael Bellman (1740–95), in his 'Fredmans epistlar' No. 59, which portrays the sailor's milieu in Stockholm's port. The expression is presented as 'Gebjörnamat' (Bellman 1916: 196).
Ёbёna is here identified as *bjørna* (bear) and *mat'* as *mat* (food), and it can

therefore easily be interpreted as 'give the bear food'. That this is the same expression as the one from the 1807 lawsuit is, however, beyond doubt. (We are grateful to Sven Strömqvist, University of Stockholm, for informing us of the occurrence of this expression in Bellman.)

16 This is only a possible hypothesis according to Fox, and it is therefore somewhat presumptuous of Hancock (1977: 290) to claim that Fox 'has shown RN to be derived in part from a northern European military pidgin ("soldier's cant") spoken in garrisons throughout Scandinavia'.

17 It is not completely clear what Högström means by 'Borgerskap' and 'borgar'. Literally translated it is 'citizenry' and 'citizen', but the context seems to indicate that these terms refer to all non-Lappish Swedes in the area. According to Nesheim (1967: 140), borgar means 'merchant'. The name Borgarmålet should then mean either 'the language of the merchants' or 'the language we use when speaking with the merchants'.

18 Translation of Broch quotation:

> Norwegian terms for the trade in and preparation of the main kinds of fish which the Norwegians had introduced were taken over by the Lapps who lived on the coast of the Arctic Sea in earlier, in part very early times. When the Russians arrived later, they did not acquire the relevant terms from the Norwegians, but first from the Lapps, and probably before they began to trade directly with the Norwegians. Much later, when RN was created, it acquired its terms for fish from the Russian, which had in turn acquired them in this fashion; however, in the recent past the present-day Norwegian terms have been in the process of penetrating RN.

19 It is probable that the term *kråkemål* was not just meant in a pejorative sense. *Kråkemål* is also used in Norwegian to describe a pig-Latin or 'secret language' which, for instance, children make up to avoid being understood by others. The easiest way to make such a pig-Latin is by adding the same prefix or suffix to all the words. When the expression 'a curious *kråkemål*' was used about RN, it is possible that this use reflected the impression that RN could be compared with these language varieties. When Lund (1842: 62) writes that RN resembles most of all 'this so-called *skøiersprog*', he most probably means by *skøiersprog* precisely the same as the definition of *kråkemål* given above. Note also that it is precisely these secret languages which are claimed to be especially developed among the Lapps (Qvigstad 1909 actually uses the term *kråkemål* about these secret Lappish jargons).

20 Translation of Broch quotation:

> ... despite certain fixed phrases can definitely not be considered as one of the normalized 'languages', but has remained a fairly amorphous mass within which there remained the greatest possible scope for subjective and spontaneous improvisations. Nevertheless there are signs of the development of distinctive grammatical features.

21 From the side of the boat we called up to the youngest Russians. Strangely enough we understood Russian, and could also sing in Russian .... We were young and therefore quickly learned to understand the language (Eriksen 1971b: 58).

> My father spoke Russian as we speak Finnish. He spoke well. He was born here (1850), and had probably played with the Russian boys and learned the language in this way (Eriksen 1971b: 74).

> The Russian fishermen, according to the Kiberg regulations, were allowed to fish from the shore in Norway. The little boys also learned Russian from them. Of course we went into their shacks and boathouses. They came from the Russian side and rented boats from the fish-buyers. We were there all the time, and it was easy to learn Russian. When the Russians left, I could speak Russian fairly well, but now I've forgotten all of it. ... Sundays they [the Russians] were on land, the skippers and crews. They walked and

looked around, talking to people. They spoke a little Norwegian, and we, the little boys, ran around with them all the time. The Russians laughed when we talked. Then they corrected us, and we learned in that way. It was like in a school. . . . We were always on board the boats. Even though we didn't have anything to do there, we rowed and *pjålska* (see note 24) with them.

As small boys, did you look forward to the Russians' arrival? Of course! We waited for them. The Russians started staying here with their boats, also through the winter. Then they came here. Many were moored in Båtsfjord, 5–6 vessels in Hammerfest and many other places (Eriksen 1971b: 81–6).

Everywhere we met Russians, we spoke to them. We met only friendliness. . . . I remember going down to the Russians' fishing huts with my father, and drinking tea. . . . We hung around their huts as much as we liked, when the Russians were on land. We liked it, and so did the Russians. We never heard anything to the contrary. Many of the boys learned Russian (Eriksen 1971b: 110).

22 This phenomenon has also been observed in other places. Hancock (1971: 512) quotes the missionary Paul le Jeune (1632) as saying of a Franco-Amerindian pidgin in and around Montreal that 'the Frenchmen who spoke it supposed it to be good Indian, and the Indians believed it to be French'. And Cole (1953: 7) says that speakers of Bantu languages who learn the pidgin Fanagalo 'fondly imagine that they are speaking the language of the White Man'.

23 In addition we have also heard RN referred to as *Pomorrussisk* (Pomor Russian).

24 Hveding's dictionary for northern Norway (1968) gives this meaning: 'To speak unclearly; especially about speaking a language one does not properly know. "-med finnan", [with the Finns] exchange Finnish and Norwegian words or use half-Finnish or half-Norwegian words to make oneself understood. Thus: "-med russen" [with the Russians] or "-Russian", "try to speak RN".' In the novel *Susanna* by Jens Hagerup (1922: 234, 235) we find the verb used twice, but without any reference to Russian or RN.

Bibliography

Adler, M. K. 1977: *Pidgins, Creoles and Lingua Francas: A socio-linguistic study.* Hamburg.

Alimova, T. A. 1976: Dva pamjatnika pis'mennosti Drevlechrianlišča Puškinskogo Domo o russko-skandinavskich svjazjach XVIII–XIX vv. '*Slovo o polku Igoreve' i pamjatniki drevnerusskoj literatury.* Trudy otdela drevnerusskoj literatury 21: 390–2, Leningrad.

Bang, Th. 1873: *Landmålerliv i Finmarken.* Kristiania (Oslo).

Bellman, C. M. 1916: *Dikter av Carl Michael Bellman. Första delen: Fredmans epistlar.* Utgivna av Richard Steffen, Stockholm.

Bergh, K. 1950: *Elisabeth Lorck.* 3rd printing. Oslo.

Bernštam, T. A. 1978: *Pomory, Formirovanie gruppy i sistema chozjajstva.* Leningrad.

Bjørgan, M. 1969: *Fragmenter av Finmarks og Alta-Talviks historie.* Vol. 1. Leirbotn.

Blom, G. P. 1830: *Bemærkninger paa en Reise i Nordlandene og igjennem Lapland til Stockholm, i Aaret 1827.* Christiana (Oslo).

Blom, H. 1862: *Indbydelsesskrift for Hovedexamen ved Tromsø Lærde og Realskole.* Tromsø.

Broch, I. and E. H. Jahr, 1980: The problem of stability in russenorsk. In E. Hovdhaugen (ed.) 1980. *The Nordic Languages and Modern Linguistics.* Proceedings of the Fourth International Conference of Nordic and General Linguistics in Oslo. Oslo/Bergen/Tromsø.

1981: *Russenorsk – et pidginspråk i Norge.* Tromsø-studier i språkvitenskap 3. Oslo.

Broch, O. 1927a: Russenorsk. *Archiv für slavische Philologie* 41; 209–62. Berlin.

1927b: Russenorsk. *Maal og Minne.* Oslo, pp. 81–130.

1928: Noen fiskenavn i 'russenorsk'. (Résumé of a paper given at the Norw. Academy of Science 18 March 1927.) *Det Norske Videnskaps-akademi i Oslo. Årbok 1927.* Oslo, p. 10.

1930: Russenorsk tekstmateriale. *Maal og Minne.* Oslo, pp. 113–40.

Brox, A. 1954: Russenhandelen i Finnmark og Troms, *Heimen* 9: 517–29.

Brun, A. W. S. 1878: Skildringer fra den norske Kyst. *Nor og Syd* 11. Trondhjem.

Bucharov, D. N. 1883: *Russkie v Finmarkene.* St Petersburg.

Cole, D. T. 1953: Fanagalo and the Bantu languages in South Africa. *African Studies* 12: 1–9.

Daa, L. K. 1870: *Skisser fra Lapland, Karelstranden og Finland.* Kristiania (Oslo).

D[ybos, V.] 1959: Tråk om tråk: Tuskhandel på havna. *Finnmarken* 30 June 1959.

Eidnes, A. (ed.) 1973: *Nord-Norge i manns minne, Dagleglic ved hundreårsskiftet.* Oslo.

Eriksen, O. G. 1971a: *Pomorhandel i pomorstrøk 1870–1922 (ca.).* Unpublished thesis, University of Trondheim.

1971b: *Tradisjon fra norsk og russisk Finnmark.* Unpublished supplement to Eriksen 1971a.

Finstad, L. 1910: Det russiske fiskemarked. Archangels import av fisk og sild. *Nordkap* 12 and 16 March 1910.

Fox, J. A. 1973: *Russenorsk: A study in language adaptivity.* Unpublished term paper, University of Chicago.

Frette, Th. 1959: *Bibliografi over skrifter trykt i Finnmark 1866–1940.* Særtrykk av Vardøhus Museums årbok 1959, Vadsø.

Gamst, L. 1967: *Loppa øy gjennom tidene og slekten Gamst.* Vadsø.

Grannes, A. and A. Lillehammer 1980: Russefiske og pomorhandel. Nyfunne russiske dokumenter til belysning av russefiske og russehandelen i Nord-Norge i det 18 århundre. *Forskningsnytt* 25: 5, 17–22.

Grøttland, K. L. 1978: *Daglig brød og daglig dont.* [Oslo.]

Hagerup, J. 1922: *Susanna.* Kristiania (Oslo).

Hall, R. A. Jr. 1966: *Pidgin and Creole Languages.* Ithaca/London.

Hancock, I. F. 1971: A survey of the pidgins and creoles of the world. In D. Hymes (ed.), *Pidginization and Creolization of Languages.* Cambridge, pp. 509–23.

1977: Recovering pidgin genesis: Approaches and problems. In A. Valdman (ed.), *Pidgin and Creole Linguistics.* Bloomington/London, pp. 277–94.

Hansen, A. 1862: *Norsk–Russisk Ordbog og Parleur.* Bergen.

Hansen, E. R. 1977: *Pomorhandelen i Finnmark.* Skoledirektøren/Høgskolen i Finnmark. Vadsø.

Hanssen, H. 1978: *Nordnorske konturer og profiler.* Trondheim.

Helland, A. 1899: *Norges land og folk. Topografisk-statistisk beskrevet. XIX: Tromsø Amt.* Kristiania (Oslo).

1905: *Norges land og folk. Topografisk-statistisk beskrevet. XX. Finmarkens Amt.* Kristiania (Oslo).

Högström, P. [1747]: *Beskrifning öfwer de til Sweriges Krona lydande Lapmarker, (etc.)* Stockholm. Reprinted Umeå 1980.

Hveding, J. 1968: *Håløygsk ordsamling.* Bodø.

Iversen, R. 1913: *Senjen-maalet. Lydverket i hoveddrag.* Videnskapsselskapets Skrifter II. Hist.-filos. Klasse 1912. No. 4. Kristiania (Oslo).

Jakobson, R. 1959: Why 'mama' and 'papa'? In *Perspectives in Psychological Theory*, dedicated to Heinz Werner, New York 1960. Reprinted in *Roman Jakobson Selected Writings* 1. Phonological Studies. 2nd edn. The Hague/Paris 1971.

Jarlsberg, F. W. Wedel, 1887: Nogle Materialier til Beskrivelse over Finmarkens Amt. *Illustreret Familielæsning* 6.

Johnsen, O. A. 1923: *Finmarkens politiske historie – aktmæssig fremstillet.* (Videnskaps-selskapets Skrifter II. Hist.-filos. Klasse. No. 3) Kristiania (Oslo).

Korneliussen, K. 1968: Streiftog i den gamle pomorhandelen. *Håløygminne* (1968) 4. (Svorkmo).

Kortfattet norsk-russisk Haandbog samt Tabel til Udregning av Melkvantum ved Russehandel. Tromsø 1899 (2nd edn. 1900).

Koškin, A. 1912: *Russko–norvežskij slovar'.* Archangel'sk.

Lönnrot, E. 1842: *Elias Lönnrots svenska skrifter utgifna af Jenny af Forselles. II. Bref, anteckningar och reseskildringar.* Helsingfors 1911.

Lund, N. 1842: *Reise igjennem Nordlandene og Vestfinmarken i Sommeren 1841.* Christiania (Oslo).

Lunden, S. Sverdrup, 1978a: *Russenorsk Revisited.* Meddelelser 15, University of Oslo, Slavic–Baltic Institute, Oslo.

1978b: Tracing the ancestry of Russenorsk. *Slavia Orientalis* 27: 213–17.

1979: Russenorsk – gammelt hjelpespråk langs ishavskysten. *Tromsø* 3 February 1979, pp. 15 and 23.

Maksimov, S. V. 1859: *God na sĕverĕ.* St Petersburg.

Mikkelsen, M. 1978: *Hundre år under pisken, fortellinger fra Finnmark.* Oslo.

Murman 1907–1909. Vardø.

Nesheim, A. 1947: Russiske og russisk-finske lånord i Finnmark-lappisk. In *Festskrift til professor Olaf Broch.* Avhandlinger utgitt av Det Norske Videnskaps-Akademi i Oslo. II. Hist.-filos. klasse 1947. Oslo, pp. 155–67.

1967: Eastern and western elements in Lapp culture. In *Lapps and Norsemen in Olden Times.* Institutt for sammenlignende kulturforskning. Serie A: Foreles-ninger 26. Oslo, pp. 104–67.

Neumann, G. 1965: Russennorwegisch und Pidginenglisch. *Nachrichten der Giessener Hochschulgesellschaft* 34: 219–32.

1966: Zur chinesisch–russischen Behelfssprache von Kjachta. *Die Sprache* 12: 237–51.

O.H. 1891: Russenorsk. *Nordlands Trompet* 2. Kristiania (Oslo), pp. 139–42.

Paine, R. 1957: *Coast Lapp Society.* Tromsø Museums skrifter Vol. 4. Tromsø.

Paulaharju, S. 1928: *Finnmarkens folk.* Uddevalla 1973.

Peterson, R. E. 1980: Russenorsk: A little known aspect of Russo–Norwegian rela-tions. *Studies in Language* 4: 249–56.

Podvysockij, A. O. 1885: *Slovar' oblastnogo archangel'skago narečija v ego bytovom i etnografičeskom primeneҥii.* St Petersburg.

Prišvin, M. M. 1908: *Za volšebnym kolobkom, Sobranie sočinenij,* 2, Moskva 1956.

Qvigstad, J. 1909: Peder Claussøn om sjøfinnernes sprog. To breve fra rektor J. Qvigstad. *Maal og Minne,* Kristiania (Oslo), pp. 129–32.

Reinecke, J. E. 1938: Trade jargons and creole dialects as marginal languages. *Social Forces,* pp. 107–18.

Reusch, H. 1895: *Folk og natur i Finmarken.* Kristiania (Oslo).

Rinnan, G. D. 1980: [Review of] Lunden, S.S. *Russenorsk revisited,* Oslo 1978. *Svantevit, dansk tidsskrift for slavistik* 5: 192–4.

Rode, F. 1842: *Optegnelser fra Finmarken samlede i Aarene 1826–1834 og senere udgivne som et Bidrag til Finmarkens Statistik.* Skien.

Ruong, I. 1980: Saglig kommentar. In [reprint of] Högström1 747. Norrländska Skrifter No. 3. Umeå.

Siljeström, P. A. 1842: *Anteckningar och Observationer rörande Norrige, i synnerhet de nordligaste delerna af detta land.* Norrköping.

Skilling-Magazin, Christiania (Oslo) 1855, p. 231.

Slobin, D. I. 1977: Language change in childhood and in history. In J. Macnamara (ed.), *Language Learning and Thought*. New York.
1979: *Psycholinguistics*. 2nd edn. Glenview, Illinois.
Sommerfelt, A. 1929: Quelques remarques sur le problème de la parenté des langues. *Donum Natalicium Schrijnen* 1929. Reprinted in *Diachronic and Synchronic Aspects of Language*. Selected articles by Alf Sommerfelt. 'S-Gravenhage 1971.
1948: *Språket og menneskene*. Oslo.
1954: Language, society and culture. *Norsk Tidsskrift for Sprogvidenskap* 17:5–81.
1960: Mixed languages versus remodelled languages. *Norsk Tidsskrift for Sprogvidenskap* 19: 316–26.
Steen, M. 1961: *Gammelt fra Kanstad-fjorden*. Ballangen.
Todd, L. 1974: *Pidgins and Creoles*. London/Boston.
Weinreich, U. 1953: *Languages in Contact. Findings and Problems*. 7th printing 1970, The Hague/Paris.
Westrheim, H. 1979: Pomorhandelen. In R. Hirsti (ed.), *Finnmark. By og bygd i Norge*. Oslo, pp. 273–80.
Ytreberg, N. A. 1940–2: Russehandelen i Troms – en brekkstang for frihandelen av 1789. *Historisk Tidsskrift* 32: 481–513.

II East Scandinavia

3 Language contact as reflected in the migration of the Finns, the Saamis and the Vikings

OLAVI KORHONEN

Introduction

The present article will deal with the geographical distribution of five lexical items used as terms in navigation in Finnish, Estonian, Swedish, Saamish,[1] and Russian. The spread of these terms around the Gulfs of Finland and Bothnia is here seen as a result of cultural contacts during the Viking Age and the early middle ages, when there were extensive migrations by the Vikings, Finns and the Saamis in the eastern and northern parts of the Baltic. The first lexical item is the term for 'a boat hollowed out of an aspen tree trunk' (cf. Finnish *haapio*, Estonian *haabjas*, east and north Swedish *håp/hap*, Saamish *hapi*, Section 1); the second is the term for 'the gunwale' of this type of boat (cp. Finnish *paarre*, and Saamish *bárda*, Section 2); the third is the term for 'an isthmus; wet moor; a strip of land on a moor' (cp. Finnish *keidas*, Section 3); the fourth is the term for 'thwart or cross plank in a boat' (cp. Finnish *piitta*, Estonian *piit*, East Swedish *bett/bette*, North Russian *bet'*, Section 4); and fifth and finally the terms *bat* and *bat'* for 'boat' in Russian (cf. Section 5).

Even if the art of hollowing boats out of long trunks of aspen trees (cf. Finnish *haapio/haaparuuhi* 'aspen dug-out') is nowadays known only in the province of Satakunta, Finland and in some places in Estonia and Latvia (see Map 1), oral tradition and written descriptions are still available for study. Terms for this type of boat are found in Finnish and Estonian and also in Swedish and the Saamish dialects of northern Sweden (Korhonen 1981, 1982). The latter dialects also possess other words which refer to boats and the component parts of boats, for which there are corresponding expressions in Finnish. The limited geographical distribution of these words in all three languages makes them a suitable subject for an areal-linguistic study.

Ethnographical material and historical sources can be drawn on to illuminate the important role of the aspen dug-out in Finnish culture. They give us information about the cultural trends which resulted in it reaching such distant areas as the province of Satakunta. In older periods it might even have been used as far north as the areas north of the Gulf of Bothnia.

Some of the questions which will occupy us here are: (a) How far to the west or

67

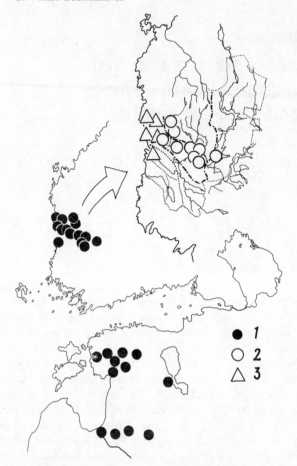

Map 1. South-western Finland, Estonia and the Baltic States with places where soft dug-outs (hollowed-out aspen boats with widened sides) have been found. The Province of Satakunta, Finland, is shown in detail. The borders of the areas of Sastamala (in the west) and Kyrö (in the east) are indicated by the broad dash-dotted lines, whereas the dotted lines indicate other neighbouring areas.

Key to symbols:

1. Aspen dug-outs in Finland, Estonia and the Baltic States.
2. Finnish *haapio* 'aspen dug-out with widened sides'.
3. Finnish *haaparuuhi* 'idem'.

north-west was the aspen dug-out used? (b) in what period did it spread from its eastern area of origin?; and (c) who were the people who brought it there? Two even more important questions which must be answered in this context are: (d) why did this people migrate into the areas around the Gulf of Bothnia? – judging from the shape of the boat they were probably of eastern origin; and (e) what were the activities which brought them so far?

By fitting together the pieces of evidence regarding conditions in this period drawn from linguistic, ethnological, and archaeological material, we are able to reconstruct a detailed picture of the period with which we are concerned. In this way we will arrive at a reliable description of Finnish–Swedish–Saamish cultural contacts in the areas situated on the northern coasts of the Gulf of Bothnia. This region has long attracted people who live in other areas because of its rich fishing and hunting.

The next section will deal with the different names for the aspen dug-out, its component parts and its function in the economy of the region.

1   The geographical distribution of the aspen dug-out

The starting point of our investigation will be the documentation of the spread of the boat in its most westerly area of distribution, Finland. It was a long time before ethnologists became aware of the fact that this type of boat, the soft dug-out,[2] existed in Finland (cf. Itkonen 1930: 189). A number of Finnish scholars had previously discovered that it was being used by Slavic and Finno-Ugric peoples who lived in areas further to the east of Finland. They had described it in detail without knowing that it was still being constructed in Finland proper – in a few remote areas in the west of Finland (see Map 1). After Itkonen had mentioned its existence, Nikkilä 1936 gave a detailed description of the dug-out in Satakunta. He documented in words and pictures the carving of a boat which is now kept at the National Museum in Helsinki (cf. Figures 1a, 1b, and 1c). Supplementary details were published in two articles in 1946 and 1947. Thanks to these publications we are well informed about the technique of constructing the boat even though this was on the point of being forgotten as a result of the death of the last boat-builders, before the ethnologists were able to carry out their field research (cf. Vilkuna and Mäkinen 1977: 306 f). Thanks to the extensive and intensive linguistic field work carried out in Finland, we also possess linguistic data on the boat. We will be concerned primarily with linguistic information on the aspen dug-out here.

1.1   The aspen dug-out in the wild-life culture of Satakunta, Finland

In material which is to be found in the Finnish Dialect Archive, S.M.S., the word *haapio* is used as the special Finnish term for a boat made of aspen wood. Some examples with the compound *haaparuuhi* are also mentioned with the same meaning (cf. *haapa* 'aspen' and *ruuhi* 'trough; a boat which resembles a trough'):

The term *haapio* or *haaparuuhi* denotes a boat made out of a thick trunk of aspen. The tool with which the dug-out is hollowed out is called the *telso* 'hollowing axe'. (*S.M.S.*, Lavia Parish, Laaksonen 1928).

After collecting all the examples of the word *haapio* (derived from *haapa* 'aspen') with the meaning 'hollowed-out aspen boat with widened sides', one finds that they are distributed along an oblong area stretching from the coast of northern Satakunta towards the interior of the province (see Map 1). Today this area does not constitute a coherent or distinctive region, but during the middle ages it was well known for its extensive hunting and fishing which contributed considerably to the maintenance of the population (cf. Jaakkola 1925). The agricultural settlements were mainly to be found along the fertile river valleys. The distances from

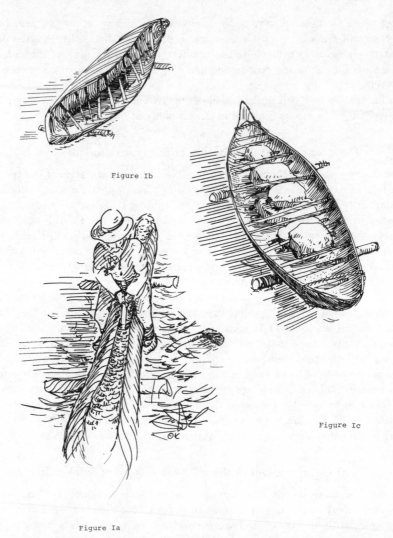

Figure Ib

Figure Ic

Figure Ia

Fig. 1. The aspen dug-out was hollowed out with an axe (1a) and the sides were stretched (1b) by covering the wood with tar and warming it. The sides were braced and stretched with stout branches so that the correct shape was obtained (1c).

the settlements to the hunting grounds and fishing waters, to which the population travelled twice each year, were often very great. In certain areas the distance from the home village to these outlying lands could be 250 to 300 km (cf. Luukko 1959). In the earliest Swedish documents the terms *erämarck*, *aeremarck*, etc. were used for the outlying lands of a given village. The terms derive from the Finnish *erämaa*, which originally denotes 'a remote isolated strip of land' (cf. Rapola 1936). The word has been borrowed into Finnish–Swedish and northern Swedish. It is used to describe the diverse way of life in the southern parts of Finland during earlier

Map 2. The provinces of western and southern Finland.

periods, and the similar way of life in Lappland in modern times. The modern
Swedish form is *erämark*.

We know very little about the hard life which the people had to lead in the
wilderness, i.e. before the brief entries start to appear in the documents of the 15th
century. The fight for survival in the wilderness consisted mainly of fishing and
hunting. However, the dominance of these activities centred on wild life had
already been diminished somewhat by the introduction of agriculture (cf. Jaakkola
1924).

The area where the boat terms *haapio* and *haaparuuhi* are found with the meaning
'hollowed out aspen boat' is a well-known *erämark*-region, called Sastamala (cf.
Jaakkola (1935) 1956: 298f; Virtaranta 1952). Sastamala and Kyrö were the two
large areas which correspond to present-day northern Satakunta (cf. Suvanto 1973:
111f).

Since old traditions of hunting and fishing lived on here for a long time, written
sources from this area have preserved important information. However, few details
of daily life are documented in these sources. In order to obtain more knowledge
about the 'wild-life culture'–the *erämark* culture–we have to rely on later investigations of Finnish folk culture and Finnish dialects.

1.2 The aspen dug-out as an ideal means of transportation

A study of folk traditions and culture helps us to understand the use and spread of
this special type of boat. Information on it gives us a good picture of an important

detail of life in the wilderness, namely the means of transportation to the hunting grounds and fishing waters and back. The *haapio* was here the most adequate means of travelling and transporting goods because of its lightness. Some examples of this type of boat with a length of 6 m, a breadth of 70–90 cm, and a height of 35 cm, have been weighed. Their weight was less than 80 kilograms (cf. Manninen 1927: 7). Such a boat could without difficulty be carried or hauled fairly long distances across land, particularly if it was even smaller than the example just mentioned. Since the *haapio* has no keel and floats high on the water it can also be used in shallow waters. The *haapio* was propelled by paddling rather than by rowing. One could also pole it, when narrow waterways made this necessary. It is easy to understand how popular this type of boat must have become. The usefulness of the boat contributed to its popularity and made it a natural part of the transportation system of the wild life area, a function which it has preserved down to the present day.

1.3   Areal-linguistic evidence of the spread of the term *haapio*

There are certain features in the areal-linguistic distribution of the term *haapio* which should be commented on (cf. Map 3). One could interpret the dispersed examples of the meaning 'small rowing-boat' (symbols 2, 5, 6, and 7 on Map 3) as traces left over from a period when dug-outs were made in these areas. But the term itself does not prove that the production of this type of boat was so widely spread as is indicated on Map 3 by the symbols just mentioned. Its production was very dependent on the great experience of the craftsmen and was therefore probably limited to a somewhat smaller area than the area of distribution of the term. The boat was certainly brought to other areas and was also called *haapio* there. For this reason the term *haapio* either in the meaning 'aspen dug-out' or 'small rowing-boat', has to be analysed in the light of other cultural and linguistic evidence.

Examples of *haapio* in the secondary meaning of 'small rowing-boat' are found in some places along the coast of the Gulf of Bothnia (see symbol 2 on Map 3 and Korhonen 1982: 33, 42). Here the term should, in my opinion, be understood as the result of some kind of knowledge of real dug-outs (cf. 1.3.5). First of all it seems impossible to explain the existence of the term in this northern area without connecting it with the province of Satakunta. It is known that cultural and linguistic characteristics, which are typical of south-western Finland, spread towards the northern parts of the Gulf of Bothnia, as these examples of the term *haapio* demonstrate. Both the type of the boat and the linguistic term for it are completely lacking in the middle and southern parts of East Bothnia – a province separating south-western Finland from the northern areas. This distributional pattern is characteristic of several cultural and linguistic phenomena which spread north from south-western Finland in ancient times (cf. Valonen 1978, 1980).

1.3.1. *In the Gulf of Finland and Estonia.* The occurrence of hollowed-out boats made of aspen in northern Satakunta (see symbol 1 on Map 3) is, of course, late evidence of a long-standing eastern influence on this area, about the extent and nature of which we do not have much information. This type of boat bears the name: Finnish *haapio* or *haaparuuhi*. These terms give us no etymological indication

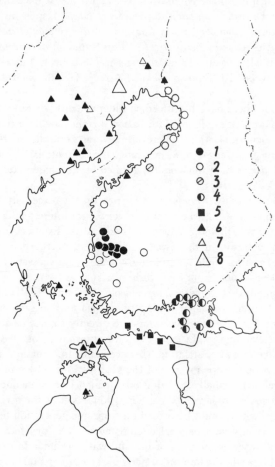

Map 3. The geographical spread of Finnish *haapio* and the corresponding terms in Estonia, Finland, and northern Sweden.

Key to symbols:
1. Finnish *haapio* 'aspen dug-out with widened sides'.
2. Finnish *haapio* 'small rowing-boat'.
3. Finnish *haapio* 'thin creature (man or horse)' or 'tall man' (secondary and pejorative meanings).
4. Finnish *haapio* 'larger or smaller fishing boat; seal-hunting boat'.
5. Estonian *haabjas* (and other phonological variants) 'small rowing-boat'.
6. East Swedish dialectal *håp* 'small rowing-boat' in Estonia, Finland, and northern Sweden.
7. Northern Swedish and Estonian Swedish *hap* 'small rowing-boat'.
8. Estonian prefixal *Haap-* in the place name *Haapsalu* and northern Swedish *Hap-* in *Hapträsk*, Norrbotten.

as to where the dug-out might have come from or when it might have been introduced into this area, but Finnish *haapio* is derived from *haapa* 'aspen' in the same way as the Russian term *osinovka* 'aspen dug-out with stretched sides' comes from *osina* 'aspen' (Aleškovskij 1969: 265–6). This type of derivation is not unusual in Finnish; it also occurs in another term for a boat, Finnish *honkio* 'boat made of fir-tree wood' (cf. Finnish *honka* 'fir-tree'; Hakulinen (1961) 1968: 127).

Therefore *haapio* could here have been formed independently in Finnish. However, it cannot be ruled out that the Russian formation was the model for the Finnish and the latter was a loan translation. There are several examples of this word formation pattern being transferred from one language to another. For example, the Finnish boat term *uisko* which was possibly formed on the same pattern as Old Swedish *snækkia* (see Vilkuna 1975).

Even if it cannot be proved that *haapio* was formed on the same pattern as the Russian word for an aspen dug-out, the term is of very great interest because of its widespread distribution: in Finland, in Estonia (both in the Estonian and in the Estonian–Swedish dialects) and in the Swedish dialects of northern Swedish. It would be natural for a term for such a useful dug-out to spread via waterways used by merchants and collectors of tribute (see Korhonen 1982: 26–7).

From Map 3 it is evident that the term *haapio* also occurs in the Gulf of Finland. Here it denotes both 'larger or smaller fishing boat' of a normal type and 'seal-hunting boat' (cf. symbol 4). Since these waters are directly connected with Lake Ladoga by the River Neva, one might expect to find information on Slavic aspen dug-outs constructed like those in Satakunta. However, such information is lacking. The need for large boats on the open waters of the Gulf of Finland led to the early disappearance of the relatively small aspen dug-outs, which I presume once existed there; they were superseded by larger boats. The production of them required a sophisticated technique, which could be passed on from one generation to another only under especially favourable ecological circumstances. The province of Satakunta was such an area, whereas the Gulf of Finland was not. Therefore, the term *haapio* for clinker-built boats in the innermost parts of the Gulf of Finland indicates that aspen boats were also used here in an earlier period, but new conditions required another technique and a new raw material. Therefore the term *haapio*, when it occurs in this area, can be said to have survived the disappearance of the type of boat it originally referred to.

The Finnish term *haapio* for an aspen boat was borrowed into northern Estonian dialects in the form *haabjas* (and in other phonological variants; cf. S.K.E.S., *haapio*). The geographical spread of the Estonian loan word (see symbol 5 on Map 3) shows that the cultural and environmental conditions throughout the inner areas of the Gulf of Finland and along the northern coasts of Estonia were of a similar nature in the past. It is natural then to assume that this Slavic boat type spread north from the coasts of the Gulf of Finland to Satakunta, although other possible explanations of how it spread must be considered as well (cf. 1.3.4).

1.3.2. *The role of Finnish traders during the Viking age.* Thus, in its construction the aspen dug-out with widened sides is eastern in origin, but the term for it originated from the dialects around the Gulf of Finland. As regards the Baltic–Finnish names for it in this area, in Satakunta, and in northern Sweden, the Baltic–Finnish population must be considered to have been instrumental in spreading this type of boat. Because of its extraordinary usefulness the type was adopted by people who were forced to travel on the waters between Lake Ladoga and the coastal strip of Satakunta and further up to the region north of the Gulf of Bothnia. In what period can the *haapio*-boat be assumed to spread, and what kind of travelling was involved?

The distribution of the boat term *haapio* corresponds well to the travelling patterns which are known to have been prevalent during the Viking age. We know that the Vikings travelled extensively through the Gulf of Finland and up the River Neva into Lake Ladoga on their expeditions to the east (cf. Arbman 1955). From here alternative routes towards the south and south-east were available on the lakes and rivers of Russia. We are accustomed to regarding the presence of the Varangians in Russia solely as a result of the activities of the Swedish Vikings from the Lake Mälar region. However, there is abundant archaeological evidence which shows that Finnish tribes were also active at an early period, in particular in the southern and south-eastern parts of Lake Ladoga. Certain types of finds indicate that the Finns maintained trade relations between the Lake Ladoga region and south-western Finland (cf. Kivikoski 1937: 243; Salmo 1956: 41; Raudonikas 1930). The participation of the Finns in the so-called Viking expeditions in the east remains an unwritten page in the history of the Varangians.[3] However, the occurrence of the soft dug-out in Finland and the spread of its Finnish names into Estonia and northern Sweden give us new perspectives on the Viking period in the east.

1.3.3. *In the Swedish dialects of Estonia and Finland.* The term *haapio* was also borrowed into the Swedish dialects spoken on the islands off the west coast of Estonia and, what is more, into the Swedish dialects of northern Sweden (see symbols 6 and 7 on Map 3). This spread of *haapio* indicates an extensive borrowing process from the east into the west and north-west of the area under consideration.

The term occurs in the form *håp* and other phonological variants on the islands of Dagö, Nuckö, Ormsö, and Runö. A few examples of this form are also found in a region situated between these two areas; namely, in the Swedish-speaking archipelago of Turku, and in Kronoby in East Bothnia in Finland. In the dialects close to the River Kalix in Norrbotten, Sweden, and in Västerbotten similar forms of *håp* occur, especially frequently in the latter case (cf. Korhonen 1982: 42).

In all the areas listed here the term refers to 'a small boat' used for various purposes. It may be the little dinghy which is used when a seine net is being hauled from the shore. The catch is then transported in the *håp*. It may also denote the light flat-bottomed dinghy used on sealing expeditions from the large mother ship. This little boat was also used at home as a normal rowing-boat after the annual sealing voyages were over, and for fishing and hay-making on swampy meadows etc. The fact that *haapio* as a term for a boat is borrowed into all these areas and is used for 'a small and light boat' – irrespective of its construction – is the reason why I consider that it was derived from an earlier term which denoted a boat which, just as the term says, was made by hollowing out an aspen trunk.

The use of this term thus goes back to an earlier method of construction, namely to the period when the technique of making real aspen dug-outs with widened sides was still known – as is documented in the province of Satakunta.

1.3.4. *The Dvina–Dniepr–Lovat origin of the aspen dug-out in Estonia.* But what about the cultural and environmental conditions in Estonia? Here too we are fortunate to find that the soft dug-out has been preserved down to the present day. In the shallow bays of the west coast of Estonia this type of boat was well known into the 20th century. It has also been described in other parts of Estonia (cf. Schneider 1929).

In this context I want to point out that this type of dug-out may also have spread as a means of transportation to the Baltic coast directly from a Slavic area along the River Dvina at a very early period (cf. Bielenstein 1918: 603). This river has its main source in the upper parts of the Dniepr, the Volga, and the Lovat, which were then inhabited by the Slavs. It is known that these rivers served as arteries of communication between the population in the western and eastern areas; even before the beginning of the Viking Period (cf. Nerman 1939, 1942). Therefore, it is not just possible but very likely that such a typically Slavic object as the aspen dug-out became known in the trading centres of the Dvina estuary in this early period. The distance from here to the western archipelago of Estonia and Finland is very short – 150 to 250 km. If this was the first route along which the Slavic soft dug-out spread, the heavy traffic through the Ladoga region during the Viking age resulted in the increasing use of this suitable boat which had been introduced earlier and come to be appreciated as an effective means of transportation for long distances.

1.3.5. *In northern Sweden.* The question now arises whether the present-day occurrence of the term *håp/hap* in northern Sweden (see symbols 6 and 7 on Map 3) reflects the fact that the hollowed-out boat really was used here in the past (cf. 1.3). Could one not interpret the occurrence of the term *håp* in northern Sweden as a parallel to the use of the north-Swedish term *eka*, which is originally derived from the term for an oak tree – Swedish *ek* 'oak' – and which is a simply built, small, often flat-bottomed rowing boat? The term *eka* 'rowing-boat' is used throughout Sweden, even in the north, where the tree does not grow and where boats made of oak cannot possibly be part of the folk tradition. For the same reason the term *håp* could be a loan from Finnish *haapio* 'little rowing-boat' without reference to dug-outs. *Haapio* is also used in some Finnish dialects to refer to a rowing-boat in general without the connotation of being made of aspen (see symbol 2 on Map 3). Neither such ethnological nor archaeological data are available which could solve the problem. There have been no archaeological finds of hollowed-out boats made from aspen tree trunks in the north (nor are there any in Finland!) and a boat-building tradition similar to that of Satakunta is not found there either.

However, the ecological and cultural background of the term *håp*, as used in northern Sweden, is clearly illuminated by our knowledge of Finnish wild-life culture – the *erämark*-culture – especially in those areas where boats and transportation by means of boats still play an important role.

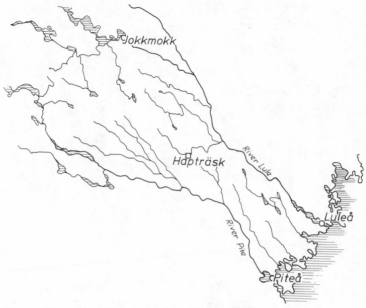

Map 4. The valleys of the River Pite and the River Lule

Therefore the occurrence of aspen dug-outs in Swedish Lappland in ancient times seems quite plausible, even though Finnish *haapio* has been found only in one single case in Saamish dialects (cp. *hapi, LÖ* 1780).

1.3.6. *The aspen dug-out as the missing link between Estonia and northern Sweden.* In this section I will discuss at some length terms for expanses of water which reflect the similar ecological circumstances under which the term *hap-* became the first item in a noun compound (see Map 3).

Although Lake Hapträsk between the Rivers Pite and Lule in northern Sweden and the town Haapsalu on the west coast of Estonia are about 1,000 km distant from each other, they demonstrate an identical prefixal noun: north Swedish *hap-* and Estonian (-Swedish) *haap-*. The north Swedish lake is very shallow and was a centre of pike-fishing before it was drained at the turn of the century. Several square kilometres of it were only about two meters deep. Using fishing nets, seine nets, willow (osier) baskets, and fishing-spears, fish were caught throughout all the seasons of the year. Lake Hapträsk is situated on the water-divide between the Rivers Pite and Lule. In this area bartering and trade between the Finns and the Saamis must have taken place from very early on, and this must be the reason why Lake Hapträsk is called *Bar'tajáv're* (cp. Saamish *jáv're* 'lake') by the Saamis in this area (see Symbol 8 on Map 3). This was probably also the main factor in spreading the term *hap-*, which now occurs only in a few place names and the names of lakes in northernmost Sweden (cp. Korhonen 1982: 106–12, 169).

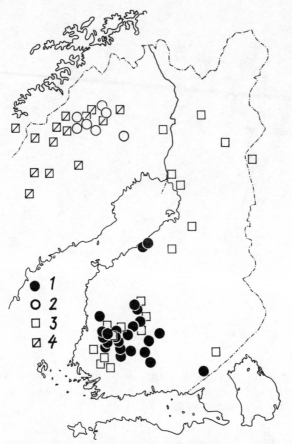

Map 5. Geographical spread of Finnish *paarre* and Saamish *bárda*.

Key to symbols:

1. Finnish *paarre* 'gunwale of a boat; reinforcing edge on other objects made of wood'.
2. Saamish *bárda* 'gunwale of a boat'.
3. Finnish *paarre* 'fur trimming or edging on clothing'.
4. Saamish *bárda* 'trimming made of dog or goat skin' on the lower part of a fur-coat.

I have already mentioned the north-Swedish term *håp/hap* borrowed from Finnish *haapio* (see Map 3), and I will now discuss west Saamish *bárda* with a parallel in Finnish *paarre* (see Map 5), and the possibility that the River Pite got its name from Finnish *piitta* (see Map 7), just as nearby Hapträsk certainly got its name from *hap*. These western Finnish words have western parallels in Swedish and Saamish dialects and in old place-names. Now it is illuminating to find that Lake Hapträsk in Saamish is called *Bar'tajáv're* (cf. symbol 2 on Map 9). The meanings of *bar'ta* are 'kiln (a log cabin with oven) for drying grain (barley)' in the Saamish dialects south of this area, and 'log cabin; the living room in a house' further north. *Bar'ta* comes from Finnish *pirtti* 'log cabin; living room' (where originally no cooking or baking took place, see symbol 2 on Map 9); in dialects it also means 'steam-bath, sauna'. There are also statements about *pirtti* with reference to drying grain in Finland.[4]

Lake Hapträsk is situated in an area which is divided administratively into two territories: those of the Lule and Pite Saamis. The boundary line follows the highlands between the rivers. It is natural to find a centre of commercial and cultural contacts here. Strangely enough the noun *håp/hap* is not known in the dialects of the Pite and the Lule River Valleys. No examples of it are to be found in the archives (e.g. D.A.U.M.), which possess dialectological data from the area. Inquiries among native informants of the Lule River Valley concerning the use of the term *håp/hap* for 'a small boat' yielded negative results, except for one or two informants, who claimed to have heard the term being used for 'a rowing-boat' in the region of Kalix, which is much further to the north and closer to the Finnish-speaking area. In fact, further to the north and to the south in West Bothnia there are several examples of the use of *håp/hap* in the sense of 'a small rowing-boat' (see symbols 6 and 7 in northern Sweden on Map 3). The point here is that the frequent use of aspen dug-outs in this area in the past seems to be reflected in the name *Hapträsk*. The name of the lake indicates a knowledge of *haapio*-boats in the past, but the term for the boat in the dialects has disappeared. The shallow waters of the lake, the low banks, and the great amount of reed and weed in it made flat-bottomed boats a most useful type of boat for fishing and transportation. The *haapio*-boat in northern Satakunta, Finland, is claimed to be especially suitable for that kind of lake.

In field work in Hapträsk I was informed that two types of boat were formerly used in log-driving. One had a distinct keel and stem and was too large to be steered easily on the river. This type of boat originated from the Lule River Valley. The other type of boat originated from the Pite River Valley and was rounder, flat-bottomed and easy to steer; indeed it was almost too lightly built for the heavy work of log-driving on the river. I see the difference between the ways in which the two types of boat were constructed as a reflection of an old cultural difference between the two river valley settlements: the knowledge of a boat, similar to the *haapio*, in the Pite River Valley on the one hand, and the existence of another boat type in the Lule River Valley on the other. The existence of a name such as *Hapträsk* for a lake between the river valleys is, in my opinion, not accidental. It reflects different trading connections across the Gulf of Bothnia in ancient times. It is possible to reconstruct early connections between the Lule River Valley and Häme or eastern parts of Finland, where neither *haapio* nor *pirtti* exist. Therefore it is only in place names (Swedish *Hapträsk* and Lule Saamish *Bar'tajáv're*) that the old terms from the western parts of Finland have survived as suffixal components. Thus the areal distribution of the two terms in question gives us information about early contacts between western Finnish and Saamish cultural centres in Finland and Sweden respectively.

An excellent parallel to the compound *Hapträsk* in North Bothnia, Sweden, is found on the Estonian mainland close to the Estonian islands where Swedish was formerly spoken. On the mainland the place name *Haapsalu* occurs (see symbol 8

on Map 3; cp. Korhonen 1982: 100–1). The town is situated north of the bay of
Matsalulaht, which is about 20 km long and 10 km broad, but only one or two
metres deep. This bay is well known for its rich fishing and the variety of its bird-
life (cf. Schneider 1929; Valmet 1970). The eastern part, which is filled with dense
beds of reeds, remains accessible here and there by means of small canals which
are kept open by the passage of boats. Here the native population pole their boats,
which are carved out of aspen trunks. They can glide noiselessly over the water in
their light dug-outs, spear fish and shoot seabirds.

In other words there are great environmental similarities between this bay in
Estonia and the lake in northern Sweden as far as the conditions for fishing and
hunting are concerned. Sastamala in northern Satakunta, Finland, is situated
between these two extreme geographical points, and a region of wild-life settlements
is to be found there. In the three areas involved here the landscape is full of smaller
rivers and lakes, which are separated from each other by swamps and moors. It
was such a network of water courses that gave rise to the type of boat which we call
the aspen dug-out. Hence the existence of the prefixal *Hap-* in the compound
Hapträsk in North Sweden and *Haap-* in *Haapsalu* in Estonia together with the
occurrence of the terms *håp/hap, haapio* and *haapjas* in the three areas which are
geographically far apart – Norrbotten in Sweden, Satakunta in Finland, and Estonia
– can be convincingly explained with the (originally Slavic) aspen dug-out as the
missing link (for further details on the spread of the prefix *Håp-* and *Ha(a)p-* see
Korhonen 1982: 100–12).

2   The terms for the gunwale built onto an aspen dug-out (Finnish *paarre* and Saamish *bárda*)

2.1   The ethnological background

The top part of the artificially stretched sides of a dug-out is not very stable. The
aspen wood is porous here and prone to bend inwards again. In the Finnish *haapio*
ribs were used to reinforce the side, and a broad plank on the top – the gunwale
(or side plank) – lent the boat stability (cf. Nikkilä 1936). Such details are completely
lacking in the Siberian boats of which we have descriptions or pictures. With the
Siberian type, in hollowing out the trunk a somewhat thicker rounded upper edge
to the side was fashioned. Straight thwarts across the boat gave it rigidity (cf.
Sirelius 1913, Figure 6; 1919: 424). This is the way the soft dug-out was constructed east of the Urals, but in the European part of northern Russia both a broad
gunwale and supports for the sides which resemble frames are found. The latter
two details have been explained as a result of the influence of western boat-building
techniques, which use planks. There are some similarities with the long-ships of
the Vikings. The combination of boat-building techniques just described is considered to have been caused by Scandinavian influence on native boat-building.
The frames in the Viking ships were attached to the cleats of the washstrakes with
cords which were run through holes in the top section of the frames (cf. Falk 1912:
46; Eskeröd 1956: 69). In some areas of Russia and the Baltic States one single
thick wooden frame, almost like a bent thwart, in the middle of the boat was attached

to the sides of the boat (cf. Manninen 1927: 14). The existence of frames of various types in the soft dug-outs in Russia is a sign of a Scandinavian boat-building technique, which must have spread very early.

2.2 The terms in Finland

The western influence was more extensive in Finland. The *haapio*-boats in Satakunta all have a large number of ribs made of bent whitewood or wood from tree roots, but the top part of the ribs is always supported by a broad gunwale – which is a western characteristic. The similarity to clinker-built boats is very great indeed.

Map 6. Geographical spread of Finnish *keidas*.

Key to symbols:
1. Finnish *keidas* 'promontory, narrow strip of land between lakes'.
2. Finnish *keidas* 'wet moor' or 'swamp'.
3. Finnish *keidas* 'narrow strip of firm ground in a moor'.
4. The broken lines indicate the borders of Sastamala (west) and Kyrö (east).

In my research on boat-terminology in Finland I observed the dialectal distribution of the Finnish term *paarre* 'gunwale of a boat' which also denotes 'a reinforcing edge on other objects made of wood' or 'edge, or trimming (e.g. of fur) on clothes' (see symbols 1 and 3 on Map 5). The spread of this term is in the west parallel to that of *haapio* (see Maps 1 and 3) and *keidas* (see symbols 2 and 3 on Map 6; cf. 3.1). On the maps we can see that in the *erämark*-area of Sastamala the occurrence of the three terms is particularly widespread.

The term *paarre* for 'gunwale of a boat' is also found along the water-course from Lake Näsijärvi and northwards, which was the route used by the people in the ancient Parish Pirkkala when travelling to their *erämark*. All the important routes in Finland which came into use during the Iron Age and continued to be used up to 1000 AD are indicated by the different distributions of the lexical items, which are plotted on Maps 3, 5 and 6. It is striking that in certain respects great similarities exist in the vocabulary of the dialects spoken in the old *erämark*-districts. In other respects, however, there are also considerable differences (cf. Valonen 1946: 186; 1980: 212). As examples of the latter I would mention: (a) the various meanings of *keidas* 'promontory' or 'wet moor', or 'strip of firm ground in a moor' (cf. 3, 3.1); (b) the few occurrences of this word found in Pirkkala in the area of Lake Näsijärvi; (c) the *paarre* 'gunwale of a boat' found frequently in the province of Sastamala, Parish of Pirkkala, and the region of Päijät-Häme, but few occurrences of it found in Kyrö; and finally (d) the term *haapio* with its original meaning 'boat made of aspen', which only occurs in Sastamala.

By means of areal-linguistic research the areas of *erämark*-culture can be mapped so as to show the regions where it was furthest developed. By doing so we are able to examine it separately from other types of Finnish folk culture and make a study of the features which distinguish it from other types of settlements. Dialectological methods have a long tradition in Finnish linguistics. The field work which has been carried out here is a continuation of this type of research.

2.3   The terms in northern Sweden

It is possible to develop dialectological research by expanding the field to include information on the ecology and economy of a given area, both of which are important underlying factors in the spread of loan words from one language to another: that is, to develop a method of interlinguistic dialectology. The result of such research can be combined with the information which is available from historical studies on trade routes, colonization or other types of migration.

The Finnish term *paarre* 'gunwale of a boat; reinforcing edge on other objects made of wood' and the corresponding form *bárda* in Saamish (see symbols 1 and 2 respectively on Map 5) are cases which give us the opportunity to develop such an interlinguistic dialectological approach. This meaning of Finnish *paarre* is geographically more concentrated than the more general meaning 'fur trimming or edging on clothing' (symbol 3). The difference is not so distinct that it would be possible to judge which of the two meanings was the primary one.

In northern Finland *paarre* only refers to 'fur trimming or edging on clothing'. In Saamish dialects *bárda* (symbol 4) usually refers to 'trimming on the lower part of a fur-coat made of dog or goat skin'. In Swedish Lapland I have also found *bárda* 'gunwale of a boat' among the Saamis (see symbol 2 on Map 5) very close to those areas where Swedish *håp/hap* 'a small rowing-boat' and Saamish *hapi* with the same meaning occur (see symbols 6 and 7 on Map 3). It is not clear whether the Saamish term is a loan from Finnish or the other way round.[5] The two main meanings 'gunwale of a boat' or 'edge of a wooden object' and 'the trimming of an article of clothing', which are found in Saamish as well as in Finnish, are too specific to have developed independently within the two languages. In addition the meaning 'gunwale of a boat' is found only in western Saamish dialects. Cultural and linguistic contacts have obviously resulted in a semantic parallel which will be further explained here.

The Saamish verb *bár'det*, from which *bárda* is derived (cp. Finnish *paartaa*, S.K.E.S.) refers either to the action 'put fur trimming on a fur-coat' or (in certain places in Swedish Lapland) 'put a gunwale on a boat'. A more general meaning of the verb is 'twine, wind, coil (a thread or rope on or round something, and to attach in this way)' (cf. Grundström 1946–54; Nielsen 1932–8; Itkonen 1958), which seems to explain the two meanings of the noun *bárda*. It is not so much the reference to an edge, i.e. the extreme part (on the side of a boat, on a wooden object or on a fur-coat) that is the essential factor, but the manner in which the edge is fastened. The fur trimming was sewed on the fur by attaching it with the thread in a loop through the lower part of the fur and the trimming. In earlier periods the gunwale of the dug-out was fastened with withies of narrow fir-tree roots. There is a great deal of old data on the use of this technique of sewing or binding in the construction of boats (cf. Linné (1732) 1913: 41; Högström (1747) 1980: 112); we also possess ethnological descriptions of such boats and finds of fragments of board secured in this way from boats with remains of wicker or root threads in the holes (cf. Hammarstedt 1908; Hallström 1909; Prins 1975).

One of the most interesting finds made so far is a boat which was found in Malå, West Bothnia, in Sweden. Pieces of threads of fir-tree root were still attached to the remains of the boat. Besides a frame with a hole in it, which was probably used for fastening, there was also a piece of wood which had a width of 42–52 mm, and a thickness of 16 mm, and the outside of which was rounded off. It has been suggested that this piece was 'a part of the gunwale, i.e. a rim or edge which ran around the outside edge of the side of the boat' (cf. Hammarstedt 1908). Such a gunwale was probably best attached with root threads which were looped around the gunwale-plank and inserted through a hole in the side of the boat. The method of attachment would explain why there is no hole in the gunwale itself. (Some other finds are discussed in Korhonen 1982: 72–81.)

This strengthening device, which is fixed in a similar way to that by which the trimming is fixed to the fur-coat, was to give rise to the Swedish term *sudbord*, i.e. 'a board attached by binding or sewing' (*sud* is derived from a stem which is also the underlying stem of the verb *sy* 'sew') and to the Swedish Saamish *bárda* with a similar meaning, from the verb stem *bár'det* 'twine, wind, coil (a thread or rope around something)'. However, north Finnish dialects have *paarre* and the Saamish dialects in the neighbourhood *bárda* in the sense of 'edging of an article of clothing', but not with the meaning of 'gunwale of a boat', which confirms the hypothesis that the western parts of Finland were in closer connection with West Bothnia. What is significant in this context is the technique of attaching the trimming to a fur-coat or the gunwale-plank to the side of a ship. Consequently, Saamish and Finnish dialects contain terms which reflect an old method of constructing boats by means of sewing the boards to each other or binding the gunwale to the side. Through the centuries the terms have been preserved in the dialects of the two languages, although the technique of attaching the gunwale-planks has changed.

3   **The geographical distribution of the Finnish term** *keidas* **'moor'**

Communication with people outside their own settlements was a necessity for the hunters and fishers of the *erämark*. Contacts were made during fishing and hunting trips, on which trade was also carried on and taxes collected in the form of furs from the Saamis who were liable to pay taxes.

During the middle ages there were a considerable number of Saamis living as far south as central Finland (cf. Itkonen 1947: 55). What had been collected on these hunting expeditions was intended to be sold. The goods were therefore brought to certain trading market centres. Here contacts were established not only with fellow countrymen, but also with people from distant countries. It was perhaps at these meeting places that the eastern soft dug-outs first became known in western Finland. Anyhow it seems as if a term of western origin – *keidas* – was introduced in the same way and became a word which was particularly used on travels to the *erämark* (cp. Old Norwegian and Old Icelandic *skeið*, Old Swedish *skeidhe* etc. and, especially as regards the meaning, Old English *shed* 'a ridge of high ground dividing two valleys or tracts of lower country; a "divide"'; Itkonen 1962: 7–15). In dealing with this word we must also consider other old Finnish settlements beside Sastamala.

The term *keidas* is still found in place names in the province of Häme (in Swedish called Tavastland) and the neighbouring areas of southern Savo (in Swedish Savolax), where it refers to 'places situated on narrow promontories or narrow strips of land between lakes'. The term occurs both in place names and common nouns (*keidas* 'promontory, narrow strip of land between lakes', see symbol 1 on Map 6). Several examples can be mentioned which indicate that the naming of the places is connected with whether it was possible to haul boats from one lake to another there.

The word does not exist in the Kokemäki River Valley or near the source of this river, these being the furthest points the settlements in the Iron Age had reached before 500 AD (cf. Kivikoski 1961: 111). For this reason it has been assumed that the word was borrowed into Finnish between 550 and 800 AD (Itkonen 1962: 34). The explanation for the uneven distribution of the word is that it was used in communication by people who were travelling in unpopulated areas or who were on their way to their *erämark*-areas. The Finnish dialects do not lack their own terms for referring to stretches over which boats have to be hauled between two lakes, but the north Germanic word spread because it became fashionable. Like most fashionable words *keidas* enjoyed a limited period of popularity, though we can see from the extent of its expansion in Häme and southern Savo (as indicated by the symbol 1 on Map 6) that it must have been in regular use for a considerable period of time.

On Map 6 (which is adapted from Itkonen 1962: 35) we also see that in the west the word *keidas* has two different meanings (see the symbols 2 for 'wet moor' or 'swamp' and 3 for 'narrow strip of firm ground in a moor'). It is interesting to see that the two areas of distribution represent northern regions of settlement, where the population originally came from two well-known wild-life culture regions of northern Satakunta: Sastamala, where the meaning of *keidas* is 'wet moor' or 'swamp' and north of Kyrö, where *keidas* means 'narrow strip of firm ground in a moor' (cf. Suvanto 1973: 69). The geographical distribution of the word has been seen as a result of the historical and ecological conditions of the two settlements involved. The two different meanings of *keidas*, as used in these two areas, have not so far been quite explained. Because they do not seem to be connected with travelling by boat, it has been suggested that the differences in meaning developed from whether it was possible to travel over open moors in winter time. The moors and the narrow strips of firm ground in a moor were, in other words, short-cuts over the terrain, just as the routes for hauling boats overland were for the traveller during summer.

In Häme and southern Savo the eastern meaning of *keidas*, i.e. 'narrow strips of land between lakes' (see symbol 1 on Map 6) can be better understood if the ecological conditions are taken into consideration. Here in the east, where the broad and open lakes made large boats necessary, the passage across the strip of land from one lake to another was much more laborious because of the heavier boats. Here we also have *keidas* referring to the places for hauling boats across necks of land and promontories. On the other hand in the west, in Satakunta, navigable water-ways were rivers and streams, and moors and swamps had to be crossed between these water-ways (see symbols 2 and 3 on Map 6).

In the settlements where aspen dug-outs or other light boats were used, even broad strips of land or promontories between the lakes caused no major difficulties. Here a man could carry his boat and his back-pack singlehanded. In places where the water in streams or in swamps was 10 cm or so deep, he simply put down his boat and could paddle for a stretch. When we consider these ethnological circumstances, it is clear that the meanings of *keidas* in the west are also to be interpreted in relation to communication by boat.

3.1 The overlapping distribution of *haapio* and *keidas*

If we compare the geographical distribution of the terms *haapio* 'aspen dug-out' (see symbol 1 on Map 3) and *keidas* in the sense of 'wet moor, swamp' (symbol 2 on Map 6) or 'narrow strip of firm ground on a moor' (symbol 3 on Map 6) in northern Satakunta and southernmost East Bothnia, we notice that the areas where *keidas* is found with these two meanings are directly to the north of the area where this type of boat is known to have been used. From our analysis of *keidas* it is evident that the meaning 'strip of firm ground in a moor' in southern East Bothnia also has something to do with travels which were undertaken in light boats. The problem is that we cannot demonstrate on Map 1 that the *haapio* was used in Kyrö as well, if we disregard the few examples of its use on the border with Sastamala. One would expect the inhabitants to have known about the aspen dug-out in southern East Bothnia, for instance, if it had really been in use there. In any case, there must have been some sort of light boat in use.

The term *keidas* for 'strip of firm ground in a moor' or 'wet moor' demonstrates that there were routes through these parts of Finland for the trade northwards. The term spread from the south through the western Finnish dialects northwards and corresponds exactly with the historical, ethnological and archaeological facts regarding the spread of the settlements (cf. Luukko 1950). The nature and extent of this movement of the *erämark*, region of the wild-life culture, northwards could be compared with the advancing frontier in the American West. There is further linguistic data, which could be referred to, which shows the rapid spread of the *erämark*, but considerations of space prevent a lengthy discussion here.

4   The term for 'thwart or cross-plank in a boat'

I mentioned in 2.1 that the Slavic soft dug-out found west of the Urals seems to have been influenced by Scandinavian boat-building techniques. The introduction of the term for the gunwale in Finnish (*paarre*) (cf. 2.2) and in Saamish dialects (*bárda*) (cf. 2.3) has been described.

Another important lexical item of western origin in the terminology connected with boats is the term for the straight planks across the boat, the thwarts, which support the sides of the boat. The frames of the soft dug-outs in the European part of Russia, and the special method of fastening them with cords to cleats on the sides of the boat, seem to have come about through Scandinavian contacts. The fact that an old Scandinavian word for the thwart of a boat is found in Finnish, Estonian and Russian, is evidence of widespread influence.

4.1   In Finland and Estonia

The Swedish term for a thwart or a cross-plank in a boat, *bett/bette*, which is also used for the beams in a house, comes from Old Swedish *biti* (cp. Norwegian *bite*, Old Icelandic *biti*). It has been borrowed into Finnish, Estonian, and Russian and yields interesting information on the early contacts between the peoples of the east. In connection with boats it can also refer to the piece of wood on which the mast stands or which is used to support the mast. In Finnish it occurs as *piitta* (cf. S.K.E.S.) referring both to 'a ceiling', 'a beam, high bench (or the edge of the high bench or platform) in a Finnish steam-bath (sauna)' (see symbol 2 on Map 7) and to 'cross plank etc. in a boat' (see symbol 3). In Satakunta it also occurs with the meaning 'steep bank (of a lake or a river)' (see symbol 5 on Map 7). In connection with what is said about the spread of *haapio*, which occurs as *håp/hap* in western Bothnia (cp. Map 3), it is interesting to find that the original form of the name of the River Pite, and the town situated by the river, is *pita* (inflected Latin forms (1339): *in pitu, in pito*). Because of the characteristic banks of the river, it is very plausible that Finnish visitors or colonists named the river by using their word *piitta* 'steep bank'. *Piitta* is a common place name in northern Satakunta (N.T.A.; see symbol 5 on Map 7). The Finnish–Swedish and Estonian–Swedish form is *bita* 'cross plank which supports the sides of the boat and to which the mast is attached'. In Estonian we find the term *püt* 'seat in a boat; board for securing the mast' (see symbol 4 on Map 7) especially in the western dialects spoken close to the former Swedish-speaking settlements. Here it occurs both on the mainland and on the islands. It is also used in northern Estonian dialects, where Estonian *haabjas* from Finnish *haapio* occurs, i.e. east of the Swedish-speaking area (cp. symbol 5 on Map 3). As regards this geographical distribution

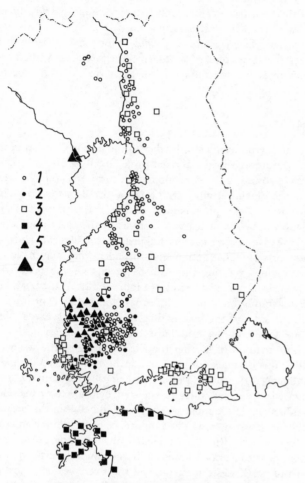

Map 7. Distribution of Finnish *piitta* and Estonian *piit* compared with *Pite*(-) in northern Swedish.

Key to symbols:

1. Finnish *piitta* 'ceiling beam in a house'.
2. Finnish *piitta* 'beam, high bench (or the edge of the high bench or platform in a Finnish steam-bath (sauna))'.
3. Finnish *piitta* 'cross plank or thwart in a boat, sometimes with a mast-hole'; 'rowing seat in a boat'.
4. Estonian *piit* 'seat in a boat; board for securing the mast'.
5. Finnish *piitta* 'steep bank (of a lake or a river)'.
6. Swedish *Pite älv* 'River Pite' (cp. inflected Latin forms 1339: *in pito, in pitu* from *pita*), probably named by the Finns because of its steep banks. (Note that *piitta* 'steep bank (of a lake or river)' occurs in Sastamala and Kyrö in Finland (acc. to *N.T.A.*)).

of the term south of the Gulf of Finland, we should note that it also occurs in the innermost areas of the Gulf (see symbol 3 on Map 7). Finnish *piitta* and Estonian *piit* are consequently in areal-linguistic correlation with each other, which repeats the parallels in the occurrence of *haapio* and *haabjas* for aspen dug-out in the two languages. The fact that examples of *piitta* are also found in Vodian (*pit*) and Livonian (*pīt'*), illustrates the general spread of the term along the coasts of the Baltic.

4.2   In Russia

The north Germanic term occurs still further to the east in Russian in the form *bet'* 'cross plank or thwart in a boat', derived from Old Russian **b't"*, i.e. a form which phonologically requires an Old Scandinavian form **biti* (cf. Vasmer 1976). In the Novgorod dialect the lowering of /ъ$^{(n)}$/to/e/ occurred in the first half of the 13th century. The time of the phonological change makes it possible that the borrowing of the term occurred at least as early as in the early middle ages (cf. Thörnqvist 1948: 25). However, there is linguistic, ethnological, and historical evidence which supports the assumption that the borrowing may have occurred earlier, during the Viking Age, i.e. the 10th century. In some texts where the term occurs the thwart is described as being cut into the side of the boat. We know that in northern Russian dug-outs the thick frames, almost like bent thwarts, were fitted into cleats in the sides of the boat and secured there with cords. There was sometimes only one frame in the middle of the northern Russian dug-out (cf. Hallström 1925). The method of lashing the ribs to cleats of the washstrakes in nordic clinker-built ships disappeared in Scandinavia during the Viking Age, but it probably had influenced the method of constructing both Russian clinker-built boats and dug-outs with widened sides in the east before a new technique was introduced in Scandinavia. There must be a correlation between the Scandinavian term and the method of construction. The importance of Scandinavian craftsmanship in boat-building in early Russia is evident from the widespread use of the construction technique with various kinds of frames and thwarts in the Slavic boats. Lake Ladoga in north-western Russia and the rivers east and north-east of the lake were the centres where this occurred. The Zyryan and Votyak peoples learned the technique of constructing and fastening a thwart-like frame (or frames) into the boat and passed it on to certain groups of the Vogul people and the East Yakuts. The use of this construction is known in many other parts of western Russia besides the Lake Ladoga area.

5   The role of the Vikings in the spread of the terminology used in connection with boats

5.1   The spread of *bat/bat'* as a term for a dug-out in Russian

The spread of the techniques of boat-building and certain terms for the boat is due to contacts between the eastern peoples and the Scandinavians which were established during the Varangian period in Russia. In Russian there are two loan words which illustrate this process: Russian *bat* 'rowing-boat hollowed-out of a trunk; narrow boat with a pointed prow' and *bat'* 'carved, oblong and narrow boat; boat hollowed-out of a pine or aspen tree trunk with a flat bottom' (cf. Thörnqvist 1948: 218f). The Scandinavian word occurs also in south-western Finnish dialects as *paatti* (S.M.S.). The words derive from Old Scandinavian *bátr* 'boat', Old Swedish *bater* 'boat'. The narrowing and labialization of *a* > *å* [ɔː] in Middle Swedish dialects took place about 1350–1400 AD, but the borrowing of the terms must have occurred much earlier. The wide distribution of the terms suggests this. (There are examples of the forms as far away as the provinces of Tomsk and Kamchatka, but these forms were probably spread later by the Russians.) From early on Scandinavians travelling into Russia made their boat-building technique known there and the Scandinavian terms for boats and their component parts were adapted into various languages and were spread together with the knowledge of the new techniques. But how is it possible that a Scandinavian word for a simple type of boat became a term for a dug-out in Russian? Other loan words on navigation always have a connection with large ships and developed boat building techniques. When analysing what sort of dug-outs *bat* and *bat'* refer to, it is striking that they are never stretched ones (Levin and Potapov 1961: 107, 110, 121). They are of the same hollowed-out type as in Scandinavia, where dug-outs with widened sides are completely unknown. The fact that a Scandinavian term was used for a dug-out in Russia is evidence of very old contacts.

5.2   Kiev as the 'city of boats'

The trade which the Scandinavians carried out using boats was considerable. In a text written in Greek dating from the middle of the 10th century we find the information that boats played a great role in trading. In Chapter 9 of his *De Administrando Imperio* (950 AD, cf. D.A.I. 9: 3–9; 9: 105–11. See Moravcsik (ed.) 1949) the Byzantine Emperor, Constantine Porphyrogenitus, described the trading expeditions of the Rus'. During the winter the leaders of the Rus' collected furs, honey, wax etc. among the Slavs and brought those products by boat to Constantinople in the early summer (see Map 8). The merchants arrived in Kiev in April and bought newly hollowed-out aspen boats (μονόξυλα) from the Slavic tribes and discarded those which were old and worn out. By this time the boats, i.e. the hulls, were equipped for trading purposes. Because of the heavy and bulky cargo they needed built-up gunwales in order to be able to pass the Dniepr rapids. Constantine describes how the various groups collected into a large convoy before they started the voyage down the Dniepr. When they reached the estuary the equipment was supplemented with sails and a rudder for the voyage across the Black Sea. This description gives us a good picture of the strenuous methods of transport which were employed. The quantities of goods transported down the Dniepr were substantial (cf. Vernadsky 1948: 30). The long trip had to be completed by November, because the journeys to the Slavs who were liable to pay tax to the Rus' started again then.

In the old Icelandic Sagas Kiev is called *Kænugarðr*, which has been interpreted as being derived from an old form of the city's name *Kijangorod*, but it is also connected by folk etymology with the Scandinavian word *kæna* 'boat' (cf. Stender-

Map 8. The route of the fur traders from the Gulf of Bothnia to Constantinople.
1. Satakunta. 2. Häme. 3. Savo. 4. Pite River Valley and 5. Lule River Valley.
6. The settlement of the farmer Ottar (see the Conclusion).

Petersen 1946: 132f; Vries 1962: 342). Since the word *kæna* (also *kana*, *kane*, and *kani*; Vries 1962: 300; Jóhannesson 1956: 291; Falk 1912: 389) refers to some kind of vessel hollowed-out of wood or to a dug-out, it was a suitable term for the boats in Kiev. But why did *bat/bat'* not fit this time? It is probably because *kæna* refers to a dug-out with a pointed prow, more like the indigenous Slavic type, although the Scandinavian type of dug-out did not have widened sides. Falk derives the boat-term from the meaning '(boat with) upstanding prow' (Falk 1912: 89; cp. Icelandic *kæna* 'small boat; bailer in a form of a boat', *kani* 'small wooden basin for liquid food; muzzle (of a cow), nose (of a dog); prow', Blöndal 1920–4: 418, 464). Consequently *Kænugarðr* was the most fitting name to characterize Kiev, a place which must indeed have been 'a city of boats', when the Rus' met there in the spring.

Conclusion

An exhaustive description of the influence of Slavic culture upon the Scandinavian and Baltic areas cannot be given in the present article. The existence of a Slavic type of boat – the *haapio*-boat – in western Finland and the spread of the terms for it (cp. Estonian *haabjas*, Estonian–Swedish and northern Swedish *håp/hap* etc.) was the reason why I chose to deal with historical evidence which indicates that cultural contacts resulted in the spread not only of this type of boat, but also of a number of other innovations. Without being able to present any supporting evidence, ethnologists have assumed that the use of the soft dug-out was wide-spread in Finland in the past (cp. Nikkilä 1946: 167; 1947: 40; Vilkuna and Mäkinen 1977: 306). This claim cannot be sustained here, however. The construction of a Finnish *haapio* in the sense of 'an aspen dug-out with widened sides' depended very much on the skill of the native craftsmen in particular areas, so that it is unlikely that this meaning of *haapio* is the original one in all other areas, where the same conditions did not exist (skills, materials etc.). Instead a semantic shift took place in the latter areas (e.g. to 'small rowing-boat' (symbol 2 on Map 3); 'large or small fishing boat' (symbol 4 on Map 3) etc.). However, in those areas where the ecological and cultural conditions for its construction prevailed, such as in the *erämark*-areas of Sastamala in Finland, the original meaning of *haapio* was retained. The intensive fur-trade during the Viking Age and early middle ages was the decisive factor in the spread of this type of boat and the terms for it. That is why I think that *håp/hap* in northern Sweden reflects a genuine knowledge of aspen dug-outs in ancient times. The boat was a cultural phenomenon which spread out over vast territories, as far as the northern coasts of the Gulf of Bothnia and to the western coast of Estonia. The province of Satakunta was the starting point for trading expeditions northwards, in a similar way to Kiev on the Dniepr. The Kokemäki River Valley, which runs south of the area in western Finland where the *haapio*-boats are found, is the route by which they spread from the south. This was the centre of the Finnish settlements during the Viking Age, from which the art of hollowing-out aspen boats must have come to northern Satakunta. The linguistic and cultural features which distinguish Satakunta from Häme are also to be found in parts of the Saamish area. These characteristics are of importance for determining the Saamish cultural provinces. Thus comparative ethnography can assist us in determining the age and origin of the northern culture. In addition a sophisticated inter-linguistic word geography can include scientific results from various fields. The latter is important for all types of arctic studies, since there are so few written documents.

However, some written documents exist on early conditions in the north, which yield information relevant to our topic. The Anglo-Saxon Chronicle tells us that as early as the end of the 9th century the farmer Ottar in northern Norway gave information to King Alfred of England on the ethnography and ecology of the north (see 6 on Map 8). For instance, he tells us about the *Cwenas*, the 'Cwens', who used to make surprise attacks on the coastal population of Norway across the mountains from the east. In the mountain range there were large lakes, 'and the *Cwenas* carry their boats across land to the lakes, and from there they make attacks on the Norwegians; they have very small boats and they are very light' (cf. Sweet (1876) 1967: 20f).[6] These *Cwenas* are considered to have been a Finnish tribe which had trading and hunting interests in the north (cf. Luukko 1964). In the Egils-saga their fur-trading is explicitly mentioned (cf. Egils-saga 1809: 56), in a passage which dates from the era of the farmer Ottar, although the text was written several centuries later (cf. Sigfússon 1958). The *Cwenas* are described as being fur-traders as well as robbers who sold the objects they had collected or stolen in the south. In this context it must be pointed out that in the days of Ottar only certain parts of Satakunta – the areas around the Kokemäki River Valley – had been settled. The settlement which had existed earlier in southern East Bothnia – around the present-day city of Vasa – had vanished by the end of the 8th century. The causes of the decline of this settlement are unknown. An expansion towards the north from Satakunta and a consequent conflict over the fur trade might have been the underlying causes.

On the basis of the present investigation I would venture to claim that the small and light boats, which Ottar mentions in connection with the Finnish tribe *Cwenas*, were some sort of soft dug-outs, perhaps a type which preceded the *haapio*-boats in Satakunta. These light and manageable boats were carried between the lakes. In this way travelling from one area to another was made easy and surprise attacks could be carried out swiftly. With larger boats of the same type considerable quantities of wares could be transported.

In the light of this information we should study the activities of the Rus' in Russia, who were also dependent upon this type of boat. Voyages between Novgorod and Constantinople were made possible by the dug-outs which the Rus' bought and equipped, and they took place despite repeated attacks by hostile tribes around the Dniepr cataracts – e.g. by the Petchenegs. Voyages on waterways in the north were less dangerous for tribes such as the *Cwenas*. If the destination of the fur-traders coming from the north was Novgorod, which is a plausible destination, then the distance from the Gulf of Bothnia to Novgorod was only half the distance which the Rus' had to cover from Novgorod to Byzantium every year (cf. Map 8). Just as Kiev was a stop-over place for the fur-traders from the north, where supplies were replenished and business was conducted, while new boats were equipped or old ones repaired, the coastal areas of Satakunta probably fulfilled a similar purpose for the traders travelling north.

Notes

1 In this article the subst. *Saami*, pl. *Saamis*, *Saamish* (the language) and adj. *Saamish* are used instead of the traditional *Lapp*, *Lapps*, *Lappish* (cf. Korhonen 1976: 64, note 1; Beach 1981: 1). The corresponding Saamish words are subst. *Sábmelaš/ sábmi* (also *Sábmi* 'Saamiland, the area where the Saamis live'). In Swedish (subst. *same*, adj. *samisk*) and other Scandinavian languages and in Finnish (subst., adj. *saamelainen*) the words (Sw.) *lapp*, *lapsk* and (Fi.) *lappalainen* are no longer in common use because of their more or less pejorative connotation.

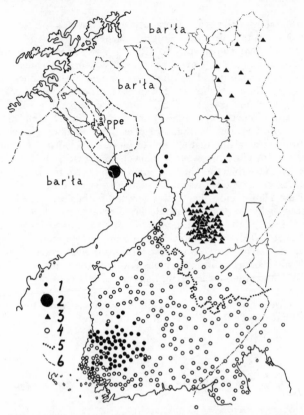

Map 9. The geographical spread of Slavic and north Germanic terms for 'log cabin/living room' in Finnish and Saamish dialects.

Keys to symbols:

1. Finnish *pirtti* 'living room where no cooking or baking takes place'.
2. Saamish *Bar'tajáv're* (*jáv're* 'lake') 'Lake Hapträsk' (cf. the map and the text about *bar'ta* with different meanings).
3. Finnish *pätsi* (in the dialects also *pätti*) in the meaning 'open air oven made of stone'.
4. Finnish *tupa* (cp. Swedish *stuga*, *stuva*) 'main living room, where both cooking and baking take place'.
5. Northeast of the dotted line, *pirtti* also occurs in the sense of 'main living room where both cooking and baking take place', i.e. with the same meaning as *tupa*, which might be a result of an influence from the latter word (Valonen 1963: 541).
6. Saamish *dåppe* from Finnish *tupa*, which is of north Germanic origin (cp. dialectal Swedish *stuva* 'small house'). *Dåppe* occurs only in the Lule Saamish dialect. The broken lines indicate the Saamish villages in that area.

2 In this text I will use the word *dug-out* for a boat hollowed out of a tree trunk. The dug-outs are made of different kinds of wood and can be called *hard* dug-outs (of oak, pine etc.) and soft ones (of aspen, poplar or ash; Eskeröd 1956: 62). The sides of a *soft* dug-out, like the aspen dug-out discussed in this paper, can be expanded by using hot water or tar. The sides of Scandinavian hard dug-outs are not stretched since the technique cannot be applied to the wood of which they are made.

3 See Lägreid's discussion of the ethnic composition of the Rus' in Novgorod and Kiev during the 9th and 10th centuries (in the present volume).

4 *Pirtti* is an old Slavic loan word (cp. Old Russian *p'rt'*, Modern Russian *pert'*; Plöger 1973; Valonen 1963). The oven of a *pirtti* was originally used only for heating the room. For cooking and baking there was an oven outdoors (Vilkuna 1945; Valonen 1963). The Finnish name for an open air oven is *pätsi/pätti*, which originates from Russian *peč'* (see S.K.E.S.). They occur in the western parts of Finland and have spread north (see symbol 3 on Map 9). Finnish *tupa* 'main living room, where both cooking and baking take place' (see symbol 4 on Map 9) is quite different from an areal-linguistic point of view. This word is of north Germanic (Scandinavian) origin (cp. Swedish *stuga*, *stuva*; see S.K.E.S.), and spread later than *pirtti*. The fact that the Lule Saamish dialect (around the River Lule) borrowed *dåppe* 'log cabin; house' from Finnish *tupa* is an indication of a strong later influence from Häme and other eastern parts of Finland. This influence is probably the reason why *håp/hap* has disappeared from the dialects in the Lule River Valley and is only left in place-names. *Dåppe* has forced its way into the Lule Saamish dialect and the word *bar'ta* is quite unknown here (see *dåppe* compared with *bar'ta* on Map 9). These word distributions indicate the correspondence between Finnish and Saamish cultural regions and how the latter can be analysed by means of what is known about Finnish dialects and folk culture.

5 See Korhonen 1982: 79.

6 ... and berað þā Cwēnas hyra scypu ofer land on ðā meras, and þanon heriað on Norðmen; hȳ habbað swyðe lȳtle scȳpa and swyðe lēohte.

Bibliography

Aleškovskij, M. Ch. 1969: Lad'ja v iz Novgoroda. *Sovetskaja Archeologija* 2: 264–9. Moscow.

Arbman, H. 1955: *Svear i österviking*. Stockholm.

Baudou, E. and K. H. Dahlstedt (eds.) 1980: *Nordskandinaviens historia i tvärvetenskaplig belysning*. Acta Universitatis Umensis. Umeå Studies in the Humanities 24. Umeå.

Beach, H. 1981: *Reindeer-herd management in transition*. Acta Universitatis Upsaliensis. Uppsala Studies in Cultural Anthropology 3. Uppsala.

Bielenstein, A. 1918: *Die Holzbauten und Holzgeräte der Letten*. St Petersburg.

Blöndal, S. 1920–4. *Islandsk–Dansk Ordbog*. Reykjavik.

Constantine Porphyrogenitus, *De Administrando Imperio*, ed. G. Moravcsik, trans. R. J. H. Jenkins. Budapest 1949.

D.A.I. = Constantine Porphyrogenitus.

D.A.U.M. = *Dialekt-, ortnamns- och folkminnesarkivet i Umeå.*

Egils-saga sive Egilli Skallagrimii Vita. Havniæ 1809.

Eskeröd, A. 1956: Early Nordic–Arctic Boats. A Survey and some Problems. *Arctica*. Studia Ethnographica Upsaliensia 11: 57–87. Uppsala.

Falk, H. 1912: Altnordisches Seewesen. *Wörter und Sachen*. Kulturhistorische Zeitschrift für Sprach- und Sachforschung 4: 1–121. Heidelberg.

Grundström, H. 1946–54: *Lulelappisches Wörterbuch*. Schriften des Instituts für Mundarten und Volkskunde in Uppsala. Series C: 1. Uppsala.

Hakulinen, L. (1961) 1968: *Suomen kielen rakenne ja kehitys*. Keuruu.

Hallström, G. 1909: Båtar och båtbyggnad i ryska lappmarken. *Fataburen* pp. 85–100.

   1925: Utriggade kanoter i Sverige? *Fornvännen* pp. 50–69.

Hammarstedt, N. E. 1908: En lappsk båt. *Fataburen* pp. 149–55.

Högström, P. (1747) 1980: *Beskrifning Öfwer de til Sweriges Krona lydande Lapmarker.* (Stockholm) Umeå.

Itkonen, T. 1962: *Keidas.* Erään maastotermin vaiheita. *Suomi* 110: 1. Helsinki.

Itkonen, T. I. 1930: Muinaisruuhistamme. *Suomi* 5: 10. Helsinki.

1947: Lapparnas förekomst i Finland. *Ymer* pp. 43–57. Stockholm.

1958: Koltan- ja kuolanlapin sanakirja 1. *Lexica societatis fenno-ugricæ* 15. Helsinki.

Jaakkola, J. 1924: Pirkkalaisliikkeen synty. *Turun Suomalaisen Yliopiston julkaisuja.* Sarja B. Osa, no. 1. Turku.

1925: Pohjois–Satakunnan vanha eräkulttuuri. *Satakunta* 5: 1–102.

(1935) 1956: Suomen varhaishistoria. *Suomen historia* 2: 229–50.

Jóhannesson, A. 1956: *Isländisches etymologisches Wörterbuch* 1–2. Bern.

Kivikoski, E. 1937: Studien zu Birkas Handel im östlichen Ostseegebiet. *Acta Archaeologica* 8. København.

1961: Suomen esihistoria. *Suomen Historia* 1.

Korhonen, O. 1976: Linguistic and Cultural Diversity Among the Saamis and the Development of Standard Saamish. *The International Journal of the Sociology of Language* 10: 51–66.

1981: Ett Sydvästfinskt Syntaxlån i Arjeplogs-och Jokkmokkssamiskan. *Tvåspråkighet.* Acta Universitatis Umensis. Umeå Studies in the Humanities 36: 184–200. Umeå.

1982: *Samisk-finska båttermer och ortnamnselement och deras slaviska bakgrund.* Skrifter utgivna av DAUM. Serie A, dialekter Nr 3. Umeå.

Levin, M. G. and L. P. Potapov, 1961: *Istoriko-etnografičeskij atlas Sibiri.* Akademija ja nauk SSSR. Moskva/Leningrad.

Lindahl, E. and J. Öhrling, 1780: *Lexicon Lapponicum.* Holmiæ.

Linné, C. von. (1732) 1913: Iter Lapponicum. *Skrifter af von Linné* 5. Uppsala.

Luukko, A. 1950: *Etelä-Pohjanmaan historia II. Keskiaika ja 1500–luku.* Helsinki.

1959: *Erämark. Kulturhistoriskt lexikon för nordisk medeltid* 4: 39–45. Malmö.

1964: *Kväner. Kulturhistoriskt lexikon för nordisk medeltid* 9: 599–602. Malmö.

LÖ = Lindahl and Öhrling.

Manninen, I. 1927: Zur Ethnologie des Einbaumes. *Eurasia Septentrionalis Antiqua* I: 4–17.

Moravcsik, G. (ed.) 1949: See Constantine Porphyrogenitus.

Nerman, B. 1939: *Die Verbindungen zwischen Skandinavien und Ostbaltikum.* Stockholm.

1942: *Sveriges första storhetstid.* Stockholm.

Nielsen, K. 1932–8: *Lapp Dictionary based on the Dialects of Polmak, Karasjok and Kautokeino* 1–3. Instituttet for sammenlignende kulturforskning B: 18. Oslo.

Nikkilä, E. 1936: Satakuntalaisen palko- eli haaparuuhen valmistus. *Satakunta* 10: 134–55.

1946: Satakuntalainen haapio sekä sen aikaisempi levinneisyys Suomessa. *Satakunta* 13: 165–74.

1947: En satakundensisk äsping och dess eurasiatiska motsvarighet. *Folk-Liv.* Acta Ethnologica et Folkloristica Europaea 11: 33–46. Stockholm.

N.T.A. = Nimitoimi:ton arkistokokoelmat (Namnbyråns arkivsamlingar. Helsingfors).

Plöger, A. 1973: *Die russischen Lehnwörter der finnischen Schriftsprache.* Wiesbaden.

Prins, A. H. J. 1975: Development in Arctic Boat Design: Efflorescence or Involution? *Netherlands–Swedish Symposium on Development in Scandinavian Arctic Culture, February 1974.* pp. 12–27. University of Groningen, Netherlands.

Rapola, M. 1936: Suomen sanat *erä* ja *erämaa. Virittäjä* pp. 106–21.

Raudonikas, W. J. 1930: Die Normannen der Wikingerzeit und das Ladogagebiet. *Kungl Vitterhets Historie och Antikvitets Akademiens Handlingar.* Del 40: 3. Stockholm.

Salmo, H. 1956: Finnische Hufeisenfibeln. *Suomen Muinaismuistoyhdistyksen Aika-kauskirja* 56. Helsinki.

Schneider, G. 1929: Ormskeppet i Matzalviken och andra ekstockar. *Terra.* Geografiska sällskapets i Finland tidskrift pp. 36–51. Helsingfors.

Sigfússon, B. 1958. Egils-saga. *Kulturhistoriskt lexikon för nordisk medeltid* 3: 522–4. Malmö.

Sirelius, U. T. 1913: Primitive Konstruktionsteile an prähistorischen Schiffen *Finnisch-ugrische Forschungen* 13: 1–6. Helsinki.

1919: *Suomen kansanomaista kulttuuria* 1. Helsinki.

S.K.E.S. = *Suomen kielen etymologinen sanakirja* 1–6. Y. H. Toivonen, Erkki Itkonen, Aulis J. Joki, Reino Peltola. Lexica societatis fenno-ugricae 12. Helsinki 1955–78.

S.M.S. = *Suomen murteiden sanakirjan kokoelmat* (Samlingar till finsk dialektordbok, Helsingfors.)

Stender-Petersen, A. 1946: Etudes varègues, la théorie de l'origine varègue de la byline Russe. *Classica et mediaevalia* 8. Copenhagen.

Suvanto, S. 1973: *Satakunnan historia.* Vol. 3. Keskiaika, Vammala.

Sweet, H. (1876) 1967: *Anglo-Saxon Reader in Prose and Verse.* Oxford.

Thörnqvist, C. 1948: *Studien über die nordischen Lehnwörter im Russischen.* Ètudes de Philologie Slave. Uppsala.

Valmet, A. 1970: Lääne-Eesti randadel. *Saaremaast sajaanideni ja kaugemalegi.* Tallinn.

Valonen, N. 1946: Yläsatakuntalaisia sanoja anastavien elinkeinojen alalta. *Satakunta* 13: 175–90.

1963: Zur Geschichte der finnischen Wohnstuben. *Suomalais-ugrilaisen seuran toimituksia* 133, Helsinki.

1978: Keskiajan kulttuurin iskostuminen Tornialaaksoon. *Kalevalaseuran vuosikirja* 58: 131–48.

1980: Den finska folkkulturen i Nordskandinavien: Särskilt skidans historia i tvärvetenskaplig belysning. In Baudou and Dahlstedt (eds.), pp. 207–33.

Vasmer, M. 1976: *Russisches etymologisches Wörterbuch* 1. Heidelberg.

Vernadsky, G. 1948: *Kievan Russia.* New Haven, Connecticut.

Vilkuna, K. 1945: Brödet och bakningens historia i Finland. *Folk-Liv.* Acta Ethnologica et Folkloristica Europaea 9: 17–56. Stockholm.

1975: *Kirkkovenelaitoksemme vanhinta taustaa* 3: 62–9 Kotiseutu.

Vilkuna, K. and E. Mäkinen, 1977: Isien työ. Veden ja maan viljaa. *Arkityön kauneutta.* Helsinki.

Virtaranta, P. 1952: Satakunnan paikannimiä III, Saastamala ja Sastmola. *Satakunta* 15: 88–122.

Vries, J. de. 1962: *Altnordisches etymologisches Wörterbuch.* Leiden.

4 · The Scandinavians in Russia: On the extra-linguistic factors in the language contact between North Germanic and East Slavic peoples in the early middle ages

ANNELIES LÄGREID

Introduction

The aim of the present article is to sketch the historical and socio-cultural framework within which the Scandinavians and the East Slavs came into contact with each other during the early middle ages, and as a result of which linguistic contacts came about between these two ethnic groups.[1] The relationship between Scandinavia and Russia is a topic which has been of great interest to scholars in various disciplines for more than 200 years. As early as the first half of the 18th century the Normanists and Anti-Normanists carried on impassioned debates with each other about the role of the Scandinavians in East Europe. As early as 1724, the year of the foundation of the Russian Academy of Sciences, the topic became the subject of learned articles. L. M. Lomonosov was one of the first convinced Anti-Normanists, whereas N. M. Karamzin could be regarded as a moderate Normanist.[2]

In Germany the historian A. W. Schlözer in Göttingen held an ultra-Normanist position with his view that the Germanic ethnic groups had played a dominant role in the establishment of civilization and in political developments in eastern Europe. Until a few years ago it seemed that the 'Normanist Problem' had been solved, the dating of the contacts between North Germanic and East Slavic ethnic groups had been clarified and a satisfactory interpretation of the name *Rus'* had been arrived at. In this context the articles of A. Stender-Petersen must be mentioned, in particular those collected in the volume *Varangica* (1953) and his article on the four stages of Russian–Varangian relations (1954).[3]

In the course of the 1970s, however, the debate was taken up again: this was certainly a result of the symposium on 'The eastern connections of the nordic peoples in the Viking period and early middle ages', which was held in Aarhus, Denmark and the proceedings of which were published in 1970.[4]

In the last two decades a great deal of research has been carried out and there has been a lively debate in the field of archaeology. There has been a controversy between the different camps in archaeology – on the one hand between the two Soviet schools, Moscow and Leningrad, and on the other hand between them and the Scandinavian archaeologists. This controversy has centred firstly on the age of the Scandinavian settlements in the East Slavic territories such as Gnezdovo, Staraja Ladoga, Černigov, Tver' etc., and secondly on the ethnic classification of the finds made. In addition to these archaeological finds new hypotheses have recently been advanced as a result of new research in east European prehistory and early history, especially those in Gothic studies: Scholars now believe that the Goths were continuously present in eastern Europe from the time of their advance to the north coast of the Black Sea and the foundation of settlements there in the 2nd and 3rd century right until the early middle ages. Scholars now identify the Goths with the people of the Rus' who founded the East Slavic State.[5]

If this Gothic hypothesis is accepted, then it is necessary to rethink and revise the chronology, which till now has dated the presence of the Scandinavians in east Europe from the 9th to the 12th century AD. As a result of taking account of this new research and of the development of new areas and methods of research in linguistics certain areas of research are now once more in the centre of current interest: areas such as the early forms of state structure and military organization, the foundation of the Kingdom of Kiev in the 9th century, and research on language contact and loan words.

1   The historical framework

The historical events, against which the contact between the Scandinavians and the East Slavs took place, are documented in a series of sources, of which the Old Russian Chronicle, which is referred to as the *Nestor Chronicle* or in English the *Primary Chronicle*, is one of the richest.[6] In an entry for the year 862 we find the Varangian Calling-in Legend and a description of the foundation of the kingdom of the Rus'. This sage-like entry in the *Nestor Chronicle* has been the starting-point of innumerable debates.[7]

Today the vast majority of historians, both in the West and in the East, agree that the East Slavs did not possess a definite state organization before the 9th century. In the cities and settlements on the trading routes along the rivers the Khazars (and possibly also the Goths) in the south and the Scandinavians in the north can be said to have exerted a sort of sovereignty over the Slavs, which the latter bore, because it also meant protection for them. Von Rimscha, the expert on east-European history, considers that it is possible that groups of the East Slavs integrated into the empire of the Khazars or were at least obliged to pay tribute to the Khagan.[8] The kingdom of Kiev, which arose later, perhaps continued in some respects the political traditions of the Khazars. As supporting evidence for this claim one can mention the use of the title 'Khagan' in the Kingdom of the Rus' in Kiev to refer to the ruler – Vladimir the Holy was thus referred to at the end of the 10th century.[9] From time to time the Slavs probably resisted paying tribute and the *de facto* control by the Khazars and drove out the local rulers. In the context of such events the calling-in of the Varangian princes may have taken place. It is no longer possible to reconstruct exactly how the calling-in came about. For

Map 1: Scandinavia and Russia during the Viking Age.

one has to assume that the Calling-in Legend is to a very large extent literary in origin. Stender-Petersen has shown this in detail in his book *Die Varägersage als Quelle der altrussischen Chronik* (1934).

Nevertheless most historians in both camps agree that the first rulers in Russia were of Varangian origin. Accordingly the Varangians occupied a privileged position in the Kingdom of Kiev, which played a decisive role in the linguistic attitude of the entire ruling upper-class: it remained bilingual up until the 11th century. However, after then the Scandinavians became linguistically and culturally increasingly integrated into Slavic society.

At the end of the 9th century the areas between Novgorod and Kiev had already developed into a political and cultural unit. Thus the foundations were laid for the economic progress and cultural flowering of the 11th century. During that century the most extensive and intensive contacts between Russia and Scandinavia existed. Yaroslav the Wise, the ruler during the Golden Age of the Empire of Kiev, was married to Ingegerd, the daughter of the Swedish King Olaf; Yaroslav was also the brother-in-law of the Norwegian king; and his daughter later married the King of Norway, Harald Hardradi.[10]

The level of education was definitely European.[11] Yaroslav himself spoke four languages: East Slavic, Old Swedish, Greek, and Latin. How much importance he attached to the education of his children – including that of his daughters – is shown in a charter dating from 1063 of the French King Philip I, whose father, Henry I, was the husband of Yaroslav's daughter Anna. In this document Anna's signature in her own hand in Cyrillic letters (Anna Reina) is found, whereas the other statesmen who signed the document only put crosses – they were apparently not able to write.[12]

At that time the clergy also consisted of Varangians to a large degree. The Cave Monastery in Kiev, the focal point of Old Russian spiritual life, had been founded by a Varangian Russian.[13] Not only in Kiev but also in other smaller princely courts, there existed what was called the 'princely *družina*' – a bodyguard, which consisted of between 2,000 and 3,000 Varangians according to the power and reputation of the prince. This bodyguard also played a significant role in transmitting language and culture.

For the purpose of research on these connections during the 11th century, the Old Scandinavian legends, in particular the Old Icelandic sagas, are an important additional source on the early history of Russia. The most information is obtained by studying the Kings' Sagas, the *Heimskringla* by Snorri Sturluson.[14]

The contribution of the Varangians to the development of the Russian state has also been acknowledged by most Soviet historians in the past few years. However, there are still a few stubborn Anti-Normanists, who regard this view of Russian history as a falsification. One of them is V. T. Pašuto, who can cite such Marxist historians as Grekow, Rybakov, and Šaskol'skij in support of his opinion that a state existed long before the arrival of the Varangians in Russia.[15] It is characteristic of the works of these Anti-Normanist historians that they ignore important parts of the historical source material, e.g. West European sources written in Latin such as the *Annales Bertiniani* or Greek sources such as the description of the Rus' by the Byzantine Emperor Konstantin Porphyrogennetos, or the reports of Arabic and Persian geographers and chroniclers of the 9th, 10th, and 11th centuries.[16]

2   The trade routes

Linguistic contacts between the Scandinavians and the East Slavs also arose as a result of trade. The Scandinavians used the trade routes which already existed before their arrival: the route to the Caspian Sea seems to have been more interesting for commercial purposes to begin with. Its route was via the Lakes Ladoga, Onega, Beloozero to the river systems of the Dvina, the Volga, and the Oka. The first section of this route ran in part through Finno-Ugric areas of settlement. Further south, half-way down the Volga, it passed through the empire of the Turkish–Mongolian Bulgars, which had been established since the 7th century, and in the lower Volga, the Khaganate of the Khazars. Like the Bulgars the Khazars were a Turkish people. They had built up a well-organized trading network, in which numerous cities with a high level of culture and civilization already existed. In these cities on the trading routes members of various ethnic groups came into contact with each other. It is reasonable to assume that some kind of *lingua franca* must have developed, to which Old Swedish along with East Slavic, Finno-Ugric and Turkish dialects must have made a considerable contribution.

The second, more recent trade route ran via the Dniepr to the Black Sea. This is described in the *Nestor Chronicle* as the road 'from the Varangians to the Greeks' (*put' iz varjag v greki*).[17]

Along these trade routes new centres were established around which settlements were developed, or those which already existed were expanded and fortified. They served as places of transshipment and bases for the merchants and were also fortified against attack; hence in Old Icelandic the term *garðaríki* is used, i.e. 'the land of the fortified towns'.

In the 9th century towns such as Smolensk, Gnezdovo, Černigow, L'ubeč and the magnificent city of Kiev, the centre of the Kingdom of the Rus', were founded along this western route via the Dniepr. As a result of their participation in the development of the first Russian state this Dniepr-trading-route became increasingly important for the Scandinavians.

The finds in archaeological excavations provide most striking evidence of the multi-ethnic and consequently the multilingual character of those trading settlements. In Gnezdovo for instance, there are numerous Baltic and Finno-Ugric graves besides Slavic and Scandinavian ones; very similar finds have also been made in the Ladoga area. Unfortunately we still know far too little about the economic and social conditions, which are so important in investigating the linguistic situation. However, it is evident that during the 9th and 10th centuries the Scandinavians were integrated into a society which was already mixed linguistically.

Within these trading systems special forms of commercial organization developed following in part Scandinavian and in part Khazar–Bulgarian models. They were founded on the principle of mutual liability and help. Here we find the explanation of one of the names for Scandinavians in Slavic territories, namely the term 'Varangians', Russian *varjazi*. The members of these commercial organizations, which carried on the trade between the Baltic areas and the Black Sea, were called in the language of the Swedish Rus' people, i.e. in Old Swedish **väring-*, which is derived from the stem *var-* 'oath' (of mutual assistance).[18] For example, in the

Russkaja Pravda, which is a Russian legal codex, written down between the 10th and the 12th centuries we find the word Russian *varjag* (singular) in the sense of a privileged foreign merchant. The term *kolbjag* was used in the same sense.[19] Later on the term *varjag* acquired the additional meaning of 'mercenary' and 'warrior from across the sea', probably because the merchants' organization was active in hiring the warriors from abroad. We know from the *Nestor Chronicle*, for instance, that in 977 Vladimir the Holy arrived in the Kingdom of Svealand in flight from his brother; and there within three years he hired a strong army of mercenaries, with which he returned to Novgorod in 980. The members of this army were called Varangians (Swedish *varjager* and Russian *varjazi*). The Greeks also called the Nordic warriors in their service *Varangoi*, 'Varangians', occasionally with the addition of the ethnic name *Rus'*: 'Ρῶς-βαραγγοι ἤ κούλπιγγοι (*Rhōs-Varangoie Koulpingoi*).[20]

3   Archaeological evidence

In the last few decades archaeological research has been able to prove the presence of Scandinavians in East Europe and give us detailed information about their life there. However, archaeologists are far from being of one opinion as to the interpretation of the objects found – various kinds of weapons, jewellery, and objects of daily use – and to the ethno-cultural origin of these objects. The differences of opinion in the Normanist and Anti-Normanist sense continue to a certain degree, even if they are not expressed with the same acrimony as in the past, when national feeling was more apparent than today in the assessment of the contribution of the Varangians to the rise of the first Russian state, and to the development of its economy and culture.[21]

The liveliness of the discussion is exemplified by the debate on the finds made at the excavations in Smolensk and Gnezdovo, which is to be found in the *Norwegian Archaeological Review*.[22] The Soviet archaeologist Avdusin, who has directed the excavations in these areas from the University of Moscow since the 1960s, claims to be able to find only a few items of evidence of a specifically Scandinavian origin here. In his opinion there are hardly any Scandinavian graves at all in Gnezdovo. The Swedes Arne (1914) and Arbman (1955), on the other hand, regard the graveyard of Gnezdovo as purely Scandinavian. They consider Gnezdovo in general to be one of the oldest and most important centres of the Scandinavian settlements in Russia, which were founded as early as in the first half of the 9th century.[23]

Beside the Slavic and Scandinavian finds archaeologists have also discovered evidence of Baltic and Finno-Ugric graves, which give us an idea of the multiethnic and hence multilingual character of these trading settlements. The same ethnic variety is found in the Ladoga area, where the early presence of the Scandinavians is undisputable. In the 9th and 10th centuries Staraja Ladoga was an important trading and manufacturing city through which trade was carried on between other trading centres such as Haithabu and Birka in the west and the Bulgarians (Bulgar) and Khazars in areas as far away as the Kama region in the east and towards the Orient. These trading links, which were still flourishing in the 11th century, are substantiated by numerous coins found throughout this area:

many Arabic, English, Danish, Byzantine, and Scandinavian coins have been found. The finds dating from the 11th century are especially rich and numerous.

4   On the chronology of the contacts

There are still many unclear questions as to the length of the period during which there were relations between the North Germanic and East Slavic peoples. Many questions regarding the ethnic origin of the people of the Rus' are also still unanswered. This leads me to my next topic – some current controversial questions regarding the ethnic composition of the population in Russia before 800 AD. I shall illustrate this problem by means of a short survey of the attempts to explain the name of the Russians.

4.1   The Roþs-hypothesis

In my view Stender-Petersen's explanation is still the most convincing.[24] Stender-Petersen (1954) based his account on the explanation of the name Rus' which was suggested by Thomsen (1877) and further elaborated by Ekblom (1915) – the Roþs-hypothesis. According to this hypothesis this ethnic name is derived from a Finnish term for the Scandinavians.

Vasmer (1941) and Kiparsky (1963) have also accepted the Roþs-hypothesis on the whole.[25] According to Thomsen (1877) the name Rus' is derived from the name Roslagen given to the coastal area of Svealand which is situated on the Baltic opposite Finland and the Baltic states. The prefixal element of this name ros- was the basis of the old term 'oarsmen' or 'sailors' living in this province: cp. Old Swedish roþs-karlar, roþs-maen, and roþs-byggiar. These words are formed from a genitive form roþ(er)s of a noun roþer meaning 'narrow strip of sea (narrows) between islands', 'water way', 'protected sea route'; the roþs-byggiar lived beside such narrow strips of water. From this word the Finns formed the short form Rōtsi (cp. Modern Finnish Ruotsi 'Sweden') to refer to the emigrants who came across the sea from Sweden and settled among the Finns and Estonians. Later on this name spread from the Finns to the Slavic inhabitants of those areas in the east, and then no longer meant just the Swedes, but also other colonizers from the north, who settled close to or amongst the Slavs over the years. From this word Rōtsi the Slavs formed a feminine collective form Rus', a formation of an ethnic name which has numerous parallels in the East Slavic dialects e.g. Ves', Čud', Sum', Perm'.

We find evidence of the name Rus' for the first time in the Annales Bertiniani, where in an entry under the year 839 there is an account of a delegation from the Byzantine Emperor Theophilos to the Carolingian Emperor Louis the Pious in Germany, in which members of the delegation are specifically mentioned, whom the Greeks call the Rhōs ('Ρῶς). Louis is surprised to realize that they are Swedes.

Another important document where this name occurs is De Administrando Imperio which was written by the Byzantine Emperor Konstantine Porphyrogennetos about 950. In the geographical description of his· empire he mentions the Dniepr rapids, which were situated south of Kiev; it was a daring and hazardous venture for travellers on boats going downstream to pass the rapids on their way to the Black Sea. Konstantine Porphyrogennetos also mentions here the traders and warriors from the north, who travelled on the Dniepr in their ships and who maintained the trade relations between Byzantium and Kiev which were at that time already well established. In his description of the empire Porphyrogennetos also mentions the seven names for the rapids both in 'Rūsian' (ῥωσιστί, *Rhosleti*), i.e. 'Scandinavian', and in 'Slavic' (σκλαβηνιστί, *Sklavenisti*) form: e.g. 'Rūsian' Οὐλβορσί (*Ulvorsi*), and Slavic 'Οστροβουνιπράχ (*Ostrovuniprach*).[26] This list is mportant for a description of the linguistic situation in the 10th century in that for a Greek at that time the term '*Rūsian*' was still synonymous with 'Scandinavian' and hence here 'Old Swedish'.[27] The Soviet philologist Trubačev has recently argued against the derivation of the name *Rus'* from Finnish *Rōtsi* – the *Roþs*-hypothesis – which is linked to the hypothesis that the Scandinavians emigrated to eastern Europe at the beginning of the 9th century (Trubačev 1978). Trubačev takes up again a comment by the German expert on East European history Marquart, who pointed out in 1903 that the ethnic name *Hrōs* first occurs on the shores of the Black Sea.[28] In Zacharias Rhetor's church history which was written in the 6th century – that is some 300 years *before* the calling-in of the Varangians – a people of this name is mentioned who settled on the Sea of Azov. Trubačev refers to the Russian expert on Byzantine history, Vasilevskij, who in his study published in 1893 quoted a reference to a tribe, the Rus' (Greek 'Ρῶς, *Rhōs*) in Tauria and on the shores of the Black Sea in the holy legends of Georgios Amastrides and Stephan Surož dating from the end of the 8th century – hence also clearly *before* the Varangian period. In fact it has been recurrently asserted that the relations between the North Germanic and East Slavic peoples go as far back as some period *before* the 6th century. For instance as early as 1837 in his *Slovanské starožitnosti* P. J. Šafařík, the Slovak Slavist and classical scholar, concluded after studying the loan words exchanged between North Germanic and East Slavic, that the relations must date back to a much earlier period, that is *before* the 6th century.[29] Further references following the same line of thought, are quoted by Knud Rahbek Schmidt in his survey of Scandinavian–Russian research.[30]

Trubačev does not support the Gothic hypothesis put forward by Marquart, Valisevskij – and recently also by Scardigli and Söderlind – that the people Rhōs in Tauria and on the Sea of Azov were of Germanic and namely Gothic origin because in his opinion the Goths were always called by their own name.[31] Trubačev, however, is mistaken on this point. In this period it was entirely usual for a people to be named not according to its ethnic origin but after the area where they had settled or after the inhabitants of a particular area, near whom they lived. Thus in the ancient writers the Goths are also referred to by the name of other peoples, namely as Sarmatians, Scythians, Getae, Tauro-Scythians and others.

Obolensky 1970 also states: 'It is true that the term Scythian was, in a vaguely geographical sense, sometimes applied by Byzantine writers to the Slavs; but it was also used as a general synonym for "barbarian".'[32] In a passage from the *Homilie* by the Patriarch Photios for instance, in which the attack by the Rhōs people on Constantinople in the year 860 is described, 'barbarians' are referred to, 'a people of the north', 'a fierce and barbarous Scythian tribe'.[33]

By the same token other ethnic groups are also subsumed under the term 'Goths' – Germanic as well as non-Germanic – such as the Vandals, the Rugians, the Herulians, and occasionally the Alans who also lived in this area.[34] In this context another explanation of the name *Rus'* should be mentioned, which was suggested as early as the 16th/17th centuries[35] and which Trubačev has recently taken up again. According to it the *Rus'* are identical with the Roxalans, who are mentioned by the Greek geographer Strabo in the 2nd century AD; and this name should be split into the two segments *Ross-Alans*. Ilovajskij 1882 and others interpret this name as being Iranian with the meaning 'The Blond Alans'.[36] Trubačev, on the other hand, suggests an Old Indian origin of the stem *Ross-* (cp. Old Indian *rukṣa* 'bright, light') and points out other names – place names and topographical terms – which also have 'bright, white' as their first component and which justify the conclusion that Indo-Aryan tribes settled on the northern coast of the Black Sea at an early date (consider *Rosso Tar* 'bright shore/bank' on the western Crimea, *Rukusta*, a village on the south-western Crimea, and also *Beloberež'e* 'white bank', which is the name for a part of the lower Dniepr Valley). All these examples must be taken into consideration. Thus Trubačev also compares the hybrid-formation *Roga-stadzans* found in Jordanes with the second component of Gothic *stadja* 'bank, shore'.[37]

Trubačev himself admits, however, that this derivation of the name *Rus'* from *Roxaláns* still leaves a number of unsolved problems of a phonetic nature. Nevertheless he tries – with little success, in my opinion – to disprove the Germanic etymology of *Rus'* and in doing so he reveals his Anti-Normanist attitude to the problem.

From the above remarks it is evident that there are still a great number of unsolved problems concerning the ethnic origin of the *Rus'*. The hypothesis has been regularly advanced that a people called the *Rhōs* existed in the south of Russia (on the northern coast of the Black Sea and on the Sea of Azov) and that another people with the name *Rus'* existed in the north and that the two were united in the 9th century. The problem is to decide which ethnic group is hidden behind the southern Rhōs? Was it the Goths, who had been settled there since their immigration in the 2nd century? Or was it a mixture of Slavs, Iranians (Indo-Aryans) and Alans or other ethnic groups, as the Anti-Normanists would like to have us believe?

4.2   The mention of 'russkij' in the 'Vita Constantini'

In this context I want to draw attention to a passage in the *Vita Constantini*, the biography of the Slavic apostle Konstantin-Kyrill. This passage has been the cause of recent reconsideration of the cultural and ethnic situation in the Black Sea area, not only in Slavic studies but also in other fields of study.

The passage in question deals with the Christian mission to the Khazars; Konstantin was on his way to them in the autumn of 860 at the head of a Byzantine delegation. He and his companions broke their journey in the Byzantine colony of Cherson on the Crimean peninsula. The *Vita* tells us that Konstantin found a gospel text and a psalmbook written in a language, which is described as *russkij*. Konstantin also met a man there, who knew this language. With his help he could distinguish 'the letters, the vowels, and consonants' more exactly and begin to understand the language.[38] Some Russian and Ukrainian Slavists took the view that the Old Russian language was to be understood by the description *russkij*. This assumption is completely unfounded, however. On the other hand Slavists such as Vaillant, Roman Jakobson and others have amended the written form *russkymi* to ⟨*syr*⟩*skymi* and claim that 'Syrian' is meant here.[39]

In his article already quoted, which deals with the ethno-linguistic situation on the northern coasts of the Black Sea, Trubačev also takes the discussion about *russkij* up again and rejects the frequently expressed opinion that it was a written language of the Goths.[40] But he surmises that the 'Pseudo-Scythians' were the inventors of this written language. He does not, however, explain which ethnic group he means by the scholarly term 'Pseudo-Scythians'.

If we consider the fact that the ethnic name Scythians was also used to refer to other groups – the Goths themselves for instance – we have to admit that the suggestion that this was a Gothic language is perhaps not so unfounded after all; and that it could possibly indeed be used to support the hypothesis that the Goths were continuously present in southern Russia.

Conclusion

Problems such as those discussed above and especially the numerous proposals for resolving them also affect research on language contact dealing with the connections between the North-Germanic and East-Slavic peoples. This language-contact research will have to take account of the results of research in Gothic studies in the last few years and will also have to consider the documents and historical evidence of the period *before* the 9th century. There are still various sources, e.g. the Arabic and Persian, which have not yet been sufficiently evaluated. It is possible that they may contain material, which can give us a more exact picture of the situation in these areas. Archaeological studies will certainly also yield new insights into this field of study.

Perhaps linguistic research will also succeed in making an important contribution to the solving of these problems by a fresh examination of the linguistic data already available (loan words, place names etc.) employing the new methods which are being developed in research into language contact.

Notes

1 This article was presented in German at the Conference in Oslo as an introduction to the paper by B. Panzer on 'Parallel Internal Development or Interference? – Post-Positive Article and Possessive Perfect in North Germanic and Northern Russian' (cf. Panzer, this volume, pp. 111–32). It was translated into English by Sture Ureland and Iain Clarkson.

2 M. L. Lomonosov (1711–65) was one of the most prominent Russian intellectuals in the 18th century, a polymath, poet, and scientist. Largely as a result of his efforts the University of Moscow was founded. N. M. Karamzin (1766–1826) was an influential Russian poet and author. As official historian at the Russian

court (from 1803 on) he was commissioned by the Czar to write *The History of the Russian State* in 12 volumes (*Istorija gosudarstva rossijskogo*).

3 cf. Stender-Petersen 1953, 1954.

4 cf. *Varangian Problems* edited by Rahbek Schmidt *et al.* 1970. In this collection of articles there are contributions by scholars of various nationalities working in several different disciplines: articles by Soviet historians, archaeologists, and cultural experts alongside articles in these fields by Scandinavian, German, and British scholars. As a result the picture of the state of research on this topic, which these articles provide, is extraordinarily rich and stimulating. For instance we are given information *inter alia* on new results of archaeological research, gained from finds of weapons dating from the 9th and 10th centuries (A. N. Kirpičnikov), on new insights into the material culture in the cities of Old Russia (D. A. Avdusin), and also new material on the Scandinavians in eastern Europe based on a fresh examination of Byzantine sources (Dm. Obolensky).

5 cf. Hachmann 1970, Scardigli 1973, and Söderlind 1978 and especially Söderlind in the present volume, in which the Red–Blond-people-hypothesis is presented as the explanation of the rise of the Kingdom of the *Rus'*.

6 The *Nestor Chronicle* was written in the first half of the 12th century; the oldest manuscript, the so-called Laurentius manuscript, dates from 1377. It is known among Slavic philologists under the title *Povest' vremennych let*. (Concerning the editions and the translations of this chronicle see the references in the bibliography under *Povest' vremennych let*.)

7 Concerning the veracity of the Calling-in-legend see the article by D. S. Lichačev 'The Legend of the Calling-in of the Varangians, and Political Purposes in Russian Chronicle-Writing from the Second Half of the 11th to the Beginning of the 12th Century' in *Varangian Problems*, pp. 170–85.

8 cf. von Rimscha 1970: 5f.

9 cf. Stender-Petersen 1954: 143.

10 cf. Birnbaum 1978 on the early connections between the royal houses of Scandinavia and Russia.

11 'In many respects the Rus' of Kiev were more open to western Europe than to the Byzantine Empire'; cf. von Rimscha 1970: 31.

12 cf. Grekow 1947: Fig. 13, p. 68f.

13 cf. von Rimscha 1970: 54.

14 A number of other texts also tell us of events in this period, e.g. *Eymundarþáttr*, *Morskinskinna* and *Fagrskinna*, *Ágrip af Noregš konunga sogum*, a compilation in Old Icelandic dating from the last years of the 12th and the 13th centuries; cf. Birnbaum 1978: 23f.

15 Pašuto supposes that this state was some kind of a confederation, which consisted of several (possibly 14) royal houses of various East Slavic tribes. The Varangian intruders had to submit to one of the established noble dynasties, which consisted partly of the Slavic and partly of the Čudian (i.e. Estonian) nobility, cf. Pašuto 1970: 51–61.

16 On the Arabic and Persian sources, see Cross 1946: 506f. Cross quotes a Jewish chronicler, Ibrahīm ben Ya'qūb (c. 965), who stresses in his account, that the *Rus'* were not Slavs and that they had learned the Slavic language through their close contact with the Slavs, ibid., p. 508.

17 cf. the informative study of this topic: Davidson 1976.

18 For the etymology of *Varangian* see Stender-Petersen 1953: 89ff.

19 For the etymology of *kolbjag* (Old Icelandic *kylfing*) see ibid., p. 148.

20 cf. Stender-Petersen 1954: 148.

21 Nevertheless, the opponents in the debate are nowadays much more prepared to consider the results of the research done by the other side. A reduction in the

intensity of the old controversy can apparently also be seen in the fact that the parties involved have been renamed the Neo-Normanists and Neo-Anti-Normanists.

22 cf. the articles by Avdusin 1969, Bulkin 1973, Klejn 1973, and Lebedev and Nazarenko 1973.

23 cf. Avdusin 1969: 54f. A great number of further archaeological publications, which appeared in the 1970s, are evidence of the current interest in the discussion as to the contribution made by and the age of the Scandinavian elements in Russia. Dejevsky 1977 gives an excellent survey of the current state of research.

24 cf. Stender-Petersen 1954: 140f.

25 cf. Vasmer 1953–8, 2 (1955): 551 and Kiparsky 1963, 1: 14.

26 cf. Falk 1951 on the etymology of the seven Scandinavian and Slavic names for the Dniepr rapids. See also Kleiber 1960.

27 cf. Forssman 1967: 67f.

28 cf. Trubačev 1978: 401f.

29 cf. the comments of Thörnqvist 1948: 6, on this point. My reference to Šafařík is also taken from this source.

30 cf. *Varangian Problems*, pp. 15 and 18. The majority of these references come from Soviet scientists, who endeavour to support their own Anti-Normanist position, e.g. Grekow 1939, Movrodin 1945 and 1953.

31 cf. Trubačev 1978: 402.

32 cf. *Varangian Problems* 1970: 151.

33 cf. *Varangian Problems* 1970: 150–1. Obolensky is of the opinion that the Varangian *Rus'* are meant here, i.e. the Scandinavians who had immigrated into Russia in the 9th century.

34 cf. Scardigli 1973: 4, 60, and 243f. Scardigli repeatedly stresses the difficulty of giving a reliable picture of the circumstances surrounding the Goths in the east after the 6th century (cf., e.g. p. 244).

35 cf. Schmidt 1970.

36 cf. Trubačev 1978: 402.

37 ibid., p. 402.

38 cf. Grivec 1960: 47f.

39 A few Syrians lived in the Byzantine colonies on the Black Sea at that time. According to Grivec, for example, it is very likely 'that Konstantin understood the Syrian language, knew the Syrian translation of the Bible and in some passages followed the Syrian translation in preparing his own translation of the gospel into Slavic' (Grivec 1960: 49).

40 cf. Trubačev 1978: 403. Recently Scardigli 1973 has also dealt with this question (p. 232f.)

Bibliography

Arbman, H. 1955: *Svear i österviking*, Stockholm.

Arne, T. J. 1914: Les rélations de la Suède et de l'Orient pendant l'Age des Vikings. *5ème Congrès Préhistorique de France.*

Avdusin, D. 1969: Smolensk and the Varangians according to the Archaeological Data. *Norwegian Archaeological Review* 2: 52–62.

Birnbaum, H. 1978: Yaroslav's Varangian connections. *Scando–Slavica* 24: 5–25.

Bulkin, V. A. 1973: On the Classification and Interpretation of Archaeological Material from the Gnezdovo Cemetery (discussion of Avdusin). *Norwegian Archaeological Review*, 6: 1, 10–13.

Cross, S. H. 1946: The Scandinavian Infiltration into Early Russia. *Speculum, A Journal of Mediaeval Studies*, 21: 505–14.

Davidson, E. 1976: *The Viking Road to Byzantium*. London.

Dejevsky, N. J. 1977: The Varangians in Soviet Archaeology today. *Medieval Scandinavia* 10: 7–34.

Ekblom, R. 1915: *Rus' et Vareg* – dans les noms de lieux de la région de Novgorod. *Archives d'Études Orientales* 11. Stockholm.

Falk, K. O. 1951: Dneprforsarnas namn i Kejsar Konstantin VII Porphyrogennetos' *De Administrando Imperio*. Lunds Univ. Årsskrift, N.F. Avd. 1, Vol. 46. No. 4.

Forssman, J. 1967: *Skandinavische Spuren in der altrussischen Sprache und Dichtung*. München.

Grekow, B. D. 1939: *Kievskaja Rus'*. Moskau/Leningrad.

1947: *Die russische Kultur der Kiewer Periode*, Moskau.

Grivec, F. 1960: *Konstantin und Method. Lehrer der Slaven*. Wiesbaden.

Hachmann, R. 1970: *Die Goten und Skandinavien*. Berlin.

Ilovajskij, D. 1882: *Razyskanija o načale Rusi*, 2nd edn. Moskva.

Kiparsky, V. 1963: *Russische historische Grammatik*. Vol. 1. Heidelberg.

Kleiber, B. 1960: Zu den Namen der Stromschnellen des Dnepr bei Konstantin Porphyrogennetos. *Zeitschrift für slavische Philologie* 28: 75–98.

Klejn, L. S. 1973: Soviet Archaeology and the Role of the Vikings in the Early History of the Slavs (discussion of Avdusin). *Norwegian Archaeological Review*, 6 (1): 1–4.

Lebedev, G. S. and V. A. Nazarenko, 1973: The Connections between Russians and Scandinavians in the 9th–11th Centuries. *Norwegian Archaeological Review*, 6 (1): 5–9.

Marquart, J. 1903: *Osteuropäische und ostasiatische Streifzüge*. Leipzig.

Movrodin, U. V. 1945: *Obrazovanie drevnerusskogo gosudarstva*. Leningrad.

1953: *Očerki istorii SSSR IX–XIII VV*. Moskva.

Müller, L. 1977: *Handbuch zur Nestorchronik*. 3 vols. München.

Obolensky, D. 1970: The Byzantine sources on the Scandinavians in Eastern Europe. In *Varangian Problems*, pp. 149–64.

Pašuto, V. T. 1970: Russko–skandinavskie otnošenija i ich mesto v istorii rannesrednevekovoj Evropy, *Skandinavskij Sbornik* 15: 51–61.

Povest' vremennych let, ed. V. P. Adrianova-Peretc, D. S. Lichačev et al., Moskva/Leningrad 1950. English translation: *The Russian Primary Chronicle: Laurentian Text*, S. H. Cross and O. P. Sherbowitz-Wetzor, Cambridge, Mass., 3rd edn., 1973. German translation: *Die Nestorchronik*, R. Trautmann, Leipzig 1934.

Rimscha, H. von 1970: *Geschichte Russlands*. 2nd edn. Darmstadt.

Rydzevskaja, E. 1934: K varjažskom Voprosu. *Nachrichten d. Akad. d. Wiss.* Petersburg (Leningrad), 7: 485–532; 8: 609–30.

Šafařík, P. J. 1837: *Slovanske starožitnosti*. Praha.

Scardigli, P. 1973: *Die Goten, Sprache und Kultur*. München.

Schmidt, K. R. (ed.) 1970: On the possible traces of Nordic influence in Russian place-names. In *Varangian Problems*, pp. 143–6.

Söderlind, S. 1978: *Rusernas Rike* (Zur Frage der Entstehung des ostslavischen Reiches). Stockholm.

Stender-Petersen, A. 1934: *Die Varägersage als Quelle der altrussischen Chronik*. Aarhus/Leipzig.

1953: *Varangica*. Aarhus.

1954: Die vier Etappen der russisch–varägischen Beziehungen. *Jahrbücher für Geschichte Osteuropas*, Bd. 2, 2: 137–57.

Sturlasson, S. 1959: *Kongesoger*. Oslo.

Thomsen, U. 1877: *The Relations between Ancient Russia and Scandinavia and the Origin of the Russian State*. Oxford and London.

Thörnqvist, C. 1948: Studien über die nordischen Lehnwörter im Russischen. *Etudes de Philologie slave. Publiées par l'institut de l'Université de Stockholm.* Uppsala, Stockholm.

Trubačev, O. N. 1978: Lingvističeskaja periferija drevnejšego slavjanstva. *Indoarijcy v severnom pričernomor'e. Slavjanskoe jazykoznanie. VIII meždunarodnyj s″ezd slavistov.* Zagreb–Ljubljana 1978. Doklady sovetskoj delegacii, Moskva, pp. 368–405.

Varangian Problems. Scando–Slavica. Suppl. I. Report of the First International Symposium on the Theme: The Eastern Connections of the Nordic Peoples in the Viking Period and Early Middle Ages, Copenhagen.

Vasilevskij, V. G. 1893: *Russko-vizantijskie issledovanija.* Vol. 2. St Petersburg.

Vasmer, M. 1931: Wikingerspuren in Russland. *Sitzungsberichte d. Preussischen Akad. d. Wiss., Phil.-hist. Klasse,* pp. 649–74.

   1941: Die alten Bevölkerungsverhältnisse Russlands im Lichte der Sprachforschung. *Vorträge und Schriften. Preussische Akad. d. Wiss.,* 5. Berlin.

   1949: Warägisch-Russisches. In *Die Sprache* 1: 213–16.

   1953–8: *Russisches Etymologisches Wörterbuch.* 3 vols. Heidelberg.

5 Parallel internal development or interference? Post-positive article and possessive perfect in North Germanic and northern Russian

BALDUR PANZER

Introduction

This article should be seen in the broader framework of the question as to whether it is possible to distinguish between loan relationships caused by language contact and internal developments which have led to identical or similar language structures in different places. Or to put it differently: how can one prove what are the results of borrowing from other languages and what are independent parallel developments? The question is that of the monogenesis or polygenesis of language phenomena: monogenesis where a phenomenon spreads out from a central point; polygenesis, where it spontaneously develops independently in different places in different languages.

1 The cultural and historical background

The cultural and historical background to a North Germanic influence on East Slavic is the contacts and connections of the Varangians with their old native country over a period of 200-300 years between the 9th and 11th centuries, before and after the (alleged) summoning of Rurik the Varangian to Novgorod (862) at least until the time of Yaroslav the Wise (d. 1054), who is often referred to as Jarizleif in North Germanic literature.[1] It is true that in general the Bulgarian and Byzantine-Greek influence on the intellectual life and thus also the language was and remained ultimately the dominant one for Russia and the Russian language, so that everything else is insignificant by comparison, but at least the place names and personal names and also the famous Dniepr river rapids in Old Russia show very clear traces of the language of the North Germanic Varangians, who probably also indirectly provided the Russians with their name. Ureland has recently shown that North Germanic probably more extensively influenced the language structure of Russian as regards the use of the enclitic reflexive particle than had previously been thought.[2] Even without Russian and Soviet researchers' aversion in principle to acknowledging any important political or cultural-historical contribution in Russia by the North Germanic Varangians, who were very quickly assimilated into the

III

Slavic ethnic framework,[3] the assessment of the linguistic interference phenomena
and their effects on Russian is made more difficult not only by the Finno-Ugric
substratum influence in the north and north-east of European Russia (which must
not be forgotten),[4] but also by the fact that all substrata first affect principally the
substandard forms of the language; it is very difficult to examine this substandard
language because it is scarcely documented. The old official language of church
books and chronicles is that of the clergy, who had been educated in Church
Slavonic and Greek, so that even the texts of the treaties between the Scandinavian
Varangians and the Byzantines are only known to us in their Greek or Russian
versions. Therefore we do not know in which language the Varangians heard or
read the treaties and hence signed or swore to them, when they were not yet able
to speak and understand Slavic. The treaties of Smolensk (1229) with Riga and
Gotland, and of Novgorod (1262–3, 1264–5) with the Germans are written in
Rus'-Slavic, with peculiar and individual features, it is true, but these can scarcely
be explained as due to foreign influence. Private documents (on birch bark) are
now available from a fairly early date from the finds just made in Novgorod, perhaps
dating from as early as the 11th century, although the majority probably date from
later times (13th–14th centuries), but they are all in good Slavic, admittedly with
many features of colloquial speech, which are revealing for the history and dialectology of Russian, but without any noticeable foreign influence. That is in itself
astonishing if one considers that precisely in the north-west and particularly in
Novgorod a considerable proportion of the population must have been of North
Germanic origin and have spoken North Germanic, so that the chronicler in the
year 862 could say of the inhabitants of Novgorod that they were of Varangian
origin (*otŭ roda Varjažĭska*), but previously they were Slavs (*preže bo běša
Slověni*).

We will have to take into consideration that in ancient times the normative
prestigious influence of the written Bulgarian-Church-Slavonic created on a
Byzantine model was dominant for all forms of written records, from private letters
on birch bark to semi-official and official contracts .This meant that the oral language actually used by the warriors and merchants of Varangian and Slavic origin
is not documented. The actual spoken language was very likely not recorded in
writing at all before the 19th century, and even then not without being considerably
polished up by the recorder, as we know from many cases. But that means that over
a long period of time the colloquial substandard language could have led an entirely
unnoticed independent life which only became apparent when particular attention
was paid to it and it was recorded in its unadulterated form. This means in practical
terms that we really do not know anything about the spoken language until the
dialects were documented in the 19th and 20th centuries. That is one reason why
frequently we can only understand the influence of the substratum after a long period
of darkness, in which it flowed on below the surface or rather below the 'level of
observation'. Thus it is not impossible that the present day dialects, or those
dialects which we have access to, display features which can be connected with
older states of the language or influences over a gap of an epoch in history which
has not been documented. Naturally this does not exactly make it easier to prove
or even produce evidence of such a connection, so that one will perhaps not get

beyond proving the identity of structures in the languages being compared and the 'missing link' will remain a matter of speculation or even of faith.

Among the many special features which characterize the North-Russian dialects and which are certainly not all a result of foreign influence, there are at least two phenomena, which at first or second glance make both the Slavist and the linguist interested in language contact think that external language factors influenced their development: the post-positive demonstrative pronoun and the active use of n/t past-participles – usually only used in the passive in Russian – in the active periphrastic perfect. The first phenomenon will only be briefly outlined here, but the second will be dealt with in more detail; both of them represent the particular problems of research into language contact in this area (or in general), so that they can and should be the occasion for reflections on methodological matters.

2   Post-positive article in North Russian dialects

It has long been known that in the Slavic language group, which did not have the article in ancient times and scarcely has it today, two areas have deviated from this type: Bulgarian has developed one post-positive article, Macedonian three. This should certainly be seen in connection with the same phenomenon in Rumanian and Albanian, i.e. the Balkan linguistic area (*Balkansprachbund*); however, a similar phenomenon is also to be found in the North Russian dialects, which are geographically distant from this area. Here it would be more appropriate to think of a connection with the post-positive article in the North Germanic languages, since the Baltic–Finnic languages on the Baltic coast have no article at all and the West European languages only have an article preceding the noun.

In Russian we find evidence of post-position as early as the 17th century in Avvakum's autobiography. Consider, for example:

. . . napiši i ty rabu *tomu* Christovu, kak bogorodica bēsa *tovo* v rukachŭ *tēchŭ* mjala i tebē otdala . . . i kakŭ bēs-*otŭ* drova-*te* sožegŭ, i kakŭ kēlija-*ta* obogrēla, a v nej vse cēlo, i kakŭ ty kričalŭ na nebo-*to*, da inoe, čto pomnišŭ.[5] (LW 220)

You too write to servant of Christ, how the mother of God crushed the devil in her hands and gave you . . ., and how the devil burned the wood and how the monastery cell became warm and everything in it and how you cried to heaven and the other things which you remember.

The post-positive demonstratives appear to be congruent in case, number and gender, much as in the languages with distinctive articles. As Avvakum was in exile for a long period in the north of Russia, he could have acquired this usage there, and have used it in some passages of his autobiography (*Vita*). Similarly even today we find forms in North Russian dialects such as:

> otec-ot 'father-the', izba-ta 'cottage-the', vedro-to 'pail-the', vodu-tu 'water-the',
> mal'čiški-ti 'boys-the' (Meščerskij 1972: 250)

also of course forms with false 'harmonized' inflections:

> domu-tu (instead of -tomu) 'to house-the', na reke-te (instead of -toj) 'on river-the',
> s raboty-ty (instead of -toj) 'from work-the' (ibid.)

In addition new and more intensive investigations have revealed that in most of the relevant dialects not only are the inflections no longer correct, but there has also been a shift of function to a more general accentuation particle with an emphatic function with a more or less harmonized outer form, which can be attached not just to substantives, but also to other types of words. Hence today it is largely impossible to speak of an article in the real sense of the word. Sometimes this leads to a downright proliferation of particles and to a generalization of forms which differ from region to region:

nynče-*to* na bol'šoj-*to* doroge ručej-*to* u bajni-*to* u Pavla-*to* doma ne tekë sej god. (Trubinskij 1970: 56; Meščerskij 1972: 280)

'now on the great path the brook at the bath at Paul's house is not flowing this year'

Compare also the statistical evaluation of questionnaires completed by informants in Trubinskij 1970 and the mapping of the regional distribution of types in Kuz'mina and Nemčenko 1971, Map 5 (our Map 1). Despite the provisional nature and incompleteness of the material surveyed until now, both show that a complete postpositive article, which is correctly inflected throughout and used congruently, is today no longer present anywhere in Russian. At most we find a differentiation between gender and number in nominative and accusative (NA) singular and plural, while the *casus obliqui* have at most 'harmonized' or neutralized forms. When we consider the regional distribution, it becomes clear that the most varied structures occur in the north-east of Russia, approximately on the line Leningrad–Vladimir–Saratov (area 1 on Map 1); the harmonized endings occur in an area to the west of this one, which lies to the east and south-east of Novgorod as far as Kalinin and in an area in south-east Russia between Ryazan–Tula and Saratov (areas marked as 3 on Map 1); the remaining areas, as far as the line Velikie Luki–Orël–Kursk, have only the unvaried *to* (area 4); further west this no longer occurs.

From this distribution it is clearly established that the phenomenon is concentrated on a medieval colonial area, not in the older settlements on the head waters of the river Dniepr. As this is an area of old Finno-Ugric settlements, it is an obvious step to think of a possible Finno-Ugric substratum influence: it is true that the Finno-Ugric languages have no article (except Hungarian), but here one can assume an indirect influence by the post-positive possessive suffixes, which in part also have an emphatic function.[6] A typological and historical connection with the north (and west) European article system need, however, not be excluded for this reason, particularly since the parallels are here much clearer; Kuz'mina and Nemčenko (1962) citing Šachmatov (p. 6, note 14) also assume that Russian was in the process of developing a system of articles from demonstrative pronouns, which would have been genetically and functionally entirely comparable with the Romance, Germanic or Bulgarian ones. The fact that this did not come about and that these tendencies toward the development of articles take a different direction in the North Russian dialects is no argument in principle against this. It can be pointed out that neither North Germanic (except Icelandic) nor Bulgarian and Macedonian combine a (synthetic) case inflection with the article!

But here the crucial question for our purpose remains unresolved: whether the development of an article or a quasi-article from a demonstrative represents a

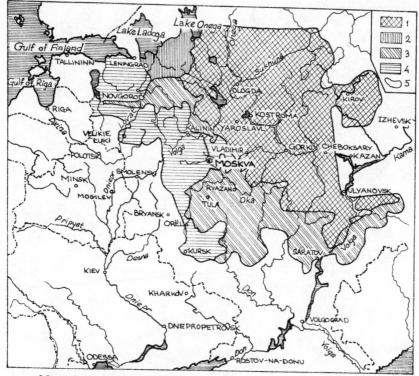

Map 1 (adapted from Kuz'mina-Nemčenko 1962).
1. Special particles with all Nominative/Accusative forms.
2. Particles -ot, -tu (-ty).
3. Post-positive particles are only harmonized, with the exception of -to.
4. Only -to is used.
5. No emphatic post-positive particles.

phenomenon which is typologically a parallel to the Germanic and Romance languages or whether there existed, in addition to this, a historical connection with these languages through language contact over an extended period with the resulting interference phenomena. This is not impossible, but it is also impossible to prove it, either with historical or with dialect-geographical evidence!

3   The possessive perfect

In most contemporary European languages the perfect is formed periphrastically with a participle and a conjugated auxiliary verb – either 'have' or 'be'; in some languages both. Thus in German, French and Italian the periphrastic perfect with 'have' is usual (with most verbs), while that formed with 'be' is restricted to a small semantic group (verbs of motion and others; details cannot be dealt with here). This is also the case with Dutch, Danish and Norwegian, whereas other languages, particularly English – but also Swedish, Spanish, Portuguese, Rumanian, Albanian (and Modern Greek) – have almost exclusively the periphrastic perfect

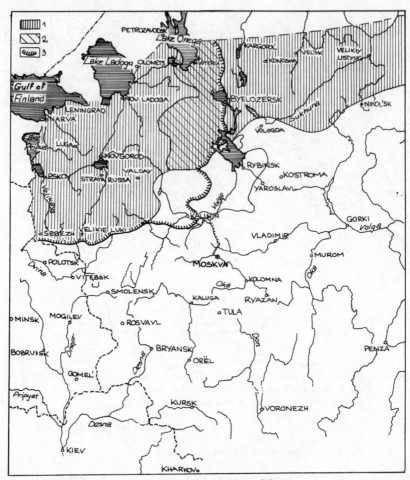

Map 2 (adapted from Kuz'mina-Nemčenko 1962).

1. Transitive verb constructions with *-no, -to* relatively widespread (*izba postavleno, izbu postavleno, vody prineseno, u nego položeno* type).
2. Intransitive verb constructions with *-no, -to* (*-nos', -tos'*) widespread.
3. Approximate furthest extent of the widespread use of constructions with past-participle forms of transitive and intransitive verbs.

with 'have'. It is generally assumed that the form with 'have' spread from Latin and the Romance languages to the Germanic languages, although there is evidence contradicting this in the very early records and in the fact that it was widespread particularly in the languages which were not in direct contact with Latin or the Romance languages, such as Old English, Old Saxon and in particular Proto-Scandinavian and Old Norse. Consequently it would also be possible to advance the thesis that the perfect with 'have' developed independently of the Romance perfect with 'have', at least in Germanic; the more so in view of the fact that there is no earlier evidence of it in the Romance languages and that in Latin it must probably be regarded as an influence from vulgar Latin.

In contrast to the great area of west and south Europe where the perfect with 'have' or with 'have'/'be' is found, there is the great Slavic language area in east and south-east Europe where all the active periphrastic forms (perfect, past perfect, conditional and partly also the future) are formed with the word 'be'. This was the case from the beginning, as we can see from the evidence of Old Church Slavonic, Old Russian, Old Serbian etc., and has in most cases remained so up to the present day, even if partly new synthetic forms have developed from 'be' – such as in Polish *czytalem* – which can be explained as developing from periphrastic 'be'. Only Macedonian is an exception here with its perfect with 'have', which is certainly due to a Balkan–Romance substratum influence.

The North of Russian also has a special status with regard to the use of verbal participles in the function of the main predicate instead of finite verbal forms as in standard Russian. To the west of a line Vyterga (on Lake Onega)–Yaroslavl'–Kalinin–Kaluga–Orёl type I *devuška uecha+vši* 'the girl departed' is found; to the north of a line Velikie Luki–Vyšnij Voloček–Vologda–Nikol'sk (area 1, Map 2) type III *izb+a/u postavle+n+o* 'cottage built', *vod+y prinese+n+o* 'water brought', *u nego polože+n+o* 'he has laid down' or literally 'with him laid down' are found.[7] The centre and starting point of this latter phenomenon, which is what we mainly wish to examine here, is obviously the area from the Estonian border to the White Lake (area 3), i.e. the old area of Novgorod, from where the colonization of the areas to the east and north-east took place.

In order to understand this phenomenon completely, let us take a brief look at the inner Slavic and historical context. Russian inherited and/or developed a relatively rich participle system from Indo-European:

Table 1. *Participle system of Russian*

	Present participle	Past participle	
Active	*-šč-*	I *-(v)-š*	II *-l-*
Passive	*-m-*	*-n/t-*	

In the past tense, which is all that interests us here, there are then three participles available: two active and one passive; the past participle active II ending in /-l-/ was from the beginning mainly predicative in use and is the periphrastic form of the perfect, past perfect, conditional and partly also the future, with tenses of *byti* 'to be';[8] the attributive use is limited; corresponding forms are regarded in Russian nowadays as isolated adjectives, for example *ustalyj* 'tired'. In most Slavic languages the past participle active I has become fixed as a gerund (the Russian term is *deepričastie*) without inflections and mostly designates the secondary predicate. The *n/t*-participle, which is morphophonologically distributed, has in old and new Slavic an almost exclusively passive function, although it was originally neutral as regards voice according to the evidence of the Latin deponent verbs and perhaps also of the Germanic languages.[9] The participles ending in *-m-* (present) and *-n/t-* (past) are, what is more, the only passive forms in Slavic at all! The situation described here is true not only of Old Church Slavonic and Old Russian, but also of present-day standard Russian. A slighter deviation, however noticeable it may seem to be, is the use in the primary predicate of the past-participle active I (*on emši* 'he has eaten', *ona uechavši* 'she (has) departed'), which can definitely be connected with older uses of this participle: Old Church Slavonic, Old Russian and Old Serbian also tend frequently to employ participles in the primary and secondary predication (cf. *inter alia* Růžička 1963).

A considerably more noticeable feature from the inner Slavic point of view is the active use of the *n/t*-participle in North Russian. Only in Macedonian do we find anything comparable, namely a normal perfect with 'have' and with the *n*-participle according to the Romance type of an analytic perfect:

> Macedonian: *imam zeme + n + o/vleze + n + o/nose + n + o/bega + n + o*
>
> Latin: habeo prehensum /intratum /portatum /fugitum
>
>   'I have taken'   /'entered' /'carried' /'flown'

This is here certainly a result of foreign influence (Balkan–Romance substratum).[10] North Russian does not have this type of active use of the past participle in connection with the verb 'have', which is probably the only possible explanation of the development from a possessive predicate structure (*habeo scriptum* – 'I have something written') to an active periphrastic perfect ('I have written'). However, here, as is general in Russian, the North Russian dialects express the possessive relationship by means of the *u*+genitive (G) construction (*u menja (est')* 'with me is'), which in turn is usually explained by a substratum influence from Finno-Ugric,[11] cf. Finnish *minulla on* = 'with me is'. As the copula in the present tense is lacking here, as usual,[12] and the indication of an agent is optional, the *n/t*-participle can also have an *active* predicate function without an auxiliary verb and agent: *izbu postavleno* = Latin: cas*am* construct*um* 'cottage built'. This construction – a neutral *n/t*-participle without an agent and with an accusative object (the criterion for *active* use) – is, however, also found (and we must draw particular attention to this here) in Ukrainian and Byelorussian[13] from the 14th–15th centuries and in Polish[14] from the 15th–16th centuries until the present day (of the type *podano herbatę* = appositum team 'tea is served'; *czerpano wodę* = haustum aquam 'water is drawn'), even if with various restrictions: in Polish only in the literary language, not in the dialects; in Ukrainian in the standard language and dialects, but to a lesser degree in the west and north-west; in Byelorussian today not in the literary language and only in the north-east dialects where they border on North Russian and in the dialects between Russian and Ukrainian in the south:

> Ukrainian: *a samoho tam zabyto* 'he himself killed there' (17th century)
>
> Byelorussian: *holovu eho . . . u ozero . . . ukineno* 'his head into the lake thrown' (16th century).

Here we will certainly have to take account of the language contact between Polish, Ukrainian and Byelorussian with the dominance of Polish in the centuries when the great Polish–Lithuanian state existed (Filin 1972: 498). However, it seems doubtful whether there is a historical connection with the related phenomena in North Russian which we will describe next.

3.1   The types of possessive perfect in the North Russian dialects

I. $NP_{Ng}+u+NP_G+PPP_{Ng}$

      g (gender) = masc./fem./neuter/plural agreement
      Nominative (N), Genitive (G),
      Dative (D), Accusative (A),
      Instrumental (I), Locative (L) = Russian cases.

i.e. congruence of the subject with the past perfect participle (PPP) (as with the passive), but with u+genitive instead of the usual agent instrumental in Russian:

(1) a.   *éto u menja vedro vzjato* (Meščerskij 1972: 216, Section 127)
           ('this with me pail taken = I have taken this pail')

    b.   *dom-ot u nego prošloj got postroen* (ibid., 223, Section 135)
           ('the house with him last year built = he built the house last year')

IIa. $NP_{Nx}+(u+NP)+PPP_{Nm}$

      x = m/f/n/pl optionally.

i.e. with a nominative subject, but without congruence of the PPP which *always* has the form of the nominative sing. masc.:

(2) a.   *tudy k beregu vsja trava skošen* (ibid. 216, Section 128)
           ('Here up to the bank all the grass mowed')

    b.   *droviški slava bogu raspilen*; *vedro prinesen* (ibid., 216, Section 128)
           ('the wood thanks to God chopped up; the pail brought')

    c.   *sčétka kuda-to byla zapichan* (ibid., 216, Section 128)
           ('the brush somewhere was stuffed in')

    d.   *a ovcy-to u menja ne zagnan* (ibid., 216, Section 128; North-west: Pskov, Novgorod)
           ('the sheep with me not driven in = I have not driven in the sheep')

In order to understand this correctly we must note here that in any case these dialects also have the object nominative:[15] *nado trava kosit* 'one must mow the grass' and the like.

IIb. $NP_{Nx}+(u+NP_G)+PPP_{Nn}$

      i.e. PPP always in nominative sing. neuter:

    e.   *bajnja u ego samogo srubleno* (ibid., 220, Section 133)
           ('the bath with him himself made = he carpentered the bath himself')

    f.   *u Griši zaborik postavleno* (ibid., 211: 'at Grisă a fence built')

    g.   *u nas lošad' kupleno* (Stecenko 1972: 88)
           ('with us a horse bought = we have bought a horse')

However, here in the case of *zaborik* 'fence', nominative = accusative, as above with *vedro* 'pail'.

IIIa. $NP_A+(u+NP_G)+PPP_n$

      i.e. accusative object with a neuter PPP.

(3) a.   *ozero teper' nebol'šoe, kudy-to étu vodu spuščeno* (Meščerskij 1972: 220)
           ('lake now small, to somewhere this water let out')

    b.   *ruku tože bylo smjato* (ibid.)
           ('the hand also it was squeezed')

c.   *u volkov tut korovu jideno/u volkov jideno korovu* (Meščerskij 1972; Kuznecov 1970: 72)
('with the wolves here the cow eaten = the wolves have eaten the cow')

IIIb. $NP_A + NP_I + PPP_n$

i.e. likewise accusative object with a neutral PPP, but with an agent instrumental (rare, cf. Kuznecov 1973: 192).

d.   *molodu ženščinu schvačeno medvedicej* (Meščerskij 1972: 223)
('young woman seized by a she-bear')

IV. $(u + NP_G) + PPP_{n\ (itr.)}$

i.e. PPP of intransitive (itr.) and reflexive verbs.

(4) a.   *u menja privyknuto*
('with me used to = I am used to it')

b.   *u nego v gorod uechano*
('with him = he has travelled into the town')

c.   *u nich na rabotu ujdeno*
('with them = they have gone to work')

d.   *u ej zamuž vydeno let 14 už*
('with her = she has already been married for 14 years')

e.   *u dočeri razojdenosja, . . . a u nego už poženenosja* (Meščerskij 1972: 221)
('with the daughter separated; with him already married = he has married already')

Whereas it is possible to explain type I as basically still a passive construction, despite the unusual u + G-construction to express the agent, type II with its now-fixed participle without inflection for gender and number is certainly more unusual, but with its patient in the nominative it can still be interpreted as a passive construction. Type III with its unchanged neuter participle and the patient in the accusative (if it is clearly distinguished from the nominative as in the case of the *a*-stems and the animate masculine forms) is the first one which can only be explained as active.[16] From type III type IV is developed which it is not possible to understand in a passive sense or to consider as a passive construction at all. As here, too, the u + G-construction only indicates the agent or the subject, we are dealing with a construction which is exactly parallel to the west and north European 'have' constructions with the past-participle,[17] in which only the 'have' or possessive element (poss.) appears in a form which is peculiar to Russian. Therefore it is possible to describe the formation of the perfect thus:

1.   Perfect → Poss. + PPP

Poss.   → $\begin{cases} \text{Germanic, Romance, Macedonian 'have'} \\ \text{Russian (dialect) } u + NP_G \end{cases}$

The morphological and syntactic structure of the above types is then:

3.   NP   + Perfect

4.   NP   + Poss.   +   PPP

I. NP_{Ng} $+ u$ $NP_G +$ PPP_{Ng}
     dom-ot   *u*   *nego*   *postroen*

IIa.	NP_{Nx}	$+u+NP_G+$	PPP_{Nm}
	ovcy-to	*u menja*	*ne zagnan*
IIb.	NP_{Nx}	$+u+NP_G+$	PPP_{Nn}
	bajnja	*u ego*	*srubleno*
IIIa.	NP_A	$+u+NP_G+$	PPP_{Nn}
	korovu	*u volkov*	*jideno*
IIIb.	NP_A	$+ NP_I+$	PPP_{Nn}
	ženščinu	*medvedicej*	*schvačeno*
IV.	$\emptyset$	$u+NP_G+$	PPP_{Nn} $(+NP_{Preposition})$
		u nego	*uechano (v gorod)*
		u nego	*poženenosja*

The differences between the syntactic structures of the sentences are best clarified in the tree diagram by the positioning of NP_N or NP_A and of the possessive element, although the linear unity of the perfect is lost as a result:

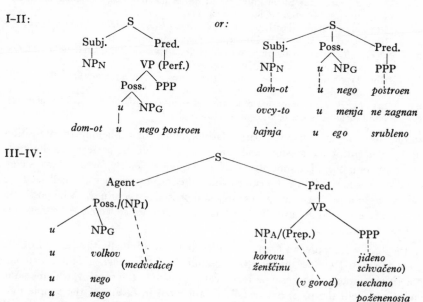

There are internal reasons why the constructions with the accusative participle (type PPP_A: 'habeo litter*as* script*as*') do not occur here, because the possessive expression always remains a 'be' and not a transitive 'have' expression. Then it is relatively unimportant whether one assumes a possessive 'have' in the strict sense of the word which has developed from the meaning 'hold' and has become generalized and recategorized to a mere time auxiliary in both Latin or Germanic,[18] or whether one restricts in a somewhat sophistic way 'possessivity' to pure 'possession' in the legal sense, so that in expressions like 'my sister' and 'my opinion' we are dealing with something different, which one would rather refer to as 'relatedness' or the like:[19] the $u+G$-construction designates the one as well as the other, the actual possession as well as the mere 'membership' or involvement in the action. Nevertheless it seems to me that the very fact that Russian goes over to accusative constructions here, which cannot be derived from 'be' sentences or from passive participle constructions without the copula, is a clear sign that another model – namely active 'have' – in an altered form underlies these constructions. Let us take a closer look at this phenomenon in Latin and Germanic.

3.2   In Latin[20]

In the classical period Latin already displayed a parallelism between *tenere* and *habere*, and even *possidere* (!) plus the accusative predicative PPP or past participle deponent (active!), in which perfect and preterite meaning are often very close to each other. Compare, for example:

(5) a.   'equitatumque omnem . . ., *quem* ex omni provincia et Aeduis atque eorum sociis *coactum habebat*, praemittit . . .' (Caes. *BG* I, 15, 1).

   b.   'Adsunt, queruntur Siculi universi; ad meam fidem, *quam habent spectatum* iam et *cognitam*, confugiunt' (Cic., *Caec.*, 4. 11).

   c.   'Rex . . . per decem dies Libero patri *operatum habuit exercitum*' (Curt. 8, 10, 17: 'had the army employed', Kühner and Stegmann 1976: 764).

   d.   'et eum locum *quem* nobilitas praesidiis *firmatum* atque omni ratione *obvallatum* tenebat me duce rescidistis' (Cic., *Leg. agr.* II, 3).

   e.   'cuius vis omnis haec semper fuit, ne P. Clodius, . . ., vi *oppressam civitatem teneret*' (Cic., *Mil.* 38).

   f.   'nam *patrimonium* domestici praedones vi *ereptum possident*' (Cic., *Rosc. Am.* 15).

   g.   'Nihil iuvant avarum opes, *quas collectas possidet*'[21]

Examples like the latter two are particularly suitable for explaining the transition from the concept of 'possessing' and 'having' to that of the perfect and the past: (f) the robbers possess the inheritance as something stolen by force = have stolen it and now possess it; (g) the treasures which the miser possesses and collected are of no use to him = he collected treasures and possesses them now = he possesses (by himself) collected treasures = he has the treasures collected = he has collected the treasures.

In the split word order in German, with what was originally the past participle in final position ('er hat die Schätze gesammelt'), this stage is still preserved, although semantically the basic perfect meaning (state in the present, which results from an action in the past) has usually disappeared in favour of the simple past meaning. The transition from the purely possessive meaning to the temporal happens most easily where the doer and possessor are the same person: he has collected the treasures and now has the collected treasures. If the doer and the possessor are not the same person (A has collected the treasures, but B (now) has the collected treasures), then the possessive constructions can only be understood in the actual possessive sense.[22]

3.3   In North Germanic

Germanic has an even greater variety of possessive constructions, which lead in the last instance to a possessive perfect: Gothic has scarcely any; Old High German, Old Saxon and Old English have more from the beginning; North Germanic has the most, however, from the Runic Scandinavian languages to Edda and later,[23] not just *hafa* 'have', but also *eiga* 'own', *láta* 'let', *valda* 'rule', *vinna* 'win', *geta* 'get', *fá* 'receive' and others occur in this way. Here are only a few examples for the purposes of illustration from the rich material gathered by Ekbo and Smirnickaja. Parallelism of *eiga* and *hafa*:

(6) a.   'Nío *átto* vit . . . úlfa *alna*' (H. H. 1, 39)
          ('we owned = had nine wolves fed')

    b.   'þar *hefir* dýrr konungr dóttur *alna*' (Fm. 41, 5)
          ('When the beloved king had the daughter fed')

Ekbo (1943) and following him Smirnickaja (1977) distinguish between three types syntactically:

Type A.   *hafa* + NPA + PPA
           i.e. with a congruent past participle in the accusative:

(7) a.   '*hafþi* burg um *brutna*' (Kjulaås, S. O. 106: SR 3)
          ('had the castle destroyed')

    b.   'nú *hefir* ek dverga rétt um *talða*' (Vsp. 12, 3)
          ('now have I the dwarfs correctly counted')

    c.   'sundr *hǫfom* Sigurd sverði *hogginn*' (Br. 7, 2)
          ('to pieces have we Sigurd with the sword chopped')

Type B.   *hafa* + NPA + PPn
           i.e. no longer (except in the case of singular neuter forms) with a congruent past participle neuter.

(8) a.   'inulfra *hafiR* ąnklati þrukial*takat*' (Yttergärdestennan, U. 344: S.R. 6–9)
          ('but Ulf has in England three times money taken')

    b.   en þú *fengit hefir* gambanreiði goda (Skm. 33)
          ('you have drawn on yourself the anger of the Gods')

Also with genitive or dative extensions or completely without an object:

    c.   Nú *hefi* ek *hefnt* harma minna (Vkv. 28, 3)
          ('now have I avenged my sufferings')

    d.   Nú *hefir* pú, Grípir, vel *gjǫrt* (Grp. 53, 5)
          ('now have you, Gripir, well done')

However, the type with the genitive object is assigned to type C by Ekbo, but to type B by Smirnickaja. In contrast to the last example in B, which is elliptical, since it could after all have an accusative object, intransitive forms, the past participles of which likewise appear in an uninflectable neuter form, make up type C:

Type C.   *hafa* + PPn (itr)

(9) a.   'saR uisitaula um *uarit hafþi* burg um brutna' (Kjulaås, S. Ö. 106: S.R. 3)
          ('the man, who has been in the west, has destroyed the castle')

    b.   'han *hafþi* (a)ustarla u(t)i *uaRit*' (Tystberga, S. Ö. 173: S.R. 3)
          ('he had been abroad in the east')

    c.   '*verit hefir* þú Giúka gestr eina nótt' (Grp. 31)
          ('you have been Giuki's guest for one night')

d.   '*hefi* ek lengi *farit*' (Vm. 8)
     ('I have travelled for a long time')

e.   'en ek *gengit hefk* inn móðurlausi mogr' (Fm. 2)
     ('and I have gone, a motherless boy')

The uninflected *t*-form of the neuter, which is today referred to as a 'supinum' in general in North Germanic (cf. Ekbo) and is today still distinguished from the participle (e.g. in Swedish), tended to become the only and unchangeable participle form as in German or North Russian (in -*n*/*t* or -*no*/*to*). The syntax also changed correspondingly![24]

Since, as we have shown, in Slavic languages (Polish (P), Ukrainian (U), Byelorussian (WR), Russian (R)) the impersonal or rather agentless constructions are also used, it should be specially emphasized that in North Germanic, impersonal constructions with the past participle are also widespread,[25] so that they should be given here as type D:

Type D.

$$vera + PP_n + \begin{cases} Adv \\ NP_D \\ Prep\ N \end{cases}$$

(10) a.   'svá *er* nú *ráðit*' (Smirnickaja 1972a: 63)
          ('so it is advised')

     b.   '*var* þar at kveldi of *komit* snimma' (ok fyr iǫtna ǫl fram borit) (Þrk. 24: 1–2)
          ('it was thither come early in the evening (and for the giants beer brought)')

     c.   'þá *var* oss *syniat* Sváfnis dóttur' (H. Hv. 5, 7)
          ('then was refused us Svafnir's daughter (GA))

     d.   '*borgit er* lófðungs flota' (H. Hv. 29, 5)
          ('saved is the ruler's fleet' (G))

Verbs governing the accusative case do not, however, seem to occur (Smirnickaja, 1972a). The genitive, dative and prepositional constructions are in any case outside the normal active–passive correlation, which only places nominative and accusative in relation to each other, e.g. Greek: καταφρονέω τινός (G) 'despise' – καταφρονοῦμαι (pass.), πιστεύω 'believe', φθονέω 'envy' τινι (D) – πιστεύομαι (pass.), φθονοῦμαι (pass.), 'people believe me, envy me' etc.

3.4   Parallel development or loan formation

These facts about North Germanic and North Russian or Slavic, together with the brief look at Latin, the Romance and West Germanic languages, force us to consider the question as to whether there is a historical connection here in the sense of language contact and a loan relationship (between languages) or whether we are dealing with parallel developments within the respective languages which are easily explicable in terms of semantic and syntactic universals and general language features, just as in phonology there are without a doubt, for example, assimilation processes such as palatalization, velarization and devoicing in different languages without there being a historical connection. The reason for this is simply that because of the physiology of articulation certain processes of change and adaptation are obvious and 'natural'. The semantic and syntactic bases here would be, on the one hand, the connection between possessiveness, perfect meaning and general past tense already dealt with and, on the other, the connection between case government, diathesis (grammatical voice) and impersonal constructions (without agents), which we will deal with next.

Miklosich (1875: 364–5) has already drawn attention not only to Old Church Slavonic, but also to parallel Greek and Latin impersonal passive constructions with an accusative object which clearly show that impersonal constructions are to be seen as a third type somewhere between the actual active and passive constructions. In this third type an impersonal (passive by inflection or in form) predicate expression is followed by an accusative object:

(11) a. Greek: ἀσκητέον ἐστὶ τὴν ἀρετήν ('to be practised is the virtue' (A))
   b. Latin: aliqua consilia reperiendum est ('some suggestions is to be found')
   c. Medieval Latin: Matthaeum legitur, psalmos erat ante legendum ('Matthew (A) is read, Psalms (A) was (!) to be read before')
   d. Old Church Slavonic: glasŭ trǫby uslyšano bǫdetĭ
       ('the sound of the trumpet will be audible')
       = Greek: σάλπιγγος φωνὴ ἀκουστὸν ἔσται (Isai. 18.3)

Havránek (1928–34, Section 229, p. 118) also compares

(12) a. Old Church Slavonic: viděti estŭ silǫ christosovǫ (Supr.) ('to be seen is the power (A) of Christ')
   b. Latin: videre est potestatem Christi ('to be seen is the power (A) of Christ') (Supr.)
   c. Old Russian: takŭ pravdu vŭzjati rusinu = takova pravda uzjati rusinu (ibid.) ('such a law each Russian (should) take') (treaty of Smolensk with Gotland in 1229).

If one understands the impersonal passives, gerunds and participles, like the infinitives, as impersonal predicate constructions with active case government (accusative), then all these structures in various languages can be very easily explained. We must once more point out here that by origin verbal adjectives, gerunds, infinitives and also the n/t-participles are indifferent to voice:[26] Latin: laudatus (pass.) – meritus (act.); New High German: geschlafen (act.) – geschlagen (act./pass.) etc. Altogether these transitions between active and passive voice seem not to be confined to particular languages or language structures, even if Slavic seems at first glance scarcely to have had active n/t-participles.

But what is the historical evidence of the possessive perfect in Russian? We already know that the impersonal active constructions in Polish, Ukrainian and Byelorussian go back to the 14th–16th centuries. What is the evidence of the possessive u + G-construction with the PPP as the possessive perfect? Kuz'mina (1979: 171) is of the opinion that the present state of the dialects of North and West Mid-Russian is the result of processes which have only taken place since the 17th century (because definite evidence of the accusative is not found until the 17th century, e.g. u nas votčinu vzjato). But this ignores not only the Ukrainian, Byelorussian and West Russian evidence from the 16th century, such as, for example:

(13) a. i bolšuju polovinu vojska pěšogo k šturmu poslano (Kuznecov 1949: 72) ('and the greater part (A) of the infantry were sent in to attack')

b.   zbira*no* . . . sperva dvadcat*uju* den*gu*, potom desjat*uju* den*gu* (ibid.)
      ('at first a twentieth (A) was collected, then a tenth' (A))

c.   i v to že vremja *u nich* podkopom *vodu* otnja*to* (Borkovskij 1968: 174)
      ('and at that time with them by digging the water (A) taken away')

but also neglects or incorrectly interprets the material which has been known at least since 1940 (Borkovskij) or 1949 (Kuznecov),[27] which was also dealt with in more detail in 1961 (Feoktistova) and cited and discussed briefly in Filin 1972: 493–4; in particular the material from the chronicles and records of Novgorod since the 13th–14th century, in isolated cases from as early as the 11th century, which it is true in part do not display any morphologically clear-cut accusatives (as is so often the case in Russian, also in present-day dialects), but nevertheless, or for this very reason, can definitely be considered as pre-forms of the constructions in question. It is true that examples with homonymous nominatives and accusatives are not decisive proof of active usage but could also be interpreted as passives with errors in congruence, but on the other hand, because of the morphological facts of Russian, where an accusative which is distinct from the nominative is the exception rather than the rule, they are not decisive proof of the passive interpretation either, but can definitely also be explained as active:

(14) a.   'medŭ dan*o* bystŭ bogomï' (Izb. 1076, Filin 1972: 493)
            ('honey was given by God')

b.   'a čto golovy poima*no* po vsei volosti Novgorodskoj, a tĕ poidu(tĭ) k Novugorodu bez okupa' (Document of Novgorod, No. 11 from 1136: Feoktistova 1961: 203 etc.)
      ('and what/that heads were captured in the whole area of Novgorod, they go to Novgorod without ransom')

c.   'a što grable(*n*)o *u moich ljudii* i tomu vsemu sudŭ (Document of Novgorod, No. 12 from 1317)
      ('and what was stolen by/from my people, must go before the court')

d.   'ubi*to u nas* pod stenoju Azova goroda na tom 1-om pristupe v tot 1-yj denï turok 6 golov jazyčeskich' (Pov. ob azov. vzjatii 72, Borkovskij 1968: 41)
      ('killed with us below the wall of the town of Azov in the first attack on the first day six heads of heathen Turks')

e.   'a pleči *u sebja* – skazalŭ – vŭ livomŭ nožemŭ kolo*to*' (Kabal'nye knigi 1594–9, Feoktistova 1961: 203)
      ('and the shoulders with himself – he said – stabbed on the left (shoulder) with the knife')

Unfortunately it is not always clear whether the meaning of *u*+genitive is ablative, locative or agent, but that scarcely prevents the reinterpretation of syntactic constructions. For we cannot expect active constructions to develop from passive ones and agentive constructions from possessive or locative ones without the borderlines, which linguists can clearly determine, becoming blurred for the speaker or writer, at least for a time. On the contrary: we positively need the ambiguous constructions in order to be able to understand a reinterpretation at all. In this light I consider the early evidence simply to be proof that something new is beginning to happen here, which is only definitely identifiable at a later stage of development.

It does not seem to be quite possible to link the possessive perfect to the very oldest period of Russian, in which a North Germanic influence is most likely, so that the hypothesis of a parallel development within Russian seems more likely. We must, however, bear in mind that it can take centuries until a colloquial usage is accepted and developed in the literary language and so is finally verifiable in documentary form. And since North-West Russian has not become the norm for the Russian standard language, the possessive perfect has to the present day been part of the 'substandard' which has now become 'literary' in the Bylina, which has a long oral tradition:

> Vo vsech gorodach *u menja pobyvano*
> a vsech knjaz'ev da *perevidano*
> a i vsem knjaginam-to *posluženo* –
> v odnom, vo Kievi ne *byvano*
> Kievskogo knjazja ne *vidano*
> Kievskoj knjagine-to ne *služeno*.[28]

In the second part of his article (p. 91ff) Maslov (1949), who considers the situation both in Latin and the Romance and Germanic languages,[29] presents the facts presented here regarding the Russian dialects as proof of the polygenesis of this phenomenon. He argues that both the great morphological differences plus the complete identity of internal form in these constructions and cultural-historical reasons exclude the possibility of any sort of influence or borrowing. Maslov considers that Marr's hypothesis of the unity of the glottogonic process is thereby confirmed, namely that various languages can develop analogous categories completely independently of each other, and, what is more, not because of inherited common features or the much-discussed 'influences' and 'borrowings', but as a result of definite and general regularities (p. 95).

This 'proof' rests on two arguments: (1) the different morphological forms; (2) the lack of a cultural-historical connection. As far as the latter point is concerned, this argument does not hold because, as has been shown, it is possible to prove Germanic–Slavic contacts from the earliest Old Russian period, not to mention the later contacts brought about by the Hanseatic League. And the first argument is really nothing more than an unproven hypothesis, which could be disproven by the case dealt with in this article: namely, the belief that only structures, which are apparently morphologically identical, can be borrowed. Here we might have a case where the identity of inner form – which has been repeatedly emphasized by Maslov and others – would have been taken over and developed differently in each case.

So it seems to me that the theoretical question of how borrowings are to be distinguished from genuine parallel developments still remains unresolved.

Notes

1 Cf. the most recent contribution by Birnbaum 1978.
2 Cf. Ureland 1977, 1979.
3 Cf. the controversy among the historians on this question, the dispute between the 'Normanists' and 'Anti-Normanists' and the extensive relevant literature; the most recent contribution is probably: Varangian Problems. *Scando–Slavica* suppl. 1. 1970.
4 Veenker 1967 reviews the research on this topic.

5 Transliteration: ъ = ŭ; ь = ĭ; ѣ = ē.
6 On this point cf. Veenker 1967: 88–90 and the literature cited there, in particular Wissemann 1939 and Schlachter 1960, and also Serebrennikov 1956a.
7 Cf. the Maps in Kuz'mina-Nemčenko 1971, in particular Map 4 = our Map 2, and the schematic diagrams between pp. 284–5; the same map in Kuz'mina 1975a between pp. 230–1, and 1975b between pp. 204–5.
8 Old Church Slavonic: *pisalŭ jesmĭ/bēachŭ/bychŭ/bimĭ* – 'I have written'/'I had written'/'I would have written'/'I would have written'; Bulgarian: *pisal săm*, Serbo-Croat.: *pisao sam*, Slovakian: *pisal som*, Czech: *psal jsem*, Polish: *pisałem*, Russian: *ja pisal*, Ukrainian: *ja pysav*, White Russian: *ja pisaŭ* – 'I have written'.
9 Cf. Brugmann 1904: Sections 387, 814; Szemerényi 1970: 297.
10 Cf. Rumanian: *am făcut* 'I have done'/*dormit* 'slept'/*fugit* 'flown'/*avut* 'had'/*fost* 'been'/*putut* 'believed'.
   Albanian: *kam vënë* 'I have laid'/*ardhur* 'come'/*dhënë* 'given'/*qenë* 'been'/*pasur* 'had' (= habeo positum/ventum/datum/(statum)/habitum)
   Modern Greek (rare): ἔχω κομμένο = ἔχω κόψει 'I have cut'
   For evidence in the vernacular of the perfect with 'have' or 'be' with the past-perfect participle, especially in southern Slavic languages (Macedonian, Bulgarian, but also Serbo-Croat, and Slovenian) and in the spoken west Slavic languages (Czech, Polish, Kashubian as a result of German influence) *see* Vasilev 1968 and the older linguistic research which he discusses.
11 The equivalents in other Finno-Ugric languages, with the exception of Voguli and East Yakut, which possess a word for 'have', are to be found in Veenker 1967: 118. Incidentally this hypothesis does not fit in with the assumption – which Isačenko 1974 particularly supports and which is latent in Veenker – that Slavic, and hence also Old Church Slavonic and Russian only introduced a word for 'have' (*imēti*) under Greek and later Romance and Germanic influence; for then *u* + G would have remained the original marker of a 'be-language' for the possessive relationship in Russian and the assumption of a Finno-Ugric substratum would be superfluous. For how else should the Slavic languages have expressed this, cf. also Latin: *mihi est liber* ('for me is a book') and the like.
   The type *u nego uechano* (Veenker 1967: 137ff.) has as far as I know no parallels in Finno-Ugric at all, because here (in any case, in Finnish) all periphrastic perfects are formed with active participles and 'verbum esse' (as also in Slavic cf. fn. 8): Finnish *on sanonut* 'has said', *oli tullut* 'had come'; other participles are used for the passive. Veenker does not cite any parallel constructions in Finno-Ugric either, only an East Yakut example, which is doubtless different because it is a genuine passive: *wersa* = 3rd singular past-passive 'was made'. Thus *habeo* – or possessive-perfects are obviously missing; they would also be quite unusual in 'be-languages'!
   Evidence of and arguments for the Proto-Slavic origin of the *u* + G possessive construction are to be found in Vasilev 1973; the numerous examples of evidence from (early) Serbian deserve particular attention.
12 Details on form and use in Safarewiczowa 1964 and Isačenko 1974.
13 Cf. Filin 1972: 491–501, in particular 496–7.
14 Cf. Brajerski 1977 and Podgórski 1977.
15 Cf. on this point Timberlake 1974, in addition to the dialectological studies.
16 Trost's (1972) interpretation is therefore inappropriate; he understands and tries to explain all these sentences as passives.
17 This has long been known. Cf. Trubinskij 1979: 154, Note 1 with a reference to Šafranov 1852: *O vidach glagolov v sintaksičeskom otnošenii*. Moskva, p. 10–11: *U menja v dome ubrano, u nego mnogo bylo posluženo* = 'I have put everything in good order in the house, he has served a great deal'. Cf. also Maslov 1949.

18 Cf. Zadorožnyj 1960. On Latin: Kuryłowicz 1931 and: 'civitatem servitute oppressam habuit/tenuit. Deus omnes homines pari amore complexus tenet' (Menge 1953: 319). See Section 3.2 below.

19 Russian *prinadležnost'*, English 'implicational' (Isačenko 1974). Even if 'have' equals 'be + transitivity' (ibid. p. 76), then $u + G + A + PPP$ equals 'have' + A + PPP.

20 Abbreviations used in the text:
Latin sources:
Caes. *BG*: Caesar, De Bello Gallico
Cic., *Caec.*: Cicero, In Q. Caecilium oratio quae Divinatio dictur
Cic., *Leg. agr.*: Cicero, De lege agraria oratio secunde contra P. Servilium Rullum
Tr Pleb. ad populum
Cic., *Mil.*: Cicero, Pro T. Annio Milone oratio
Cic., *Rosc. Am.*: Cicero, Pro Sex. Roscio Amerino oratio
Curt.: Quintus Curtius Rufus, Historiae Alexandri Macedonis

Old Norse and Runic sources:
H.H.: Helgakviða Hundingsbana
Fm.: Fáfnismál
S.R.: Sveriges Runinskrifter
Vsp.: Vǫluspá
Br.: Brot
Skm.: Fǫr Skírnis
Vkv.: Volundarkviða
Grp.: Grípisspá
Vm.: Vafrúðnismál
H.Hv.: Helgakviða Hiǫrvarzsonar
Þrk.: Þrymskviða

Slavic sources:
Isai.: Isaiah
Supr.: Codex Supraliensis
Smol. gr.: Smolenskaja gramota
Izb. 1076: Izbornik Svjatoslava of 1076
Nov. gr.: Novgorodskaja gramota: Gramoty Velikogo Novgoroda i Pskova, ed. Valka. Moskva/Leningrad 1949.

21 Menge 1953: 319. Further model sentences from classical sources can be found here. Compare also the evidence in Kühner and Stegmann 1976: 763–4; Thielmann 1885; Tammelin 1889: 98–104, 157–8.

22 Cf. also Trubinskij 1979, especially p. 165, in general, and in particular on North Russian.

23 Cf. in particular the works of Ekbo, Johannisson, Smirnickaja and Zadorožnyj.

24 The morphological distinction is no doubt more theoretical than real, cf. the 'errors' from the Swedish press of that time quoted in Lindberg 1937: 198–9: 'har lektor NN fått infört en artikel, som' instead of 'har lektor NN fått en artikel införd, som' and the like.

25 Cf. in particular on this point Smirnickaja 1972a; 1977: 44.

26 See note 9 above and also Blümel 1979: 77–125.

27 Cf. Kuznecov 1949: 71, fn. 1.

28 'In all towns with me (= I have) been/and all the princes (have I) seen/and all the princesses served/only in Kiev (have I) not been/the princes of Kiev (I have) not seen/the princesses of Kiev not served' (from: Gil'ferding, Onežskie byliny 3: 222; after Kuznecov 1970 (1949), p. 69.

29 With somewhat forced polemics against west European 'bourgeois' scholarship

he points out that the old perfect is not a tense but an aspect and not in the narrow sense of a 'possessive perfect', but a form which denotes a particular interest of the person in the action or its results, somewhat in the sense of the function of a *dativus ethicus* (p. 96).

Bibliography

Benveniste, E. 1960: 'Être' et 'avoir' dans leurs fonctions linguistiques. *Bulletin de la Société de Linguistique* 55: 113–34.

Birnbaum, H. 1978: Yaroslav's Varangian Connection. *Scando-Slavica* 24: 5–25.

Blümel, W. 1979: Zur historischen Morphosyntax der Verbalabstrakta im Lateinischen. *Glotta* 57 (1–2): 77–125.

Borkovskij, V. I. (ed.) 1968: *Sravnitel'no-istoričeskij sintaksis vostočno-slavjanskich jazykov*. Tipy prostogo predloženija. Členy Predloženija. Moskva.

Brajerski, T. 1977: O orzeczeniach typu *jedzono* i *pito*. *Roczniki Humanistyczne* 25 (4): 5–36.

Brugmann, K. 1904: *Kurze Vergleichende Grammatik der Indogermanischen Sprachen*. Strassburg.

Ekbo, S. 1943: *Studier över uppkomsten av supinum i de germanska språken*. Uppsala.

Feoktistova, A. S. 1961: K istorii sostavnogo skazuemogo s prisvjazočnoj čast'ju, vyražennoj pričastiem stradatel'nogo zaloga prošedšego vremeni (na materiale Novgorodskich pamjatnikov pis'mennosti XII–XVI vv.) *Issledovanija po leksikologii i grammatike russkogo jazyka*. Moskva, pp. 194–208.

Filin, F. P. 1972: *Proischoždenie russkogo, ukrainskogo i belorusskogo jazykov. Istoriko-dialektologičeskij očerk*. Leningrad.

Havránek, B. 1928–34: *Genera verbi v slovanských jazycích* 1–2, Praha.

Isačenko, A. V. 1974: On 'Have' and 'Be' Languages (A Typological Sketch). In M. S. Flier (ed.), *Slavic Forum*. The Hague, pp. 43–77.

Johannisson, T. 1945: *Hava och vara som tempusbildande hjälpverb i de Nordiska språken*. Lund.

Kühner, R. and K. F. Stegmann, 1976: *Ausführliche Grammatik der lateinischen Sprache*. Part 2: *Satzlehre*. 5th edn. Darmstadt.

Kuryłowicz, J. 1931: Les temps composés du roman. *Prace Filologiczne* 15: 448–53. (Also in: *Esquisses linguistiques* 1960, pp. 104–8.)

Kuz'mina, I. B. 1975a: O meste sočetanij tipa (*est'*) *postavlen, byl* (*budet*) *postavlen*; (*est'*) *vstavši, byl* (*budet*) *vstavši* v grammatičeskoj sisteme sovremennych russkich govorov. *Obščeskavjanskij lingvističeskij atlas*. Materialy i issledovanija 1973. Moskva, pp. 219–58.

1975b: Ešče raz o konstrukcijach tipa *kartoška vykopano, koni zaprjaženo, pol pomyto* v russkich govorach. *Russkie govory. K izučeniju fonetiki, grammatiki, leksiki*. Moskva, pp. 202–34.

1979: K istorii dvukomponentnych konstrukcij s pričastnymi formami na -*no*, -*to* v russkom jazyke (v svjazi s voprosom 3127 'Voprosnika Obščeslavjanskogo lingvističeskogo atlasa'). *Obščeslavjanskij lingvističeskij atlas*. Materialy i issledovanija. Moskva, pp. 153–74.

Kuz'mina, I. B. and E. V. Nemčenko, 1962: K voprosu o postpozitivnych časticach v russkich govorach. *Materialy i issledovanija po russkoj dialektologii*. Novaja serija t. 3, Moskva, pp. 3–32.

1971: *Sintaksis pričastnych form v russkich govorach*. Moskva.

Kuznecov, P. S. 1970 (1949): K voprosu o skazuemostnom upotreblenii pričastij i deepričastij v russkich govorach. *Materialy i issledovanija po russkoj dialektologii*. t. 3: 59–83.

(ed.) 1973: *Russkaja dialektologija*. Moskva.

Lewicki, A. M. 1966: Geneza struktur typu *podano herbatę. Poradnik językowy* 5. Warsaw.

Lindberg, N.-H. 1937: *Lehrbuch der schwedischen Sprache.* 3rd edn. Göteborg.

LW = Lehr-Spławiński, T. and W. Witkowski, 1965: *Wybór tekstów do historii języka rosyjskiego.* Warsaw.

Maslov, Ju. S. 1949: K voprosu o proischoždenii possessivnogo perfekta. *Učenye Zapiski LGU Nr.* 97. *Serija filologičeskich nauk,* 14: 76–104.

Menge, H. 1953: Repetitorium der lateinischen Syntax und Stilistik. *Elfte Auflage besorgt von Andreas Thierfelder.* Leverkusen.

Meščerskij, N. A. (ed.) 1972: *Russkaja dialektologija.* Moskva.

Miklosich, F. 1875: *Vergleichende Grammatik der slavischen Sprachen.* Vol. 4. Wien.

Neckel, G. (ed.) 1914: *Edda.* Heidelberg.

Nemčenko, E. V. 1975: K voprosu o morfologičeskoj protivopostavlennosti pričastnych form v russkich govorach. *Russkie govory. K izučeniju fonetiki, grammatiki, leksiki.* Moskva, pp. 178–89.

1977: K istorii stradatel'nych pričastij prošedšego vremeni v russkom jazyke. *Obščeslavjanskij lingvističeskij atlas.* Materialy i issledovanija. Moskva, pp. 135–74.

Podgórski, A. 1977: Passivum i orzeczenia typu *jedzono, pito* w tekstach z 2. połowy XVI w. *Roczniki Humanistyczne* 25, (4): 37–53.

Růžička, R. 1963: *Das syntaktische System der altslavischen Partizipien und sein Verhältnis zum Griechischen.* Berlin.

Safarewiczowa, H. 1964: *Oboczność* ja imeju *i* u menja est' *w języku rosyjskim dziś i dawniej.* Wrocław/Warszawa/Kraków.

Smirnickaja, O. A. 1972a: The Impersonal Sentence Patterns in the Edda and in the Sagas. *Arkiv för nordisk filologi* 87: 56–88.

1972: Morfologizacija analitičeskich glagol'nych konstrukcij v germanskich jazykach. *Istoriko-tipologičeskie issledovanija morfologičeskogo stroja germanskich jazykov.* Moskva, pp. 70–90.

1977: Evoljucija vido-vremennoj sistemy v germanskich jazykach. In V. N. Jarceva (ed.), *Istoriko-tipologičeskaja morfologija germanskich jazykov. Kategorija glagola.* Moskva, pp. 5–127.

Stecenko, A. N. 1972: *Istoričeskij Sintaksis Russkogo jazyka.* Moskva.

Sveriges Runinskrifter (S.R.): Kungliga Vitterhets Historie och Antikvitets Akademien, Stockholm. Vol. 3 (1924–36), ed. E. Brate and E. Wessén, *Södermaniglands Runinskrifter* (S.Ö.); Vols. 6–9 (1940–58), ed. E. Wessén and S. B. F. Jansson, *Upplands Runinskrifter* (U.) 1–4.

Szemerényi, O. 1970: *Einführung in die vergleichende Sprachwissenschaft.* Darmstadt.

Tammelin, E. J. 1889: *De participiis priscae latinitatis quaestiones syntacticae.* Dissertation. Helsingfors.

Thielmann, Ph. 1885: Habere mit dem Part. Perf. Pass. *Archiv für lateinische Lexikographie und Grammatik,* 2: 372–423, 509–49.

Timberlake, A. 1974: *The Nomitative Object in Slavic, Baltic, and West Finnic.* Munich.

Trost, K. 1972: Zur Struktur passivischer Sätze im Russischen, namentlich in den nordgroßrussischen Dialekten. *Die Sprache* 18: 9–23.

Trubinskij, V. I. 1970: Ob učastii postpozitivnoj časticy *to* v postroenii složnogo predloženija (po materialam pinežskich govorov). *Severnorusskie govory* 1: 48–66

1979: O russkom razgovornom possessivnom perfekte. *Severnorusskie govory,* 3: 154–73.

Ureland, P. S. 1977: Some Comparative Aspects of Pronominal Cliticization in the Baltic Language Area. *Akten der 2. Salzburger Frühlingstagung für Linguistik.* Tübingen, pp. 301–19.

1979: Prehistoric Bilingualism and Pidginization as Forces of Linguistic Change. *Journal of Indo-European Studies,* 7: 77–104.

Varangian Problems 1970: *Scando-Slavica* Suppl. 1. Report on the First International Symposium on the Theme: The Eastern Connections of the Nordic Peoples in the Viking Period and Early Middle Ages. Copenhagen.

Vasilev, C. 1968: Der romanische Perfekttyp im Slavischen. *Slavistische Studien zum VI. Internationalen Slavistenkongress in Prag* 1968. München, pp. 215–30.

1973: Ist die Konstruktion *U Menja Est'* russisch oder urslavisch? *Die Welt der Slaven*, 18: 361–7.

Veenker, W. 1967: *Die Frage des finnougrischen Substrats in der russischen Sprache.* Bloomington.

Zadorožnyj, B. M. 1960: Pervičnoe značenie konstrukcii 'pričastie II + glagol "imet"' v drevnegermanskich jazykach. *Voprosy Jazykoznanija*, 6: 74–82.

6 The realm of the Rus':
A contribution to the problem of
the rise of the East-Slavic kingdom

STEFAN SÖDERLIND

Introduction

For the last 260 years, scholars have been actively interested in the rise and development of the East Slavic kingdom.[1] New works dealing with historical, philological
and archaeological aspects of this topic have appeared in a continuous stream.

The result of this industry is a considerable, almost unmanageable body of
literature, the size of which puts the present-day scholar in a difficult position. It
would naturally be impossible to master all the various aspects of research on this
topic. There is a hazard resulting from this state of affairs – what seem to be new
insights may already have been presented by earlier scholars. As a matter of fact,
I do not know whether the present article discusses any aspects of the problem
which are completely new. It does, however, suggest a solution to the great historical
enigma regarding the rise of the kingdom of the Rus' in the 9th and 10th centuries
AD.

From a historical and philological viewpoint it is quite unlikely that the problem
of the origin of the kingdom of the Rus' should pose a series of troublesome or
insoluble questions. In the 10th century AD, this state was one of the great powers
of the period. At that time the humanities flourished in both Byzantium and the
Arab world. Many of the humanist scholars were historians, chroniclers or ethno-
graphically oriented geographers. One cannot imagine that observers like these
were ignorant of the historical facts regarding the existence of their powerful
neighbour. There is no obvious reason why we should have any great difficulty
in understanding the information which these scholars convey. In any case why
should we expect a series of enigmatic philological problems? Surely, modern
linguistic scholarship should be capable of throwing light on the basic philological
problems of a topic which has been so thoroughly researched and extensively
commented on.

Any one who reflects along these lines has to realize, however, that there are
historical discussions which are so deep and interesting that they attain a scientific
importance of their own. This is certainly the case with the exciting discussion on
the rise of the East Slavic kingdom. Therefore I have presented my report here in
the form of a survey of the present state of research, supplemented with some
scattered critical remarks of my own.

The present article is therefore divided into three major sections, in which the various hypotheses as to the origin of the Russian state are reviewed. The Normanist and Anti-Normanist hypotheses are discussed in detail in 1.3. Then the traditional etymological derivations of the names *Ruotsi* and *Rus'* in Finnish, Russian, Arabic, Greek, and West European languages are dealt with in 1.4.1 to 1.4.3. The origin of the designations Varangians and Kolbjazi for Scandinavians in Russia is treated in 1.4.4.

In 1.6 and 1.9 the Gothic hypothesis, suggested by Strube de Pyrmont 1785 and Latham 1863, which claims that the East Slavic kingdom was founded by the Goths is introduced. This hypothesis seems the most plausible one to this writer and it has therefore been expanded into the Red–Blond-People hypothesis in Section 3 of this article (cf. especially 3.1). The latter hypothesis claims that the Old Russian forms *Rus'* and **Rud'* are forms derived from the Proto-Slavic stems **rusu* and **rudu* 'red', which in the collective feminine singular form (**Rusi* and **Rudi* 'the Red–Blond People', i.e. the Goths) began to spread among the Slavs in the period 150–350 AD and which were accepted by the Goths as ethnic names for themselves around 400–600 (cf. 3.1). In the palatalized form **rusu* occurs in Old Russian as *Rus'*, a form which I consider was borrowed directly into Arabic as *Rūs* (cf. 3.2).

However, in order to explain the Middle Greek form *Rhōs* (839) (cf. 3.1), the Estonian *Roots* and Finnish *Ruotsi* forms (cf. 1.9) on the one hand, and the Old Russian *rus'* and Arabic *rūs* forms on the other, two stem variants of the ethnic name have been posited here. In the former case the stem is Gothic **rauþs* [ro:þs] whereas in the latter case the stem is Proto-East-Slavic **rusi*. The spread of the former stem of the ethnic name into Estonian and Finnish is discussed in 1.9. In some Finno-Ugric languages the semantic development was different from that of Russian, Greek, and Arabic in that the stem in the Finno-Ugric languages denotes neither 'Gothic' nor 'Russian' but 'Sweden' and 'Swedish' (cf. Estonian *Roots* and Finnish *Ruotsi*). On the other hand the Scandinavian languages developed a meaning of the stem *Rus'* which is common to all West European languages: 'Russian' (cp. Swedish *ryssar*, Danish and Norwegian *russer*, and Icelandic *rússar*, all meaning 'Russians', cf. 3.3).

In order to be able to understand this great difference in both meaning and form of the ethnic name *Rus'*, the history of the Goths and Scandinavians in Russia must be taken into consideration. The spread of the forms *Rhōs* and *Rus'* through Greek, Arabic, and West European languages is discussed in detail in 3.1–3.4.

To support the Gothic hypothesis and its extended version – the Red–Blond-People hypothesis – as developed here, an extensive survey of the present state of research is presented in 1.2 and 2, in which historical and philological evidence for and against the latter hypothesis is summarized. Direct quotations from Latin, Old Russian, Old Swedish, Old Icelandic, Old High German, Middle Greek, Classical Arabic, and Persian sources are included in this survey. In the conclusion the historical evidence for the Red–Blond-People hypothesis is summarized.

1   The origin of the name *Rus'*

1.1   The early hypotheses

Between 7–11 October 1968, the First International Symposium on 'The eastern connections of the nordic peoples in the Viking period and early middle ages' was held in Denmark. A large number of experts from the Scandinavian countries, England, France, Poland, Czechoslovakia, Bulgaria, and the Soviet Union attended the symposium and gave papers on Varangian problems or participated in the ensuing discussions. The papers and the discussions were published in 1970 edited by Rahbek Schmidt, who also surveyed the research into Varangian problems carried out until then in his introduction to the volume.[2] Rahbek Schmidt first delimits the topic in accordance with Stender-Petersen 1953 to: 'The problem of the part played by the Nordic–Scandinavian ethnic element in the history of the political and cultural creation and early development of the ancient Russian state.'[3] Then he takes the *Nestor Chronicle* (Kiev 1111–13, Codex Laurentianus 1377) as a starting point and discusses the Calling-in legend of how Rurik and his brothers founded the East Slavic kingdom after being invited into the area by Slavic and Finno-Ugric tribes. The versions of this legend vary somewhat from manuscript to manuscript. Rahbek Schmidt also points out that modern scientific research into the subject began as late as 1724, the year of the foundation of the Russian Academy of Sciences.

A survey of the historical and ethno-linguistic research on the Scandinavians and the Goths in the east will be necessary before I introduce the Red–Blond-People hypothesis.

Th. S. Bayer is one of a long line of Russian scholars who have dealt with the problem of the origin of the Russian state. In 1736 he drew attention to an entry in the *Annales Bertiniani*, dated 839, which has been quoted ever since. In this passage Bishop Prudentius of Troyes reports that Emperor Theophilos of Constantinople had sent a delegation to Emperor Louis I of the Holy German Empire who received them in Ingelheim on 18 May of the same year. Some people who were not Greeks arrived along with the Byzantine delegation. The former said 'that they, i.e. their people, were called *Rhōs* and confirmed that their king, who was entitled *Chacanus*, had sent them to Theophilos with the aim of promoting friendly relations'. Theophilos, however, did not want to let them return to their country by the route by which they had come to Constantinople, as it was considered to be too dangerous. He therefore requested that Louis should permit them to travel home across German territory. Louis had an investigation carried out as to why these Rhōs had come and he was told that they belonged to the nation of the Swedes (*comperit eos gentis esse Sueonum*). This statement led to further investigations.[4]

There have been numerous suggestions as to how this passage should be interpreted, but I see no reason for this variety of alternative interpretations. It is evident that it was a delegation from the Chaganate of Kiev that arrived in Ingelheim. It is also clear that the judgement of the Germans was founded on their examination of the language of the members of the delegation from Kiev, since the Svear have never called themselves Rhōs.

The language of the delegation was considered to be of the same type as that of the Svear, that is, East Scandinavian. Right down to the present day, some philologists have attempted to claim that Middle Latin *chacanus* was derived from the Scandinavian name *Håkan*. Collinder 1975, however, pointed out once and for all that the word is a Latin written form of Middle Greek καγᾶνος (kagānos) 'Khan', a title of Chinese origin.[5] Therefore, no further discussion of *Chacanus* is necessary here.

1.2   The Scandinavian evidence in Byzantine and Old High German sources

Bayer 1770 was also familiar with other, extremely important material *inter alia* a number of passages and dates in the work of Constantine VII: *De Administrando Imperio* (c. 950) and also in a text written by Bishop Liutprand of Cremona (died c. 970). The Emperor reports on the Rhōs and the Slavs, and on the Dniepr rapids (in both languages – ῥωσιστί (Rhōsistí) and σκλαβινιστι (Sklavinistí)) which modern scholars have found of great interest, especially the section on the Dniepr rapids. Bishop Liutprand writes in one passage that Constantinople's neighbours include among others, 'the *Rusii* whom wec all by another name Northmen' (*Rusios, quos alio nos nomine Nordmannos appellamus*).[6]

Bayer's examination of the material concerning the Varangians in the works of Saxo Grammaticus, Snorri Sturluson, Byzantine authors, and in the *Nestor Chronicle* led him to conclude that the Varangians were prominent men from Sweden, Norway and Denmark who entered the service of the Rus' as mercenaries. This conclusion of Bayer's was to influence a specific development in future research which manifests itself in the claims of the Normanists or Scandinaviomaniacs.

1.3   The Normanist and Anti-Normanist hypotheses

Among the Normanists of the 18th century, G. F. Müller 1749 must be mentioned; he was the first scholar to discover the etymological similarity between Old Russian *Rus'* and Finnish *Ruotsi*. But when he also asserted that the Rus' were a Scandinavian people, the polyhistorian V. M. Lomonosov (died 1765) objected that such a claim was an insult to the honour of the Russian people. This objection made Lomonosov the first of the so-called Anti-Normanists.

A hypothesis that the Rus' were of Finnish origin was presented by V. N. Tatiščev (died 1750): the Varangians were Finns, who were called *russy* because their hair was *rusyj* 'blond'.

In 1785 a remarkable suggestion was made by a member of the Russian Academy, F. H. Strube de Pyrmont. He claimed that there was no doubt that the Scythians, Goths or Normans – called ῥῶς 'Rhōs' by Greek historians – and the Varangians, whom the Russian chronicle writers call *Rus'*, were one and the same people.[7] Moreover he introduced a cultural-historical perspective which was of great importance for later discussions: the Varangians brought culture to the East Slavs;

the oldest Russian collection of laws, *Russkaja pravda*, was simply Old Scandinavian law. Strube also traced the derivation of the North Germanic names of the Dniepr rapids from Old Scandinavian languages. However, as far as these derivations are concerned, he had a predecessor, the Swede J. Thunman 1774 who had made some important observations in the same direction around 1770. Thunman was of the opinion that the denotation *Rus'* derived from Finnish *Ruotsi* and that this name in its turn derived from a Swedish tribe on the Swedish east coast, *Roslagen*. This way of thinking was to prevail for a long period of time.

Somewhat later, at the beginning of the 19th century, the German historian A. L. Schlözer 1802–9 took an ultra-Normanist position. He got involved in a polemical argument with J. F. G. Ewers 1814, who maintained that *Rus'*, both the people and the name, had existed in South Russia long before the era of Rurik. Ewers thought that the Khazars had called the East Slavs in the south *Rus'*.

As time elapsed, the number of historical and philological sources increased and were to stimulate scientific discussion. The results of research based on Oriental, Russian and Scandinavian material began to appear. The long debate, which until then had been conducted mainly between historians, began to change its character; in the 1840s it merged into the so-called Great Philological Controversy. E. Kunik 1844–5 can be said to have initiated this epoch. In an extensive treatment of the topic, which was strongly philologically oriented, he discussed a series of controversial expressions, among others, *rus'*, *varjag* and *ruotsi*, which he claimed to be of Scandinavian origin. These Scandinavian claims provoked strong criticism from another philologist, S. Gedeonov 1862. The latter claimed that *rus'* was a purely Slavic word and was of the opinion that a people called *Rus'* or *Ros'* had existed as early as the 7th and 8th centuries in southern Russia on the Black Sea coast. (See 1.7, 1.8.1, 1.8.2 for further details on the river-name hypothesis.)

V. Thomsen 1877 was the scholar who was to continue the debate later in the 1870s. Rahbek Schmidt points out that the works of Thomsen contain very little which is actually new. It is, however, customary to take them as the starting point for a more detailed orientation in the topic and this practice will also be followed here.[8]

1.4   Thomsen's (1877) contribution

1.4.1. *The origin of* ruotsi *and* rus' *in Finnish and Russian.* Thomsen is of the opinion that the arguments of the Anti-Normanists are not entirely implausible. In particular he points out that nowhere within Scandinavia proper is a Scandinavian tribe to be found which calls itself Rus'. This term only occurs in the east during the Viking Age when it is a common name for the peoples who in the west are called Normans. These are the Rus' who had settled in Novgorod and Kiev and who were to lay the foundation of the Russian kingdom. Drawing on earlier research results Thomsen manages to develop a new synthesis of earlier hypotheses. The crucial element here is the name for Sweden in the Baltic–Finnish languages: cp. Finnish *Ruotsi*, Estonian *Roots*, Votian *Rootsi*, Livian *Ruots(l)i*, also cp. Vepsian *Ruottš* meaning 'Finland'. Thomsen considers Old Russian *rus'* to have been clearly derived from the Finnish word for Sweden, *Ruotsi*. It is logical to assume that the Finns must have had a name for their North Germanic neighbours before the East Slavs came into contact with them.

At this point the question of the etymology of Finnish *Ruotsi* arises. Thomsen writes that neither can Finnish *Ruotsi* be plausibly derived from Finnish, nor Old Russian *rus'* from a Slavic language; it is, in all probability, a Scandinavian word. There is, however, no direct etymological one-to-one relationship between the *Ros-* of *Roslagen* in East Sweden on the one hand, and *ruotsi* or *rus'* on the other. The point of contact has therefore to be reconstructed via compounds of the type *roþ(r)s+mæn*, *roþ(r)s+karlar*, *roþ(r)s+folk* or similar compounds with the prefixal *roþ(r)-s-* 'rowing'. These compounds designate the main activities and the way of life of the coastal Swedes. Thomsen believes that Swedish emigrants may have referred to themselves in a similar way, using compound names of this type. With the exception of the usage in learned East European circles, no sign of Svear or the like is to be found in the east. The Finns, however, retained only the first part of the compound. The suffix *i-*, which was added, shows that the word belongs to the more recent series of North Germanic loan-words in Finnish and is not older than the Viking Age. According to Thomsen this explanation of Finnish *ruotsi* is quite satisfactory; it offers in all respects 'harmony and logical context' (Thomsen 1919: 346).

The convenient Finnish short-form spread slowly eastwards and was first borrowed by the East Slavs as the form *rusi, rus'*. At this stage of his discussion Thomsen makes two important comments: Finnish *uo* from earlier *ō* was a sound which was lacking in Proto-Slavic. Therefore it is rendered as *u* in Old Russian (cf. Finnish *suomi* and Old Russian *sum'*). Furthermore, the Finnish origin of the suffix *-i* in *rusi* and the ensuing palatalization of *s* into *s'* (*rus'*) are dealt with, a phonological phenomenon in Slavic which presupposes the typical Finnish suffix *-i*. In addition to this phonological evidence of a non-Slavic origin of the word an interesting observation as to the usage of names in Old Russian must be made: *Rus'* is always used as a collective name in the feminine singular. In Old Russian this is the rule in adopting foreign names – especially those referring to Finno-Ugric tribes – or for the names of peoples borrowed from *Finno-Ugric* languages, where the suffixal form is a common morphological characteristic. Thomsen reports a series of illuminating examples of this type of name:

> Old Russian *jam'* 'the Tavastians' (cp. Finn. *hämäläinen* 'Tavastian')
> *ves'* 'the Vepsians' (cp. Finn. *vepsäläinen* 'Vepsian')
> *perm'* 'the Permians' (cp. Finn. *permalainen* 'Permian')
> *čud'* 'the Chuds' (cp. Finn. *tšuudi* 'Chud').

An important phonological feature is the assimilation of the dental cluster *ts* in Finnish, which appears in Old Russian as *s*. Thomsen points out that in south-eastern Finland there is evidence of a dialectal pronunciation of *ts* as *ss*. Above all he stresses the impossibility of a Slavic *i*-stem ending in *-si* or *-s'*. However, a folk-etymological derivation from the adjective *rusŭ* (Russian *rusyj* 'blond') might have been a contributory factor in the choice of the forms *rusĭ, rus'*.

1.4.2. *In Arabic, Greek and Hungarian.* In Classic Arabic of the period the vowel in *Rūs* is normally long. Here Thomsen suggests a development *ō > ū* as in Latin

Roma > Arabic *Rum*, but he also believes that ō might have remained unchanged here and there in the eastern areas. (See 2.2, where the Arabic terms *Ar-rūs* and *Al-madjūs* are also discussed; compare also the derivation of the latter term in 2.6.)

Of greater interest is the study of Byzantine terminology used to refer to the Scandinavians. Thomsen's merit in this context is that he takes an overall view and does not just examine a detail here and there, even though such details may be important. He deals with the expressions Scythians, Tauro-Scythians, Dromites, ῥῶς (Rhōs), ῥούσιοι (Rhoúsioi), Varangians, and Kolbjazi.

The first three of these names are 'learned-names' – Thomsen reminds the reader that these names occur in Greek sources referring to geographical areas, where the Greeks knew that the ῥῶς (Rhōs) lived (Thomsen 1919: 258). He devoted much time and energy to dealing with the remaining four.

Thomsen stresses a peculiarity of the Middle Greek ῥῶς (Rhōs): the word is generally used without inflection; only in a later period is it sometimes found in an inflected form. Such morphological deviation is found in Byzantine literature only in names of Oriental – predominantly Turkish – origin. Thomsen also makes a comment concerning the ῶ-vowel. If the name ῥῶς (Rhōs) had been borrowed directly from a Slavic language into Middle Greek, the resulting form would have been *ῥοῦς (Rhous). Therefore, the ῶ-vowel points to a Turkish or Khazar intermediate form. Here Thomsen gives as an example the Hungarian form *orosz* 'Russian', the o-prefix of which demonstrates that the word was borrowed into Hungarian via a Turkish language (cf. p. 349f.).

Instead of ῥῶς (Rhōs) another Byzantine expression, ῥούσιοι (Rhoúsioi) begins to occur in the middle of the 10th century. Thomsen is of the opinion that the new term is more closely connected to the Slavic *rus'*, but supposes that the Greeks also thought wrongly that this name had to do with Middle Greek ῥούσιος (rhoúsios) 'red, red-haired'. Thomsen here supports his claim by referring to a statement by Bishop Liutprand mentioned above (cf. pp. 266, 350).

1.4.3. *In West European languages.* In the late Middle Ages the name *rus'* came to the West European peoples via Germany. Thomsen points out that the Swedish y-quality (cf. *ryss* 'Russian') has its origin in German *iu* [y] (cf. Middle High German *riuze* 'Russian'). The form in Middle Latin is first *russi*, *ruzzi*, *ruci* or similar forms, later also *rut(h)eni*, a form not further commented upon by Thomsen. The term *rus'* was thus spread over vast areas of Europe and Asia, but its ethnic content was completely changed as time elapsed. Thomsen concludes: 'It was once the old Slavic term for the Normans, but in its final meaning it was used to refer to a purely Slavic nationality' (cf. p. 350f. and p. 355).

1.4.4. *The origin of the names of the* Varangians *and the* Kolbjazi. In the extended and recurrent discussions concerning the origin of the expressions *Varangians* and *Kolbjazi* Thomsen stresses the following points:

(a)   The *Nestor Chronicle* refers to the Rus' as a group who were subjects of the Varangians. The word Varangian means here 'a Scandinavian'. However, in Russian chronicles a distinction is sometimes made between Varangians and Rus'. The question is what the relationship between the two names is. Thomsen 1919 answers that the Varangians constituted a kind of 'surplus' in the Scandinavian migrations to Russia (ibid.: 357). The expression Varangians is always used in Russian sources in an ethnic sense: 'Scandinavians, especially Swedes'. Consequently, from the very beginning it did not mean a military institution. It is evident from the name of the Baltic in the *Nestor Chronicle*, *varjažskoe more* 'The Varangian Sea', that the meaning 'Scandinavian' or 'Swede' for Varangian is of ancient origin in Russia. The ethnic meaning of the name survives till about 1200 AD, but was known for a much longer period – it was in use as late as 1613 (cf. ibid.: 357ff and 364f).

(b)   In *Greece* the form βάραγγοι (Várangoi) or βάραννοι (Várannoi) was used. Thomsen claims that the original meaning was the same as in Russia and refers to the fact that the name βαραγγία (Varangia) is found in the 11th century with the meaning of 'the Scandinavian peninsula' (Norway). In the same century βάραγγοι (Várangoi) gained the upper hand, whereas ῥῶς (Rhōs) lost ground contemporaneously with the continuing Slavification of the Rus'. Sometimes the two terms fuse into a compound of the type ῥῶς βαράγγων (Rhōs Varángōn). The outcome of the semantic development was that βάραγγοι (Várangoi) was used to denote the members of the Varangian Guard, the Imperial Body Guard in Byzantium (cf. ibid.: 358, 364, 368, 370f., and 371f.).

(c)   In *Arabic* sources the Baltic is also called *bahr warank* and the Warank people are said to live on its coasts. Here Thomsen also discovered the same ethnogeographical use of 'Varangian' at the beginning of the 11th century (p. 365f).[9]

(d)   In *Scandinavia*, according to Thomsen, the term 'Varangian' is semi-foreign. It refers mainly to the mercenaries in the Imperial Guard of Byzantium, but sometimes also to Scandinavians in general. The former meaning can be explained as a result of language usage among Scandinavians who had returned home from Byzantium, the latter meaning can be regarded as a result of semantic borrowing from East Slavic (p. 373).

The etymological derivation of Varangian has caused many problems. Thomsen derives the name Varangian (Swedish *väring*) from a North Germanic stem *vár*, plural *várar* 'pledge' (cp. Old English *wær* 'pledge'). He points out, however, that *várar* was never used to any great extent in Scandinavia as a term for a warrior's pledge. Although it may appear as if the word contains the derivational suffix *-ingi*, Thomsen is of the opinion that it is a compound (cp. Old English *wær+genga*, 'a man who offers his service to another master, another people' or the like). The loss of the initial consonant *g* of the second part of the compound is parallel with that of Old Norse *foringi* from **forgengi*.[10] The normal military interpretation 'guard, sentinel' etc. appears to him completely unsatisfactory. Instead he claims that those Scandinavians who settled on the other side of the Baltic originally called themselves Varangians (Swedish *Väringar*). Then the content of the name changed in Russia, perhaps quite early, and it was used here instead to refer to the inhabitants of Scandinavia, especially those of Sweden (p. 374ff). As regards the phonological similarity between Swedish *Väring* and Russian *Varjag* (Old Russian *varęgŭ*), Thomsen makes an interesting observation. The Old Russian word-formation suffix *-jag*, i.e. *ja* from an older suffix *-en* or *-ę*, is borrowed from an East Germanic language (Gothic?), as in most words containing this suffix, but it occurs *several centuries before the Viking Age*. This word-formation suffix has been transferred by analogy to the word which was to become *Varjag* in Russian; this did not happen in the case of more recent Scandinavian names in Russian like *Igor* (Old Swedish *Ingvarr*) and *Emig* (Old Swedish *Hemingr*) (cf. p. 363, footnote 1). According to Thomsen, the other expression in Swedish, *Kylfing*, which in many respects is parallel with *Väring*, is the term used for a certain part of the Scandinavian population in Russia during the Viking Age, perhaps that in Novgorod in particular. Among the mercenary forces in Byzantium there were also troops of *Kylfingar*, Middle Greek κούλπιγγοι (Koúlpingoi) or κούλπιννοι (Koúlpinnoi) during the latter part of the 11th century. The Old Russian form for this name was *kolbjag* (< *kŭlbęgŭ*), plural *Kolbjazi*. In Scandinavia this name is known from the runic inscriptions and from the saga literature. In one passage in *Hauksbók* we find that *Kylfingaland* was called *Garðaríki*. Accordingly the role played by the Kolbjazi was so prominent that they could lend their name to Russia. Thomsen's opinion is that the word *kylfing* was probably derived from Old Norwegian *kylfa* 'club' and it therefore means 'man with a club' (cf. 1919: 386f).

The course of events in the history of the Rus' and their accomplishments as founders of states in Finno-Ugric and Slavic territories is described by Thomsen in roughly the following way: The Scandinavians began to settle in Novgorod, but it did not remain the major Scandinavian centre in Russia for long. Instead, the conquest of Kiev led to the founding of a truly Russian state. Here, above all, the name *Rus'* had been firmly established for a considerable time. However, by the middle of the 11th century the Slavization of Kiev was far advanced, while a strong Scandinavian element was still to be found in Novgorod; in the 13th century this element yielded to an ever-increasing German influence (cf. p. 355 and 380ff). Thomsen's research and conclusions have been widely accepted by Swedish historians and philologians. It is therefore entirely appropriate to examine his results critically here.

1.5 Critical examination of Thomsen's 1877 *Roþs*-hypothesis

Thomsen's reflections on the possible derivation of Middle Greek ῥούσιοι (Rhoúsioi) and the folk-etymological influence of Old Russian *rusŭ* 'red' are of doubtful value. His etymological explanations of Swedish *väring* and *kylfing* are difficult to reconcile with the actual use of these names – especially in the former case. Why should the Varjazi, a race with a dominant political role, call themselves by a name which was identified with a race which had submitted to another chief and to a different people? Furthermore, if the forms in Old Russian *Varjazi* and *Kolbjazi* point towards a far older period than the Viking Age, why should we assume that these names developed by analogy at a later date? The objection to Thomsen's conclusions about the derivation of Old Russian *rus'* are even stronger. His starting point is Old Norse *roðr* and Old Swedish *roþer*, masculine; genitive *roðrar*, *roðar* 'rowing'. A compound containing this prefixal morpheme of the modern Swedish type *rodds-män* 'rowing men' is not found during the Viking Age, since during this period the word-formation morpheme was /-a-/ not /-s-/; the *a*-genitive in noun compounds still existed in the era of the Swedish provincial laws between 1250–1350, e.g. *roþa+rum* 'space for rowing' and *roþa+rætter* the 'law of rowing'. Thus the prefixal form *roþa-* cannot be the source of a Finnish short form *ruotsi*, which has preserved a genitive *s*-form.

Moreover, a deletion of the nominative suffix /-r/ in *rōþr* to *rōþ-* during the Viking Age is not very plausible either. But even if such an early deletion had occurred, the triple consonant-cluster in compounds of the type *roþs+mæn* would have given rise to the form **rosmæn*; the dental fricative of the stem /-þ/ would first have been deleted, since the genitive /-s/ is stable.[11] Here one can compare Finnish *puosu* 'boatswain' from Swedish *båtsman* which Thomsen exemplifies as one of the loan words in Finnish containing syncopized short forms. The tendency in Swedish towards a weakening of /-t/ in the cluster /-tsm-/ may have caused a deletion of the dental stop in the Finnish pronunciation of *puosu*. Finnish *ruotsi* cannot possibly be derived from the Old Swedish genitive **roþ(r)s-* as a prefixal noun in a compound.

Hjärne 1947 has suggested another solution, drawing upon an idea of Ekblom's 1915.[12] He reconstructs a word **rōþr*, neuter, 'ship'; its plural form **rōþrin* is supposed to have been reinterpreted as a singular masculine form with the loss of the suffixal /-r/. Ekbo 1958 tested this proposal and draws the following conclusion: The word probably existed before 1000 AD in Scandinavia, at least in the west; it is possible that it had the meaning of 'rowing' or that it denoted something more concrete 'that which is used to row with', and also – though less probably – '(rowing) ship' or 'rowlock'. This hypothesis is, however, based on 'very uncertain evidence and the compounds suggested for such a word naturally appear even less plausible'.[13] Such claims must lead to a negative view of Hjärne's first idea of a recategorization of the plural form.

Another hypothesis which departs from the reconstructed plural form mentioned above stresses the administrative function of the word. The underlying meaning of the word is 'ship'. Now if an area (Roden) acquires the name 'The Ships', because it consists of a number of administrative units called 'ships' or 'ship-sokes', the term must necessarily have been very frequently used. This usage of the word led to a conservation of the original form.

It is hardly likely that the word **roþrin* changed its plural form or gender, or that the original word was lost. However, Hjärne's proposal that Finnish *ruotsi* might be used as a point of departure for an investigation of the name *Roden* is completely wrong. The two words have nothing in common. Nor is Ekblom's suggestion that Finnish *ruotsi* lost its /-t-/ as a loan word in Slavic and developed into the palatalized form *rus'* of interest for our purposes.[14] There was no /-t-/ of Old Swedish origin which could have been borrowed into East Slavic.

Another phonological observation can be included in this context. Wiklund 1947 made some observations and drew some conclusions regarding a North Lappish form *ruoššа* 'Russian' or 'Russia'. He was of the opinion that this form could not have been an underlying form of modern Finnish *ruotsi* or Russian *rus'*, but must necessarily have been a much older borrowing from Finnish. In 1948 Collinder pointed out that 'Russian *u* as a rule changes into *uo* in older East Finnish and Karelian loan words from Russian' and 'that Russian intervocalic *s*, in palatalized or unpalatalized form, appears as *šš* in Karelian'. He reaches the following conclusion: 'It is reasonable to assume that *ruošša* probably entered the East Lappish language area and from there it spread to North Lappish via the province of Karelia.'[15] The underlying form is consequently Old Russian **rusi* or *rus'*. Is it likely that these phonological structures in East and North Lappish were of no interest to Thomsen, who was well aware of the existence of a Finnish dialectal pronunciation *ruossi*? As regards Thomsen's main semantic point – that Finnish *ruotsi* denotes the main activity and way of life of the Swedes as *roþ(r)smæn*, etc. – no further comments are necessary. At the time of the Birth of Christ the names of Gotones (in Swedish: Gutar, Götar) and Suiones (Svear) were well known to the peoples of the ancient world as the names of important tribes in Scandinavia. It is an implausible hypothesis that the names of these major Scandinavian peoples were forgotten by their Finnish neighbours 800 years later simply because the Scandinavians spent a lot of time on ships.

However, it is understandable that Thunman (and also for a time Kunik) was fascinated by the idea of connecting *Roslagen* with Russia. The conclusions of Thomsen's investigation are very difficult to understand in the light of the linguistic and historical evidence we have of the period he examined. It is an enigma how this investigation could have been so influential among Swedish scholars and, in particular, among the philologists.

1.6 The Gothic hypothesis

In 1863 the English scholar R. G. Latham tried to evaluate the evidence for and against the various hypotheses concerning the rise of the East Slavic kingdom. He suggested that the most plausible hypothesis was that the Rus' were Goths. Thomsen 1877 rejects this hypothesis as 'a view involving a confusion which cannot be sufficiently deprecated'.[16] He asserted this, although he was aware that the *-ing* suffix in *kylfing* is still reflected in the Old Russian form *kolbjag* and although he knew that this form had been borrowed from an East Germanic language, very likely from Gothic.

Some evidence, which we owe to the work of 20th-century archaeologists and place-name researchers, can be added here. Above all Ekblom's 1915 study of the nouns *rus'* and *varęg* in the place names of the Novgorod area should be mentioned. He found some 50 examples of these nouns – admittedly statistically a very small corpus.

1.7 The Neo-Anti-Normanists and Neo-Normanists

The Neo-Anti-Normanists appeared on the scene in the Soviet Union in the mid-1930s. This group of scientists placed great emphasis on the research carried out by Gedeonov but added some interesting modifications. Their theory is that both a southern Rhōs and a northern Rus' might have existed which had later been united. The Khazars or the Byzantines were the main foreign influence on the Rus'. In the west Neo-Normanism was a reaction to the Neo-Anti-Normanists. Norrback 1943 presented arguments (the *Law of the Rus'*) based on legal and historical evidence. Karlgren 1947 and Falk 1951 presented linguistic ones (the names of the Dniepr rapids). Stender-Petersen 1953 stressed that a Varangian Khaganate in the north (Ladoga–Novgorod) had been united with another one in the south (Kiev). The direction in which cultural contacts took place was from south to north, not vice versa. With his publication *Svear in the East*, Arbman 1955 made an important archaeological contribution which attracted a good deal of attention. He concludes *inter alia* that archaeological material is lacking which would prove that the Varangians founded the East Slavic kingdom.

1.8   The international symposium on Varangian problems in 1968

The present state of research is accurately reflected in the comments made at the international symposium in 1968 (cf. *Varangian Problems* 1970).

1.8.1. *Šaskol'skij's contribution.* In particular Šaskol'skij's contribution, 'Recent developments in the Normanist controversy', in the same volume is captivating and is also an excellent example of the point of view of the Russian historians dealing with the *rus'*-problem today. Šaskol'skij points out that the problems have now become more complicated than they were previously because numismatic, philological and especially archaeological research has produced so much additional information that was not available in Thomsen's day. The exception is the literary material which has remained unchanged since his day. Moreover new Soviet theories concerning the rise of the Russian state have been proposed since Thomsen's time. To the question as to whether Scandinavian kings and their mercenaries founded the kingdom of Kiev in the 9th and 10th centuries, the Russian scholars suggest the following answer.

Where no state organization existed before, one cannot claim that such a state was founded solely as the result of the activity of a few persons and a detachment of foreign troops. The state as such came into being and developed in a long and complicated process. In every country economic development created new social classes, whereby the state developed in such a way that those new social classes could use it to achieve a dominant political influence for themselves. In the area from Ladoga to the Lower Dniepr the primitive form of civilization ended in the 9th and 10th centuries and a class system developed. This was the reason why a new state was founded. The events leading to its foundation occurred, at the latest, at the beginning of the 9th century. Byzantine sources mention the first state or the 'pre-state' in the southern part of the East Slavic territories and refer to it by the name of Rus' (*Ros, Ros'*) – it had attacked the Byzantine possessions Surož and Amastrida by sea. The development of the state then continued until the first half of the 10th century, when the large East Slavic kingdom was united by a strong ruling class. The Scandinavians took part to a greater or lesser degree in this major 'socio-economic and political' process. However, in ancient Russia there was no network of Scandinavian colonies; the Varangian kings came on the scene at a rather late stage in the development of this state. A comparison between the Scandinavian kingdoms and West European states during the Viking Age and Russia is not possible because states with a definite class structure had existed in the west several centuries before the Vikings made their contribution.

Information exists on the Scandinavians as far back as the 10th and 11th centuries, but scarcely anything from the 9th century. That is why it is so difficult to interpret the passage dated 839 in the *Annales Bertiniani*. As far as the Arabic literary sources are concerned, it is still a mystery whether they should be considered to contain information on the Scandinavians in eastern Europe. No Arabic chronicler states that the Rūs are Scandinavians; some of them tell us that they were partly Slavs.

The judgement of Russian scholars on the results of the archaeologists is similar. The earliest Scandinavian finds were made in the Ladoga area which was part of East Slavic territory at the end of the 9th century. Here some difficulties arise in connection with the passage in the *Annales Bertiniani* just mentioned. Šaskol'skij comments on this point: 'This conflict is one of the main problems at the present stage of Normanist studies and it is not easy at the moment to find a satisfactory solution' (cf. 1970: 32). Although both the passage and the finds must be reliable, Šaskol'skij is of the opinion that 'the resolution of this conflict is the task of future scholars' (cf. ibid.: 33). In considering the linguistic problem with *rus'*, Šaskol'skij says that a reference to Finnish *ruotsi* is not sufficient evidence to prove that *rus'* is a Scandinavian word, nor that it is derived from *ruotsi*.

1.8.2. *The river-name hypothesis.* During the past few years an old hypothesis has been revived, i.e. that *rus'* is originally a term for a southern river which has no connection with the Scandinavians (cf. especially Knauer 1912–13). Some 40 passages in various chronicles are quoted to lend support to the hypothesis that *Rus'* meaning 'Russia' was used in ancient times in a limited sense to refer to the central area of the Dniepr and was later used in a more extended sense for the entire Russian state; the former use of the word is considered to be the original one and occurs above all in the East Slavic states which were founded *before* the Scandinavians arrived; and consequently they cannot have been involved in founding these states.

1.8.3. *The Swedish names of the Dniepr rapids.* Šaskol'skij agrees with Falk's 1951 and Karlgren's 1947 view that the names of the Dniepr rapids, which occur in the description of Constantine VII, are 'Swedish', but he still has reservations: 'It is still a mystery why the "Russian" names in the work of the Byzantine emperor derive from Swedish' (Šaskol'skij 1970: 34).

1.8.4. *The derivation of the name* Rus' *– an unsolved problem.* In his conclusion Šaskol'skij writes:

By and large, the question of the origin and semantic content of the word *rus'* remains one of the most complex and intractable problems of the Normanist controversy. The innumerable, mostly valuable and fundamental enquiries of the last decades have provided a greater insight into this question, but have also shown that the difficulties facing scholars are more serious than previously believed (1970: 34–5)

it is at present impossible to see, as some writers still do, the Normanist problem with Vilhelm Thomsen's eyes and consider it to be long solved (ibid.: 37).

Šaskol'skij goes on to propose international interdisciplinary research and hopes the increasing amount of archaeological material will continue to be researched.

In the discussion of Šaskol'skij's important paper Rahbek Schmidt points out that in the Soviet Union the documentary material is now being more realistically evaluated. It is now officially admitted that dynasties of Scandinavian kings existed in ancient Russia. At the symposium another participant stressed the fact that the kings of Scandinavia maintained connections with the rulers of Novgorod and Kiev right down to the days of the Valdemar kings of Denmark – and that without any apparent linguistic difficulties![17]

1.8.5. *Obolensky's contribution.* At the symposium on Varangian Problems in 1968 D. Obolensky presented another interesting study entitled: 'The Byzantine sources on the Scandinavians in Eastern Europe'. Some aspects of this paper will be discussed here.

Not until 860, when the Kiev state launched a sea attack with 200 ships against Byzantium, does the denotation ῥῶς (Rhōs) appear regularly in the sources. Obolensky notes further attacks in the years 907, 941, 944, 970, 989, and 1043. For two centuries the Byzantine Greeks used the expression Rhōs specifically for 'the ruling classes of Kievan Russia'. The earliest use of the term Rhōs is for the Scandinavian dynasty and the Scandinavian Vikings in its service, but later it is also used for the Slavic subjects in the kingdom.

During Vladimir's attack in 1043 the names Scythians and Tauro-Scythians are used as synonyms for Rhōs; the soldiers were Scandinavians from northern Russia, Slavs and Scandinavian auxiliaries.

Obolensky points out that the Byzantine sources completely ignore the Slavization process to which the Scandinavian element in the Kingdom of Kiev was gradually subjected. The choice of first names in the royal house shows that the trend in the middle of the 10th century was in favour of the Slavs. But what Obolensky calls 'the Old Swedish language' had not yet died out in Kiev; evidence for the survival of this language until about 950 is provided by the names of the Dniepr rapids as written in *De Administrando Imperio*. The names are rendered both in the language of the Rus' and Slavic. Of course the vital question is which of the two languages was the primary one. Obolensky stresses the following fact: At the time when the Greek text was written, *the area of the rapids was outside the Slavic region of settlement*. Obolensky is of the opinion that the fact that the Dniepr rapids have *Rūsian* names in a Greek graphemic representation must mean that the Rhōs were considered to be Scandinavians in this period. (According to Obolensky the name *Varangian* is found for the first time in the works of Georgios Kedrenos (1034) in the form of βάραγγοι (Várangoi). The word is a synonym for Rhōs in this period. Both names are actually combined (Rhōs–Várangoi) during the 11th century in eight imperial golden documents. He underlines the importance of complementing the Byzantine data with Slavic, Arabic and Western European facts when the *rus'*-problem is being studied as a whole. He summarizes his own point of view in the following way:

Next to the *DAI* and the *Russian Primary Chronicle* considerable importance should be attached to two early medieval texts, which, though not Greek, go back to information derived from Byzantium: the Bertinian Annals, which state that in 839 the Rhōs were recognized as Swedes; and the statement of Liutprand, Bishop of Cremona, who in describing his visit to Constantinople in 968 enumerates the northern neighbours of the Byzantine Empire: among them he lists 'Rusios quos alio nomine Nordmannos appellamus' (cf. Obolensky 1970: 164).

1.9   Recent contributions from Scandinavian philological research

In two articles which both appeared in 1958, Ekbo and Mägiste investigated the place-name *Roden* and Finnish *ruotsi* respectively.[18]

Ekbo presents some strong arguments against Thomsen 1877. He points out the long period of time which separates Thomsen's examples of loan words in Finnish containing short forms, (e.g. *puosu* 'boatswain' derived from Swedish *båtsman*, *huovi* 'a court servant' from Swedish *hovman*, *riksi* 'a coin' from Swedish *riksdaler*) and the word *ruotsi*, the short form which Thomsen assumed to be the underlying form of *rus'*. Even more remarkable is the following passage in Ekbo's article: 'It is important to note that Thomsen's proposal that compounds were the underlying forms of the Finnish word (*ruotsi*) is based on assumptions which cannot be sustained in the face of evidence which has since come to light' (1958: 196). Ekbo does not reject the compound hypothesis entirely, however: It is possible that in compounding Old Swedish **roþer-* might have acquired a second noun which began with an /-s/, i.e. of the type **roþ-sæssar* 'men who sit together on the rowing bench'. He himself commented on such a hypothesis in the following critical terms: 'One is in fact moving here far out on the insecure grounds of the swamps of hypothesis' (ibid.: 196f).

Ekbo states that we know practically nothing about the compounds of this type from the 7th and 8th centuries. Moreover we do not even know whether they could be rendered as *ruotsi* in the Baltic-Finnish of this period. In order to trace the development of this form one has to take as a semantic starting point Old Swedish *roþer* in a concrete sense 'a war fleet' and as a morphological starting point the older form **roðR*, 'the R of which has been replaced in Finnish by *s*, and the suffix *i* was added later' (ibid.: 197). However, there is no corresponding example of a North Germanic loan word in Baltic–Finnish, 'which would demonstrate the case of a nominative suffix from the Nordic source combining with the Finnish *i*-suffix' (ibid.: 199). Ekbo seems to be of the opinion that the Estonian form *roots*, which acquired its *i*-suffix subsequently, is later than the Finnish form *ruotsi*. This seems unlikely.

Ekbo summarizes his work thus:

One could say that no North Germanic word has been discovered which could be considered to be an indisputable source of Baltic–Finnish **rōtsi*. Thus it has not been shown that Finnish *ruotsi* and the words derived from it were borrowed from Old Swedish, although such an assumption is very plausible on the basis of internal evidence. One might be able to justify the hypothesis that it was of Swedish origin, as long as there are no formal obstacles to such a hypothesis. Among the proposals suggested so far, all very far-fetched, the presumably least vague would be that the *-tu*-stem *roþer* is considered to have been an independent word and in an older form the source of Baltic–Finnish **rōtsi* which achieved such widespread acceptance among the East European peoples (ibid.: 199).

Mägiste (1958) also suggests that **rōtsi* was the underlying form of Baltic–Finnish *ruotsi* in the 9th century and the beginning of the 10th century. Corresponding loan words in a number of Finno-Ugric and Samoyedic languages are derived from this form. The characteristic differences in meaning between 'Swedish' or 'Sweden' on the one hand, and 'Finnish' or 'Finland' on the other derive from the original Finnish meaning of 'Swedish Varangian'. Mägiste regards the *i*-stem *rōtsi* as Baltic–Finnish which was very probably one of the Germanic words borrowed into Baltic–Finnish during the period up to 1000 AD. It is not necessary to insist that its suffix exactly corresponds to that of the North Germanic source noun. 'The main point is that an appropriate North Germanic stem is reconstructed, from which the Baltic–Finnish form *rōts-* can be derived, e.g. North Germanic *rōþs-* or *rōðR-*, where R is pronounced as ž or rž, or from something which corresponds to this form' (cf. Mägiste 1958: 207). A Finnish etymon has been suggested but is very implausible; 'this suggestion could be considered, only if every proposed North Germanic origin of the term *rōtsi* were rejected by Scandinavianists'. From Wiedemann's dictionary (1869) Mägiste excerpts the Estonian form *root's*, genitive *root'si*, *rood'zi*. As can be seen, this form is identical with the Baltic–Finnish stem *rōts-* which Mägiste suggests was the original stem. Consequently, I regard the form *rōts* (*rōþs*) as a common basic Finnish form.

Judging from Ekbo's and Mägiste's studies the word *rōts* or *rōþs* is neither a Finnish word nor a North Germanic loan. What Ekbo refers to as a less vague hypothesis in his defence of the second possibility is still too vague to be taken seriously. In view of the tremendous impact which the word *rōts* (*rōþs*) had, it is necessary to explain the linguistic circumstances in terms of very simplistic but strong arguments.

Almost all philologists agree that the original word underlying Finnish *ruotsi* must be Scandinavian. It is a well-known fact that Germanic settlers were the dominant political force in Kiev and Novgorod during the Viking Age. The Scandinavian names of the Dniepr rapids are evidence of this fact. Therefore the word *rōts* (*rōþs*) in common Finnish should be regarded as an ethnic name borrowed from the *Scandinavian masters of the Finnish tribes in Russia*. According to the passage in the *Annales Bertiniani* of 839 they called themselves Rhōs (in the Greek written form) (cf. 3.1). Since we know that the Proto-Slavic stem form was something like *rusi* 'the red–blond', which yielded *rus'* in Old Russian (cf. 3.1), we need another stem form for Finno-Ugric which yields in its turn *Roots* in Estonian and *Ruotsi* in Finnish, both meaning 'Sweden', that is the Gothic form *rauþs* 'The Red–Blond Man', which is the masculine, singular form in the nominative.

The naming of the Goths in the feminine singular (*rusi*) by the Slavs might to some extent have had an influence on the Gothic language spoken in Russia in the past. This is the third alternative for an explanation of the forms *Roots* and *Ruotsi* in Estonian and Finnish respectively.

In his monograph study of Swedish commerce and politics in the period around 1000 AD, Collinder made an important contribution to the problem in focus here (cf. 1975: 78ff.). He quotes a passage in the introductory section on the geography of the world in Snorri Sturluson's *Heimskringla*: 'North of the Black Sea Great or Cold Sweden is situated' – *Svíþjóð in mikla eða in kalda*. 'Some say that Great Sweden is no smaller than Great Serkland; some compare it with great Blackland. The northern part of Sweden is uninhabited on account of the frost and cold, just as the southern part of Blackland is desolate because of the burning sun. In

Sweden there are many peoples and many languages' . . .[19] Collinder points out that the archaeological investigations around Grobin in 1929–30 seem to confirm that a Swedish Gutnish colony existed there during the period 650–850 and that the fortifications were Swedish, which supports the correctness of Rimbert's report of successful Swedish military activities in Kurland in the middle of the 9th century.

Collinder does not consider the story of Rurik in the *Nestor Chronicle* to be very reliable source material since it has too many of the stereotyped features of a Calling-in Legend. The chronicle has, however, preserved two well-known treaties between the Rus' and the Greeks in 912 and 945. According to Collinder the Rūsian personal names in the texts of 912 are completely Scandinavian; in those of 945 they are as a rule Scandinavian but they are also interspersed with Slavic names. There are no unmistakably Finnish names. Collinder explains that the Rūsian names of the Dniepr rapids unmistakably demonstrate that Old Scandinavian was the language of the Rus'. In addition to these points Collinder cites Ekblom's 1915 observations on Scandinavian place-names in the Novgorod area, the passage in the *Annales Bertiniani*, and the information contained in Liutprand's works. On the strength of all this evidence Collinder concludes that during the first half of the 10th century the leaders of the Rus' were Scandinavians, in particular Swedes, and that they exerted a military and commercial dominance in the east.

Concerning Finnish *ruotsi* Collinder writes that the word is derived from a common Finnish *rōtsi or rōþsi, a word which also entered Lappish, probably via Karelian. The name should be treated as a loan from Old Swedish into Finnish perhaps during the 8th century. It corresponds to the prefixal roþs- in *Roþsland 'the coastal area of Uppland (and Gästrikland)'. Then Collinder discusses the linguistic development of the word and its spread into Proto-East-Slavic along the same lines as Thomsen 1877 and Ekblom 1915. He concludes: 'die Identifikation schwed. rōþs-, finn. *ruotsi*, russ. *rus'*, griech. ῥῶς, arab. *rūs* ist ganz einwandfrei. Die Versuche, die man gemacht hat, das Wort rus' anderweitig zu erklären, sind gescheitert' (cf. 1975: 83).[20]

In addition to this major philological problem Collinder also deals with several other problems. He discusses Russian *varjag*, which occurs in Runic Swedish in the form of VIRIKR (= *väringR*). The word is consequently Scandinavian; it is derived from *vár* 'oath, pledge' and its meaning is – in Ekblom's 1915 formulation – 'gens engagés par serment à s'entr'aider'.[21] In Russia the Varangians were active as merchants, also as soldiers, and in Byzantium as bodyguards of the emperor. Russian *kolbjag* is considered by Collinder to be a Scandinavian word: *kylfing*, a derivation from *kolv* 'blunt arrow', a weapon used in hunting smaller furred animals. He regards the Kolbjazi (Swedish Kylfingar) as Swedish free-booters who possibly lived in southern Finland and were competitors of the Norwegians, Finnish Cwens, and Karelians in the fur-trade in Lappland (cf. ibid.: 76 and 85).

1.10   Scandinavian philological research on north and east European place names: an overview

It is hardly an overstatement to say that Collinder 1975 succeeded in summarizing the major viewpoints to be found in Swedish historical and philological research.

A remarkable observation can be made here: Thomsen modified his earlier view as to the connection between the stem *roþs-* and the words *ruotsi* and *rus'*, which he had at first thought to have been of a geographical nature. Later he suggested that these names should be connected with 'the main occupation and way of life' of the coastal Swedes (cf. 1977: 345). Nowadays Scandinavian philologists – such as Collinder, Svennung and Kiparsky – seem to stick to the old theory which Thomsen himself had long since abandoned – the *Roþs* hypothesis. However, the province of Roslagen has never been such an important political, demographic or economic force that the hypothesis suggested by the linguists above would seem even approximately plausible. Collinder's interpretations of the names *Ruotsi*, *Varjazi*, *Kolbjazi*, etc. have been commented upon indirectly above (cf. 1.4.4 and 1.5).

In the research on the rise of the East Slavic kingdom the importance of the place names and hydronymy has been stressed. Swedish contributions in this field have attracted international attention, *inter alia*: Ekblom 1915, Falk 1951, and Karlgren 1947. Russian scholars on the other hand have concentrated on the elements *rus-*, *ros-* and *ras-*. Strangely enough names of this type also occur in South and West Slavic areas which generally are not thought to have had any connection with the activities of the Varangians. One scholar pointed out in 1964 that 46 such names were found in the second half of the 19th century within Slovakia and a further 24 names of this type in Carpato-Ukraine.[22] In Hungary *várong-* names from the 11th century have been discovered. Such discoveries show that the Varangians lived there as well as in the Novgorod area. There are also place names which contain the word *kölpény* (South Slavic *kulpin*), i.e. *kolbjag* (cp. Swedish *kylfing*).[23]

The form *kolbjag* is also found in the place names of the area between Tichvin, Novgorod, and Pskov; that is probably a relic of the role which the Kolbjazi played in the East, as described in the *Nestor Chronicle*, the *Russkaja pravda*, and the *Hauksbók*.[24] In fact the names *Rus'*, *Varangian* and *Kolbjag* occur side by side in the place names and hydronymy of a vast geographical area in eastern Europe.

2   Ethnic characteristics of the Goths and the Rus' in Russia

2.1   Accounts by the Byzantine Greeks

Besides the information already referred to here, Prokopios also makes several interesting observations on the Goths and their way of life. Earlier they were also called Sarmatians, Melanchlains (Black Coats), Scythians or *Gétai*. They all have white skin, red–blond hair, are sturdy, tall and good-looking. When a crowd of Ostrogoths are standing before the Emperor Justinian, he admires their tall stature and physical beauty. Prokopios believes that they all originate from one and the same people.[25] Long before him Tacitus gave a similar description.

2.2   Accounts by the Arabs

In mentioning Prokopios we have reached the period when Russian scientists claim that they found the Rus' mentioned for the first time in a Syrian text. The passage referred to here cannot, however, be used as historical evidence.[26] Another mention of the Rus' is in an account dating from the 6th century and this is documented in an Arabic description from the end of the 14th century. At the coronation of the ruler of the areas around Derbent on the Caspian Sea he was acknowledged as having authority over the countries which belonged to the Rūs, the Khazars and the Slavs. The use of the term Rūs here can be seen as an example of anachronistic use of names by Arabic authors.[27]

Some decades later, in 626, the Avars attacked Byzantium. A Byzantine chronicler of the 12th century gives us some information about this attack, which Gedeonov investigated with great interest. He found the Tauro-Scythians mentioned, evidently as allies of the Persians and the Avars. The Byzantine chronicler identified them with the Rus', which was a natural reaction, since he wrote his thoughts down in the 12th century. Gedeonov finds it especially striking that the Tauro-Scythians were characterized as a sea-faring people. This is not a characteristic of the Turks. Therefore he considers the passage to be important and not just an invention. It is true that Prokopios also speaks of Tauro-Scythians, but Gedeonov says that he does not understand which people Prokopios is referring to.[28] It should be noted in this context that if the Tauro-Scythians referred to Rus' in 626, it is unlikely that the name could have had any other meaning in the middle of the 6th century. The meaning of the term 'Scythians on the Crimea' is clarified by the fact that Prokopios used Scythians as a synonym for Goths. Their skill as sailors was not doubted by anyone who lived on the Black Sea. In a manuscript of Tabarī's Arabic chronicle translated into Persian by Belamī in the 10th century, there is some information about the Rus' in connection with an Arabic war in Azerbaydzhan in 644. A comparison with the Arabic original shows, however, that the term Rus' has been inserted by the translator.[29] Of course Gedeonov also refers to this text in order to support his hypothesis, which was not accepted everywhere in his day, that the Rus' lived on the Black Sea (čornomorskaja rus') as early as the 7th century.[30] The Rus' are also mentioned a couple of times in the Epic Shāhnāme by Firdosī. One mention is at the beginning of the 5th century, another is during the period 590–628; neither of these is convincing, however.[31] The passages containing Rus' in the historical sources just mentioned have not greatly interested Swedish scholars. This lack of interest is a consequence of the following premise: No man from Scandinavia can possibly have visited southern Russia before the Viking Age. With the same reasoning Gedeonov came to the following conclusion in line with his own view on this matter: Since the Rus' existed on the Black Sea in the 7th century and since the Scandinavians appear there at the earliest in the 9th century, the Rus' must be of Slavic origin.

The term Rus' cannot be said to be used in any Arabic or Persian historical source before it occurs in the entry of the Annales Bertiniani in 839. Only a few years later, in 845, Ibn Khordādbeh gives a report on the Ar-rūs and their trading journeys, for instance, to the Caspian Sea and Bagdad. In this text it is stated that the Rus' were a type of Slav.[32] But in 891 another Arabic chronicler writes about the Viking attack on Seville in 844, that the attack was carried out by the Al-madjūs, i.e. Northmen, 'who are called Ar-rūs'. Birkeland 1954 comments on this passage: 'This commentary of Jakūbi's is extremely interesting and extraordinary in that he identifies madjūs with rūs; how could he know this?'

Marquart 1903 assumes that Jakūbi (died 897) in Egypt heard of the raid by the *Al-madjūs* through the Mediterranean in 859, when some scattered groups of Vikings are said to have penetrated even as far as Alexandria. To associate these pirates with the Rus' was a natural thing to do.[33] But why raise this question at all? Does not Bishop Liutprand state some decades later that *rusii* – Arabic *rūs* – are Northmen? The information provided by the Arabs that the Rūs are 'some type of Slav' does not contradict this assertion. It depends on the fact that the Rus' were the leading political power in the countries where the Slavs lived, or – as a later Arabic chronicler expressed it – 'the Varangians are the most prominent of the Slavs'.[34]

An important account from a cultural-historical point of view is preserved from the year 860. The apostle of the Slavs, Konstantinos (Kyrillos), set out for a missionary journey to the Khazars who lived close to the Crimea in order to convert Muslims and Jews. The following Latin passage is quoted:

Invenit vero ibi evangelium et psalterium *rossicis litteris* scriptum, et hominem invenit loquentem illa lingua et locutus cum eo vim sermonis accepit, et cum sua lingua conferens discrevit litteras et vocales et consonantes, et ad deum orationem mittens mox coepit legere et loqui, et multi eum admirabantur, Deum laudantes.[35, 36]

What Konstantinos found was a gospel-book and psalter written 'in Rus' script'. By talking to a person who spoke the language he succeeded in analysing the texts, so that he could finally read them and speak in the same language. Scardigli (1973) makes the following comment on this point: 'Wir finden es weder schwer vorstellbar noch verwunderlich, einen in gotischen Buchstaben geschriebenen Text mit Worten dieser Art charakterisiert zu sehen.'[37] We can only agree with this statement. In the 830s a letter written in runes (*more ipsorum* by King Björn of Sweden to Emperor Louis) is mentioned for the first time.[38] But is it likely that Vikings from Svealand occupied themselves with writing down gospel-books in runes on the Crimea? The Rus'-script mentioned above was Gothic.

2.3   Accounts by Ibn Fadlan and Ibn Rusteh

The well-known descriptions of the Rus' by Ibn Fadlan (922) and Ibn Rusteh (after 922) also give us important insights into the physical and psychological characteristics of the people: They are a tall handsome people with splendid physique, reddish hair and skin colour. No attention is paid to medical care – a sick person is left isolated in a tent with only bread and water; and the illness is allowed to take its course. The wife or a female slave accompanies the husband into the grave. Alcoholism is common.[39] This misuse of alcohol is also mentioned in the *Nestor Chronicle*. In 986 Vladimir heard some Muslims describe their religion and he reacted utterly negatively on one special point: 'The part which dealt with prohibition against drinking displeased him entirely. But circumcision and abstinence from pork and wine were also disagreeable to him. "Drinking", he said, "is the joy of the Rus'. We cannot exist without that pleasure"' (cf. *Nestor Chronicle* 986).[40, 41]

2.4   The attacks on Constantinople and on the Caspian Sea area

The fierce attack on Constantinople by the Rus' in 860 marked the beginning of a series of military encounters between the Rus' and the Eastern Roman Empire. These attacks are recorded in a number of interesting accounts and descriptions in Byzantine historical literature. In this context no closer study of such descriptions is intended here, but some remarks seem to be justified. Shortly after the attack of 860 the Patriarch Photios of Constantinople sent a letter to the Bishops of the Orient. He writes in this letter that the Rus' had dared to attack the Roman Empire *after having subdued the peoples who lived around them.*[42] It is evident that what is meant here is the consolidation of their kingdom which had taken a long time. This point is supported by an argument which is particularly stressed by Russian historians: We are confronted with extensive organizational accomplishments and military operations on such a large scale that a handful of warriors called in from Scandinavia hardly could have carried them out. In order to illustrate the magnitude of these undertakings one only need refer to Arabic sources. In a geographical description Masūdi (died 956) reports on a naval expedition undertaken by the Rus' in the Caspian Sea for several months in 912–13 after an agreement with the Khazars. At the outset of this enterprise their strength is reported to have been 500 ships, each with 100 men on board; after the decisive defeat their losses are estimated at 30,000 men. Ibn Miskawaih (died 1030) describes a major naval expedition in 943–44; this time the attack was directed at a place in Azerbaydzhan.[43]

In a chapter of his geographical dictionary Jakūt (died 1229) deals with the Rus' using information drawn from Ibn Rusteh. He estimates the numbers as 100,000; his predecessors give no comparable figures, however.[44]

2.5   Ethnic information in the *Nestor Chronicle* and other sources

What can we establish as the likely date when Scandinavians of the Viking Age appear for the first time in the kingdom of the Rus'? The first information which we possess from historical sources on their appearance is the Calling-in Legend in the *Nestor Chronicle*. It is written here that 'Varangians from beyond the sea' in 859 demanded tribute from the Čuds, Slavs, Maris, Ves' (Vespians) and Krivichi. In 862 after the Varangians had been expelled and forced back to their native country, the above-mentioned tribes with the exception of the Maris asked the three Varangian brothers, Rurik, Sineus, and Truvor in Sweden, to bring their Swedish countrymen (Rus') with them and to come and be their masters (lords).[45] The chronicle is to be seen as having been edited on the basis of old annals, Khazar sources, and oral tradition.[46] The origin of the legend can probably be traced to fragments of the annals. No great credibility can be attached to the continuation of the Calling-in Legend which is too stereotyped to be reliable. But a faint relationship with the facts is still recognizable – a distinct wish to explain why the same Varangians or Rus' were to be found in Russia as well as in Sweden.

The chronicle mentions the Scandinavian Varangians again in connection with Igor's attack on Constantinople in 944 – in a trivial context though: during his preparations for war Igor sent messengers to Sweden to hire men on the other side of the sea for his army which consisted of many ethnic elements: Slavic, Finno-Ugric, and Scandinavian etc.

All the information we have about these Scandinavian travellers in the east is primarily from archaeological data, which give us evidence of their presence in the Ladoga area by the end of the 9th century. In addition to this archaeological material, we have all the information on Scandinavian warriors in Russia which was gleaned from the runic inscriptions of the 9th century and later, from the Icelandic sagas, and from Byzantine, Arabic, Slavic and West European historical texts. In spite of all this varied information we cannot find anything that proves that the Scandinavians were the founders of the East Slavic kingdom which was capable of challenging the Byzantine superpower in the middle of the 9th century, no doubt after a long period of consolidation.

Some geographical names must be mentioned in this context. In Arabic descriptions the Don and the Black Sea are sometimes called the River Rus' and the Rus' Sea respectively.[47] Apart from this Snorri Sturluson used the term *Svíþjóð in mikla* (*Heimskringla* 4.9) 'Great Sweden' for an enormous territory north of the Black Sea. What is a plausible explanation for names such as these being used to refer to vast geographical concepts and specific hydronymy?

The scattered Viking expeditions during the 10th century cannot be the single cause of these names. The *Nestor Chronicle* tells us the following about the relationship between the Rus' and the Slavs: 'But the Slavs and the Russes are one people, for it is because of the Varangians that the latter became known as Rus', though originally they were Slavs' (*Nestor Chronicle* 898).[48] This must mean that the name *Rus'* actually referred to the Varangians, but little by little – as a consequence of a terminological development – it was transferred to the Slavs. The term ῥῶς βαράγγων (Rhōs Varángon) in Greek confirms the words of the chronicle. It was also a natural result that the Scandinavian peninsula was called βαραγγία (Varangía) in Greece, because the information on Scandinavia grew. The expression 'The Varangian Sea' for the Baltic was equally natural in the *Nestor Chronicle*, as it was known that the Varangians in Russia belonged to the same tribe as the Scandinavians.[49]

The Germans came to the same conclusion in Ingelheim, when the delegation of the Rus' were found to be Swedish, which Bishop Liutprand and Jakūbi later confirm with their observations.

However, when the Russian chroniclers wanted to explain this strange identification of the Rus' with the Svear, a pseudo-historical account of three brothers from Scandinavia was a convenient solution – a later counterpart of the native emigration saga of the Goths preserved by Jordanes. The information in the *Nestor Chronicle* that the Varangians were also called Rus' in Scandinavia, is probably due to the incorrect application of a Russian term to Scandinavian ethnic conditions by the Russian chronicler.

2.6   Recent ethnic hypotheses on the origin of names for the Vikings

Legends as to the origin of the Scandinavians are to be found in the west as well. Wikander 1963 stresses the fact that the Arabs of Spain and northern Africa called them *Madjūs*, whereas the Arabs in the east used the term *Rūs*. *Madjūs* with the meaning of 'magician' was a well-known ancient term among the population of Iran who were adherents of Zoroastrianism. Some religious historians have tried to explain why *madjūs* means 'Viking' in the west but not in the east. Could it be that the adoration of fire among the Scandinavians reminded people of the Zoroastrians? Wikander rejects this hypothesis. There were almost no Zoroastrians in the west and, what is more, the adoration of fire in Scandinavian religion occurs in a different form than in Zoroastrianism. The difference between Scandinavians and Zoroastrians was so marked that their ethnic identity could not possibly have been confused. According to Wikander the word *madjūs* seems to 'have lost its original meaning and become a vague term for infidels in general' (cf. 1963: 75).[50] A complete analysis of this strange collection of legends has still to be carried out. The *madjūs* of the western chronicles are by no means Zoroastrians, but are to be understood as prototypes of the Vikings who started harrying the coasts of Spain in the 9th century.

It seems that Arabic scholars in Spain tried to explain the difference in meaning of *madjūs* by interpreting the word in the context of an authentic traditional oral legend which states that the *madjūs* will come from the north and harry Spain every 200 years.[51] According to Wikander the *Madjūs* of the legend are not Zoroastrians. It is also evident that the Visigoths were the prototypes of the Vikings to the inhabitants of Spain. They could not clearly distinguish one Scandinavian tribe from another.

Thus, it is implausible that Arabic *madjūs*, meaning 'Vikings', are understood as being identical with Arabic *madjūs* in the sense of 'Zoroastrian adorers of fire'. Rather we have a case of a homonym with two different meanings.

As far as the derivation of the word *madjūs* in the sense of 'Vikings' is concerned, one can refer to Isidore of Seville (died 636), who claims that both Goths and Scythians originated from Japhet's son Magog. At a much earlier date, this ethnic derivation had caused Josephos to call the Scythians οἱ μαγῶγαι (hoi magōgai) – the name Magog in the plural.[52] A term for the Scandinavians was needed in Spain by the 9th century and the name *Madjūs* 'the Magogs' seemed natural, since the Visigoths were already a nation within Spain and since the name Scythians was inappropriate for geographical reasons. Its Latinized form, *almuiuces*, was probably one of the most remarkable terms for the Scandinavians in antiquity.

3 Ethnic, linguistic and historical evidence for the Gothic origin of the kingdom of the Rus'

After the Goths had reached their new areas of settlement in the Black Sea region the authors and chroniclers of the period developed an ethnic terminology for the Germanic settlers. It is scarcely possible here to uncover much more information about the main stages of this linguistic development. However, it is clear that Prokopios' information is correct on one major point: There was a main term – the Goths – and a number of special tribal names. Among the latter, two names – Latin *greutungi* and *tervingi* – were established as variants of the names Ostro- and Visigoths respectively. These linguistic developments in the west of Europe remind us of the results of a corresponding terminological development in eastern Europe. The main term *Goths* is replaced by the term *Rus'*. This term and the tribal names Varangians (Old Russian Varjazi) and Kylfings (Old Russian Kolbjazi) spread to many peoples in the east. With the exception of Goths, all of these ethnic denotations still require further philological research.

3.1   The Red–Blond-People hypothesis

In a dissertation on the terms for colours in Slavic languages, Herne 1954 investigated the words for the colour red. Among these, two series of expressions occur which can be derived from the Proto-Slavic stems **rūdŭ* and **rūsŭ* for 'red'.[53]

Rūdŭ is claimed to have been derived etymologically from Proto-Indo-European **reudho-* or **roudho-*. It has an exact cognate in Gothic *rauþs* 'red' and Latin *rufus* 'light-red'. (Probably also in Latvian *ruds*, plural *rudi*, 'brown–red'.) The stem is represented also in Russian dialects (southern and western Russia) by the adjective *rudyj* 'red-brown', in Polish by the adjective *rudy* 'brownish, red–yellow', and in Czech by the adjective *rudý* 'dark–red'.

Rūsŭ belongs etymologically to the Proto-Indo-European stem **roudh-so-* or **reudh-so-*. Exact equivalents are lacking in other non-Slavic Indo-European languages. The stem is represented in Russian by the adjective *rusyj* 'light brown', in Polish by the adjective *rusy* 'brown–red', in Czech by the adjective *rusý* 'red–yellow'. The word is to be found in all the major Slavic languages and is used to refer to the colour of the hair.

In Proto-East Slavic (Old Russian) the stems might have given rise to the words **rudi* and **rusi* respectively. The palatalized forms **rud'* and *rus'* arise through assimilation of the plural suffix *-i*, when the words are used in the singular feminine form to denote a collective noun; then they denote 'the red–blond people'. These two words which were both used to denote various shades of redness among the eastern peoples were used to describe the *qualitas corporis* among the Goths (red–blond hair and fair complexion) which, according to Liutprand, was the reason why the Greeks called them ῥούσιοι (Rhoúsioi). As mentioned above in section 1.9 the entry of 839 in *Annales Bertiniani* shows that the Goths themselves accepted the ethnic name Rhōs which was given to them by the Slavs. This Greek form derives from Gothic **rauþs* [roːþs] 'red', which from an etymological standpoint is the exact corresponding form of the Proto-Slavic stem **rudŭ* 'red'. It took a long time before this term **Rauþs* for 'the Goths in Russia' among the Goths themselves was arrived at, partly because Gothic could not automatically adapt to the rules in Proto-Slavic to form collective feminine nouns ending in the suffix *-i*. In Middle Greek the earliest occurrence of the new name (Rhōs) is in 839; it came into common use during the later half of the same century.

3.2   Philological evidence in Russian, Greek and Arabic

It is natural that the Greek spelling ῥῶς (masculine) (Rhōs) like the Arabic form *rūs* should raise many questions. Even if these questions are of limited interest to historians, since nobody denies the connection of these forms with Old Russian *rus'*, some philological observations seem justified. There is no reason to assume that Middle Greek ῥῶς (Rhōs) contains any other vowel than *ō*. This sound did not occur in Proto-Slavic. Therefore Middle Greek ῥῶς (Rhōs) should – like Estonian *Roots* – be considered as identical with Gothic **rauþs*. This form was somewhat simplified, as Middle Greek had no corresponding sound for Gothic þ. The tendency in Middle Greek to inflect the indeclinable word is an indication that the linguistic intuition of the Greeks created resistance to the foreign form. During the 10th century the Rhōs-form was exposed to increasing competition from Middle Greek ῥούσιοι (Rhoúsioi) – a late borrowing in Middle Greek from Latin *russeus* 'reddish'. This etymological relationship tells us a lot about the real meaning of the word *Rhōs*. It would seem very likely that the lack of an *ō*-sound in Proto-East Slavic must have blocked the possibility that Greek influenced the Rus' with regard to the form of the name of their country. On this point, however, the accentuation of the Middle Greek form of the name in the 10th century, ῥωσία (Rhōsía), might have been of some importance, since the unstressed sound ω was certainly pronounced *ŏ*. The consequence was that the Middle Greek form could bring about a variation between the vowels *u* and *o* because of the strong position of Greek as a literary language. Both terms *Rusija* and *Rosija* are found about 1500 (the spelling -ss- about 1700). The name of White Russia was spelled *Belaja Rossija* during the 17th century. The modern spelling is *Belorussija*.[54]

Arabic possessed both long *ū* and short *ŭ*. Arabic *rūs* is most similar to Russian *rus'*. In Jakūt (died 1229) there is a note: '*Rūs* is written with a long *ū*, but (the people) are also called *rŭs* with a short *ŭ*.'[55] It is hardly possible to question the long vowel quality of the name borrowed into Arabic. Arabic *rūs* seems to have been borrowed either from Russian *rus'* or from Middle Greek *Rhōs* with the substitution of Arabic /u:/ for Middle Greek /ō:/. Later on the long vowel in literary Arabic was not quite stable (cf. the quotation from Jakūt).

3.3 Evidence from other European languages

The forms for 'Russia' and 'Russian' in other European languages also seem to support the Red–Blond-People hypothesis. In Old Swedish the early *y*-form of *rysser*, *ryze* (possibly an *Umlaut*-form of **rūssi*, cp. the Proto-Slavic form **rusi* or Old Russian palatalized form *rus'* with Icelandic *rússi* 'Russian, *rússar* Russians'). The *i*-mutated form also occurs in Middle High German as *riuze* 'Russian' (*iu* = [y]) besides the form *rûz* (Old High German *rûzo*, Middle High German *rûze*).[56] In Norwegian *russer* (Old Norwegian *ruzzar*) and Danish *russer* the non-mutated form has prevailed, whereas in Swedish the mutated form *ryssar* 'Russians' became the only accepted form, perhaps also as a result of influence by the Middle High German form *riuze* [ry:(t)sə]. In Middle High German *riuze* the *z* has the sound value of *s*.[57] Numerous similar spellings of the kind, exemplified by *rytzen* in Early New Swedish, are an indication that variants in the pronunciation existed for a long time, at least as far as Scandinavian languages are concerned.

The linguistic circumstances regarding the rise of the various forms for 'Russia' and 'Russian' in European languages are unclear. More philological research is needed to clarify the specific forms in the course of the centuries. Several mixed forms may have entered the ethnic terminology of the European languages.

3.4   The rise of the ethnic name *Rus'* among the Slavs

It was the Slavic neighbours of the Black Sea Goths who introduced the new ethnic name *rus'* to refer to the Goths in the east. It was slowly accepted by other peoples as a loan word and it spread to the rest of the world after a semantic change. From denoting 'the red–blond', i.e. 'the Goths' it acquired the meaning of 'the people of the state in the east'.

In the Old Scandinavian language this denotation 'Rus'' occurs as a loan word. It has nothing to do with the Old Swedish organization of the war-fleet (*ledungs-väsendet*) or with the Medieval name *Roþin* for a coastal area north and south of Stockholm in Sweden (cp. the *Roþs*-hypothesis by Thomsen 1877 in 1.5). It must be stressed in this context that Finnish makes a clear distinction between *venäläiset* 'Russians' and *ruotsalaiset* 'Swedes'. The Finnish tribes of the past knew very well how to make an ethnic distinction between Slavs and Goths. The fact that they referred to the Swedes by the same name as the Goths is not due to an inability to distinguish between these peoples. From a passage in the *Nestor Chronicle*: 'They accordingly went overseas to the Varangian Russes: these particular Varangians were known as Russes, just as some are called Swedes, and others Normans, English, and Gotlanders, for they were thus named.'[58]

This quotation shows that the Slavs knew that the people Rus' in their own country also lived in Scandinavia. The Finnish tribes were just as well, if not better, informed. Thus Finnish *Ruotsi* 'Sweden' and *Ruotsalaiset* 'Swedes' are conclusive linguistic proof of the Scandinavian origin of the Goths.

3.5   The origin of other terms for Scandinavians in the east

The tribal names *greutungi* and *tervingi* in the west (cf. Swedish *grytingar* and *tyrvingar*) and Russian Varjazi and Kolbjazi (cf. Swedish *väringar* 'Varangians' and *kylfingar*) are all Gothic and they are all formed in a similar way, i.e. as nominalizations with an *ing*- suffix. The name form *greutungi* in Latin and *gryting* in Swedish derive from the Germanic stem **greuta-* 'stone ground' (cp. also Swedish *gryt*). The derivation of *tervingi* is unclear, however.

The name *Varjazi* 'Varangians' was so wide-spread in Russia that it tended to become the overall term for the people of Sweden – 'the Varangians beyond the sea'. The etymological derivations suggested so far are misleading. It is most certainly a noun used to refer to settlers and of the same type as *greutungi*, which had possibly been formed from Old Swedish *vara* 'high situated area' etc. It is, however, impossible to trace a tribe with a name of this type in Scandinavia. It is striking that the term seems to have become so frequently used in Scandinavia to refer to the Goths in Russia that *Umlaut* of the stem vowel occurred (cf. the Old Icelandic plural *Væringjar*).

The name Kolbjazi (Swedish *kylfingar*) shows the same features as the name Varangians. In Russia they occur less frequently than the Varangians. This is also the case in Constantinople. Both tribes were represented in the Imperial Germanic Bodyguard (the *Hetaireia*) in the 11th century. This bodyguard is known as the Varangian Guard, but there were some Kolbjazi serving in it, too, in this period. The mercenaries in the guard who came from Scandinavia were even fewer in number than the Kolbjazi. In Russia the terms Varjazi and Kolbjazi are also known with the meaning of 'merchants'; the word Varjazi also denotes 'persons of high stature' in Ukrainian.

3.6 Historical evidence

In the 370s AD the Goths in the east (see Map 1: 362 AD, p. 162) were defeated but their power increased again after the fall of the Huns in the 450s AD. This was the beginning of *The Second Great Gothic Kingdom* in the east which arose in the vast geographical space extending north of the Black Sea. Almost three centuries of continuous efforts were necessary to permanently establish the Khaganate of Kiev, an enormous area which became an extraordinarily strong power in the east. It was populated by a number of different races, but the political power remained in the hands of the Goths. Its military capacity was such that warlike conflicts with Byzantium were a recurrent phenomenon in its political life. In the north a new Gothic centre was built in the area of Novgorod (see Map 2: 923 AD, p. 163). In the east control of the Don Valley was gained as a result of the victory over the Khazars in 969. The situation in the west is illustrated by a strange passage in the *Nestor Chronicle* in which the Khagan Svjatoslav (died 972) says: 'I do not care to remain in Kiev, but I should prefer to live in Pereyaslavets on the Danube since that is the centre of my realm'.[59]

Among an increasing number of eastern peoples Rus' became the common Slavic term for all Varangians and Kolbjazi and was used for all the races who lived in this new kingdom. Rus' is here a parallel to the Gothic name used in the west for all East Germanic tribes.

This semantic expansion of the name Rus' also had a deeper background. Wherever the Goths migrated to they demonstrated the same characteristics: an extraordinary military and organizational capacity together with a high level of cultural development, but offset by an almost total inability to set up political systems which could remain stable for longer periods of time. From a historical viewpoint the states of the Herulians, Gepids, Ostrogoths, Visigoths and the Vandals had political systems which did not last long. Such was also the pattern in the kingdom of the Rus'. Among all the Gothic states their kingdom was to last the longest. As late as the 11th century the major Gothic element is still discernible (see Map 3: 1071 AD, p. 164). The ethnic, linguistic, and cultural process of Slavization prevailed, however. In addition to this we should also mention the fateful effects of the system by which the leadership was passed on.[60] The endless wars must also be considered as a factor contributing to the decline of the kingdom of the Rus'. After the victories of the Tatars in the 1240s the last traces of the Gothic origin of the Khaganate of Kiev disappeared in the south.

In the north the development of Novgorod was somewhat different. Here, too, the Slavization process took place in all spheres of life, but the connections with the North and West Germanic peoples remained intact, in particular as a result of increasing German interest in political and commercial activities in the east – the Hanseatic League. Large areas in the north were governed from Novgorod. When the Egils Saga speaks of trading competition between the Scandinavians and the Kolbjazi, this is to be interpreted as a reflection of the great period of the Goths of Novgorod. The population of the northern state was predominantly Finnish. The state was conquered and destroyed in 1478, when its territories were absorbed by the Grand Duchy of Moscow.

By standard Scandinavian perspective *Svíþjóð in mikla* 'Great Sweden' in the east was an enormously large and rich state, which was both politically and culturally superior to Sweden itself. This 'Great Sweden', as it was called by Snorri Sturluson, cannot possibly have been a result of political activities on the part of the Swedes alone. Snorri Sturluson has been misunderstood by those historians who interpret 'Great Sweden' in this sense. 'Great Sweden' must rather be interpreted as referring to the extremely large Germanic/Gothic kingdom in the east, which was a leading nation, whereas Sweden, as a part of Scandinavia, was one of the small nations. In relation to Scandinavia the Rus' were as a rule the creative partner culturally.

Important economic connections between Sweden and the kingdom of the Rus' can also be reconstructed. A host of numismatic finds throughout Scandinavia, but especially on Gotland and in East Sweden, give us archaeological evidence of intensive trade connections.

The activities of the Scandinavians as mercenaries in the armies of the Rus' or as Varangians in the Imperial Bodyguard of the Byzantine Emperor give us evidence of political involvement in the east. However, in wars against the Khaganate of Kiev, the small Scandinavian states could only marginally influence the outcome in one area, that around Novgorod. Any other strategic influence was impossible for geographical and political reasons.

Conclusion

In modern Gothic studies historians, philologists, and archaeologists working from a variety of evidence have claimed that a subgroup of the Germanic peoples – the East Germanic branch – inhabited the regions on the Lower Vistula around the Birth of Christ. This East Germanic subgroup was dominated by North Germanic tribes.

A common ethnic name for all these East and North Germanic tribes was 'Goths'. It is etymologically derived from the same root as the ethnic names *gautar* and *gutar* in Old Swedish (cp. Swedish *götar* and *gutar* in East and West Götaland and on Gotland).[61] Because of its early appearance in Greek and Latin literature the common name 'Goths' became the dominant ethnic name in the west. A number of other ethnic names for Gothic tribes existed as well.

At the beginning of the 3rd century after the Gothic hordes had emigrated from the areas of the Lower Vistula to those of the Black Sea, where they settled, the *Foundation of the First Great Gothic Kingdom* in the east took place, the most famous ruler of which was Ermanarik. This kingdom was destroyed in battles against the Huns between 370 and 380. In the course of historical events (250–500) the Gothic tribes became increasingly separated from each other geographically. Many tribes had converted to Arianism. Some of them marched west and became famous for their military achievements; others remained in the east. Here some very strong tribes, which had remained heathen, were to play an important historical role. They were to initiate *The Foundation of the Second Great Gothic Kingdom* in the east after the fall of the empire of the Huns. The Varangians and the Kolbjazi were the foremost representatives of this new kingdom. Their Slavic neighbours and subjects called their Gothic masters by a common name: the Rus' 'The Red–Blond People'. The following chronology is suggested to explain the rise of the name Rus' and its spread to the south, north, east, and west:

1   150–350 AD. The Slavic name for the Goths is formed with two variants from the Proto-Slavic stems *rūsŭ and *rūdŭ 'red'. This name begins to spread among the Slavs in the form of *Rusi and *Rudi 'the Red–Blond (People)'.

2   Ca. 450 AD. The palatalized Proto-Slavic forms *Rus' and *Rud' (a collective noun in the feminine singular formed in analogy to other ethnic names such as Ves', Čud' etc.) is now a common name among the Slavs for Goths, irrespective of the ethnic origin of the latter. The Proto-Slavic name *Rus' corresponds to the western denotation for 'Goths' (Ostrogoths, Visigoths etc.), but it is different from the latter in that it is of Slavic origin.

3   Ca. 400–600 AD. The Goths in Russia accept the Slavic name for themselves, i.e. *Rus', which they render as *Rauþs [roː þs] in their own language.

4   Ca. 600–800 AD. The Greeks in the south and the Finno-Ugric tribes in the north borrow the *Gothic* form of the ethnic name (*Rauþs) which gives rise to Greek *Rhōs* and Estonian *Roots* 'Sweden' and Finnish *Ruotsi* 'Sweden', the *uo* of Finnish being a later diphthongized form. However, the Arabs borrowed the *Slavic* form *Rus' directly into *Ar-Rus* 'the Rus'.

5   Ca. 800–1100 AD. (a) The Finns as well as the Slavs use the ethnic name also for the inhabitants of Sweden (cp. the forms for Sweden above in Estonian and Finnish and in the *Nestor Chronicle* the mention of the Rus' as being Swedes, year 862).

(b) In Old Russian the ethnic name Rus' denotes to begin with 'people of a Germanic or Scandinavian origin' (cf. the *Nestor Chronicle*, years 860–862), but as time passes and the kingdom of Kiev is established, the name denotes 'the people of Russia'.

(c) In the Scandinavian languages only the latter meaning of *Rus'* has been preserved. Two vowel variants occur, which may reflect two different periods of borrowing: Icelandic *rússi* 'Russian' and *rússar* 'Russians'; Danish and Norwegian *russer* 'Russians'; Swedish *ryss* 'Russian' and *ryssar* 'Russians'.

A long period of expansion marked by continuous military campaigns ended in the foundation of the Khaganate of Kiev. This kingdom conquered in succession enormous geographical areas and acquired tremendous political power. In the south the Khagan of the Rus' competed for power with the Byzantine emperor; in the north Novgorod dominated vast areas up to the Arctic Sea and in the east to the Urals, which were primarily inhabited by Finno-Ugric races. The kingdom of the Rus' reached its peak of power and influence between 700 and 1050 AD. The Goths in Russia demonstrated the same qualities as founders of states as the Goths elsewhere: a military and naval strength which was incomparable and which was coupled with a remarkable inability to maintain their political and cultural independence. As a result of this over-willingness to integrate with other cultures they

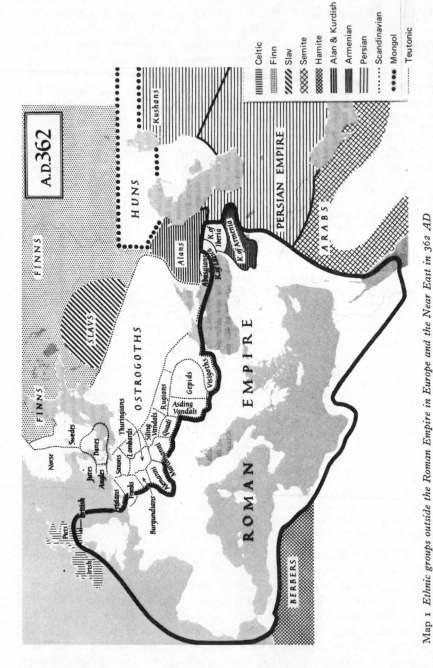

Map 1 *Ethnic groups outside the Roman Empire in Europe and the Near East in 362 AD*
From: C. McEvedy (ed.) *The Penguin Atlas of Medieval History*, Penguin Books, 1961, p. 15. (Reprinted by permission
of Penguin Books Ltd. Copyright © Colin McEvedy, 1961.)

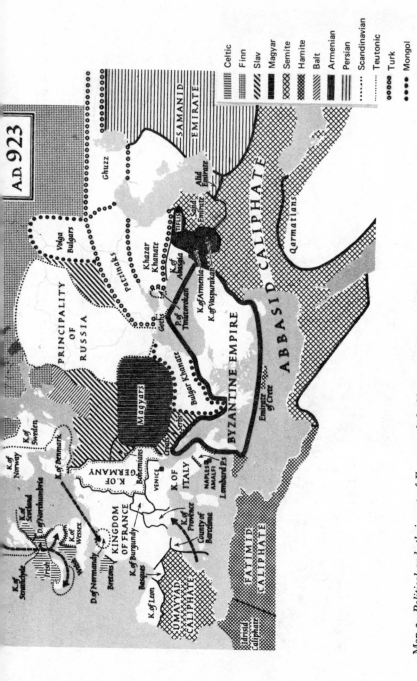

Map 2. *Political and ethnic map of Europe and the Near East in 932 AD*

From: C. McEvedy (ed.), *The Penguin Atlas of Medieval History*, Penguin Books, 1961, p. 51. (Reprinted by permission of Penguin Books Ltd. Copyright © Colin McEvedy, 1961.)

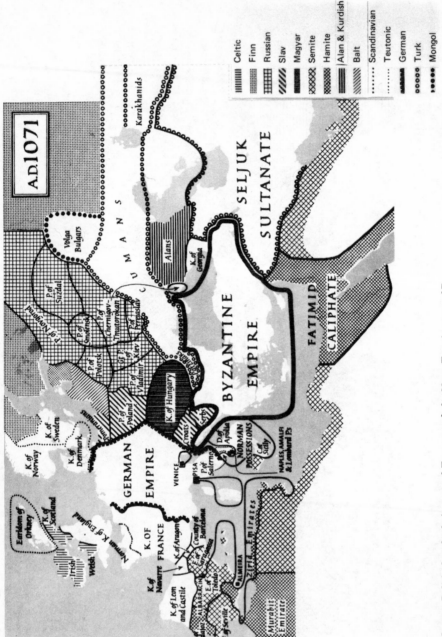

Map 3. *Political and ethnic map of Europe and the Near East in 1071 AD*

From: C. McEvedy (ed.) *The Penguin Atlas of Medieval History*, Penguin Books, 1961, p. 61. (Reprinted by permission of Penguin Books Ltd. Copyright © Colin McEvedy, 1961.)

gave up their ethnic identity, their religion, their language, and their culture. In the east where the mechanisms of decline were slower than in the west, this attitude resulted in a total Slavization and an extremely strong religious and cultural dependence on Byzantium.

The rulers of the Rus' had dynastic connections with the royal families of Scandinavia over a long period. It is the kingdom of the *Rus'*, which Snorri Sturluson still called *Svíþjóð in mikla eða in kalda* (Heimskringla 4.9) – 'Sweden the Great and the Cold'.

The Normanists have interpreted the great military and commercial activities of the Scandinavian Vikings as leading to the foundation of the East Slavic Kingdom (cf. the *Roþs*-hypothesis). However, these activities were of a limited nature. They were only possible within the framework of the Gothic kingdom of the Rus' which was already in existence. Since these activities lasted for a considerable length of time, they had major political, economic, and cultural consequences for Scandinavia as a whole. The kingdom of the *Rus'* was in most respects the creative partner in this historical process.

Notes

1 For valuable information on the Scandinavian philological aspects I would like to thank Dr B. Westlund, Stockholm. While I was working with sources and references written in Russian, Dr I. Kalnins gave me continuous assistance with important references and in interpreting texts. I am most grateful to him for his generous help. The present article is a shorter version of a long article originally written in Swedish with the title: 'Rusernas rike. Till frågan om det östslaviska rikets uppkomst' (cf. Söderlind, 1978). It was translated into English by Sture Ureland and Iain Clarkson.

2 Cf. Schmidt (ed.) 1970 and Schmidt 1970.

3 Cf. Stender-Petersen 1953: 5. A more detailed survey of the Varangian problems and the literature dealing with them is to be found in this publication.

4 The original Latin text in the *Annales Bertiniani* reads as follows under the year 839:

Venerunt etiam legati Graecorum a Theophilo imperatore directi. . . . Misit etiam cum eis quosdam, qui se, id est gentem suam Rhos vocari dicebant, quos rex illorum, Chacanus vocabulo, ad se amicitiae, sicut asserebant, causa direxerat, petens per memoratam epistolam, quatenus benignitate imperatoris redeundi facultatem atque auxilium per imperium suum totum habere possent, quoniam itinera, per quae ad illum Constantinopolim venerant, inter barbaras et nimiae feritatis gentes inmanissimas habuerant, quibus eos, ne forte periculum inciderent, redire noluit. Quorum adventus causam imperator diligentius investigans, comperit eos gentis esse Sueonum. Exploratores potius regni illius nostrique quam amicitiae petitores ratus, penes se eo usque retinendos iudicavit, quod veraciter invenire posset, utrum fideliter eo necne pervenerint; . . . *Annales Bertiniani*, ed. G. Waitz 1883: 19–20.

(Some Greek delegates who were sent by Emperor Theophilos also came. He also sent some others who said that they, i.e. their people, were called Rhōs. Their king, who had the title *Chacanus*, had sent them to him (Theophilos) in order to promote friendly relations, they assured the emperor. Theophilos asked in the letter that they should be given the opportunity and help with the goodwill of the Emperor (Louis) to return through his entire territory (that of Louis), since the route by which they had come to him in Constantinople, had brought them in contact with barbaric and extremely wild and inhuman tribes; he (Theophilos) did not wish them to return by this route so as to avoid them meeting with great danger. In a careful investigation concerning the reason for their arrival the Emperor (Louis) discovered that they belonged to the people of the Swedes (*Sueonum*). Since he was of the opinion that they were spies in his (Theophilos') and our empire rather than persons who wanted to promote friendly relations, he decided to keep them until he could find out with certainty whether they had arrived with good intent or not.)

5 Cf. Collinder 1975: 80. Cp. also the Arabic expression *ḫāqān-rūs* 'the Rus-Chacanus' (cf. Birkeland 1954: 16).

6 Cf. Thomsen 1919: 266, fn. 1. It must be added here that Bishop Liutprand is the author of another famous passage, which deals with a Greek victory over the Rus':

gens quedam est sub aquilonis parte constituta, quam a qualitate corporis Greci vocant ρούσιος [Rhoúsios], nos vero a positione loci nominamus Nordmannos (cf. Thomsen 1919: 267).

(In the north there lives a people whom the Greeks call the Red–Blonds on account of their appearance, but whom we call Northmen, because of the geographical position of their settlements.)

Here it is also evident that the Bishop considers the Rus' who lived in the north in the 10th century to be the people who were called Northmen in the west in the same period.

7 Cf. Strube de Pyrmont 1785: 11:

Il n'est donc guères douteux, que les Scythes, Goths ou Normans, que les Historiens Grecs & l'Evêque de Crémone ont nommés Roos & les Varéges que nos Annalistes ont appellés Rouss, n'aient été les mêmes.

(There is scarcely any doubt that the Scythians, Goths or Normans, which the Greek Historians and the Bishop of Cremona referred to as the 'Roos', and the Varangians which our Keepers of Annals (annalists) called the 'Rouss' were not the same people.)

8 The following points are taken from Thomsen 1919: 339ff.

9 In Birkeland 1954 the following Arabic authors are mentioned who call the Baltic by the name *bahr waṛank*: Nasir ad Dīn (died 1274), al-Qazwīnī (died 1283), Aš-Šīrāzī (died 1311), Abu-l-Fidā (died 1331). Cf. pp. 98, 103, 105, and 118 respectively.

10 Thus according to Thomsen **forgengi* and **wárgengi* should be interpreted as *forgangsmaðr* 'a man who goes in the first line' and 'a man who offers his service to another master' respectively.

11 Cf. Wessén 1951: Section 57.

12 Cf. Hjärne 1947: 28ff.

13 Cf. Ekbo 1958: 192, 196 and Section 1.9.

14 Collinder 1975: 82f. quotes Ekblom's 1915 text.

15 Cf. Wiklund 1947: 32f. and Collinder 1948: 146ff.

16 Cf. Thomsen 1877: 19.

17 Cf. Hammerich 1970: 142.

18 Cf. Ekbo 1958 and Mägiste 1958.

19 Cf. *Heimskringla* 4.9.

20 'The identification of Swedish *rōþs*, Finnish *ruotsi*, Russian *rus'*, Greek ρῶς, and Arabic *rūs* is absolutely certain. Other examples to explain the word *rus'* have been unsuccessful.' (Trans. of German text in Collinder 1975: 83.)

21 'People who are committed by oath to assist each other' (Trans. of Ekblom 1915: 39).

22 Cf. Selnes 1970: 141f.

23 Cf. Székely 1975: 10f.

24 Cf. Johansen 1964.

25 Cf. Prokopios, according to Haury 1905–13, Vol. 1: 311 and Vol. 2: 504 and 298.
26 It is a passage in a work on church history (555) by Zacharias Rhetor. In enumerating various peoples he speaks of a people *herôs* or *hros* (cf. Zacharias Rhetor. German translation ed. by K. Ahrens and G. Krüger 1899: 253). Vernadsky stresses the fact, that, according to A. P. Diakonov, Syrian *hros* is an exact transcription of Middle Greek ῥῶς (Rhōs) (cf. Vernadsky and Karpovich 1943: 258). But the context makes this information worthless. Cf. also Zernack 1958: 18, fn. 22:

In der Gegenwart kamen die sowjetischen Gelehrten immer mehr zu der Auffassung, daß der ethnische Terminus *Rus'* südlicher Herkunft ist. Der bolschewistische Sprachneuerer Marr stand hinter dieser These, die sich auf syrische Quellen des 6. Jahrhunderts beruft.

(In modern times Soviet scholars have increasingly realized, that the ethnic term *Rus'* is of southern origin. Marr, the Soviet linguistic reformer, supported this hypothesis, which is based on Syrian documents dating from the 6th century AD.)

27 Cf. Frähn 1823: 36f.
28 Cf. Gedeonov 1862: 54ff and Gedeonov 1876: 378.
29 Cf. Wikander 1963: 77.
30 Cf. Gedeonov 1862: 54ff.
31 Cf. Wikander 1963: 77.
32 Cf. Birkeland 1954: 10f.
33 Cf. ibid.: 135.
34 Cf. ibid.: 115.
35 Cf. Liewehr 1951–2. The original text is Slavic: see Pastrnek 1902 and 1933.
36 And he found there a book of gospels and a book of psalms written in Rūsian letters and he met a man who spoke in this language. In the conversation with the latter he understood the meaning of this speech. He compared it with his own language and discovered the letters, both vowels and consonants. And with a prayer to God he at once began to read and speak and many people wondered at him and praised God.
37 Cf. Scardigli 1973: 232f. 'We consider it neither difficult to imagine nor astonishing to see a text, which was written in Gothic letters, characterized in such terms.'
38 Cf. Liestøl 1969.
39 Cf. Birkeland 1954: 16ff.
40 Cf. translation of the *Nestor Chronicle* by Cross and Sherbowitz-Wetzor 1953: year 986.
41 A comparison between this description and that of Tacitus and Prokopios shows us that the characteristics of the Goths, the Herulians and other Germanic tribes are very similar.
42 Cf. Thomsen 1919: 255.
43 Birkeland 1954: 34ff and 54ff.
44 Ibid.: 82.
45 Cf. *Nestor Chronicle*, years 859 and 862.
46 Cf. Davidson 1976: 62.
47 Cf. Birkeland 1954: 11 and 116.
48 According to the translation into English by Cross and Sherbowitz-Wetzor 1953: 898. Russian original text according to *Laurentius manuscript*:

A Sloven'skyj jazyk"i Ruskyj odno est', ot" Varjag"bo prozvašasja Rus'ju, a pervoe běša Slovene (*Die Nestor Chronik*, ed. Dimitrij Tschiževskij, 1969: 28).

49 Cf. the passage in the *Nestor Chronicle* which demonstrates the ethnic identity between the Varangians and the Rus'. The Russian text: *Nestor Chronicle*, year 862.

I ot″ těch″ (Varjag″) prozvasja Ruskaja zemlja, Novugorod′ci, ti sut′ ljud′e Novogorod′–ci ot″ roda Varjaž′ska, preže bo běša Slověni (*Die Nestor Chronik*, ed. Dimitrij Tschiževskij 1969: 19).

Translation into English: (cf. Cross and Sherbowitz-Wetzor 1953: 862) 'On account of these Varangians the district of Novgorod became known as the Land of the Rus'. The present inhabitants of Novgorod are descended from the Varangian race, but aforetime they were Slavs.'

50 In the west the name *madjūs* – in Latin *almuiuces* with a great number of variant spellings – gave rise to a 'learned legend-making'.

51 Cf. Wikander 1963: 75f.

52 Cf. Jordanes 1882: 61 fn. 1. Mommsen has incorrectly emended Jordanes' text here from *ab hoc loco* to *Magog*. See also Svennung 1974: 216, fn. 4.

53 Cf. Herne 1954: 24ff and 28f.

54 Cf. Tschernych 1957: 70.

55 Cf. Birkeland 1954: 82.

56 Cf. Hellquist 1948: 859. Compare also the now obsolete *Reuße* 'Russian' in the expression *Zar aller Reußen* 'the tsar of all Russians'.

57 Cf. ibid.

58 Cf. the *Nestor Chronicle*, translated by Cross and Sherbowitz-Wetzor 1953: year 862 Russian text:

I idoša za more k″ Varjagom″, k Rusi; sice bo tii zvachusja Varjazi Rus′, jako se druzii zovutsja Svie, druzii že Urmane, An″gljane, druzii G″te, tako i si. (*Die Nestor Chronik* ed. Dimitrij Tschiževskij 1969: 18–19).

59 Cf. the *Nestor Chronicle*, ibid. year 969, p. 86.

60 Cf. *Svensk uppslagsbok*, Ryssland, 891.

61 Cf. the form *gautar* in Old Icelandic.

Bibliography

Arbman, H. 1955: *Svear i österviking*. Stockholm.

Bayer, Th. S. 1770: Opuscula ad historiam antiquam. C. A. Klotz (ed.) Halle; especially 'De Varagis', 335–70.

Birkeland, H. 1954: *Nordens historie i middelalderen etter arabiske kilder. Oversettelse til norsk av de arabiske kilder.* Norsk Videnskaps-Akademi Skrifter 2. Historisk-filosofisk Klasse. 2. Oslo.

Collinder, B. 1948: Review of K. B. Wiklund 1947: Lapparna. *Svenska landsmål* 71: 137–48.

    1975: Schwedische Handelspolitik vor 1000 Jahren. *Saga och sed*, pp. 76–95.

Cross, S. H. and O. P. Sherbowitz-Wetzor (eds.) 1953: *The Russian Primary Chronicle. Laurentian Text.* Cambridge, Mass.

Davidson, E. 1976: *The Viking Road to Byzantium*. London.

Ekblom, R. 1915: *Rus′ et Vareg dans les noms de lieux de la région de Novgorod. Archives d'Études Orientales.* Vol. 2. Stockholm.

Ekbo, S. 1958: Om ortnamnet Roden och därmed sammanhängande problem. En översikt från nordisk synpunkt. *Arkiv för Nordisk Filologi* 73: 187–99.

Ewers, J. F. G. 1814: *Kritische Vorarbeiten zur Geschichte der Russen*, 1–2. Dorpat.

    1826: *Das älteste Recht der Russen*. Dorpat/Hamburg.

Falk, K. O. 1951: Dneprforsarnas namn i Kejsar Konstantin VII Porphyrogennetos' *De Administrando Imperio*. Lunds Univ. Årsskrift, N. F. Avd. 1, Bd 46, Nr 4.

Frähn, C. M. 1823: *Ibn-Foszlan's und anderer Araber Berichte über die Russen älterer Zeit*. St Petersburg.

Gedeonov, S. A. 1862: *Otryvki iz izsljedovanjij v varjazskom voprose*. St Petersburg. 1876: *Varjagi i Rus'*. St Petersburg. (Originally this work appeared as a series of articles in the years 1862–3.)

Hammerich, L. L. 1970: Discussion contribution after H. C. Sørensen's paper. *Varangian Problems*, p. 142.

Hellquist, E. 1948: *Svensk etymologisk ordbok*. Malmö.

Herne, G. 1954: *Die slawischen Farbenbenennungen*. Publications de l'Institut slave d'Upsal 9. Uppsala.

Johansen, P. 1964: Kylfinger. In *Kulturhistoriskt lexikon för nordisk medeltid*. Vol. 9. Malmö.

Hjärne, E. 1947: Roden. *Namn och bygd* 35 (1947–8): 1–96.

Jordanes: Iordanis Romana et Getica recensvit Th. Mommsen (ed.) (1882). Berolini. (= M.G.H., Auct. antiquissimi, T. 5. P. 1.).

Karlgren, A. 1947: Dneprforsernes nordisk–slavisk navne. *Festskrift for Københavns Universitet i Anledning af Universitetets Aarsfest November 1947*. 5: 139.

Kiparsky, V. 1963: Russische historische grammatik. I. *Die Entwicklung des Lautsystems*. Heidelberg.

Knauer, F. 1912–13: Der russische Nationalname und die indogermanische Urheimat. *Indogermanische Forschungen* 31: 67–88.

Kunik, E. 1844–5: *Die Berufung der schwedischen Rodsen durch die Finnen und Slaven*, 1–2. St Petersburg.

Latham, R. G. 1863: *The Nationalities of Europe*. London.

Liestøl, A. 1969: *Runebrev*. Kulturhistoriskt lexikon för nordisk medeltid. Vol. 14. Malmö.

Liewehr, F. 1951–2: Wie Konstantin-Kyrill mit Wulfilas Bibelübersetzung bekannt wurde. In *Beiträge zur Namensforschung* 3 (1951–3): 287–90.

Liutprand. 1930: *The works of Liutprand of Cremona*, trans. F. A. Wright. London.

Lomonosov, V. M. 1955: Zapiska o plane naučnych rabot. A.-L. Šlěcera. In *Polnoe sobranje sočinenij* 9: 426–7. Moscow/Leningrad.

Mägiste, J. 1958: Fi. *Ruotsi*, estn. *Rootsi* m. m. i de finsk-ugriska språken. *Arkiv för nordisk filologi* 73: 200–9.

Marquart, J. 1903: *Osteuropäische und ostasiatische Streifzüge. Ethnologische und historisch-topographische Studien zur Geschichte des 9. und 10. Jahrhunderts (ca. 840–940)*. Leipzig.

Müller, G. F. 1749: *Om Rysslands urinnevånare*. Translated into Russian by J. Dorinsky, 1788: *O narodachizdrevte v Rossii obitavšich*. St Petersburg.

Nestor Chronicle (The Russian Primary Chronicle, Laurentian Text) trans. and ed. by S. H. Cross and O. P. Sherbowitz-Wetzor (1953). Cambridge, Mass.

Noreen, Adolf, 1898: Review of R. Loewe 1896: Die Reste der Germanen am Schwarzen Meer. *Historisk Tidskrift* 18: 32–5.

Norrback, A. 1943: *Rusernas rätt och de svenska landskapslagarna*. Stockholm.

Obolensky, D. 1970: The Byzantine sources on the Scandinavians in eastern Europe. In *Varangian Problems*, pp. 149–64.

Pastrnek, F. 1902: *Dějiny slovanských apoštolů Cyrilla a Methoda*. Prag. 1933: *Les légendes de Constantin et Méthode, vues de Byzance*. Prag.

Prokopios, 1905–13: J. Haury (ed.), *Procopius Caesariensis opera omnia recognovit Jacobus Haury* 1–3. Lipsiae.

Rhetor, Z. 1899: *Die sogenannte Kirchen – geschichte des Zacharias Rhetor*, eds. K. Ahrens and G. Krüger. Leipzig.

Šaskol'skij, I. P. 1970: Recent developments in the Normanist controversy. In *Varangian Problems*, pp. 21–39.

Scardigli, P. 1973: *Die Goten, Sprache und Kultur*. München.

Schlözer, A. L. 1802–9: Nestor. *Russische Annalen* 1–5. Göttingen.

Schmidt, K. Rahbek (ed.) 1970: See *Varangian Problems*.

1970: The Varangian problem. A brief history of the controversy. In *Varangian Problems*, pp. 7–20.

Schwarz, E. (1953): Die Krimgoten. In *Saeculum*. Jahrbuch für Universalgeschichte 4: 156–64.

Selnes, K. 1970: Discussion contribution. *Varangian Problems*, p. 141.

Söderlind, S. 1978: Rusernas rike. Till frågan om det östslaviska rikets uppkomst. (Stencil.) Stockholm.

Stender-Petersen, A. 1953: *Varangica*. Aarhus.

Strube de Pyrmont, F. H. 1785: *Dissertations sur les anciens Russes*. St Petersburg.

Sturluson, Snorri. 1941–51: Heimskringla, *Íslensk Fornrit*, ed. B. Aðalbjarnarson. 3 vols. Reykjavík.

Svennung, J. 1974: *Skandinavien bei Plinius und Ptolemaios*. Skrifter utg. av Kungl. Humanistiska vetenskapssamfundet i Uppsala 45. Uppsala.

Svensk uppslagsbok, 1947–55: Ryssland. 863–1031. eds. C. Quist and J. Carlsson. Malmö.

Székely, G. 1975: Hungary and Sweden – historical contacts and parallels in the Middle Ages. *Swedish–Hungarian Historical Studies. Hungary and Sweden. Early Contacts – Early Sources*. Budapest.

Tatiščev, V. N. 1962: *Istorija rossijskaja* 1. Moscow/Leningrad, pp. 107ff; *Polnoe sobranie russkich letopisej* 9: 8–9.

Thomsen, V. 1877: *The Relations between Ancient Russia and Scandinavia and the Origin of the Russian State*. Oxford/London.

1919: Det russiske riges grundlæggelse ved Nordboerne. *Samlede Afhandlinger* 1: 231–414. (= Revised Edition of Thomsen 1877.)

Thunman, J. 1772: *Untersuchungen über die alte Geschichte einiger Nordischen Völker*. Berlin.

1774: *Untersuchungen über die Geschichte der östlichen europäischen Völker*. Erster Theil. Leipzig.

Tschernych, P. J. 1957: *Historische Grammatik der russischen Sprache*. Halle.

Tschižewskij, D. (ed.) 1969: *Die Nestor Chronik*. Wiesbaden.

Varangian Problems, 1970: ed. K. Rahbek-Schmidt *et al*. Report on the First International Symposium on the Theme, 'The Eastern Connections of the Nordic Peoples in the Viking Period and Early Middle Ages'. Univ. of Aarhus 7–11 October 1968. Copenhagen.

Vernadsky, G. and M. Karpovich (eds.) 1943: *A History of Russia*. Vol. 1, *Ancient Russia* by G. Vernadsky. New Haven, Conn./London.

Waitz, G. (ed.) 1883: *Annales Bertiniani*. Hannover.

Wessén, Elias 1951: *Svensk språkhistoria*. Vol. 1. *Ljudlära och ordböjningslära*. Stockholm.

1969: Nordiska folkstammar och folknamn. En översikt. *Fornvännen* 64: 14–36.

Wiedemann, F. J. 1869: *Estnisch–deutsches Wörterbuch*. St Petersburg.

Wikander, S. 1963: Orientaliska källor till vikingatidens historia. *Historisk Tidskrift* 83: 72–9.

Wiklund, K. B. 1947: Lapparna. *Nordisk Kultur*. Vol. 10.

Zernack, K. 1958: *Studien zu den schwedisch–russischen Beziehungen in der 2. Hälfte des 17. Jhs. Teil* 1 (1958): Die diplomatischen Beziehungen zwischen Schweden und Moskau von 1675 bis 1689. Osteuropastudien der Hochschulen des Landes Hessen. Reihe 1. Gießener Abhandlungen zur Agrar- und Wirtschaftsforschung des europäischen Ostens. Bd 7. Gießen.

III *West Scandinavia*

7 Language contact in the Faroes

BJÖRN HAGSTRÖM

1 Introduction

The Faroe Isles are an archipelago of some 20 steep and rocky islands in the North Atlantic half-way between Scotland and Iceland, with a total land area of about 550 square miles. Language contact in the Faroes is primarily a question of the impact of the Danish language on Faroese, which has led to bilingualism, linguistic borrowing, and interference.

In the following article an attempt is made to give an overall description of Faroese–Danish language contact. First the historical and socio-cultural background and the basis of bilingualism in the Faroes in the Middle Ages is dealt with. I then outline the history of the Faroese language with regard to its status in relation to Danish in the islands, from the Reformation, when Danish was introduced as the language of the church, up to the present day, when Faroese is officially recognized as the principal language of the Faroes. Faroese bilingualism is then characterized in a few paragraphs, in which the functions of the two languages in modern Faroese society, and the degrees of bilingualism in the two mother-tongue groups are described. The effects of language contact in the Faroes is treated next. Linguistic borrowing and interference are illustrated with examples from the lexicon, morphology and phonology. The article is rounded off with a section on Faroese language policy.

2 Historical and socio-cultural background
2.1 Colonization

The first Nordic colonists, the *landnámsmenn* (landtakers), probably settled in the Faroes about 800 AD. Today's Faroese dialects have most in common with those of south-western Norway – which is linguistic evidence that the islands were populated mainly from that area. The *Færeyinga saga* ('The Saga of the Faroese', in Icelandic ms. from about 1380) relates the history of the islands up to the middle of the 11th century. A *þing* was held at Tinganes in Tórshavn from about 900 AD, forming a kind of parliament for the Faroe Isles, which at that time were a free state, founded in the Norwegian legal tradition and with competing chiefs as leaders. In 1035 the Faroes lost their independence and became a tributary country under the Norwegian crown.

In the Middle Ages Bergen in Norway was for the Faroese the most important connection with the outer world. A trade monopoly was established in 1273. As

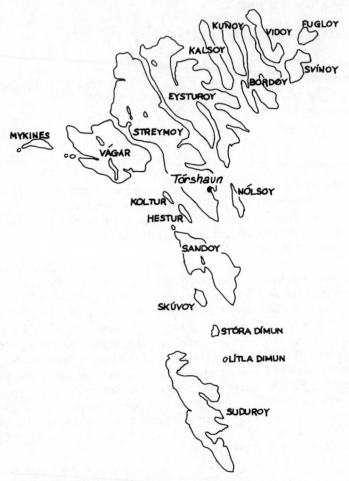

Map 1: The Faroe Isles.

by that time the Faroese no longer had seagoing vessels, they were dependent on the import of provisions from abroad, above all grain. Two merchant ships a year were to supply the Faroes with those necessities of life they could not raise themselves, and for long periods these ships were the only contact between the islands and the outside world. This trade monopoly lasted in various forms until 1856, a period of nearly 600 years of isolation and stagnation.

As a result of the Nordic Union in 1380 the Faroes became a part of the great Dano-Norwegian kingdom, but this brought about no immediate change in the status of the islands, which were still looked upon as a Norwegian colony. Norwegian law was in force in the Isles, with certain additional amendments, e.g. the famous *Seyðabrævið* (sheep-letter), a decree containing, among other things, detailed rules for sheep-breeding in the Faroes. The scanty medieval documents which have been preserved are written in Old Norwegian, but some peculiarities show that a distinctive Faroese dialect was beginning to emerge. Unfortunately it is impossible to follow in detail the development from Old Norse to Faroese. The oldest post-Reformation texts in Faroese are the manuscripts of the Faroese scientist and folk-lore recorder Jens Christian Svabo (1746–1824). The language reflected in his collection of ballads differs considerably from Old Norse and is almost identical with present day Faroese as regards pronunciation and grammatical structure.

2.2 Danish becomes the written language of the Faroes

The capital of the Dano-Norwegian kingdom was Copenhagen and the language of the royal chancellery was Danish. Subsequently the language of administration in both Norway and the Faroes became Danish, particularly after the Norwegian State Council was abolished in 1536.

It is no overstatement to say that the Reformation resulted in a linguistic catas-trophe for Norway and the Faroes. In countries such as Denmark and Sweden the Reformation Bibles supported the development of a national standard language, and gave the mother tongue uniformity and prestige.

In the Faroes the effect of the Reformation was quite the opposite. As in Norway, the Danish Bible was introduced, and with it Danish as the language of the church. From then on, Danish was the only written language in the Faroes, and so both ecclesiastical and legal documents were written exclusively in Danish. In this period the basis for bilingualism in the Faroes was laid. West-Nordic Faroese and East-Nordic Danish were by now so different that Danish clergymen and officials could not understand the language of the Faroese. So the Faroese had to learn Danish to be able to communicate with the officials and to understand what was said in church.

As a consequence of Danish being the language of the church, of the authorities and of literature, a Faroese vocabulary did not develop in lexical fields that lay outside the interests of the old agrarian community. All new impulses from the outside world were conveyed through Danish, and, as time passed, the Danish influence grew so strong that it threatened to ruin the Faroese language. In the 1780s Svabo wrote about the linguistic situation in his native country: 'Danish may be considered the principal language, and it is understood by everyone, as they [i.e. the Faroese] learn Christianity in Danish, and this language is used in church services and in court. Many speak it fairly well.' So pessimistic was Svabo about the future of his mother tongue that he proposed that the Faroese should learn to speak Danish correctly and give up Faroese, thus avoiding the disturbing mixture of Faroese and Danish, which was the result of constant linguistic inter-ference. A true child of the Age of Rationalism, Svabo reasoned that it would be an advantage to use the same language in all parts of the Danish kingdom.

2.3 Survival of the Faroese language

Had Svabo been able to look 200 years ahead, he would certainly have been astonished. Faroese did not share the fate of her sister languages in the Orkneys and Shetland. Today the Faroese language has established a stable written norm; it is the language of the local administration, the church, the primary school, the newspapers and the radio. In relation to the size of the population, book production is abundant and covers all genres of literature and many branches of learning and science.

The development of the Faroese language during the last two centuries is all the more remarkable in view of the fact that the Danish influence was actually intensified in the 19th century, both as a result of increasing governmental bureaucracy and of the introduction of compulsory schooling in the 1840s, with Danish as the language of instruction.

How could the Faroese language survive without a written standard norm throughout nearly 400 years of Danish administration in spite of the unfavourable circumstances mentioned above? The answer is to be found in the socio-cultural structure of Faroese–Danish society. The strongest resource of the Faroese language was the unique treasure house of its oral tradition, the most precious cultural heritage of the Faroese people. This included fairy tales about supernatural beings and stories about strange adventures, which were told during the *kvøldseta* (evening-sitting) in the *roykstova* ('smoke-room', i.e. the combined working-, cooking-, and sleeping-room of the old Faroese farmhouse), while wool was spun and woollen clothes were knitted in the winter evenings, and in particular the long, medieval epic ballads, the famous Faroese *kvæði*.

Narrative lays sung while dancing were popular entertainment in all the Nordic countries in the Middle Ages, but only in the Faroes has the chain-dance survived to the present day, and throughout the ages it has been the most popular form of social entertainment. Since the singing of the dancers is the only music and the texts are mainly the medieval *kvæði*, these have been perpetuated in oral tradition through century after century by the dance. About 200 old ballads have been preserved in this way. Loyalty to tradition is an essential trait in reproducing the tales and ballads. They should be told and sung word for word as they were by 'the old folks'. This has preserved the linguistic form and excluded Danish influence.

Another important factor that prevented Danish from replacing Faroese entirely was the fact that the Danish language of the clergy, officials and merchants belonged to another social level than the Faroese of the native population, who had never used Danish as their domestic language. The Faroese vocabulary had developed under special conditions in an environment where Danish was an inferior means of communication. Thus the Faroes (particularly in earlier centuries) are an excellent example of *diglossia*.

2.4   Faroese acquires a written norm

When in the 1770s Svabo started to prepare a dictionary of Faroese and to write down ballads, his ultimate aim was purely scientific and historical: he wanted to save a piece of interesting folklore and at the same time convey to posterity an impression of what the Faroese language had once been like. As no document written in Faroese existed in Svabo's time, he constructed his own orthography for his transcriptions. Not bound by tradition, he chose the phonetic principle of writing.

Though pessimistic about the future of his mother tongue, Svabo inspired others to write down ballads in a phonetic spelling, and in the 19th century several collections of *kvæði* were made. Among Svabo's early followers we may mention Johan Hendrik Schröter, a Faroese clergyman, whose manuscript *Sjúrðarkvæði* was the principal source used by H. C. Lyngbye, who edited *Færöiske Quæder om Sigurd Fofnersbane og hans Æt*, the first book printed with extended texts in the Faroese language (1822).

In 1823 a translation of the Gospel of St Matthew by Schröter was printed in Denmark and distributed in the Faroes, where it reached practically every home. In *The Faroese Book*, as the translation was called, the islanders could see their own language in print for the first time in texts prepared for practical use – for most of them a strange experience! Schröter's praiseworthy attempt to give his fellow countrymen biblical texts in their own language was not appreciated. The vocabulary of his translation was criticized for being both too profane and too foreign. However, the real cause of the aversion was probably prejudice: since the Faroese only knew the Holy Scriptures in Danish, this version was considered sacred and any Faroese translation would have been looked upon as a profanation.

In the history of the Faroese language 1846 was a decisive year. In Copenhagen in that year the young Faroese theologian V. U. Hammershaimb published a number of Faroese folklore texts in an entirely new orthography, which was based not on pronunciation but on etymology.

A consequence of the Svabonian way of writing was that the spelling varied to as great an extent as the dialects. (The degree of regional variation in Faroese pronunciation is remarkable.) Hammershaimb's orthography was an answer to the call for an overall Faroese norm to challenge Danish as the only written language of the Faroes. In the years 1846–55 Hammershaimb published a number of ballads, riddles and tales in his etymological spelling, and in 1854 his *Færøisk Sproglære* appeared, the first grammatical description of Faroese to appear in print.

The orthography of 1846 is a true product of the time when it appeared: the age of Romanticism, of Scandinavianism, of historically oriented philology. It may be characterized as a reconstruction of a past stage in the history of the Faroese language, since it conceals significant sound changes.

Thanks to its supraregional nature, Hammershaimb's orthographic system turned out to be a success. In spite of the criticisms that have been directed against it, only slight revisions of the system have been made to this day.

2.5   National revival

The abolition of the trade monopoly in 1856 marked a turning-point in the history of the Faroes. The era of free trade and unrestricted navigation to other countries brought about radical social and economic changes. The royal trade was replaced by private Danish commercial firms, which also functioned as shipping companies. People began to be more mobile; farm-hands without property became professional fishermen, and the old agrarian society, which had been practically self-supporting, began to disintegrate.

In the 1870s fishing on a large scale with ocean-going vessels started in the Faroes. That marked the beginning of the rapid progress of Faroese society to a modern welfare state. The development is reflected in the population figures: up to 1800 the population had stood at about 5,000 for hundreds of years; the period from 1850 to 1900 showed an increase from 8,000 to 15,000 inhabitants, and the census for 1976 reported 41,211.

Material progress also brought about better conditions for a richer and more varied cultural life for the Faroese people. In the 1870s there was a considerable colony of Faroese students in Copenhagen. In their circle a patriotic movement arose under the inspiration of the recently established Danish Folk High Schools, the Icelandic struggle for independence, and the Norwegian folk-language movement. The lyrical songs about the mother tongue and the far-away homeland, which were the result of their literary activities, marked the birth of modern Faroese poetry.

A prior condition for the growth of the Faroese literature was Hammershaimb's firm standard for written language. The etymological spelling proved a handy tool for the young poets, and it provided a worthy form for their patriotic songs. The most prominent of the Faroese students in Copenhagen was Friðrikur Petersen (1853–1917; later Próstur, i.e. Dean of the Faroes), whose poem Eg oyggjar veit (I know of islands) became a national anthem in the Faroes. In 1881 the Føringafelag (The Faroese Society) was founded in Copenhagen, and this society soon became the centre for the cultural activities of the Faroese in Denmark.

When the patriotic movement was transferred to the Faroes, it became more concerned with practical questions. From the 1880s to 1906, when the first political parties were formed, there was a period of growing national consciousness and political disturbance. As the Faroese language was felt to be the most important unifying symbol for the Faroese as a nation, linguistic patriotism was combined with political claims for self-determination. One of the leading nationalists was the young Jóannes Patursson (1866–1946) of Kirkjubøur, who was filled with ardent love for his country and his language. At a meeting arranged at Christmas 1888 'for the protection of the language and morals of the Faroes', his poem Nú er tann stundin komin til handa (Now the decisive moment has come) was recited, received with enthusiasm and immediately adopted as a manifesto for the patriotic movement.

In the 20th century the language struggle has played an important part in Faroese politics. Up to the First World War the Unionist Party (Sambandsflokkurin) was the dominant force in Faroese political life. Their opponents were the Home Rule Party (Sjálvstýrisflokkurin), which aimed at Faroese autonomy and at the acceptance of Faroese as the official language of the islands. With the growth of Faroese literature and the increasingly widespread use of written Faroese in private life, it gradually began to be accepted in public life as well. However, not until the Home Rule Act came into force in 1948 was Faroese legally declared the chief language of the islands. This happened after the Faroes had been separated from Denmark for five years during the Second World War and after a severe political crisis in the Islands. In 1948 there was also a change in the political status of the islands, which were now defined as 'a self-governing community within the Danish kingdom'.

Since the turn of the century Faroese has been marked by an increasing purity, richness and stylistic refinement, thanks to a large number of inspired and patriotic writers. At the same time Danish is learnt at school more thoroughly than ever before and as a result of modern communication and universal literacy the constant Danish influence is overwhelming.

3 Functions of Faroese and Danish in the Faroes, and degrees of bilingualism

Since there are as yet no systematic investigations of bilingualism in the Faroes, the following report is based principally on my own observations. However, valuable information can be drawn from Ulla Clausén's dissertation *Nyord i färöiskan* (Clausén 1978), in which the use of puristic Faroese neologisms and their competing variants is investigated.

The *functions* of the Faroese and Danish languages in the Faroes, and the *degrees* of bilingualism, are determined by the historical and political background and the socio-cultural setting of language contact, as well as by the character of the two mother-tongue groups.

In the Faroes today there are about 42,000 people whose mother tongue is Faroese. On the other hand, the group with Danish as mother tongue is a small minority, perhaps less than 1,000 people. (Exact figures cannot be obtained, since both Faroese and Danes living in the Faroes are registered as 'Faroese'. Nor are there statistics to indicate how many Faroese-speaking people live in Denmark; there they are 'Danish' citizens.) Most Danes in the Faroes went there as adults, and many of them stay for only a short period (as administrators, medical officers, teachers, skilled workers etc.).

3.1 Functions

The areas of contact to be considered in relation to the functions of the two languages include all the media through which the languages are acquired and used, the most important ones being language-usage in the home, the community, the school, and the mass media (Mackey 1962).

3.1.1. Home. In most Faroese homes Faroese is the only language used in speech, contact with Danish being confined to reading. In a small number of homes Danish is the only language used. In mixed-marriage families there are as a rule two home languages; I know some families in Tórshavn where the Danish wife speaks exclusively Danish, whereas the husband and the children always speak Faroese. In such cases all members of the family understand both languages well.

In other families the Faroese – but not the Danish – members switch between Faroese and Danish, depending on whom they are addressing. A well-known example of such regular alternation between the two languages is the Tórshavn home of the Faroese author Jørgen-Frantz Jacobsen (1900–38). When he was a boy, he and his brothers and sisters spoke Faroese with each other and with their Faroese mother. With their Danish father they spoke Danish. The parents addressed each other in Danish (Jacobsen 1958).

3.1.2. *Administration.* Within the administration great linguistic changes have taken place in this century, particularly after the Home Rule Act was passed by the Danish Parliament in 1948. Now the Faroese language is used both orally and in written communication within the sections of administration that have been taken over by the *Løgting* (a publicly elected assembly with legislative powers) and the *Landsstýri* (the local government). On the other hand Danish is the language used by the Danish administration in the Faroes, e.g. the *Rigsombudsmand* (resident state commissioner) and his office. This means that Faroese employees of these departments hear, speak, read and write Danish daily. The Danish government has jurisdiction, for example, over the judicial system and the police service. Thus the judges are Danish, as is the judicial language, and Faroese policemen write their reports in Danish.

3.1.3. *Church.* As mentioned above, a pioneer in the use of Faroese in a religious context was J. H. Schröter. However, it was to take almost a century to overcome the prejudice which had obstructed the completion of his planned translation of the New Testament and to introduce Faroese as the language of the church. When V. U. Hammershaimb used Faroese instead of Danish in the church of Kvívík on New Year's Eve, 1855, the congregation was so indignant that he dared not repeat the experiment. Nevertheless the work on a Faroese version of the Bible was recommenced. The most prominent among the translators was Jákup Dahl (1878–1944). In the 1920s and 1930s he translated most of the Holy Scriptures into Faroese, and he also translated the order of service and the general prayer-book. Thus he may really be said to have created the Faroese liturgical language. He also composed and translated a large number of hymns. The complete official Faroese Bible was published in 1961; a hymn-book appeared in 1960.

The use of Faroese in church services was first permitted in 1903, but then only to a very limited degree. It was not until 1939 that general permission was given when an ordinance was issued which allowed the individual minister to use whichever of the two languages came most naturally to him. Today the whole divine service is as a rule conducted in Faroese.

3.1.4. *School.* A government proposal in 1844 that compulsory schooling should be introduced in the Faroes (on the Danish model) was the chief motivation for Hammershaimb's attempt in 1846 to construct a universal Faroese orthography. Since the Faroes had the status of a Danish county (*amt*, 1816–1948) and there was no officially accepted norm for written Faroese, it was taken for granted by the Danish authorities that the language of instruction as well as the 'mother tongue' in the Faroese schools should be Danish. This aroused vehement opposition from the Faroese and gave rise to a lively debate on the whole linguistic situation of the islands. The liberal impulses of the 19th century and ideas of cultural autonomy were making an increasing number of Faroese conscious of the absurdity of speaking one language and writing another.

The opposition against the Danish compulsory schooling was so strong, that until 1872, when a new Local Government Act prescribed schools with permanent teachers, the Faroese were allowed to arrange the schooling as they wished, provided that all children over seven received instruction in religion and reading, which of course meant instruction in Danish.

The position of the Faroese language in education was a question of immediate importance, especially in the compulsory schools, and as time passed it became even more urgent. However, not until 1912 was oral Faroese introduced as a special subject, and instruction in written Faroese was not compulsory until 1920.

A vivid picture of school life in Tórshavn at the time of the First World War is given by the famous Faroese poet and novelist William Heinesen in a sketch, *Fra min skoletid* (*From my school days*):

The school with its garden was a world of its own. Although its name was 'Farøernes Mellem- og Realskole' [Middle and Secondary School of the Faroes], it did not have much to do with the Faroes. It was a Danish school where the pupils were taught Danish geography and Danish literature. The language of instruction was Danish even if the teacher was Faroese. We learnt everything about Danish history from the Stone Age to our days, but nothing of the history of the Faroes. As for the other subjects it was just the same. We could give detailed descriptions of the heaths of Jutland and of the granite of Bornholm, but the basalt of the Faroes was never mentioned.

The Education Act of 1920 allowed the teachers to use Faroese while instructing the younger children, 'but in order to provide the required competence in the Danish language, it is necessary that the language of instruction in the various subjects is principally Danish, especially in the case of the older children'. This very unpopular paragraph was in force until 1938. Today the language of instruction is Faroese throughout the lower forms, but all children must learn to read and write not only Faroese, but also Danish – for most Faroese children a foreign language – which is studied from the third form. Thus bilingualism in the Faroes is codified by the Education Act.

In one school the language of instruction was Faroese from the very beginning: the Faroese Folk High School, started in 1899 by Símun av Skarði and Rasmus Rasmussen, and located in Tórshavn since 1909. For generations this school has been a centre of Faroese linguistic patriotism and has made a large number of young people in the Faroes conscious of the value of their cultural heritage.

A serious problem in the schools has been the difficulty of supplying all the different forms with suitable textbooks on various subjects in Faroese. Among the first schoolbooks to appear were Joen Poulsen's *Biblical History* 1900, A. C. Evensen's Faroese readers, Jákup Dahl's *Faroese Grammar* 1908, and Rasmus Rasmussen's *Botany* 1910. These pioneering works were published while Danish was still the language of instruction. Today the lower forms are fairly well supplied with books in Faroese, but in secondary education, the lack of appropriate text-books sometimes affects the quality of the instruction. To mention just one example: there are no Faroese dictionaries to or from a single foreign language except Danish. English, German, French etc. must be studied with the aid of Danish dictionaries, which has the effect that Faroese is often totally by-passed when translations are being made.

3.1.5. *Mass media.* As a consequence of the political status of the Faroes, the islands are part of the Danish book-market. Although Faroese literature is flourishing and book production has been impressive in recent years, the Danish language has a very important contact area in the printed word. Most books sold in the Faroes are printed in Denmark, and even Swedish and Norwegian fiction appears in Danish translations. As regards weekly magazines, the Danish dominance is overwhelming.

Five Faroese newspapers are published in Tórshavn. In the biggest of them, *Dimmalætting*, with a circulation of about 10,000 copies, items in Danish and items in Faroese are printed side by side. This means that most Faroese grown-ups read both Danish and Faroese almost every day.

The copies of films that are shown in the Faroes are imported from Denmark, and have Danish subtitles, if they are not of Danish origin; films in which the actors speak Danish are not subtitled.

Since 1957 there has been a broadcasting station in Tórshavn, *Útvarp Føroya*, with daily programmes comprising news, weather reports, readings etc. The language used is exclusively Faroese, with the exception of interviews with Danes.

After years of discussion as to whether or not television would be a danger to Faroese culture, T.V. transmissions have recently started in the Faroes. The majority of the programmes are imported from Denmark, and consequently subtitled in Danish, if the language spoken is not Danish.

3.2   Degrees of bilingualism

When it comes to estimating the degrees of bilingualism we have to consider several factors, viz. the proficiency in the two languages in listening, reading, speaking and writing, as well as the linguistic levels of phonology, grammar, vocabulary and semantics.

3.2.1. *The Faroese population.* Among the Faroese population competence in Danish varies considerably, depending on age, education and place of residence in the town or in the country. Most Faroese children grow up in almost unilingual surroundings and do not learn Danish until they begin school, where all pupils are required to learn to read, speak and write Danish as the first foreign language.

Many Faroese spend several years in Denmark in order to obtain higher education. There they acquire a very good command of Danish, particularly in reading and writing. When speaking Danish, most of them retain a slight accent.

In the Faroes the traditional pronunciation of Danish is based on the phonological system of Faroese, i.e. Danish on a Faroese substratum. This mode of pronunciation was stabilized early and recognized as a regional standard norm for the Faroes. It has even acquired its own name, *gøtudanskt*. Nowadays, there is a whole range of pronunciations of Danish as regards correctness, but under certain circumstances it may be considered improper for a Faroese to speak Danish without an accent instead of the regional standard: *gøtudanskt*. Thus the linguistic situation in the Faroes parallels that of Norway, where Danish on a Norwegian substratum ultimately developed a regional standard norm, which was acknowledged as Norwegian *riksmål*.

To summarize we can say that all Faroese adults are bilingual, most of them with good competence in Danish. A characteristic feature is that their reading skill in

Danish is as a rule far greater than their speaking skill. Due to the literary dominance of the Danish language, many Faroese have in fact a more extensive reading vocabulary in Danish than in Faroese in some semantic areas.

A number of pressures force the Faroese to remain bilingual. For practical, cultural, and political reasons they simply have to learn Danish. There is a common saying that the Faroese language does not reach beyond *Borðan* (the southern headland of *Nólsoy*), an expression that shows how well aware the Faroese are of the isolation that would be the consequence of Faroese unilingualism. To the Faroese people the Danish language is an open window on the world.

The amount of space which Faroese newspapers can give to articles and reports translated into Faroese is by no means sufficient to give detailed information from the international scene. Those who have wider political, literary or scientific interests are dependent on books, magazines and newspapers imported from Denmark. The Danish language, written and spoken, is also the medium the Faroese can use when communicating with people from the other Nordic countries. In fact, the way Faroese – and Icelanders – speak Danish makes them easier for Norwegians and Swedes to understand than Danes speaking their mother tongue.

On the other hand, the Faroese language is felt to be an indispensable part of the Faroese cultural heritage and a symbol of national identity. Therefore the Faroese will remain bilingual.

3.2.2. *The Danish population.* Unlike the Faroese population, the Danes in the Faroes are bilingual only to a very small degree. Although some Danes acquire some listening and reading skill in Faroese, speaking and writing skills are rare.

The conclusion is that the burden of bilingualism is borne almost entirely by the Faroese mother-tongue group, while the Danes can always expect to be addressed in their own language in all situations of intergroup communication. In this respect, however, attitudes have gradually changed since the Second World War. While a generation ago it was considered downright rude if a Dane was addressed in Faroese, bilingual conversations may be accepted today, viz. if people know each other well and the Faroese knows that the Dane understands Faroese.

4   Effects of language contact in the Faroes

4.1   Effects on the Faroese language

As a consequence of language contact in the Faroes, all types of linguistic borrowing and interference are found in present-day Faroese. This can be illustrated with examples from the lexicon, from morphology and phonology.

4.1.1. *Lexicon.* As might be expected, the Danish influence on Faroese is strongest on the lexical level. Due to the isolation of the islands before the trade monopoly was abolished in 1856, and the diglossia that was a result of the cultural and social stratification of Danish–Faroese society, there were large gaps in the Faroese vocabulary when modern civilization reached the islands.

The vocabulary of Faroese and of standard Danish may be illustrated by means

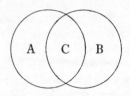

Fig. 1.

of circles, where A symbolizes the genuine lexicon of Faroese, B that of Danish (see Fig. 1). In section A we find words for fishing, keeping fowls, sheep-breeding, Faroese topography, weather and sea currents, and Faroese folk culture – areas where Faroese vocabulary is extremely rich and varied.

This may be exemplified by the following list of words, which all denote different kinds of movements of the sea (such as waves, stream, surf etc.): *bára, aldubára, alda, gerð, bullingur, drabb, tvætl, jagg, ragg, grugg, gjálv, driftingur, hevjan, kjak, kjøkr, krak, meldur, ris, rupul, rumbul, skol, skvagg, skvalp, slafs, slups, svolg, sæld, vas, grefstur, rótan, ódn, ásingur, dyningur, kembingur, rembingur, ribbingur, sig, strembingur, rensl, run, brim, gøing, mysing.* The list was made up by the Faroese philologist Jakob Jakobsen (1864–1918), who points out that it is by no means exhaustive (Jakobsen 1901).

Another illustrative example: In Robert Joensen's book on sheep-breeding in the Faroes, written in Danish, a word-list is added, explaining the Faroese technical terms used in the text. This list comprises more than 600 headwords, most of which have to be explained by a whole sentence in Danish (Joensen 1979).

In section B we find words for administration, technology, the vast range of sciences etc. – in short, words for every area of experience outside the interests of the old Faroese agrarian society. Section C represents the large overlapping area, where both languages have well-developed vocabularies.

Since the Faroese are bilingual, the gaps in Faroese vocabulary are easily filled by numerous lexical loans from Danish.

Common international words are as a rule transferred unanalysed in their Danish form, which is gradually adjusted in accordance with the morphological and phonological structure of Faroese. Thus Danish *globus* (globe), *marmelade, maskine* (machine), *sabotage* are rendered *globus* ['glo:ḅus], *marmuláta* [marmu'loaḍa], *maskina* [ma'ʃi:na], *sabotasja* [sabo'ta:ʃa] in Faroese. More examples: *alkohol* (alcohol), *arkitektur* (architect), *atom, battarí* [bata'ruĩ] (Da. *batteri*) (battery), *diskotek* (discotheque), *medisin* (medicine), *telefon* (telephone). Many words of this category may be considered mere additions to Faroese vocabulary, causing no interference in the semantic system.

A constant cause of lexical interference is the fact that the bilingual Faroese has the total vocabulary of the Danish language at his disposal, at least in theory.

Loan translations from Danish are abundant. Of particular interest is the semantic–morphological coding system that has developed: a combination of Faroese morphemes may refer to the meaning of the equivalent combination of morphemes in Danish, quite apart from the meaning of the single morphemes in Faroese. Thus in a translation from Swedish, 'nattskärra' (i.e. 'nightjar', *Caprimulgus europæus*) is rendered *náttaravnur* with reference to the Danish word for this bird, *natteravn*, which certainly has no resemblance to a raven. Swedish 'kaffekask' – i.e. coffee with spirits in it – is translated *kaffipunsur*, because the beverage in question is called *kaffepunch* in Danish, although the kind of liquor put into the coffee is never referred to as 'punch' in Scandinavia.

Other examples of loan translations are Faroese *skaðastova* and *vøggustova*. The Faroese who hears or reads these words for the first time will probably understand their rather special meanings at once, because he knows Danish and associates the combination of the Faroese morphemes with the corresponding Danish ones: *skadestue* (casualty ward or emergency room), *vuggestue* (literally 'cradle room', i.e. day nursery).

A third type of linguistic influence is the frequent occurrence of lexical interference in informal speech, where Danicisms are used as synonyms for common Faroese words. (See section C of Fig. 1.) The use of such Danicisms is above all a question of style. Many of them are never used in print, and they are less common in formal speech than in low-style speech, where almost any Danish word may be used as Faroese, and pronounced as a Faroese word (Poulsen 1977). Instead of *syrgin* (sad), *óneyðugur* (superfluous), *øki* (area), *vanliga* (generally), one may hear *bedrøvaður*, *yvirflødigur*, *umráði*, *í almindeligheit* – from Danish *bedrøvet*, *overflødig*, *område*, *i almindelighed*.

Lexical interference is also extended to conjunctions and phrases. In spoken Faroese the conditional conjunctions *dersum* and *viss* (Danish *dersom*, *hvis*) are not infrequent, although they are very rare in print (Sandquist 1980). The use of the phrase *Veitst tú hvat?* meaning 'Just listen' or 'By the way' is certainly influenced by the corresponding Danish *Ved du hvad?* The Danish habit of adding the negative *ikke* to formally affirmative clauses, meaning 'don't you' etc., as well as the use of the adverb *endelig*, meaning 'absolutely, definitely' instead of 'at last', is also taken up in Faroese speech: *ikki*, *endiliga*. In fact these are cases of semantic interference.

4.1.2. *Morphology*. Together with lexical loans a stock of affixes has been adopted, e.g. Danish *be-*, *for-*; *-eri*, *-else* – Faroese *be-*, *for-*; *-ari*, *-ilsi/-ulsi* as in *betala* (pay), *forferdiligur* (terrible), *bakarí* (baker's shop), *bangilsi* (fears). To some extent the suffix *-ilsi* is productive in Faroese; thus, e.g. we get *rokilsi* (hullabaloo) from *rok* (with the same figurative meaning, originally 'blowing').

On the whole, however, the morphological system of Faroese is resistant to Danish influence. Foreign suffixes are as a rule transformed or substituted, if they do not accord with Faroese morphological structure. Examples of this are given below.

Loan words ending in unstressed -e in Danish usually take -a and feminine gender in Faroese (Clausén 1978: 62), e.g. Danish *bacille* (bacillus), *kadence* (cadence), *kapitalisme* (capitalism) – Faroese *basilla*, *kadanca*, *kapitalisma* (cf. also on p. 182 above). The choice of feminine -a in such nouns has a parallel in the correspondence between Danish -e and Faroese -a in the old common vocabulary: Danish *gave* (gift), *kone* (woman), *side* (side), *kirke* (church) – Faroese *gáva*, *kona*, *síða*, *kirkia*.

An interesting case of suffix substitution in Faroese occurs in loan words ending in Danish *-er*, where several old suffixes have merged, among others Latin *-er*, svarabhakti vowel before *r*, and Latin *-arius*. The suffixes in Faroese corresponding to Danish *-er* are *-er*, *-ar*, *-ur*, and *-ari*. Only a few foreign words keep *-er*, e.g. the names of the months: *september* etc. (The distinction between *-er*, *-ir*, and *-ur* is chiefly a graphic one, and spellings like *oktobir* and *oktobur* also occur, reflecting dialectal pronunciations (Hagström 1967 and 1977b).) Most loan words exchange the suffix *-er* for *-ur* or *-ari*.

The derivational suffix *-ari* has a high frequency in modern Faroese and is especially productive in forming *nomina agentis*. From *keypa* (buy) is formed *keypari*, from *velja* (elect) *veljari* etc. Many *nomina agentis* denote professions, e.g. *bakari* (baker), *múrari* (mason), *prentari* (printer). Some words, which were originally *nomina agentis*, have no corresponding verbs in Faroese, e.g. *snikkari* (joiner), *skómakari* (shoemaker), *skraddari* (tailor). With such words as models the Danish ending *-er* in names of professions is regularly transformed to *-ari* in Faroese loan words, e.g. *apotekari* (pharmacist), *elektrikari* (electrician) – Danish *apoteker*, *elektriker*. The next step is that the ending *-er* in all words denoting persons is replaced by *-ari* in Faroese. For Danish *politiker* (politician), *fanatiker* (fanatic), *svensker* (Swede), *gangster* (gangster), *neger* (negro) we get Faroese *politikari*, *fanatikari*, *svenskari*, *gangstari*, *nekari*.

The suffix *-ari* in Faroese is not used exclusively in words referring to human beings. Other words in *-ari* are e.g. *flúgvari* (airplane), *trolari* (trawler), and *tikari* (tiger).

Unlike words ending in *-ari*, those ending in *-ur* with a radical *r* are often abstract, denoting qualities or conditions, e.g. *hungur* (hunger), *heiður* (honour), *myrkur* (darkness). Consequently the choice between *-ari* and *-ur* for Danish *-er* is principally a semantic one. Therefore Danish *neger*, denoting a person, is transformed to *nekari*, whereas Danish *feber* (fever) is rendered *fepur* (Hagström 1977b).

The inflectional system of Faroese is not affected by Danish. Loan words adopt Faroese endings throughout for gender, number, case, and definite article. So we find definite forms of nouns like *politikkurin* (nom. masc.), *basillan* (nom. fem), *fanatismuni* (dat. fem.), *mekanismurnar* (nom. fem. pl.).

4.1.3. *Phonology*. The phonological system of Faroese is, on the whole, resistant to Danish influence. Loan words are generally pronounced in accordance with Faroese phonology. (Cf. gøtudanskt 3.2.1 above.) There are, however, a few cases where the phonological system is affected by the impact of Danish, e.g. stress in loan words, and the pronunciation of the vowels *a* and *y* as [aː] and [yː].

In native Faroese words the first syllable is stressed. In loan words the stress as a rule falls on the same syllable as in Danish. Thus the second syllable is stressed in words like *studentur* (student), *romantiskur* (romantic), *politikari* (politician) (unlike Icelandic, where the stress is always on the first syllable).

Old Norse *a* has become the Faroese diphthong [ɛa], when lengthened; Old Norse *á* has become [ɔa] in Faroese, if not shortened by the quantity shift. The pronunciation [aː] does not occur in native Faroese words (except in a few northern dialects for long Old Norse *á*). In many loan words, however, the letter *a* is pronounced [aː], corresponding to the long Danish monophthong spelt *a*. As many of the loan words with [aː] are very common and accepted as good Faroese, [aː] must be regarded as an addition to the phonemic inventory of Faroese. Examples with [aː]: *roman* (novel), *statur* (state), *barbarur* (barbarian), *sabotasja* (sabotage). In other words a Danish long *a* is replaced by [ɛ̃a], e.g. *hospital*, or, more frequently, by [ɔ̃a]: *dáma* (Da. *dame*) (lady), *generálur* (general), *soldátur* (soldier), *marmuláta* (marmalade). The phonemic status of [aː] may be shown by a series of words like *havi* ['haːvɪ] (Da. *have* garden), (*eg*) *havi* ['hɛ̃avɪ] (1 have), *hávi* ['hɔ̃avɪ] (noise).

Danish [yː] has no counterpart in native Faroese words, as Old Norse *i* and *y* have merged into [ɪ]/[iː], and Old Norse *í* and *ý* into the diphthong [ʉ̃ɪ]. In most loan words Danish [yː] is replaced by *ý* [ʉ̃ɪ], e.g. *ævintýr* (fairy tale, Da. *eventyr*). In a few recent loan words Danish *y* is pronounced [yː], e.g. *typa* ['tyːpa] (Da. *type*) – also *typuhús* (standard house) – and *myta* ['myːta] (myth). In these words there is a conflict between spelling and pronunciation, as the letter *y* in native words is pronounced [iː] when long. On the other hand, a short Danish *y* in loan words is identified as an equivalent of the shortened *ú* in native words, and a Danish word like *cykel* (bicycle) is transformed to *súkkla* ['sYk.la] in Faroese.

Like Danish, Faroese has two series of plosives, fortes (*p, t, k,*) and lenes (*b, d, g*) but the distribution of the plosives differs on an important point in the old common vocabulary of the two languages. Postvocalic *p, t, k*, are still plosives in Faroese (e.g. *grípa* (seize), *eta* (eat), *taka* (take)), whereas the consonants are weakened in Danish, first to lenes, and later, in the case of *d* and *g*, to fricatives, [ð] and [ɣ] (*gribe, æde, tage*). In Faroese there is regional variation in the pronunciation of postvocalic plosives. In Vágar, Nólsoy and large parts of Streymoy and Eysturoy they are clear fortes but in other parts of the islands, as a rule, lenes. There is no opposition between fortis and lenis in this position in Faroese.

A typical case of phonic interference in *gøtudanskt* is the pronunciation of postvocalic *b, d, g*. The Danish fricatives [ð] and [ɣ] are identified with the corresponding plosives and pronounced accordingly. As postvocalic plosives in native Faroese words are spelt with *p, t, k*, loan words with *b, d, g* are in conflict with Faroese orthography; large groups of such loan words are consequently transformed to accord with Faroese linguistic structure. Thus Danish *neger* (negro), *jæger* (hunter), *lejder* (ladder), *tiger* have become *nekari, jekari, leytari, tikari*. From older sources – among others the newspaper *Føringatíðindi* 1890–1906 and Jakob Jakobsen's biography of Poul Nolsöe (1912) – we can see that the substitution of the suffix *-ari* for *-er* is the first step in the process of integration. Later, lenes plosives are exchanged for fortes; Danish *neger* becomes *negari*, and finally *nekari* in accordance with the phonotactic structure of Faroese.

Other examples of phonic substitution in Faroese are *fepur* (fever), *fipur* (fibre), *putur* (powder), *kápil* (cable), *tok* (train) from Danish *feber, fiber, pud(d)er, kabel, tog*, and *sjokuláta, marmuláta* from Danish *chokolade, marmelade*.

Some words keep the Danish spelling, e.g. *radar, grad* (degree), *soda, globus* (globe). In other loan words the plosives are written as fortes in *Dictionarium Faeroense* by Svabo, whereas modern Faroese has adopted the Danish spelling, e.g. *prædika* (preach), Svabo *preátika*; *edikur* (vinegar), Svabo *etikur* (Danish *prædike*, *eddike*). In Faroese there is no difference in pronunciation between words spelt with postvocalic *b*, *d*, *g* and words with *p*, *t*, *k* (Hagström 1977b).

4.2   Effects on the Danish language

Gøtudanskt was characterized above as Danish on a Faroese substratum (3.2.1). Not only is the pronunciation based on Faroese phonology, but there are also cases of lexical and syntactic interference in the Danish of the Faroese.

On the other hand, we can hardly expect a strong influence of Faroese on the mother tongue of the Danish-speaking group, in view of the socio-cultural situation (cf. 3.2). Since they can use Danish in intergroup communication, their contact with Faroese is often superficial. (In fact, in the 1950s I met a woman teacher in Tórshavn who did not even understand spoken Faroese after ten years in the country!) However, some Faroese loan words may appear in Danish, even in print. For example: Fa. *vágur* (small bay) Da. *våg*; Fa. *hagi* (outfield), Da. *hauge*; Fa. *eystfall* and *vestfall* (eastgoing and westgoing tidal currents), Da. *østfald* and *vestfald*. In other cases we may speak of semantic interference, for instance when Da. *fjord* (fiord) under the influence of the corresponding Fa. *fjørður* is used also about sounds and straits between the islands. In a similar way Danish dialectal *hammer* (stony slope, hillside) is used in the Faroese sense (Fa. *hamar*) about the horizontal basalt ledges, which are a characteristic feature of the mountainous Faroese landscape.

5   Faroese language policy

We have now traced the development of the Faroese language from being purely a spoken language, used by peasants and fishermen, and with a low status within the Danish kingdom, to its recognition as the principal language of the country. This goal was not reached without a struggle and a consistent language policy.

One aim of the national movement was to secure for the Faroese language its rightful place in the schools, the church and the administration. Another was to cultivate the language.

In modern times the two most serious problems in the cultivation of the Faroese language have been how best to resist the constant Danish influence and how best to develop a vocabulary to satisfy the demands of modern international culture. As language is one of the most important symbols of national identity, the primary trend in Faroese language cultivation has been to 'purify' the language, i.e. to replace Danish and international loan words with native words.

This puristic approach is evident in most periodicals edited in the Faroes. Of great importance was the first newspaper printed in Faroese, *Føringatiðindi*, which appeared as a monthly from 1890 to 1906. Among more recent periodicals *Varðin* is outstanding (from 1921 to the present day, 47 volumes). Most Faroese authors have published their stories, poems, and articles on various subjects in this magazine.

In 1912 an epoch-making experiment in language cultivation appeared – Jakob Jakobsen's biography of Poul Nolsöe, in which the author demonstrates the viability of Faroese as a language for scholarly matters. Jakobsen's didactic aim is apparent in the way he introduces new Faroese words: they are followed by their Danish or Danish–Faroese equivalents within parentheses. Thus e.g. *einahandil (monopol)*, *kodlvelting (revolution)*, *mentir (kultur)*, *skjalasavn (arkiv)*. Today these neologisms form part of the common Faroese vocabulary.

Important work in language cultivation has been carried out by Faroese lexicographers. The first dictionary printed was prepared by Jakob Jakobsen in 1891 and registered the vocabulary of Hammershaimb's Faroese Anthology and ballad collections. In 1927–8 M. A. Jacobsen and Christian Matras published a modern Faroese dictionary with pronunciation, grammatical information, and translations into Danish, *Føroysk–donsk orðabók*. The approach is puristic – common Danicisms are replaced by Faroese equivalents. Even more puristic is the Danish–Faroese dictionary of Jóhannes av Skarði (1967), a useful book for those who write Faroese for practical purposes, since much of what is printed in newspapers etc. is translated from Danish.

Since the Second World War there has been an increasing use of Faroese in scientific and scholarly matters. In 1952 *Fróðskaparfelag Føroya* (the Faroese Society for Higher Learning) was established. In its annual journal, *Fróðskaparrit* (1952–), articles on medicine, geology, philology, folklore, etc. are published in Faroese. In 1958 the *Málstovnurin* was established, i.e. the Faroese Language Institute of the *Fróðskaparfelag*, and since then the language cultivation programme has been in the hands of that institute.

Outstanding scholarly work in Faroese philology and language cultivation has been produced by Professor Christian Matras (born 1900), who was director of the Faroese Language Department of *Fróðskaparsetur Føroya* (The Faroese Academy) from 1965 to 1970.

Without doubt those involved in Faroese language cultivation have been successful in their efforts to guide the development of the Faroese language in the puristic direction they have chosen. Faroese has shown its viability not only as a literary language but also as a medium for all kinds of cultural and scientific purposes. Most authors accept the trend to linguistic purity and avoid Danicisms when writing. On the other hand, Danicisms are abundant in conversational Faroese, and there is often a wide gulf between the written and the spoken language. However, if the neologisms created by puristic authors are sometimes felt to be 'highbrow' and 'difficult' at the beginning, they are often finally adopted as normal via the newspapers and the radio.

The Faroese people are unique in that they are probably the smallest language community in the world with an extensive printed literature. This is not the place to discuss Faroese fiction, but it might be mentioned that it has a decidedly national character, giving detailed pictures of Faroese life and scenery in poetry and prose. However, attention should be drawn to the large number of recent translations from other languages. In the Faroese language's struggle for survival the printed word is a mighty weapon. A demand for reading matter is not the sole motivation for supplying Faroese readers with world literature in their mother tongue, since everything printed in Danish is accessible. The motivation for translating into Faroese springs from linguistic policy: skilfully made Faroese versions of masterpieces from world literature are supposed to contribute to the enrichment and development of the Faroese language. Thus the *Iliad*; *Hamlet* and *The Tempest* by Shakespeare; *Candide* by Voltaire; *The Brothers Karamazov* by Dostoevski; *Antigone* by Anouilh; *The Plague* by Camus; most of William Heinesen's novels and short stories and a collection of the old Chinese poetry are available in Faroese translations – to mention only a few.

What inspires such laborious, self-sacrificing work on translations is the conscious belief that the mother tongue is the most indispensable part of the Faroese cultural heritage and not only a means of communication, which might just as well be replaced by another.

In bilingualism there are always two possibilities: to dominate or to be dominated. In the optimistic and energetic struggle for the strengthening of the Faroese language, Danish pressure has been challenged. Without the patriotism and linguistic conscience of its users, the Faroese language would certainly have been submerged and would now only remain as a substratum in the spoken Danish of the Faroe Isles.

Bibliography

Clausén, U. 1978: *Nyord i färöiskan. Ett bidrag till belysningen av språksituationen på Färöarna.* Stockholm Studies in Scandinavian Philology. New Series 14. Stockholm.

Føringatíðindi 1890–1906. (Offset reprint. Tórshavn 1969.)

Fróðskaparrit. Annales Societatis Scientiarum Færoensis. Tórshavn 1952–.

Hagström, B. 1967: *Ändelsevokalerna i färöiskan. En fonetisk–fonologisk studie.* Stockholm Studies in Scandinavian Philology. New Series 6. Stockholm.

1977a: The Faroese Language. *Faroe Isles Review.* Vol. 2, No. 1. Tórshavn.

1977b: Hví hevur nekarin fepur? *Fróðskaparrit* 25. Tórshavn.

1978: *On Language Problems and Language Planning in the Faroes.* The Nordic Languages and Modern Linguistics 3. Proceedings of the Third International Conference of Nordic and General Linguistics, ed. J. Weinstock. Austin, Texas.

Hammershaimb, V. U. 1846: *Færøiske Trylleformularer. Færøiske Sagn.* Annaler for Nordisk Oldkyndighed og Historie. Copenhagen. (Offset reprint. Tórshavn 1969.)

1854: *Færøisk Sproglære.* Annaler for Nordisk Oldkyndighed og Historie. Copenhagen.

1891: *Tekst samt historisk og grammatisk Indledning. Færøsk Anthologi I.* Copenhagen. (Offset reprint. Tórshavn 1969.)

Heinesen, William 1964: *Fra min skoletid.* Fra Færøerne: Ur Føroyum 1. Copenhagen.

Jacobsen, J.-F. 1958: *Jørgen-Frantz Jacobsen i Strejflys af hans Breve,* ed. W. Heinesen. Copenhagen.

Jacobsen, M. A. and C. Matras, 1927–8: *Føroysk–donsk orðabok.* Tórshavn. (Second enlarged edition by C. Matras. Tórshavn 1961.)

Jakobsen, J. 1891: *Ordsamling og Register. Færøsk Anthologi II.* (Ed. V. U. Hammershaimb; offset reprint. Tórshavn 1969.)

1901: *Lidt om Sproget og Retskrivningen.* Færøske Folkesagn og Æventyr. Copenhagen 1901. (Offset reprint in Jakobsen, *Greinir og ritgerðir.* Tórshavn 1957.)

1912: *Poul Nolsøe. Lívssøga og irkingar.* Tórshavn/Copenhagen. (Recent edition Tórshavn 1966.)

Joensen, R. 1979: *Fáreavl på Færøerne.* Færoensia. Vol. 12. Copenhagen.

Lyngbye, H. C. 1822 (ed.): *Færöiske Quæder om Sigurd Fofnersbane og hans Æt.* Randers.

Mackey, W. F. 1962: The Description of Bilingualism. *Canadian Journal of Linguistics* 7: 51–85.

Matras, Christian 1939, (ed.): *Svabos færøske Visehaandskrifter.* Samfund til Udgivelse af gammel nordisk Litteratur 59. Copenhagen.

1951: *Det færøske skriftsprog af 1846.* Scripa Islandica 2. Uppsala.

1953: ed.: *J. H. Schrøters Optegnelser af Sjúrðar Kvæði.* Færoensia. Vol. 3. Copenhagen.

Poulsen, J. H. W. 1977: *Det færøske sprogs situation.* De nordiska språkens framtid. Bidrag vid en konferens, ed. B. Sigurd. Lund.

Sandquist, C. 1980: *Studier över meningsbyggnaden i färöiskt skriftspråk.* Lundastudier i nordisk språkvetenskap. Serie A, Nr 32. Lund.

Schröter, J. H. (trans.) 1823: *Evangelium Sankta Matthæussa.* Randers. (Offset reprint. Tórshavn 1973.)

av Skarði, Jóhannes 1967: *Donsk–føroysk orðabók.* Tórshavn.

Svabo, J. C. 1966–70: *Dictionarium Færoense. Færøsk–Dansk–Latinsk Ordbog I–II.* Færoensia VII. Chr. Matras (ed.). Copenhagen.

Varðin. Føroyskt tíðarskrift. Tórshavn 1921–.

IV   *South Scandinavia*

8   Statistical investigations of language death in a North Frisian community

NIELS-ERIK LARSEN

1   Introduction

The present paper illustrates with statistical material some features of the language shifts which are taking place in the multilingual community of Rodenäs, which lies just south of the Danish–German border in the extreme north-west of the Federal Republic of Germany (Kreis Nordfriesland). At the present time it is difficult to describe these language shifts convincingly within the theoretical framework put at our disposal by the sociology of language. My aims are restricted to demonstrating the present-day incidence of the five language varieties (Standard German, Standard Danish, North Frisian, Low German, and (South) Jutlandish) in this particular rural community. I also attempt to indicate some trends and developments that will determine the incidence of the language variants and language shifts in the future.

However, this paper casts relatively little light on the causes and effects of these language shifts. So, what is offered here is not a close-up picture in great detail but only a profile, a silhouette of a multilingual speech community, a description on a rather abstract level.

The linguistic situation in Rodenäs is examined in the light of a relatively new concept within the sociologically orientated examination of languages, namely language death. This article is not intended as a contribution to a much-needed clarification of this concept but as a statistical case study of language death in progress. Language death provides us with the perspective, the angle from which the statistical data are seen.

After a brief discussion of the concept of language death (Section 2) the paper describes what could be called the quantitative aspect of language death, namely the diminishing numbers of dialect speakers in relation to different age groups in the population (Section 3 through 3.2). This decline is accompanied by a parallel deterioration in the quality of the spoken dialect. This deterioration, which we could call the qualitative aspect of language death, is here seen in a steadily growing proportion of dialect speakers who are unable to speak their dialect fluently (Section 3.4). These two aspects of language death have severe consequences for bilingual and multilingual speakers in the area. The disappearance of multilingual competences is described in Section 4.

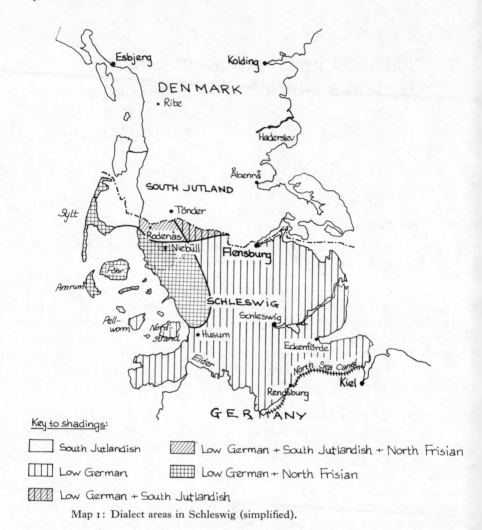

Key to shadings:

- [ ] South Jutlandish
- [/////] Low German + South Jutlandish + North Frisian
- [||||] Low German
- [####] Low German + North Frisian
- [/////] Low German + South Jutlandish

Map 1: Dialect areas in Schleswig (simplified).

1.1   Brief outline of the ethnolinguistic situation in Rodenäs

In Rodenäs five languages are spoken: two standard languages, namely High German (HG), and to a much lesser degree Danish (*rigsdansk*), and three languages which have dialect status: North Frisian, Low German (LG) and (South) Jutlandish, a local Danish dialect, the last three of which are in a very exposed position. The Frisian spoken in Rodenäs is the northernmost ramification of the dialect of the Wiedingharde and is spoken in the Frisian–Danish contact area (see Map 1). The Wiedingharde–Frisian dialect has been described by Peter Jensen in both a grammar and a dictionary (Jensen 1925; 1927). The particular variants of the other languages of Wiedingharde have not so far been the subjects of linguistic descriptions.

Generally speaking, little research has been carried out on aspects of language change and language shifts in the North Frisian language communities. Some present-day changes in Frisian dialects have been briefly discussed by Steller 1959 and Walker 1978; 1979, but neither the Wiedingharde dialect nor the other dialects spoken there are mentioned in these articles.

1.2 Some methodological considerations concerning language censuses

The older, now mostly obsolete statistics (cf. bibliography in Walker 1977), are not adequate to present a picture of the language shifts which were taking place in earlier periods; the reason being that these statistics almost without exception assume as a starting point the existence of a supposed uniform family language (*Familiensprache*). When speaking to their children parents often consciously sacrifice their own dialect in favour of the official language of the country, and consequently the children do not learn their parents' language as a first language. Therefore language shifts within the family are extremely important in establishing the real situation as regards change in the linguistic attitudes of the community, and especially in making predictions about the future situation. It is insufficient simply to cite a number of families in which two or more languages are used (so-called 'gemischtsprachige Familien'; cf. Selk 1937: 9–10). Therefore, as was emphasized by R. Böckh as early as 1869, the description of the linguistic situation in the home must focus on the individual case.[1] However, a numerical survey of which languages are spoken in the family (*Familien-* or *Haussprache*), although it does not give a sufficiently detailed survey of the situation, can be very valuable, i.e. when statistics are employed in a wider sense to describe diachronic and diatopic phenomena. An example of this approach is Århammar 1975, until now the only up-to-date statistical investigation of a North Frisian linguistic community. By using the data of the language censuses of 1889, 1909, and 1924 Århammar is able to present his own census of 1969 in an extended diachronic perspective. In addition, the distinction between language use and language competence has to be borne in mind: establishing the language used in the family at home is always a matter of determining present-day language use in a specific domain, which is very important as regards future linguistic development. By questioning informants individually it is possible to pursue both questions of language use and language competence.

A survey of informants according to age-groups is in my opinion the most advantageous way of presenting facts concerning language shift (Århammar 1975 uses this method, too). In this paper I shall not incorporate the findings of older language censuses. A discussion of some of this older material with particular reference to Rodenäs can be found in Spenter 1977.

The material of the present investigation was obtained by means of questionnaires, which were distributed from 14 to 26 May 1975 after previous announcements in the local press.[2] Where possible every household was contacted directly; only summer residents and children between 0–2 years of age were left out of consideration. The investigation was based on 470 questionnaires which is an almost complete coverage of the population. Unfortunately it was impossible to obtain the exact population figures at the time the survey was carried out from the residents' registration office. The *Statistisches Landesamt* of Schleswig-Holstein in Kiel kindly gave me the information that the community had a population of 499 on 31 May and of 496 persons on 30 June 1975. The differences are most likely to be a result of disregarding infant children (0–2 years). The number of the persons omitted can not be considered as affecting the reliability of the results of the investigation.

The information concerning the linguistic competence of the people who were questioned is based on their own estimates. This was potentially a major source of error, but in this first phase of the investigation it was practically impossible to test the competence of all informants. In a later phase some supplementary material concerning the competence of the allegedly multilingual persons was collected. Since this material has not yet been evaluated I am not able to present any results here. The data concerning active competence, i.e. whether a particular person assesses his own speech as being 'fluent', 'fairly good' or 'bad' is no indication that the qualitative aspects of language death, which will be discussed later in Section 2, are present; this survey simply states whether or not the person claims to speak the particular language with reasonable fluency. Nor is this classification to be considered as a contribution to the solution of the intricate question as to whether a bilingual person can achieve equal fluency in his two languages. That almost 100% of the population speak Standard High German fluently does not mean that it is spoken faultlessly by everybody. The older age-groups, in which the informants mostly did not learn this language until later in life, are most certainly not capable of doing so. Only awareness of this fact on the part of the informants prompted some subjects to assess their mastery of Standard High German as 'fairly good' although they certainly speak this language just as well as the majority of informants in their age-group who asserted that they spoke Standard High German 'fluently'. The situation is probably similar in the case of the three dialects, but in these cases the numbers of 'fluent' speakers indicating 'fairly good' or 'bad' are most certainly lower, because unlike High German these idioms are not continually contrasted with a codified norm, which is propagated daily by the mass media, as in the case of High German. Accordingly the figures given in Section 3 present the number of persons who are capable of using the particular languages as a medium of communication, whether 'fluently', 'fairly well', or 'badly' – without taking account of possible changes in the language.

2   Language death in Europe

What is usually called language death[3] is not just a recent phenomenon. If we recall that our knowledge of several languages has been handed down to us solely in written sources, it seems probable that language death has taken place throughout history all over the world, whenever a particular language expanded at the expense of other languages. Only the names of many languages which never achieved a written form are known. Nowadays several languages are likewise threatened with extinction and this trend is continuing at a faster pace than ever before – especially in the case of languages spoken in small remote areas – and this is a result of the opening-up of these areas by modern means of communication and of the economic and social effects of increasing industrialization and centralization. In Europe alone Haarmann (1973: 455ff) designates six languages – Karaim, Kashubian, Ingrian, Livonian, Manx and Votic – as 'dying languages', which are likely to become extinct within the next 20 or 30 years, if this has not, to all intents and purposes, already happened, as in the cases of Manx Gaelic in Great Britain and of Votic in the Soviet Union. According to Haarmann (1975: 19), 20 of a total of 69 European languages and 'culture dialects' are indicated as having negative growth rates. Certainly this fact in itself does not mean that they are about to become extinct. Other factors, such as the number of speakers, are likely to be decisive here (cf. Haarmann 1979: 279f). In addition, in areas of linguistic contact or bilingual regions, processes of assimilation may result in a reduction in the number of speakers, this reduction being limited to a particular area; not to mention the increasingly frequent tendency of speakers to shift from the vernacular to a standard language. Linguists have been aware of these problems for a long time, especially of the processes of linguistic disintegration which were thought to precede actual and final language death. This can be seen in the case of traditional dialectology, which, for example, in describing a rapidly changing local dialect simply neglected those linguistic phenomena that might be interpreted as a sign of such disintegratory tendencies. Methodologically this was the result of concentrating on informants drawn from the oldest living generation who had lived most of their lives in the community, and whose parents also came from the same place. These conditions were thought to warrant terming this a description of the 'pure' dialect. This linguistic structure, arrived at by abstraction from the actual spoken language, was considered to have been 'rescued' when the compilation of grammatical and lexical descriptions was accomplished. The method reminds one of the theoretical approach of some of the newer approaches to language study.

The extensive development of sociolinguistic research during the last few decades, in particular investigations into so-called language maintenance and language shift in plurilingual communities, has brought about a more intensive interest in threatened languages, not only in the internal processes of this last phase of their existence, but also in the conditions, mostly related to the nature of society, that determine their death. Various aspects of language death have been examined in the contributions to a volume of readings, published a few years ago (cf. Dressler and Wodak-Leodolter 1977b).

These investigations into language death, which should not be compared with the previous linguistic Darwinism, have drawn attention to the fact that the extinction of a language is quite often accompanied by a pidginization of its linguistic structure, brought about by a restriction of the language in decline to fewer domains.

Just as a language acquires a more differentiated structure when it extends to larger social domains, similarly, a language can be generalized (simplified) when restricted to a few domains. In this connection Hall talks about a 'linguistic life cycle'. First of all pidgin, then evolution to a creole language, and finally, reduction to pidgin.

Language death therefore can be looked at as a sort of pidginization: obligatory rules change to variable ones, the polystylism of a normal language (to which the creole languages belong as well) moves to monostylism, of a sort we can observe in the case of many young Bretons whose Breton vocabulary is also highly restricted. (Dressler and Wodak-Leodolter 1977a: 37).[4]

Disorganization occurs at all linguistic levels. On the phonological level obligatory rules become optional, the result being phonetic insecurity and disintegration. Other possible results are the simplification of morphophonological rules, shrinkage and calques in syntax, shrinkage and adaptation of the lexicon, and loss of stylistic flexibility.

The reduction and adaption of linguistic structures are signs of threatening language death. But they also hasten language death, as an undermined, reduced, and alienated language may seem to its speakers less worthy of being spoken, and is thus even less likely to be preserved . . ..   (Dressler and Wodak-Leodolter 1977a: 9).

In spite of this fundamental remodelling of its linguistic structures the functionality of the language is quite often preserved. Nancy Dorian's investigation of a dying Gaelic dialect in eastern Scotland shows that informants can speak the dialect fluently irrespective of whether the modifications of structure found in some parts of the linguistic community have occurred or not. For example it was found that one of the young men who most consistently spoke Gaelic was at the same time also one of those who most frequently used the modified form of the dialect (cf. Dorian 1973: 438). Frequently it is noticeable that there is no discussion of the possibility that there is a fundamental difference between the structural modifications caused by language death and the normal developments which many languages undergo in the course of their history. An example of the latter might be the radical reduction in the number of grammatical categories and in the morpheme inventories of most Germanic languages during their development from a synthetic to an analytic structure.[5]

Norman Denison in particular has pointed out the independence of loss of rules and preserved functionality. He emphasizes that the thorough-going modifications of a dying structure can only be a concomitant phenomenon, not the actual cause of death. The decisive cause is in all cases increasing disuse as a medium of communication, abandonment of the language as means of primary socialization:

languages die, not from loss of rules, but from loss of speakers. . . . More typically, the direct cause of 'language death' is seen to be social and psychological: parents cease transmitting the language in question to their offspring. (Denison 1977: 21–2).

As a linguistic concept language death still requires much clarification, but it already seems that it has a quantitative as well as qualitative aspect. Although the relationship between these two aspects is very close it has not yet been clarified. However, although the two aspects are closely connected they do not seem to be equally decisive for the future of threatened languages.[6]

3   Language death in Rodenäs

In this section 1 shall analyse the data collected in Rodenäs in the light of the concept of language death. From the references mentioned in Section 2 it appeared

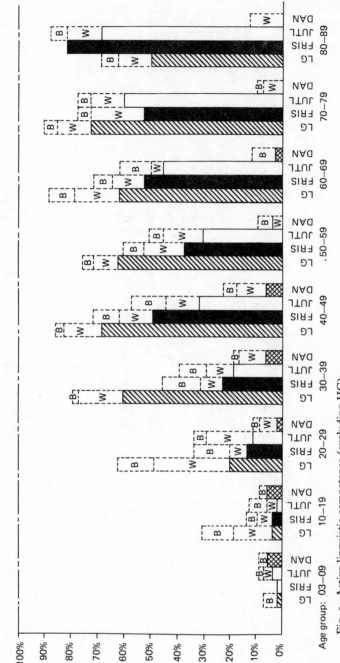

Low German (fluently)

Frisian (fluently)

☐ Jutlandish (fluently)

▨ Standard Danish (fluently)

Fig. 1. Active linguistic competence (excluding HG).

W = 'fairly well'.   B = 'badly'.

Table 1. *Which of the following languages can you speak?*

Age group	High German Fl.	W	B	Total	Low German Fl.	W	B	Total	Frisian Fl.	W	B	Total	Jutlandish Fl.	W	B	Total	Danish Fl.	W	B	Total	Total
03–09	57	—	—	57	1	—	3	4	—	1	—	1	2	2	1	5	3	—	2	5	57 P.
	100.0	—	—	100.0	1.8	—	5.3	7.0	—	1.8	—	1.8	3.5	3.5	1.8	8.8	5.3	—	3.5	8.8	100%
10–19	104	—	—	104	4	15	13	32	4	6	4	14	2	4	7	13	6	—	3	9	104 P.
	100.0	—	—	100.0	3.8	14.4	12.5	30.8	3.8	5.8	3.8	13.5	1.9	3.8	6.7	12.5	5.8	—	2.9	8.7	100%
20–29	45	—	—	45	9	13	6	28	6	3	6	15	5	8	2	15	1	3	1	5	45 P.
	100.0	—	—	100.0	20.0	28.9	13.3	62.2	13.3	6.7	13.3	33.3	11.1	17.8	4.4	33.3	2.2	6.7	2.2	11.1	100%
30–39	46	1	—	47	29	8	1	38	11	4	7	22	9	5	5	19	3	5	1	9	48 P.
	95.8	2.1	—	97.9	60.4	16.7	2.1	79.2	22.9	8.3	14.6	45.8	18.7	10.4	10.4	39.6	6.3	10.4	2.1	18.7	100%
40–49	63	—	—	63	43	9	2	54	31	8	6	45	20	8	8	36	4	7	3	14	63 P.
	100.0	—	—	100.0	68.3	14.3	3.2	85.7	49.2	12.7	9.5	71.4	31.7	12.7	12.7	57.1	6.3	11.1	4.8	22.2	100%
50–59	52	1	—	53	33	5	2	40	20	8	4	32	16	8	3	27	—	2	3	5	53 P.
	98.1	1.9	—	100.0	62.3	9.4	3.8	75.5	37.7	15.1	7.5	60.4	30.2	15.1	5.7	50.9	—	3.8	5.7	9.4	100%
60–69	41	1	—	42	26	7	4	37	22	5	3	30	19	2	5	26	1	—	4	5	42 P.
	97.6	2.4	—	100.0	61.9	16.7	9.5	88.1	52.4	11.9	7.1	71.4	45.2	4.8	11.9	61.9	2.4	—	9.5	11.9	100%
70–79	38	2	—	40	29	5	2	36	21	8	2	31	24	5	2	31	—	3	1	4	40 P.
	95.0	5.0	—	100.0	72.5	12.5	5.0	90.0	52.5	20.0	5.0	77.5	60.0	12.5	5.0	77.5	—	7.5	2.5	10.0	100%
80–89	16	—	—	16	8	2	1	11	13	—	—	13	11	2	1	14	—	2	—	2	16 P.
	100.0	—	—	100.0	50.0	12.5	6.3	68.8	81.3	—	—	81.3	68.8	12.5	6.3	87.5	—	12.5	—	12.5	100%
	462	5	—	467	182	64	34	280	128	43	32	203	108	44	34	186	18	22	18	58	468 P.
	98.7	1.1	—	99.8	38.9	13.7	7.3	59.8	27.4	9.2	6.8	43.4	23.1	9.4	7.3	39.7	3.8	4.7	3.8	12.4	100%

Fl. = fluent; W = fairly well; B = badly.

that this concept has a twofold character, and this consequently determines the approach in the following account. In the present case, where some language varieties have lost almost all their speakers, the application of the concept 'language death' seems appropriate. The declining numbers of speakers is what I call the quantitative aspect of language death. But in addition language death also has a qualitative aspect. What should be understood by this term is to some degree open for discussion. It is not possible to examine phenomena like those mentioned in Section 2 on the basis of my data. Therefore I shall analyse the steadily growing percentages of dialect speakers who are unable to speak their dialect properly. These semi-speakers in fact also represent a qualitative aspect of language death.

The results of the survey as to active competence and the replies to the question: 'Which of the following languages can you speak? (Standard German, Low German, Frisian, Jutlandish, Standard Danish)' are presented in Table 1 and in the corresponding histogram (Fig. 1). The speakers were also asked to evaluate their own ability in the language using the three categories: 'fluent' (Fl.), 'fairly well' (W), and 'bad' (B). The table presents the absolute numbers broken down by age groups and the corresponding percentages in each age group.

In the histogram Standard German has been omitted, because all the values approach 100%. Persons aged 90 and over – in actual fact a female of 91 and a male of 102 – have also been omitted, as they cannot possibly be representative of an age group. In addition their linguistic abilities have proved to be quite untypical, because they were born outside the area. Accordingly the following discussion is based on 468 persons whose distribution by age groups can be seen in Table 1.

3.1 The situation of Low German, North Frisian and Jutlandish

As already mentioned (in 1.2), we are dealing here with the assessments by the interviewees themselves of their own ability on the scale 'fluent', 'fairly well', and 'bad'. No instructions as to how they were to place themselves on the scale were given. It must be emphasized that in this way the question was directed at their own opinion of their language competence and not at the actual use of particular languages or language varieties.

The dialect with the widest distribution is clearly Low German (in the questionnaires it was referred to as 'Plattdeutsch'). Starting with the fluent speakers, Low German has the highest percentage, in part by a significant margin, which is most marked in the 30–59 age groups. Here the percentages for competence in Low German are from 19.1% to 37.5% higher than for Frisian and from 32.1% to 41.7% higher than for Jutlandish, but the Low German speakers are also in the majority in the other age groups. Only in the 80–89 age group could more informants speak Frisian and Jutlandish than Low German (on account of the small number of dialect speakers, the figures for the youngest age groups are scarcely of significance). Hence it seems that Low German is still favoured to a certain degree by middle-aged people. In other words the decline of Low German seems not to be so rapid as that of the two other language varieties.

However, all three dialects are in continuous decline. This fact corresponds to the general situation revealed by investigations into the conditions under which

Table 2. *Which of the following languages can you speak? (only persons born in North Friesland considered)*

Age group	High German				Low German				Frisian				Jutlandish				Danish				
	Fl.	W	B	Total	Fl.	W	B	Total	Fl.	W	B	Total	Fl.	W	B	Total	Fl.	W	B	Total	
03–09	53	—	—	53	1	—	3	4	—	1	—	1	1	2	1	4	3	—	2	5	53 P.
	100.0	—	—	100.0	1.9	—	5.7	7.5	—	1.9	—	1.9	1.9	3.8	1.9	7.5	5.7	—	3.8	9.4	100%
10–19	97	—	—	97	4	15	13	32	4	6	4	14	2	3	7	12	5	—	3	8	97 P.
	100.0	—	—	100.0	4.1	15.5	13.4	33.0	4.1	6.2	4.1	14.4	2.1	3.1	7.2	12.4	5.2	—	3.1	8.2	100%
20–29	38	—	—	38	7	12	5	24	6	3	5	14	3	7	2	12	1	1	—	5	38 P.
	100.0	—	—	100.0	18.4	31.6	13.2	63.2	15.8	7.9	13.2	36.8	7.9	18.4	5.3	31.6	2.6	2.6	—	5.3	100%
30–39	32	1	—	33	23	6	1	30	11	4	5	20	6	5	4	15	2	2	1	5	34 P.
	94.1	2.9	—	97.1	67.6	17.6	2.9	88.2	32.4	11.8	14.7	58.8	17.6	14.7	11.8	44.1	5.9	5.9	2.9	14.7	100%
40–49	51	—	—	51	37	9	—	46	30	8	4	42	19	8	7	34	3	6	3	12	51 P.
	100.0	—	—	100.0	72.5	17.6	—	90.2	58.8	15.7	7.8	82.4	37.3	15.7	13.7	66.7	5.9	11.8	5.9	23.5	100%
50–59	34	1	—	35	25	5	1	31	21	7	1	29	14	8	3	25	—	2	3	5	35 P.
	97.1	2.9	—	100.0	71.4	14.3	2.9	88.6	60.0	20.0	2.9	82.9	40.0	22.9	8.6	71.4	—	5.7	8.6	14.3	100%
60–69	31	1	—	32	19	7	2	28	22	5	—	27	17	1	3	21	1	—	3	4	32 P.
	96.9	3.1	—	100.0	59.4	21.9	6.3	87.5	68.8	15.6	—	84.4	53.1	3.1	9.4	65.6	3.1	—	9.4	12.5	100%
70–79	32	2	—	34	24	5	2	31	19	8	2	29	22	5	2	29	—	3	—	3	34 P.
	94.1	5.9	—	100.0	70.6	14.7	5.9	91.2	55.9	23.5	5.9	85.3	64.7	14.7	5.9	85.3	—	8.8	—	8.8	100%
80–89	13	—	—	13	6	2	1	9	13	—	—	13	10	2	1	13	—	—	—	—	13 P.
	100.0	—	—	100.0	46.2	15.4	7.7	69.2	100.0	—	—	100.0	76.9	15.4	7.7	100.0	—	—	—	—	100%
	381	5	—	386	146	61	28	235	126	42	21	189	94	41	30	165	15	14	15	44	387 P.
	98.4	1.3	—	99.7	37.7	15.8	7.2	60.7	32.6	10.9	5.4	48.8	24.3	10.6	7.8	42.6	3.9	3.6	3.9	11.4	100%

Fl. = fluent; W = fairly well; B = badly.

Table 3. *Total number of dialect speakers in relation to dialect speakers born in North Friesland (only fluent speakers are considered)*

Age group	Low German			Frisian			Jutlandish		
	Total %	Born in NF %	Diff. %	Total %	Born in NF %	Diff. %	Total %	Born in NF %	Diff. %
03–09	1.8	1.9	+0.1				3.5	1.9	−1.6
10–19	3.8	4.1	+0.3	3.8	4.1	+0.3	1.9	2.1	+0.2
20–29	20.0	18.4	−1.6	13.3	15.8	+2.5	11.1	7.9	−3.2
30–39	60.4	67.6	+7.2	22.9	32.4	+9.5	18.7	17.6	−1.1
40–49	68.3	72.5	+4.2	49.2	58.8	+9.6	31.7	37.3	+5.6
50–59	62.3	71.4	+9.1	37.7	60.0	+22.3	30.2	40.0	+9.8
60–69	61.9	59.4	−2.5	52.4	68.8	+16.4	45.2	53.1	+7.9
70–79	72.5	70.6	−1.9	52.5	55.9	+3.4	60.0	64.7	+4.7
80–89	50.0	46.2	−3.8	81.3	100.0	+18.7	68.8	76.9	+8.1
03–89	38.9	37.7	−1.2	27.4	32.6	+5.2	23.1	24.3	+1.2

the majority of dialects exist in modern industrialized societies. Nevertheless the decline of Frisian and Jutlandish in the 50–59 age group seems to be unusually great; so great that these languages (and Low German) could attain a higher percentage in the 40–49 age group. This decline in the 50–59 age group must be the result of special causes, which doubtless lie in the resettlement of refugees from the former German territories in eastern Europe. In this age group ten people, i.e. 18.9%, were born in the eastern territories, a percentage which exceeds by far that in the other age groups: the second highest percentage of refugees is 8.3% in the 30–39 age group. In order to clarify the influence of these resettled outsiders on the linguistic composition of the population, statistics for the linguistic competence of the people who were born in North Friesland only are given in Table 2.

These statistics – which exclude, in addition to the refugees from the east, people born in other provinces of Germany, in other parts of Schleswig-Holstein and in Denmark – make it possible to see the overall statistics in perspective.

Not unexpectedly, among those born in North Friesland the proportion of Frisian speakers in all age groups is greater than in the total population (cf. Table 3 which shows the differences between Table 1 and Table 2 (in %); only fluent speakers have been considered). Above all in the 50–59 age group, which is otherwise that with the highest proportion of refugees from the east, the figure rises from 37.7% to 60.0%, that is by as much as 22.3%, but the increase is also high in the case of the 60–69 age group: 16.4%. As a result of an increase of 18.7% the 80–89 age group even becomes 100% 'fluent' Frisian speakers! Of course these findings are closely bound up with the fact that the area under consideration here, North Friesland, comprises at the same time the entire North Frisian language area (except a small Frisian speaking proportion of the population of the island of Heligoland). Therefore there is no question of an influx of North Frisian speakers who were born elsewhere. And since linguistic assimilation into the Frisian language has occurred only in very few cases (in contrast to the Island of Föhr, cf. Århammar 1975), North Frisian can only stand out the more strongly when the settlers from outside Friesland are disregarded.

The relatively weak position of Frisian in the 70–79 age group is remarkable. This is already observable in the statistics for the total population and is still clearer when the people not born in North Friesland are excluded. When the figures in Table 1 are compared with those in Table 2 an increase of only 3.4% is registered in this age group, compared with, for example, 16.4% in the 60–69 age group and 18.7% in the 80–89 age group. The difference compared with other age groups is less marked when the 'fairly well' and 'bad' speakers are included: the percentage increases are then: 60–69: 13.0%; 70–79: 7.8%; 80–89: 18.7%. Likewise the proportion of the total number of Frisian speakers is more in line with the next oldest and next youngest groups (the comparative figures for the total population and those born in North Friesland are: 60–69: 71.4%/84.4%; 70–79: 77.5%/85.3%; 80–89: 81.3%/100%).

The underlying cause of the low rate of increase shown for Frisian in the 70–79 age group in Table 3 is essentially that only fluent speakers were included. But it is difficult to find the reason why precisely in this age group the proportion of 'fluent' speakers in relation to the total number of speakers of Frisian should turn out to be so unfavourable to the former, since an examination of the place of birth and social data of the people who state that they only speak Frisian imperfectly reveals nothing exceptional. If it was not simply chance, the cause is possibly to be attributed to weaknesses in the self-assessment methods used in the investigation.

In the case of Jutlandish the differences are smaller by comparison: for all age groups they remain below 10%. However, an upward tendency can be established in the 40–89 age groups. The younger age groups (3–39) register, with one exception, small decreases. The explanation of the fact that the differences between the figures for the total population compared with those born in North Friesland turn out to be smaller than was the case with Frisian lies undoubtedly in the fact that it is to be expected that people born outside North Friesland also have knowledge of Jutlandish; this is particularly true of people who were born in Denmark and also of those who came from areas of Schleswig in which Danish is spoken. As the German–Danish border was farther north of the present one until 1920, this explanation is particularly valid for people born before then. As a result of these factors the differences between the two surveys remain within a narrow margin.

In the case of Low German Table 3 shows only small differences between the figures for the total population and that for the persons born in North Friesland. For the informants aged 3–59 the values are with one exception higher in the case of persons born in North Friesland, but only the 30–59 age groups show any significant deviations. In contrast the lower figures in the 60–89 groups are remarkable, as they occur precisely in those age groups where Frisian and Jutlandish have shown remarkable increases. Although these decreases would diminish if the less than 'fluent' speakers of Low German were also included, it cannot be denied that the position of Low German in the oldest age groups is relatively weak. This observation is reinforced by the weaker position in general of Low German in comparison to Frisian and Jutlandish in the 80–89 group and also in comparison to Frisian among those fluent speakers in the 60–69 group who were born in North Friesland. The reason for this relatively weak position of Low German in the older age groups probably lies in the special role of Low German in the North Frisian language area, which researchers have often pointed out: namely as a *lingua franca*, used throughout the entire area, but with relatively few people speaking it as a mother tongue (cf. below).

3.2   The function of Low German in North Friesland

We have seen that Low German maintains a strong position only in the middle age groups (30–59). Here one could refer to the research of Paul Selk, who holds that Standard German appears in the first stage of language shift, so paving the way for Low German later (Selk 1937: 11–12):

Es ist ja allgemein bekannt, daß die plattdeutsche Sprache sich als die stärkere erweist; denn ihrem Vordringen weichen das Plattdänische und das Friesische. Aber der hochdeutschen Sprache fällt hier eine bestimmte Rolle zu:

Sie fällt zunächst in den Bereich des Plattdänischen ein durch Schule, Kirche, Rundfunk, Zeitung usw. Sie ist also gewissermaßen Wegbereiterin. Die Tabellen bieten Belege in Fülle: Wenn ein Sprachenwechsel eintritt, so tritt als 'Kindersprache'

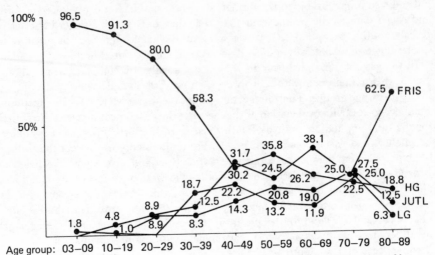

Fig. 2. Answers to the question: 'In what language were you brought up?'
The percentages from Spenter 1977: 173 (some combinations of languages have been omitted).

zunächst das Hochdeutsche auf, wohl niemals oder selten aber gleich das Plattdeutsche. . . . Die hohe Bedeutung des Hochdeutschen für das Vordringen des Platt-
deutschen steht außer allem Zweifel . . . Dem Eindringen des Hochdeutschen, das
zunächst die Bresche schlägt, folgt nun die plattdeutsche Sprache, das vorbereitete
Terrain sprachlich endgültig eindeutschend. . . . Die plattdeutsche und die hochdeutsche Sprache gemeinsam veranlassen das Zurückweichen des Plattdänischen.[7]

Paul Selk's account is primarily directed at the situation in the former and present-
day Danish linguistic area where, before the language shift, Low German did not
have the role of a *lingua franca* to the same extent as was the case in the Frisian
language area, where this role was a result of the marked differences between the
individual dialects, which were a major obstacle to inter-Frisian communication
through the medium of the Frisian language. It would therefore be reasonable to
consider whether Selk's explanation of the language shift might also be valid in the
linguistic situation in Rodenäs. When Selk carried out his survey in 1936 it was
not, for he had to conclude 'daß Rodenäs sich . . . heute noch im Anfangsstadium
des sprachlichen Wandlungsprozesses befindet, in dem Stadium also, in dem das
Hochdeutsche seinen ersten Einbruch vollzieht, das Plattdeutsche aber noch sehr
zurücksteht und ohne eigentliche Bedeutung ist' (1937: 101).[8]

If Paul Selk's theory were now also valid in the case of Rodenäs then the first
language (mother tongue) would have to have changed to Low German during
the 40 years that have elapsed between his investigations and mine, particularly in
the case of the people in the 3–49 age groups. This is plainly not the case. If one
considers the answers to the question 'In what language were you brought up?',
the percentages for which are published in Spenter 1977: 173 and are presented
here in Fig. 2 (the very low percentages for some combinations of languages have
been omitted), a distinct preference for High German as the language for bringing

Table 4. *Statistics on 'mother tongue' and 'fluent' speakers in North Friesland*

	Low German	Frisian	Jutlandish
Number of persons speaking the language as their mother tongue	50	93	52
Total number of persons speaking the language	280	203	186
Total number of persons speaking the language 'fluently'	182	128	108
'Mother tongue' speakers in relation to total number of speakers	17.9%	45.8%	30.0%
'Mother tongue' speakers in relation to the 'fluent' speakers	27.5%	72.7%	48.1%

up children starting exactly with the 30–39 age group is clearly apparent. The result is that from that age-group on Standard German is the mother tongue of most of the children. At the same time the percentages for all three dialects in this role are steadily declining, and are approaching o for the youngest children. This state of affairs does not necessarily make Selk's theory less convincing. It only means that during these last 40 years the position of Low German has been so greatly weakened that the language shift from Frisian/Jutlandish to Standard German and then to Low German does not enter this last phase. At other places in Schleswig a similar situation can be found. In Achtrup, a community outside the Frisian language area, a steady decline in Low German as mother tongue is also clearly observable starting with the 30–40 age group (Petersen 1975: 75).

The different functional position of Low German in relation to Frisian and Jutlandish, in particular its function as a *lingua franca*, can be supported by some figures. This function, which still has to be more exactly defined, is reflected in the marginal position of Low German in primary socialization which is in turn reflected statistically in the correspondingly low percentages of persons with Low German as their mother tongue in relation to the total number of Low German speakers. The number of persons who have learned any particular language as their first language can easily be ascertained from the table in Spenter 1977: 173 (in this case the combinations of languages have been distributed over the individual languages). By comparing these with the number of speakers of each particular language drawn from Table 1 in this paper, the percentages of persons with a particular language as their mother tongue can be calculated. I have here taken the data for both the 'fluent' speakers and the total number of speakers as a basis and have calculated two values for each language, which differ accordingly. The percentages can be seen in Table 4. The language with the largest percentage of persons speaking it as their mother tongue is clearly Frisian: among the 'fluent' speakers 72.7% in comparison to 27.5% for Low German. Jutlandish lies between the two with 48.1%. The percentages based on the total number of speakers show corresponding percentage relationships between the three languages. And a

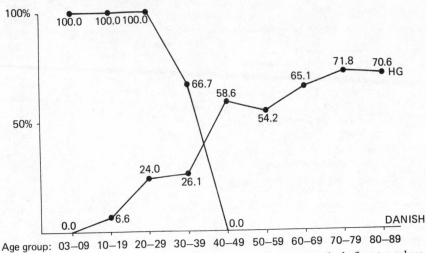

Fig. 3. The factor 'teacher' in the learning of the languages (only fluent speakers are considered).

break-down according to age groups – not given here – also only shows minor differences in the percentage relationships between the three language varieties.

3.3   The situation of the standard languages

As regards the two standard languages spoken in the area of investigation I only want to draw attention to the following points.

The replies about competence in Standard German are discussed briefly above (see 1.2): the proportion of fluent speakers in relation to those who speak fairly well or badly is attributed to varying attitudes as to what the linguistic norm is. Only one informant, a mentally retarded person in the age group 30–39, could not speak Standard German. There was no other informant who was monolingual or bilingual and was unable to speak Standard German.

Standard German – spoken by almost everybody in all age groups – has undergone a remarkable change in the way it is learned. The facts emerge from the answers to the question 'From whom did you learn which language?' The older half of the population (40–89 years old) answered that they had learnt Standard German from their teacher at school. The younger half of the population (3–39 years old) has significantly lower values for this factor; in the youngest age group it is even 0. The lower percentages for school as the socialization factor occur in those age groups where high percentages of informants gave Standard German as their mother tongue (cf. Fig. 2). The two curves for High German in Figs. 2 and 3 are in an inverse relationship to each other. The children are now taught Standard German by their parents and they have already mastered this language when they enter school. What was formerly a foreign language has now become the mother tongue. Standard Danish, on the other hand, has to be considered a foreign language in this area.

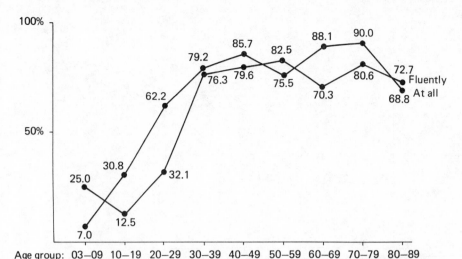

Fig. 4. Low German. Correlation between the percentage of Low German speakers, who speak Low German fluently, and the percentage of the total population capable of speaking Low German at all.

It is taught almost exclusively in the Danish minority schools – there is one in the nearby village of Neukirchen. It has to be kept in mind, however, that Standard Danish is in a very weak position numerically; the total number of speakers is very low (cf. Fig. 1).

3.4 Qualitative aspects of language death in Rodenäs

Having discussed and commented on some material which illustrates the quantitative aspect of language death in Section 3.1 I shall now turn to the qualitative aspect. As has already been mentioned, no corpus of recorded speech has been analysed in order to establish the degree to which the four language variants involved are really spoken and understood throughout the population. Nevertheless, I shall try to throw light on this aspect of language death as well by means of an examination of the informants' self-assessment of their degree of competence in the particular language, i.e. whether they consider their ability to speak the language to be fluent, fairly good or only bad. I have already emphasized that these characterizations cannot reveal whether or not internal developments in the language are taking place which are connected with language death. Nevertheless the answers to this question do illustrate one qualitative aspect of language death, namely, what is called the 'semi-speaker' (Dorian 1977). Even if the linguistic habits of the semi-speakers are principally characterized by radical deviations from the existing norm – the awareness of which on the part of the speaker can only be established by special methods of elicitation – other characteristics are usually present as well, e.g. hesitant and impeded speech, or gaps in vocabulary that must necessarily be noticed by the speaker himself and

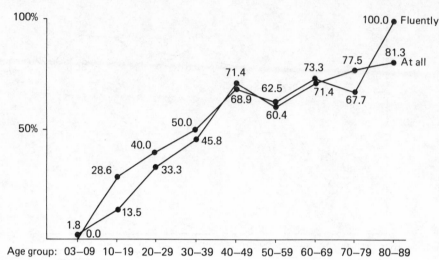

Age group: 03–09 10–19 20–29 30–39 40–49 50–59 60–69 70–79 80–89

Fig. 5. Frisian. Correlation between the percentage of Frisian speakers, who speak Frisian fluently, and the percentage of the total population capable of speaking Frisian at all.

cause him to assess his competence in the language concerned as fairly good or bad.[9]

Certainly, the informative value of evaluations like these should be considered as limited; however, in the interest of the further development of methods of carrying out language censuses, it is worthwhile examining whether it is possible to find criteria which would make possible the elicitation of qualitative aspects of linguistic knowledge and use. The following discussion is intended as an attempt to contribute to establishing such criteria.

In the 70–79 age group 77.5% speak Frisian 'fluently', 'well' or 'badly', the fluent speakers being 52.5% of the total (cf. Table 1). Or to put it in another way: if the total number of Frisian speakers in this age group (i.e. 'fluent' + 'fairly good' + 'bad') is taken as 100% (i.e. 31 speakers), then 67.7% of these speakers are capable of speaking Frisian 'fluently' (i.e. 21 speakers). According to their own estimation the competence of the great majority of informants in Frisian seems to be excellent in this particular age group. On the other hand, in the 10–19 age group, for example, only 13.5% speak Frisian at all and only 3.8% of this age group speak it 'fluently'; in other words, only 28.6% of the Frisian speakers are capable of speaking this language 'fluently' (four of 14 speakers), a much lower percentage compared to the 70–79 age group. On the basis of this sample one is drawn to the conclusion that the decline in the number of speakers of Frisian and of the other 'dying' languages, Low German and Jutlandish, and the resulting reduction in the use of these languages as active means of communication, is accompanied by a corresponding deterioration in the quality of the spoken idiom, which is to be seen in the steadily increasing proportion of semi-speakers. In actual fact this does seem to be the case, because the percentages of the total number of people in an age group that speak

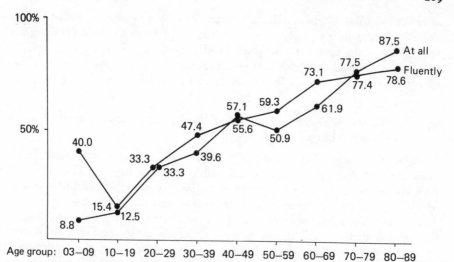

Fig. 6. Jutlandish. Correlation between the percentage of Jutlandish speakers, who speak Jutlandish fluently, and the percentage of the total population capable of speaking Jutlandish at all.

a particular language correlate with the percentages of speakers in that age group who speak this language 'fluently'. Thus, when the majority in a particular age group speak a particular language, a relatively high proportion of them speak it 'fluently'. On the other hand, when only a small minority in an age group speak a particular language at all, only relatively few of these speakers are capable of speaking this language 'fluently'. This state of affairs is clearly demonstrated in Figs. 4, 5 and 6 where the correlation between the two sets of values is shown. By the calculation of the Spearman Rank Correlation Coefficient (r_s, cf. Siegel 1956: 202–13) generally high values are achieved.[10] In the case of Low German $r_s = 0.70$; of Frisian $r_s = 0.95$ and of Jutlandish $r_s = 0.93$. The hypothesis advanced above that there is a correlation between the number of speakers and the quality of the language spoken seems to be confirmed by the high coefficients of correlation.

The percentages displayed in Figs. 4, 5 and 6, show that the values for the total number of speakers of a particular language and the values for the 'fluent' speakers are in most cases very close. Specific characteristics of this particular speech community may well be a factor here, because the relationship between the values, which are not decisive for the correlation of the two variables, may be different in the different situation in which (unstable) bilingualism occurs. All that is significant is that, when two or more age groups are compared, an increase or decrease in the overall number of speakers of one language is accompanied by a corresponding increase or decrease in the number of fluent speakers.

In line with the scope of the present study I shall restrict myself to demonstrating the statistical interdependencies just outlined and not attempt to inquire further into the causes of them. If they should be confirmed by other investigations – which would be very welcome – the importance of these interdependencies for the question of active measures to promote language maintenance is evident. It has to be considered whether such measures are still possible in view of the high percentage of semi-speakers among the young people and also of the advanced stage that the processes of linguistic deterioration have presumably reached among a significant number of speakers, who are in any case not so very numerous.

4   Trends in the development of multilingualism in a situation of advanced language death

I shall now consider the material just presented concerning language death in the community of Rodenäs in relation to multilingualism in this area. The extent of multilingualism has not been mentioned so far. However, in view of the large numbers of speakers of some of the languages spoken here there must be a significant number of bilingual or multilingual speakers, among the older members of the population at any rate. But in view of the decline in the number of speakers of varieties which have the status of dialects, the numbers of bilingual or multilingual speakers in the youngest age groups must be very low. Yet how this process takes its course in a multilingual North Frisian community has been little investigated until now. In his paper 'Historisch-soziolinguistische Aspekte der nordfriesischen Mehrsprachigkeit' (1976) Århammar presented a typological division of the North Frisian language into monolingual, bilingual and multilingual communities. This typology was of a 'purely areal nature' (*rein arealer Natur*), but information regarding the qualitative and quantitative structure of the individual speech communities in relation to the linguistic competences of their members could not be given, since material was only available from the island of Föhr. Therefore there is little definite information as to the distribution of multilingualism over the various age groups in the speech community.

Petersen has published a typological study of multilingualism with detailed statistics for another village in Schleswig, Achtrup, which lies south of the border (Petersen 1975: 49, 52; see also Wilts 1978: 166). Unfortunately the break-down of the data according to age groups has not been published and so the diachronic situation with respect to multilingualism remains unclear. Since in addition Achtrup is situated outside the North Frisian linguistic area a diachronic account of the typology of multilingualism in a North Frisian community has hitherto been a desideratum. I will now attempt to give such an account here.

4.1   The problem of language and dialect

Naturally an important question is the choice of model for the study since this will have a direct and decisive effect on the typology. Natural languages are heterogeneous. For example, the functional varieties of High German form a continuum which ranges from the pure dialect at one extreme to the theoretical construct of the standard language at the other – this extreme form of the standard language is seldom met with in reality, at any rate not in the particular area under investigation here. Some abstractions, which are necessary for theoretical purposes, were absolutely essential in questioning the informants during the survey. The reason is that it cannot be left to someone without linguistic training to make distinctions between the finely graded range of varieties of a single language, in as much as these distinctions have been worked out at all. The classification of language varieties used throughout this article is the one laid down in the questionnaire. On the basis of this classification, the informants answered the questions as to their proficiency in the varieties that they themselves speak and the statistics of their answers are given here.

There are great difficulties involved in allocating the language varieties spoken in the North Frisian linguistic area to the categories of languages and dialect. Which variety is a language in its own right and which is only a dialect in relation to another language? For example, the views of the theoreticians are contradictory as to whether it is legitimate to classify Low German within the overall system of German. The question of the relationship of North Frisian to the German system is also controversial.

These problems have been discussed by Heinz Kloss and Jan Goossens in particular (Kloss 1978; Goossens 1973, 1977). Since their discussions are of little practical value in the present case, I shall not discuss their conclusions here. But seeing that their theoretical concepts are to a large extent similar, it is all the more striking that they arrive at totally different results. Both of them use two criteria: the first concerns the sociological functions of language (Kloss's *Ausbau*- language criterion corresponding to Goossens's roofing criterion (*Überdachung*)); the second the structural (dis)similarities of the varieties involved. To Heinz Kloss High German, Low German and North Frisian are three distinct languages, whereas to Jan Goossens they can all be grouped within one German diasystem which reveals the partial differences and partial similarities of these related varieties, thus pointing out the systematic nature of the correspondences between them. These differences of opinion are not the result of a fundamental incompatibility of linguistic concepts; the most important reason is that these concepts are not related to some method of measuring linguistic similarity. Consequently it is a matter of personal judgement as to whether two varieties can be subsumed into one diasystem or not.

As the position of the language varieties in relation to each other cannot be definitely established on the basis of these linguistic models, I shall refrain from arbitrarily adopting a particular solution, even in a situation where this could really be done without difficulty – as in the assigning of Jutlandish to the Danish overall system. Accordingly I shall continue to treat the five language varieties as separate entities without attempting to assign them to larger units. Therefore in the following discussion I shall take 'bilingual, trilingual' or 'bilingualism, trilingualism' etc. to mean possible multilingual configurations the components of which could be languages as well as dialects.

4.2   The measurement of trends in the development of multilingualism

In the following statistical account of the distribution according to age groups of the configurations of multilingualism I have somewhat reduced the amount of material examined in order to achieve greater clarity. Consequently I have only

Table 5 *Configurations of multilingualism in North Friesland*

		persons
1 monolingual:	HG	211
3 bilingual:	HG/LG	77
	HG/Jutlandish	24
	HG/Frisian	21
2 trilingual:	HG/LG/Frisian	33
	HG/Frisian/Jutlandish	16
1 quadrilingual:	HG/LG/Frisian/Jutlandish	51
Total		433

considered informants who are active fluent speakers, because to also include those who spoke 'fairly well' and 'badly' would have multiplied the number of multilingual configurations[11] to the extent where it would have become confusing and would also have obscured the fact that certain configurations dominate.

Of a total of 32 possible configurations only 19 are represented in the material. Many are only encountered in the case of a limited number of persons and, for reasons of clarity, I have disregarded configurations of multilingualism which do not exceed 10% of persons in any age group. We are then left with seven configurations shown in Table 5. This total of 433 persons represents 92.5% of the total number of informants (468).

In presenting the distribution over the age groups of these seven configurations I have not used the method of presentation employed until now – the indication of percentages in the age groups concerned. The reason is that, even after the reduction in the amount of material, there are small numbers of speakers in some age groups, and, as a result of this, the percentages for some multilingual configurations are liable to be to a large extent fortuitous. In addition the new method of presentation has been chosen with the consideration in mind that it should not just convey mere average values, but really throw light on the distribution of a particular multilingual configuration over the age groups.

Simply to present the lowest and highest values, i.e. the range, would have the disadvantage that the overall picture of the distribution might be distorted and possible focal points and tendencies would not be revealed. For example, the highest and lowest values for High German monolingualism are found at the ages of 3 and 80 respectively. These figures do not reveal the fact that there is a concentration of scores in the youngest age groups. In the presentation of the multilingual situation throughout the age groups, I have therefore used the concept of the range between percentiles.

The percentile is defined as being a point or value below which a given percentage of all the values or scores are located. By means of the 25th, 50th and 75th percentile (P_{25}, P_{50} and P_{75}, also called quartiles) a frequency distribution is divided into four parts, each of which covers a quarter of the measured values. By the 10th, 20th, 30th, etc. percentile (i.e. deciles) a frequency distribution is divided into tenths.[12] The concept of the percentile has the advantage that only the number of values, not the measured values themselves, are taken into consideration. Therefore the

Table 6. *Percentile values for the configurations of multilingualism*

	P_{25}	P_{50}	P_{75}
HG	10.2	16.1	26.5
HG/Frisian	27.7	45.8	59.3
HG/LG	35.5	46.8	59.9
HG/LG/Frisian	41.6	51.9	63.0
HG/Jutlandish	25.0	54.0	67.5
HG/LG/Frisian/Jutlandish	46.2	60.8	74.9
HG/Frisian/Jutlandish	60.0	68.0	82.0

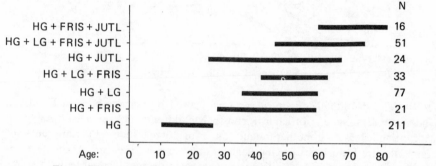

Fig. 7. The range between quartiles (P_{25}-P_{75}) of the commonest configurations of multilingualism.

percentile values are not influenced by extreme scores. The range between percentiles is the range between P_x and P_y (Sorenson 1936: 105-23). Here I have chosen the range of quartiles between P_{25} and P_{75}, thereby showing the middle 50% of values of a frequency distribution; furthermore the values of P_{25} and P_{75} are used in calculating the quartile deviation or semi-interquartile range, which is not to be done here, however. The values which were calculated for P_{25}, P_{50} and P_{75} are shown in Table 6. The ranges between P_{25} and P_{75} are shown in Fig. 7.

As expected, the calculations demonstrate distributional differences in the configurations of multilingualism in relation to age. The clearest difference is to be seen in the relation between the genuine bi- or multilingual groups and the monolingual speakers of Standard German. As a result of their concentration in the youngest age groups, the monolingual group is distinctly separated from the multilingual groups, their P_{75} value being, with a single exception, below the P_{25} values of all the other configurations of multilingualism. In other cases there are several places where the ranges overlap, as can be clearly seen in Fig. 7; I shall therefore not discuss this in more detail. In two types of bilingualism the difference according to age groups seems less pronounced. This absence of concentration in a particular age group, which is expressed by the largest ranges between the percentiles, is seen in the HG/Jutlandish and the HG/Frisian bilingual groups, the two configurations with the lowest numbers of speakers. The wide spread of the

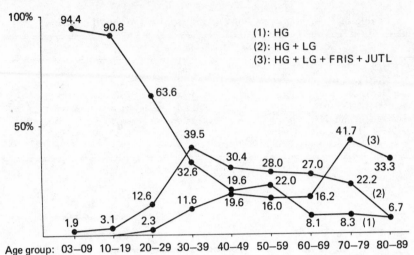

Age group: 03–09 10–19 20–29 30–39 40–49 50–59 60–69 70–79 80–89

Fig. 8. Three configurations of multilingualism by age group in percentages.

HG/Jutlandish bilinguals is most certainly caused by persons born in Denmark, whose mother tongue is Jutlandish, and their children who have been brought up with Jutlandish as their mother tongue. Their loyalty to others in the same language group who are Danish citizens has enabled them to resist the trend of the development seen in other groups of bilinguals to a certain degree. Undoubtedly the same tendency in the HG/Frisian bilingual group is an expression of a parallel resistance among the Frisians.

These two groups only influence the picture of the multilingual situation to a slight degree; but when they are left out of consideration, the trends in the development in multilingualism in this area do not emerge very clearly from the data presented in Fig. 7. Only when we concentrate on the numerically largest configurations, namely HG, HG/LG, and HG/LG/Frisian/Jutlandish, do any distinct trends emerge. With a total of 339 persons these groups represent 72.4% of the total number of 468 speakers. Over the age groups a tripartite division can be observed in the graphic presentation in Fig. 8. In the two oldest age groups (70–89) quadrilingualism is the most common type; in the middle groups aged 30–69 HG/LG bilingualism is predominant, while the youngest group aged 3–29 are almost exclusively HG monolingual:

    1st phase   (70–89 years):   HG/LG/Frisian/Jutlandish
    2nd phase   (30–69 years):   HG/LG
    3rd phase   (03–29 years):   HG

This trend of development demonstrated by these three phases – which after all take account of three quarters of the population – has been abstracted from the diversity of the multilingual situation in Rodenäs. However, in places where a comparison is possible, this trend is compatible only in part with the thesis advanced by Wilts (1978: 149) that 'ein mehrsprachiger Sprachzustand jeweils nur eine Etappe darstellt auf dem Wege von dem alten zu dem neuen einsprachigen

Sprachzustand, daß extreme Mehrsprachigkeit erst unmittelbar vor dem endgültigen Umschlagen in die Einsprachigkeit auftritt'.[13]

In Rodenäs a period of bilingualism seems to have intervened between the stage of extreme multilingualism and that of monolingualism. In Rodenäs this HG/LG bilingualism is naturally in part a result of the influence of the refugees, who came from areas where the predominant combination was Low German as the first language and High German as a second language. However, this fact in itself does not explain the phase of HG/LG bilingualism. In order to find an explanation we have to go back to the low number of persons who speak Low German as their mother tongue in relation to those who speak Low German as their second language (27.5%, see Section 3.2 Table 4). If only the HG/LG bilinguals are considered, the percentage is of course greater, but it still does not amount to more than 53.2%. The rest are divided between 42.9% with High German as their mother tongue, 1.3% with Frisian as their mother tongue (which they are now no longer able to use actively) and 2.6% who could not decide in favour of either High German or Low German.

Precisely in the 30–39 age group, which has the highest percentage of HG/LG bilingualism, 39.5%, the percentage of speakers with High German as their mother tongue rises to 58.3%, and that of speakers with Low German as their mother tongue falls to 18.7% in comparison with the next age group (40–49) where the percentages are 31.7% and 22.2% respectively (cf. Fig. 2; the percentages are not fully comparable, because in Fig. 2 the total of informants is 468, and here, 433). Hence the figures show that HG/LG bilingualism is only partly maintained by persons with Low German as their mother tongue and that the temporary increase in the number of bilingual speakers in certain age groups is not a result of an increasing number of persons with Low German as their mother tongue. On the contrary, a more likely explanation seems to be that this temporary increase in HG/LG bilingualism is a result of the ever increasing number of persons with High German as their mother tongue. This hypothesis approaches the limit of what can be proved by statistical evidence. It goes back to Paul Selk's view that High German is the 'forerunner' (*Wegbereiterin*) of Low German. But whereas Selk sees the last phase of the language shift as a germanization accomplished by persons with Low German as their mother tongue, which was preceded by a period when High German was the mother tongue, here we only find a phase when there is an increase in the number of persons who speak Low German as a second language. Thus it seems to be the case that Frisian and Jutlandish can only continue to exist in situations where a relatively high percentage of the population speak them as their mother tongue. With the increasing preference for High German as the first language the only function left for these two languages is as a medium of communication in the home, particularly among the older generations. However, the consolidation of the status of High German as the mother tongue seems to result in a temporary strengthening of the position of Low German as second language which can only be partly explained by the immigration of refugees who speak Low German. For those people who speak High German as their mother tongue Low German is apparently taking over some of the functions which were performed by Frisian and Jutlandish until now.

The explanation of these phenomena goes far beyond what can be achieved with the statistical approach. I nevertheless think that a likely explanation is that the relatively slight distance between the language systems of High German and Low German (they might be described within a joint system, a diasystem) has made it fairly easy for Low German to extend its function in this way. New investigations concentrating on this question would be necessary to provide convincing evidence for this hypothesis. The psychological reality which may be assumed for a diasystem seems to make it easier for persons with High German as their mother tongue (who are in the majority) to use Low German for these functions than Frisian or Jutlandish. That socio-cultural factors are also involved is evident from the fact that only very few people in the youngest age groups have Low German as a second language. The question must remain open as to whether the psychological reality of the distance between systems[14] could be a criterion for delimiting what is to be included in the diasystem, so that High German and Low German would be combined in one diasystem, but Frisian and Jutlandish would not.

It seems evident to me that the role of Low German in the North Frisian linguistic area cannot solely be accounted for by the function as a supra-regional *lingua franca*, which has until now been assigned to it; perhaps it is also used for stylistic purposes. In this language area, which raises many difficulties for the linguist, the status and role of Low German seems from the functional point of view to present the greatest but also the most stimulating problems, which can only be solved by further research.

5   Conclusion

The present paper has tried to outline the linguistic situation in the little community of Rodenäs in the German–Danish border district. As already mentioned in the introduction we have been able to cast only a little light on the causes of the decline of the minority languages. Probably it would not be so wrong to conclude that the most prominent causes are the parents' attitude towards these languages, which they consider to be obstacles to their children's social progress, and the general disinterest in the fate of the minority languages. But even if these are the main reasons the motives for giving up these languages are indeed very complex. Walker (1980: 25) mentions 20 possible factors for the dynamics of language decline in North Friesland. In addition to those mentioned above, the more important factors are: the small area in which a dialect can be used, the great influx of refugees after the Second World War, the growth in the number of tourists, and improved communications and mobility. The situation in the northern part of the area, where Rodenäs is situated, is complicated by the fact that we are involved with three languages which have dialect status. Therefore most of the criteria traditionally used to classify groups of speakers are not very helpful when we try to establish the different functions of the various dialects, because very often the choice of language is person-orientated in a seemingly unsystematic way. A certain refinement of methods is necessary. There is therefore ample reason for further research, but a brief examination of the tables and figures in this paper shows that the situation will change radically within a generation's time. There is therefore no time to be lost.

Notes

1 Cf. Böckh 1869, partly reprinted in Haarmann 1974; see especially pp. 81–2.

2 Those who planned and took part in the project were Professor Arne Spenter, Maike Lohse, Flemming Schroller and Niels-Erik Larsen from the University of Copenhagen. Occasionally Dr Alastair Walker (Kiel) participated.

3 For terminological considerations see Dressler and Wodak-Leodolter 1977b:5; Denison 1977: 13f.

4 Cf. also: Dorian 1973: 437–8; 1977: 23–4, 29; with reservations also Dorian 1978.

5 An exception in that respect is Dorian 1978.

6 Cf. Haarmann's criticism of the use of the term 'language death' in Dressler and Wodak-Leodolter 1977b. (Haarmann 1979: 273ff: 'Inflationierung, Sinnentlehrung'). Haarmann, who wants to confine the concept of language death to the total linguistic assimilation of some small ethnic groups, what he calls 'Mini-Ethnien', does not take account of particular regional developments in linguistic islands and fringe areas. Besides the six 'Mini-Ethnien' he apparently only acknowledges language death as taking place in the case of the Kildin–Lapps on the Kola peninsula and the East Frisians (1979: 275ff). Although Haarmann previously puts the bilingualism profiles of several Polish groups living in the Soviet Union on a par with those of the 'Mini-Ethnien', mentioning 'die mehr oder weniger stark ausgeprägte Tendenz zur Sprachassimilation, deren Endphase der vollständige Sprachwechsel ist (d.h. Wechsel der Primärsprache als gruppendynamischer Prozeß)' (the more or less marked trend to language assimilation, the final phase of which is a complete language shift (i.e. shift of the first language as a dynamic process within the language group)), he apparently does not associate these preliminary stages of total assimilation with language death, probably because of the vitality of the Polish language in general. Since Haarmann's material, which mainly derives from Soviet language censuses, does not take into consideration the actual ability in the language at present (1979: 20), he is unable to consider qualitative aspects of language death, such as the steadily growing numbers of 'semi-speakers' (Dorian). Consequently he restricts the application of the concept of language death – in my opinion, to too great an extent. Haarmann (1979: 277–91) puts forward eight features which characterize total linguistic assimilation: (1) the decline in the number of speakers; (2) the overwhelming influence of the language of the mass media; (3) the status of a non-written language; (4) the lack of schooling in the minority language; (5) the great dialect differences; (6) the high ratio of old people who are fluent speakers; (7) the lack of linguistic identity; and (8) the transition from bilingualism to monolingualism (Haarmann 1979: 273–93). Most of these features would almost certainly also be valid in the case of the three language varieties (Low German, Frisian, Jutlandish) and the conditions under which they exist in my area of investigation, and I therefore consider it legitimate to deal with the linguistic situation in Rodenäs from the point of view of language death.

7 It is a well-known fact that Low German proved to be the stronger language; for Jutlandish and Frisian lost ground as it advanced. But High German played a definite role here in that it first penetrated the sphere of Low Danish through the schools, the church, the radio, the newspapers etc. Thus it was to a certain degree a forerunner of Low German. The tables provide plentiful evidence: Whenever a language shift begins to take place, High German first appears as a first language ('Kindersprache'); however, Low German never or seldom appears at the same time. . . . The great importance of High German for the penetration of Low German is beyond doubt. After the penetration of High German, which makes the first break in the defences, so to speak, Low German

then follows and completes the Germanization of the prepared ground. . . . Together Low and High German force Jutlandish back.

8 that Rodenäs is today at the first stage of language shift; that is, at the stage in which High German achieves the first penetration, but Low German has still made very little impact and is not of any real importance.

9 Cf. Dorian 1973: 414:

These younger Embo bilinguals express doubt about the 'correctness' of their Gaelic, and often remark that their Gaelic is inferior to that of their parents and grandparents. Explicit comment on the decline in the quality of their Gaelic focuses almost entirely on the lexicon, however; the younger speakers feel sure their elders had many more 'words for things' than they have themselves. There is much lower awareness of only one instance of ongoing analogical leveling in the morphology, and some sporadic note is taken of certain phonological developments; but there is no awareness at all in the community of developments currently underway in the grammar of the so-called 'initial mutations'.

Cf. also Dorian 1978: 592 fn. 2:

The communities do show some explicit recognition of a group corresponding to the s.s. [i.e. semi-speakers] here, and these community judgements of less-than-fluent proficiency prove to have demonstrated linguistic correlates. Very fine discriminations can be made by the community and confirmed by linguistic testing.

10 We compute the value of r_s by this formula (Siegel 1956: 204):

$$r_s = 1 - \frac{6 \sum_{i=1}^{N} d_i^2}{N^3 - N}$$

where N = the number of paired values
d_i^2 = the squares of the differences in the ranks.

11 In the following account I shall also include in configurations of multilingualism some types of monolingualism where I consider them in relation to real bilingual or multilingual language competence.

12 The formula for finding a percentile is (Sorenson 1936: 111):

$$P_n = L + \frac{pN - S}{f'} \times i$$

where L = the lower limit of the percentile interval
p = the percent equivalent of the percentile, e.g. p = 10 when the 10th percentile is wanted
S = the sum of the cases below the percentile interval
f' = the frequency of the percentile interval
i = the size of the interval.

13 that in each case a multilingual language state only represents a stage on the way from the old to the new monolingual language state, that an extreme degree of multilingualism only occurs immediately before the final change to monolingualism.

14 On the existence of the different degrees of distance between languages cf. Kremnitz 1977: 43 fn. 32, who is, however, concerned with the shift of the first language:

It seems to us that the shift takes place more easily in the Romance languages than in the non-Romance minorities in France; possibly the line separating the languages is less sharp. Evidence for this could only be provided by research on a large scale.

Cf. in addition Haarmann 1979: 110 on similar phenomena in the Baltic Republics of the Soviet Union:

The national group which is linguistically most closely related to the respective titular nationality [titular nationality, i.e. Estonian in the Estonian SSR, Russian in the Russian SSR, etc.] is attracted to the nearest language as a dominating first language as regards the population both in the town and in the country. This is true of speakers with Finnish as their mother tongue, who are shifting to Estonian as their first language in the Estonian SSR, those with Latvian as their mother tongue who are shifting to Lithuanian as their first language in the Lithuanian SSR and also those with Lithuanian as their mother tongue who are shifting to Latvian as their first language in the Latvian SSR. In these national groups the attraction of Russian as a first language is weaker than the respective neighbouring language. It is an obvious step to conclude that there is a connection between the close relationship between the languages involved (Finnish/Estonian and Lithuanian/Latvian) and the attraction exerted by the closely related language of the titular nationality. However at the moment the question must be left open as to the nature of the interrelationship between the factor of the close relationship between the languages and the factor 'socio-cultural and socio-political importance of the titular language' in its own territory.

It is likely that both factors combined determine the intensity of the assimilatory effect and that neither of the two factors on its own causes the first language attraction of the titular language which has been established here.

(Cf. also Chambers and Trudgill 1980:41).

Bibliography

Århammar, N. 1975: *Die Sprachen der Insel Föhr*. Münsterdorf.

1976: Historisch-soziolinguistische Aspekte der nordfriesischen Mehrsprachigkeit. *Friesisches Jahrbuch* 12: 55–76.

Böckh, R. 1869: *Der Deutschen Volkszahl und Sprachgebiet in den europäischen Staaten. Eine statistische Untersuchung*. Berlin, pp. 19–44; also in Haarmann 1974, pp. 81–116.

Chambers, J. K. and P. Trudgill, 1980: *Dialectology*. Cambridge.

Denison, N. 1977: Language death or language suicide? In Dressler and Wodak-Leodolter 1977b, pp. 13–22.

Dorian, N. C. 1973: Grammatical change in a dying dialect. *Language* 49: 413–38.

1977: The problem of the semi-speaker in language death. In Dressler and Wodak-Leodolter 1977b, pp. 23–32.

1978: The fate of morphological complexity in language death: evidence from East Sutherland gaelic. *Language* 54: 590–609.

Dressler, W. and R. Wodak-Leodolter. 1977a: Language preservation and language death in Brittany. Dressler and Wodak-Leodolter 1977b, pp. 33–44.

(eds.) 1977b: *Language Death*. International Journal of the Sociology of Language 12. The Hague. (Introduction, 5–11.)

Goossens, J. 1973: Niederdeutsche Sprache – Versuch einer Definition. In J. Goossens (ed.), *Niederdeutsch. Sprache und Literatur. Eine Einführung*. Vol. 1: *Sprache*. Neumünster.

1977: *Deutsche Dialektologie*. Sammlung Göschen 2205. Berlin/New York.

Haarmann, H. 1973: *Soziologie der kleinen Sprachen Europas*. Vol. 1: *Dokumentation*. 2nd edn. Hamburg.

(ed.) 1974: *Sprachpolitische Organisationsfragen der Europäischen Gemeinschaft*. Schriftenreihe zur europäischen Integration 13. Hamburg.

1975: *Soziologie und Politik der Sprachen Europas*. München.

1979: *Elemente einer Soziologie der kleinen Sprachen Europas*. Vol. 2: *Studien zur Multilingualismusforschung und Ausbaukomparatistik*. Hamburg.

Jensen, P. 1925: *Die nordfriesische Sprache der Wiedingharde*. Halle (Saale).

1927: *Wörterbuch der nordfriesischen Sprache der Wiedingharde.* Neumünster.

Kloss, H. 1978: *Die Entwicklung neuer germanischer Kultursprachen seit 1800.* 2nd edn. Sprache der Gegenwart 37. Düsseldorf.

Kremnitz, G. 1977: Sprachliche Minderheiten: Das Beispiel der Romania. *Studium Linguistik* 3: 27–47.

Petersen, S. Ryge, 1975: *Dansk eller tysk? En undersøgelse af sprogforholdene i en flersproget sydslesvigsk kommune 1973.* Flensborg.

Selk, P. 1937: *Die sprachlichen Verhältnisse im deutsch–dänischen Sprachgebiet südlich der Grenze.* Beiträge zur Heimatforschung 3. Flensburg.

Siegel, S. 1956: *Nonparametric Statistics for the Behavioral Sciences.* New York.

Sorenson, H. 1936: *Statistics for Students of Psychology and Education.* New York/London.

Spenter, A. 1977: Zur Mehrsprachigkeit in der Gemeinde Rodenäs. *Nordfriesisches Jahrbuch* 13: 167–77.

Steller, W. 1959: Generationsunterschiede im Friesischen. *Phonetica* 3: 39–50.

Ureland, P. S. (ed.), 1978: *Sprachkontakte im Nordseegebiet. Akten des 1. Symposions über Sprachkontakte in Europa, Mannheim 1977.* Linguistische Arbeiten 66. Tübingen.

Walker, A. G. H. 1977: Die Mehrsprachigkeit Nordfrieslands. Eine Bibliographie. *Nordfriesisches Jahrbuch* 13: 223–30.

1978: Nordfriesisch – eine sterbende Sprache? In Ureland 1978, pp. 129–48.

1979: Toochte am e frasche spräke diling. In A. G. H. Walker and O. Wilts (eds.), *Friesisch heute. Beiträge zu einer Tagung über nordfriesische Sprache und Sprachpflege.* Schriftenreihe der Akademie Sankelmark, Neue Folge 45/46, pp. 46–57. Sankelmark.

1980: North Frisia and Linguistics. In *Nottingham Linguistic Circular* 9: 18–42.

Wilts, O. 1978: Dänisch, Nordfriesisch, Hoch- und Niederdeutsch in Schleswig-Holstein. Zur Dynamik sprachlicher Entwicklungen in einem Mehrsprachenland. In Ureland (ed.) 1978, pp. 149–66.

9 Language contact in the German – Danish border region: the problems of interference

BENT SØNDERGAARD

Introduction

Like other bilingual combinations in other countries, bilingualism on both sides of the German–Danish border involves problems of various kinds: linguistic, psychological, social and pedagogic. In the following article I will try to analyse linguistic problems only. The experience of teachers and recent scientific studies – listed in Søndergaard 1980d – have shown that there are three main problems: firstly *bilingualism–diglossia*,[1] secondly *deficiencies in vocabulary*,[2] and thirdly *interference*.

The subject of the present study is the problem of interference. I must, however, make clear in advance that research into interference in this area is still at the elementary stage of observation, notation and simple classification of cases of interference at the different levels of language.

1 The pattern of interferences between five Germanic languages

Let me make a few introductory remarks about some linguistic factors which make the situation here difficult for people who want an interference-free command of Danish and German. It is a well-known hypothesis that the more closely the two languages which are in bilingual combination are related to each other, the greater is the likelihood of interference.[3] Furthermore, in the case of German–Danish we have originally three, and later five, Germanic languages existing side by side over a long period in the same contact region and therefore exerting a far-reaching influence on each other. They are Low German, North Frisian, 'Sønderjysk' or Southern Jutlandish (i.e. the dialect of South Jutland), High German and Standard Danish. These influences have been intertwined with each other, and in some cases the threads are so entangled that it is difficult or quite impossible to decide which language is the original source of many common features ('Gemeinsamkeiten'), Kuhn 1963: 75. Not only has Low German, and later High German, exerted a great influence on Southern Jutlandish, but also vice versa: there are traces of Southern Jutlandish in Low German in the whole area. In the course of time Southern Jutlandish has also had a dominating influence on North Frisian,

221

Map 1: Schleswig and linguistic areas.

cf. Hofmann 1956: 95ff., Århammar 1966: 302ff., and in some cases vice versa, Hofmann 1956: 103, while the influence of Low German upon North Frisian is a later phenomenon, and that of High German later still, cf. Hofmann 1956: 104ff., Århammar 1966: 303.

Here we have a linguistic situation which is not static, but dynamic: a language shift in South Schleswig,[4] whose main line of development is from Southern Jutlandish and North Frisian via Low German to High German. I will not explain this in detail here – in Søndergaard 1980b there is a survey of the central shift from Southern Jutlandish to Low German – but I will only mention what is of great importance, namely that such a shift leaves a substratum of the 'defeated' language in the 'conquering' one: see the detailed discussion in Bock 1933. In the northern part of South Schleswig there are still Danicisms in spoken High German. The examples quoted in Kuhn 1963: 75 show that this substratum occurs mainly in two fields – in vocabulary and in syntax.

Typical examples are: *flütten* 'umziehen' < Da. flytte (move), and *ihm ist es gut mit* < Da. ham er det godt med (he is (doing) well), cf. Section 3.

To summarize, it can be said that, as far as potential for interference is concerned, the situation is quite different from and more difficult than the situation where a person whose mother tongue is High German learns Standard Danish (and vice versa).

2   The present state of Danish-German interference research

After this short survey of the linguistic situation in the region I should like to characterize the occurrences of interference in bilingual speakers' Danish as they appear in Danish–German research at the moment. I must, however, make it clear that no specific studies of interference in adults have been carried out yet. Thus my account can be considered mainly as a description of interference at various stages of interlanguage. There are descriptions of interference in the following groups of informants:

1.   Godau (1979) described this phenomenon in the spontaneous speech of five to six-year-old kindergarten children in South Schleswig. Most of these children speak German at home.

2.   Horn (1972) described *inter alia* the interference in the speech of 80 mono- and bilingual five-year-old children in North and South Schleswig.

3.   Petersen's study (1972) was based on a large amount of written material obtained from twelve to fourteen-year-old pupils in a German school in North Schleswig.

4.   David (1976) studied the occurrence of interference in 250 pages of material written by bilingual North Schleswig youngsters who were around 16 years old.

5.   Christophersen (1979) did not describe his group of South Schleswig informants in detail, but it would appear to have been rather heterogeneous, as it consisted of both school children and adults. There are examples of both written and spoken Danish, particularly of the spoken language.

If these sources are taken as a whole, what general impression of interference from German to Danish do we get? Let us consider the phenomenon at different levels of language.

2.1   Phonological interference

There are not many cases of *phonological* interference and they are not of profound significance, even when they occur at the elementary stages of interlanguage, among young children for instance. This aspect has not been described systematically; only fragmentarily by Godau 1979 and Thrane and Dibbern 1973. However, interference is very clear in the speech of bilingual children and adults in one area in particular, namely in intonation. Mackey is right when he says: 'Of all phonological features, intonation is often the most persistent in interference and the most subtle in influence', Mackey 1962: 577. No detailed research into this has been done in the region under discussion, but it can be stated generally that the intonation of a bilingual speaker from North Schleswig who has learned High German and Southern Jutlandish relatively early – a combination of High German and Standard Danish is rare – is not normally different from that of a monolingual speaker who speaks Southern Jutlandish at home. If he has learnt these languages fairly early – the order of learning is not important – his intonation falls within the range of general tolerance for monolinguals, cf. Søndergaard 1980c.

A South Schleswigian is a different case. The reasons for this are certainly complex. One of the most striking features is the different distribution of stress. As a result of interference from German, unstressed syllables are given more stress by a South Schleswigian than by a monolingual Danish speaker, whereby the difference between stressed and unstressed syllables is smaller than in Standard Danish. The intonation of South Schleswigian Danish normally falls outside the range of general tolerance for monolinguals.

2.2   Morphological interference

There is not very much *morphological* interference from German in North Schleswig. It occurs, for instance, to some extent in gender, in regular and irregular verbs, in the use of prepositions and of pronouns (especially *hans/sin* 'his/his'). At an elementary stage of bilingualism in South Schleswig, gender, in particular, causes problems. Typical examples:

(1)   Der er kun *en træ* i haven 'et træ' < ein Baum (There is only a/one tree in the garden).

(2)   Tom har slået *en vindue* i stykker 'et vindue' < ein Fenster (Tom has broken a window).
        (Godau 1979)

These examples are analysed as follows: There is no contamination of the Danish common gender and the neuter gender, but *ein*, the neuter indefinite article in German, is transferred to Danish: en (= common) instead of et (= neuter). The same strategy is also common in Danish as a foreign language in much older learners, cf. Carstensen 1980: 31f.

2.3   Syntactic interference

Interference is much more common in *syntax*. At an elementary stage of the South Schleswigian interlanguage, for instance, one finds the incorrect placing of infinite verb forms in compound tenses:

(3)   Peter *har en mark fået* 'Peter har fået en mark' < Peter hat eine Mark bekommen (Peter has received a mark).

(4)   Else *vil bil køre* 'Else vil køre bil' < Else will Auto fahren (Else wants to drive a car).
        (Godau 1979)

However, at more advanced levels it is not in the spoken but in the written language that syntactic interference is the greatest problem. A typical example:

(5)   fordi elever *i dag ni år i skole skal gå* 'fordi elever i dag skal gå ni år i skole' < weil Schüler heute neun Jahre zur Schule gehen müssen (because nowadays pupils have to go to school for nine years).
        (David 1976).

Very few bilingual adults in North and South Schleswig completely master the syntax of Standard Danish. They are inclined to transfer the more complex syntax of German to Danish, which is rather unfortunate, because the syntactic patterns of German and of Danish are very different. (The German syntax patterns are so dominant that even teachers who have had a monolingual upbringing and education in Denmark often have interference after a few years' stay in South Schleswig.)

2.4 Lexical and phraseological interference

However, the material clearly shows that it is *lexical* interference that is the greatest problem for all age groups, both in speech and writing. From Dethlefsen's study (1979) we know that the Danish vocabulary of bilingual speakers in South Schleswig is as a rule – at the interlanguage stage – much smaller than their German vocabulary. Therefore it is not surprising that German words appear in the informants' speech where the corresponding Danish words are unknown. Examples:

(6)   Du er *den Feuerwehrmann* 'brandmanden' (You are the fireman). (Godau 1979).

(7)   Det er en *mutter* og vinker på hendes *jung* 'mor – dreng' (This is a mother and she is waving to her boy).

(8)   Der *sucher* hun *pilze* 'leder efter svampe' (There she is looking for mushrooms).

There are also examples of hybrid formations such as *schuldreng* 'skoledreng' (schoolboy) and *franskbrot* 'franskbrød' (French bread, white bread) (Horn 1972). The problem is also considerable in other age groups, with a much higher degree of balanced bilingualism. Typical examples:

(9) a.   kongen *bestod på* at 'holdt fast ved' < bestand darauf (the king insisted on).
    b.   han *havde rappet sig op* 'havde rejst sig op' < hatte sich aufgerafft (he had got up).
    c.   vi *havde gjort af* 'havde aftalt' < hatten abgemacht (we had decided). (Petersen 1972)
    d.   lommepengene *rækker ud* 'slår til' < reicht aus (there is just enough pocket money).
    e.   jeg kan *læste mig* 'har råd til' < kann mir leisten (I can afford). (David 1976).

On closer examination, howeyer, some of these examples of interferences – which were initially recorded as 'Germanisms' – turn out to be interference from Southern Jutlandish, which is the most frequently spoken language throughout North Schleswig. Against this background the following conclusion can be drawn:

Der unmittelbare Einfluß der deutschen Sprache auf die schriftlichen Darbietungen der Schüler im Dänischunterricht ist wesentlich geringer als der Dialekteinfluß. (The direct influence of the German language on the written Danish of the pupils is considerably less than the influence of the dialect.) (Petersen 1972: 53).

Typical examples:

(10)   vi *bruche* ikke at hjælpe ham 'behøver' < Southern Jutlandish bruҳe (we need not help him).

(11)   nu er der ikke *mere* heste 'flere' < Southern Jutlandish meːr (now there are no more horses).

From a diachronic point of view, it can, of course, be maintained that in such cases there is interference from German in Southern Jutlandish, but what is decisive for the present-day native speaker is that such words (and also words like *sat* 'mæt' (satisfied after eating), *møts* 'hue' (cap), *mantel* '(regn)frakke' ((rain)coat), *ler* 'tom' (empty), which I recorded myself) have a homely feel, i.e. Southern

Jutlandish. The problem is increased by the weak position of Standard Danish in the whole region; the population's familiarity with its vocabulary is consequently not great.

Christophersen's material (1979) gives by and large the same picture of interference by Danish in South Schleswig, but as the material was collected outside the small area where Southern Jutlandish is still spoken to a certain extent, cf. Søndergaard 1980b: 302f., there cannot be any direct interference from it – like in North Schleswig – although a Southern Jutlandish substratum cannot be entirely excluded from the picture (cf. Section 1). On the other hand, direct interference from Low German can be found. A typical example: *det kan han* (læreren) *ikke af* 'det kan han ikke tåle' < dat kann he ni af (he cannot tolerate it). Typical examples of interference from German in Danish spoken in South Schleswig are the following:

(12) a.   selv om det skulle *passere, bruger* du ikke komme 'selv om det skulle ske, behøver du ikke komme' < passieren – brauchen (even if it should happen you won't have to come).

   b.   han *kastede mig for*, at 'bebrejdede mig' < warf mir vor (he blamed me for it).

   c.   må jeg *lave med*? 'være med' < mitmachen (may I take part in this?).

   d.   den slags *giver det ikke* mere 'findes ikke' < gibt es nicht (there is nothing like that any more).

The dimensions of the problem can be seen, for instance, in the Germanisms in the vocabulary of Danish teachers after they have lived for a few years in South Schleswig. Examples:

   kanister 'reservedunk' < Kanister (petrol can)
   foranstaltning 'arrangement' < Veranstaltung (event)
   (Christophersen 1979).

Examples of the opposite case – lexical interference from Danish in German in the speech of German teachers living in North Schleswig:

   Nummernplatte 'Nummernschild' < Da. nummerplade (number plate).
   Knallert 'Moped' < Da. knallert (motor scooter).
   (Riese 1961: 32).

3   The degree of interference and the nature of bilingualism

The material presented here (see also the supplementary material in the Appendix) should be sufficient to give a representative picture of interference from German to Danish in the language of bilingual persons in the border region. Now I will classify these cases of interference according to the main categories of interference suggested by Mackey 1962: 571ff.:

A.   Cultural interference: –
B.   Semantic interference: –
C.   Lexical interference: + + +
D.   Grammatical interference: + +
E.   Phonological interference: +

The scheme clearly shows that the highest degree of interference is lexical and the next highest is grammatical (especially syntactic), which is in agreement with Mackey's observations elsewhere (Mackey 1977: 342f.). Only to a small extent does phonological interference exist, except in the case of intonation.

Finally, I want to consider the role interference plays in the understanding of the concept of bilingualism. In this region *bilingualism* is defined as a *native-like command of two languages*; see Søndergaard 1980c. Therefore it is understandable that it is a central pedagogical task to reduce interference to a minimum. It will hardly be possible to avoid it completely because the fundamental linguistic conditions of bilingualism are as described in Section 1, but a considerable reduction of it is an aim in itself, *inter alia* because, even to a layman, interference (especially lexical interference) is the most obvious feature in bilingual Danish and that is why it is not treated with great tolerance, especially outside the border region itself.

Appendix: Supplementary material

(1)   de skal lære *at gå om med dem* 'at omgås dem' < damit umzugehen (they must learn to associate with them).

(2)   hr.e. *fik det meste af* 'det gik hårdest ud over hr.E.' < bekam das meiste ab (Mr. E. had to suffer most).

(3)   Cassius Clay *ruser ud* 'glider' < rutscht aus (slips/slides).

(4)   hvis han igen *antager gaver* 'tager imod gaver' < Geschenke annimmt (if he accepts gifts again).

(5)   den anklagede *blev sagt fri* 'blev frifundet' < wurde freigesprochen (the accused was found not guilty).

(6)   hvad der *står en for* 'hvad man kan vente sig' < was einem bevorsteht (what you can expect).

(7)   *hedder det*, at jeg . . .? 'betyder det' < heißt das (does that mean that I . . .?)

(8)   den *lod sig tid* 'gav sig tid' < liess sich Zeit (it took its time).

(9)   det *går ikke om* sygdom 'det drejer sig ikke om' < es geht nicht um (it is not a question of illness).

(10)   han *skød den død* 'skød den' < schoss ihn tot (he shot it).

(11)   *for mange* år blev der stjålet 'for mange år siden' < vor vielen Jahren (many years ago something was stolen).

(12)   et bord, *ved det vi spiser* 'som vi spiser ved' < an dem wir essen (a table at which we eat).

    (Petersen 1972)

(13)   han *giver hende at forstå* 'lader hende forstå' < gibt ihr zu verstehen (he makes her understand).

(14)   han *lader sig aflænke* 'lader sig aflede' < läßt sich ablenken (he is easily distracted).

(15)   i haven *forbringer jeg* . . . 'tilbringer jeg' < verbringe ich (in the garden I spend . . .)

(16)   jeg *nytter det ud* 'udnytter det' < nutze es aus (I make use of it).

(17)   [det] *afspiller sig* 'foregår' < spielt sich ab (it takes place).

(18)   det *gik opad* 'gik fremad' < ging aufwärts (things were improving).

(19)   *forlængst ikke alle* 'langtfra alle' < längst nicht alle (far from everybody, not everybody).

(20)   [at] *køre på ski* 'stå/løbe på ski' < Schi fahren (to ski).
    (David 1976).

Notes

1 Cf. Søndergaard 1981.
2 Cf. Wieczerkowski 1973 and 1978 and Søndergaard 1980a.
3 Cf. e.g. Andersen *et al.* 1978: 69 and the model outlined in Søndergaard 1979: 60.
4 Following local usage, I shall refer to 'Landesteil Schleswig' of Schleswig-Holstein as South Schleswig, and to the southern area of Jutland as North Schleswig, thus reflecting the former unity of this whole area, cf. Fig. 1.

Bibliography

Andersen, E., M. Fredberg, T. Vestergaard and F. Østergaard, 1978: *Temaer i anvendt lingvistik*. København.

Århammar, N. 1966: Nordische Lehnwörter und lexikalische Stützung im Nordfriesischen. *Nordfriesisches Jahrbuch* 2: 302–16.

Bock, K. N. 1933: *Niederdeutsch auf dänischem Substrat*. Kopenhagen/Marburg.

Carstensen, U. 1980: '*Intersprache*'. *Charakteristik einiger wichtiger Fehlertypen bei Schülern mit Dänisch als Fremdsprache*. Examensarbeit. Landesschulamt Kiel. (Unpublished ms.)

Christophersen, H. 1979: Det danske sprog i Sydslesvig. *Mål og Mæle* 6: 8–16.

David, A. 1976: *Germanismen in schriftlichen Arbeiten der Schüler im Fach Dänisch an deutschen Schulen in Nordschleswig*. Examensarbeit. Pädagogische Hochschule Flensburg. (Unpublished ms.)

Dethlefsen, A. 1979: *Wortschatzdefizit der zweisprachigen Schüler im deutsch–dänischen Grenzraum*. Examensarbeit. Pädagogische Hochschule Flensburg. (Unpublished ms.)

Godau, H. 1979: *Deutsche Interferenzerscheinungen in der dänischen Sprechsprache bilingualer Kinder in Südschleswig*. Examensarbeit. Pädagogische Hochschule Flensburg. (Unpublished ms.)

Hofmann, D. 1956: Probleme der nordfriesischen Dialektforschung. *Zeitschrift für Mundartforschung* 24: 78–112.

Horn, A. S. 1972: *Tosprogethed*. Specialeopgave. Åbenrå Børnehaveseminarium. (Unpublished ms.)

Kuhn, H. 1963: Die Sprachen im deutsch–dänischen Grenzraum. *Grenzfriedenshefte* 2: 69–77.

Mackey, W. F. 1962: The description of bilingualism. *Canadian Journal of Linguistics* 7: 51–85. (See also J. A. Fishman (ed.), *Readings in the Sociology of Language*, pp. 554–84. The Hague/Paris 1968.)

    1977: Free language alternation in school. In W. F. Mackey and T. Andersson, *Bilingualism in Early Childhood*. Rowley.

Petersen, H. 1972: *Der Einfluss der Haussprache auf die schriftliche Gestaltung des Dänischunterrichts*. Prüfungsarbeit zur 2. Lehrerprüfung, Landesschulamt Kiel. (Unpublished ms.)

Riese, I. 1961: *Die Wirkung der Zweisprachigkeit auf die geistige Entwicklung des Kindes in Nordschleswig*. Prüfungsarbeit zur 2. Lehrerprüfung. Landesschulamt Kiel. (Unpublished ms.)

Søndergaard, B. 1979: Tosprogethedsproblemer i det dansk–tyske grænseområde. With a summary in German. In *Mødet mellem sprogene i det dansk–tyske grænseområde*. Aabenraa.

    1980a: *Sprogligt deficit. Sprogpædagogiske betragtninger over den dansk–tyske bilingualisme*. With a summary in German. Aabenraa.

    1980b: *Vom Sprachenkampf zur sprachlichen Koexistenz im deutsch–dänischen Grenzraum*. In P. H. Nelde (ed.) 1980: *Sprachkontakt und Sprachkonflikt*, pp. 297–305. Wiesbaden.

    1980c: Tosprogethed, fremmedsprog, modersmål – et forsøg på begrebsafgrænsning. In *Nordic Linguistic Bulletin* 4 (3–4): 4–10.

    1980d: *En begyndende udforskning af den dansk–tyske bilingualisme. En bibliografi*. With summaries in German and English. København.

    1981: Tosprogethed med diglossi højtysk, rigsdansk, sønderjysk i Nordslesvig. With a summary in German. *Danske Studier* 76: 73–90.

Thrane, H. and W. Dibbern 1973: *Aspekter ved undervisning på fremmedsprog fra skolestarten*. Kandidatopgave (pæd.-psyk.) Danmarks Lærerhøjskole. København. (Unpublished ms.)

Wieczerkowski, W. 1973: *Verbale Fertigkeiten bilingualer Schüler im deutsch–dänischen Grenzgebiet*. Hamburg.

(ed.) 1978: *Zweisprachigkeit und Schule*. Stencileret. Hamburg.

10   French transferences with nasal vowels in the graphematics and phonology of the Germanic languages

HORST H. MUNSKE

Introduction

The change of paradigm in research on language contact which was initiated in particular by Weinreich and Haugen, with the new emphasis on contrastive work, on research on interference and into bilingualism, has resulted in one of the traditional themes in language contact being pushed into the background: how loan words are integrated into our standard languages. How lexemes borrowed from other languages are to be written and pronounced was not just one of the major points of discussion in the development of national linguistic norms of spelling and pronunciation. Rather this question has again acquired topical significance as a result of present-day global communication, in particular as a result of the dominant role of just a few international languages. However, the study of the integration of loan words into the Germanic standard languages is influenced to a large extent by the older tradition of discussions of orthographic reform with special emphasis on language cultivation, and has not yet systematically taken account of the regular patterns of linguistic interference which occur here.

The topic of this article is to analyse from the point of view of interference linguistics the processes by which and conditions under which the French loan words are integrated phonologically and graphematically into the major Germanic standard languages and thus to apply the change of paradigm in this traditional area.

For this purpose the French loan words with nasal vowels in the Germanic languages were selected, since the general patterns of integration can be particularly well observed by comparing a group of 190 French lexemes which are encountered in almost all Germanic languages.[1] It will be explained why, for example, French *pardon* is pronounced as [par′doːn] or [par′dɔŋ] in German, as [par′duːn] or [par′dɔŋ] in Swedish, as [par′dɔn] or [par′dun] in Dutch and as [pɑːdn] in British English; why French *alliance* is written ⟨Allianz⟩ in German, ⟨alliantie⟩ in Dutch, ⟨allianse⟩ in Norwegian and ⟨allians⟩ in Swedish. The second example demonstrates that, in addition to phonetic and phonological integration, graphematic integration and the interaction between the two play an important role. It is this in particular that I intend to emphasize in the article – to supplement existing studies on linguistic interference.

First I will sketch my methodological approach as applied to selected examples (section 1); I will then present a survey of the transference and integration of the nasal vowels in English, Dutch, German, Danish, Norwegian and Swedish (section 2); and in conclusion I will summarize the results (Section 3). In an appendix the corpus of loan words is given with their present written norm and their pronunciation as indicated in the standard dictionaries. This may be a certain source of mistakes, since dictionaries tend to be somewhat out-dated as a rule. They are, however, a more representative and more uniform source of information than intuition-based judgements obtained from a native speaker for any linguist who is not in a position to carry out extensive empirical investigations. The more critically-minded reader who is guided by his own pronunciation may observe certain trends in the change in pronunciation.[2]

In the following text the examples quoted are as a rule presented in a simplified phonological transcription, as this is adequate for the purposes of the study and makes it possible to subsume the numerous phonetic variants under one form. (In special cases the phonetic transcription is indicated by [ ].) The corpus, which is arranged in related groups, makes it possible to examine and establish special features in each individual case and is intended to present a clear picture of transference and integration phenomena.

1   Methodology and terminology

The following observations provide my starting point.[3] In loan words interference occurs in two respects:

(a) In the first instance loan words are infringements of the norm of the recipient language in that they import foreign lexical items, foreign morphemes, sememes, phonemes, graphemes and specific rules for combining those items into the recipient language. These imports can be described as *transferences* on the level in question e.g. the nasal vowel [õ] in German *pardõ* as a phonemic transference.

(b) On all levels these transferences are exposed to interference from the recipient language, in some cases as early as at the stage of their perception and first realisation, but above all in the course of their continued use in the recipient language by monolingual speakers. Following Clyne 1975: 17ff., I describe such interferences as *integration phenomena*. For example, when French *pardõ* is integrated as *pardoŋ*, phenomena appear which we know from foreign language teaching are infringements of the norm of the target language, French.

The difference in the classification lies simply in the fact that in examining loan words the normative point of reference is not the source language but the recipient language. Transferences contradict the norms of the recipient language in the context of which they are used, as long as they are not integrated into it or accepted as innovations.

The transference and integration phenomena on the phonological level can be divided into three groups: *prosodic*, *phonemic* and *phonetic* transference and integration.[4]

I refer to *prosodic transference* when, for example, French final-syllable stress is retained in a loan word, as in German or Swedish *par'dɔŋ*, and to *prosodic integration* when this stress is replaced by that of the recipient language, as, for example, in English *'paːdn*.[5]

I refer to *phonemic transference* when the nasal vowel is retained in the loan word as in German *par'dõ*. Thus a sound occurs in German speech which does not exist in the phonological system of German. Such sounds are generally classified as 'peripheral phonemes'. This special status can be explained by the fact that such sounds are not backed up by minimal pairs. They only have genuine phoneme status in the source language, not, however, in the recipient language. They are not backed up by the network of phonological oppositions in the language in which they are used but they are orientated in an imitative way towards their source language, as a result of loyalty to the source language. It is significant that such phonemic transferences only occur in the languages of countries which border on France, in German and Dutch, and more rarely in English; not, however, in the Scandinavian languages. They particularly occur in lexemes which refer to what are supposedly specifically French cultural phenomena, e.g. *chanson, rendezvous*, etc. or which have the character of a quotation[6] such as *en passant, en face*, etc. Their regular occurrence is limited mainly to the speech of bilingual or partly bilingual speakers and, as phonetic variants, they serve the stylistic function of marking educated speech.

This influence of cultural loyalty on the status of peripheral elements results in them being exposed to interference from the recipient language in the case of monolingual speakers, i.e. to *phonemic integration*. In the case of nasal vowels this integration is carried out by biphonematic substitution with the bundle of distinctive features of the source language phoneme being 'unwrapped', as it were.[7]

$$
\text{French } /\tilde{o}/
\begin{bmatrix}
+ & \text{vocalic} \\
+ & \text{nasal} \\
+ & \text{round} \\
+ & \text{back} \\
- & \text{low} \\
- & \text{high}
\end{bmatrix}
\rightarrow \text{German } /o/ + /\eta/
\begin{bmatrix}
+ & \text{vocalic} \\
o & \text{nasal} \\
+ & \text{round} \\
+ & \text{back} \\
- & \text{low} \\
- & \text{high}
\end{bmatrix}
+
\begin{bmatrix}
- & \text{vocalic} \\
+ & \text{nasal} \\
o & \text{round} \\
+ & \text{velar} \\
o & \text{low}
\end{bmatrix}
$$

Fig. 1. Biophonematic substitution of French nasal vowels by 'unwrapping' the bundle of distinctive features

By *phonetic transference* I mean the transference of phonetic realizations in the case of phonemes which are interlingually identical, e.g. the German pronunciation of /r/ as an uvular vibrant [R] or fricative [ʁ]. These, following in part the French example, became generally accepted in preference to the apical [r] in educated speech in Germany in the 18th century. Conversely by *phonetic integration* I mean the replacement of the uvular fricative in French *pardon* [paʁdõ] by an apical [r] in Swedish *pardon* [par'dɔŋ], which is assimilated with the following [d] to a retroflex dental ([pa'dɔŋ], see below p. 256). In general it can be said that all loan words are phonetically integrated as a rule. This is also true in the case of the specific realization of nasal vowels in English, German and Dutch, which can be different from that in the source language as regards quantity and quality, for example.

The important distinction between paradigmatic and syntagmatic interference, as proposed in Weinreich 1957 and taken up in Szulc 1973, Morciniec 1976 and Tesch 1978, is also scarcely relevant in our area. All allophonically diverging realizations of an interlingually identical phoneme which were caused by distribution rules of the recipient language are to be considered cases of *syntagmatic phonetic integration* (in contrast to paradigmatic which has been dealt with above), e.g. the vocalization of *r* in final position in German *imaginär* [imagiˈnɛːɐ] in comparison to French *imaginaire* [imaʒiˈnɛːʁ].

In a corresponding way those cases in which a phoneme was substituted on the basis of the distribution rules of the recipient language are to be classified as *syntagmatic phonemic integration*, e.g. when the velar nasal in Swedish *pension* [paŋˈʃuːn] is integrated as a dental nasal [panˈʃuːn] as a result of assimilation with the following alveolar fricative. Other cases are better known, e.g. when English *smuggle* [smʌgl] is integrated into German as *Schmuggel* [ʃmʊgəl], because in German [sm-] is not an indigenous sequence in initial position. Conversely we can refer to *syntagmatic phonemic transference*, i.e. to the importation of a phonemic distribution rule, when English *smog* [smɔg] is accepted into German as *Smog* [smɔk].

So far I have remained within the framework of well-known linguistic studies of interference in spoken language. However, in this way the actual situation regarding the transference and integration of loan words is only half covered, for in addition there are corresponding phenomena on the grapheme level which are partly conflicting and partly complementary; they are on the one hand the result of what is called the 'reading' or 'spelling pronunciation' (e.g. in Swedish [parˈduːn], English [ˈpɑːdn]) and on the other, the result of the substitution of the written form of the recipient language for that of the source language, as, for example, in Swedish ⟨följetong⟩, German ⟨Allianz⟩ and Norwegian ⟨refreng⟩. Until now research on language contact has only touched in passing on these extremely common phenomena.[8] Therefore I must deal with them at greater length here in order to explain their wide-ranging significance.

Nowadays the speaker of a language has a two-fold competence in his native language. As Figure 2 shows, he possesses an oral and an auditory competence in the spoken language and – after he has attended school – a writing and reading competence in the written language.

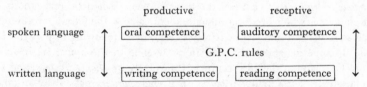

Fig. 2. Two-fold language competence, connected by grapheme–phoneme correspondence rules (G.P.C. rules)

These two competences are connected by a rule system between orthography and orthoepy, i.e. by rules for the reciprocal conversion of phoneme and grapheme sequences. Following Bierwisch 1973, I call such rules *grapheme–phoneme correspondence rules*, abbreviated to G.P.C. rules.

Loan words may be perceived by the present-day speakers of a language in two ways: auditory or visual, i.e. by hearing or reading. In each case the way in which the foreign lexeme is assimilated is different. With auditory perception foreign phones are borrowed into the language (phonemic transference) and in some cases are integrated phonemically according to the patterns of the system of the recipient language (phonemic integration); with visual perception the foreign grapheme sequence is interpreted phonemically according to the G.P.C. rules of the recipient language. Thus, for example, the grapheme sequence French ⟨-ment⟩ is not transferred as /mã/ or integrated as /maŋ/ but is reproduced as /ment/ in Dutch and partly also in German and Swedish. I call this phenomenon, which is known as 'spelling pronunciation', *grapho-phonemic integration*.

This term is designed to indicate that starting from the graphemic representation of a lexeme on the phonological level a process of integration takes place, i.e. phonemes from the source language are replaced. We encounter this sort of integration particularly in the case of monolingual speakers, who are not aware that a particular grapho-lexeme has to be converted into a phono-lexeme following other G.P.C. rules than the lexical items they know in their mother tongue. But it is possible that in language use the application of mother-tongue G.P.C. rules to particular graphemes in individual cases or in all loan words becomes so widespread that this is regarded as the norm and, by comparison, the application of source language G.P.C. rules seems noticeably foreign. (We shall see that this phenomenon is also frequently based on a morphological interpretation.)

The different pronunciations of Latin in England, Germany, Sweden, etc. can be cited as a well-known example of a general implementation of grapho-phonemic integration. Here the G.P.C. rules of the respective mother tongues are applied without hesitation in a dead language, which is only written and is rarely spoken any longer.

This is a simplification in the form of a model of the primary types of transference and integration in the phonological area, which occur in the reproduction of loan words. Since all loan words are written – irrespective of the way in which they are perceived – we should in addition examine what consequences these types of transference and integration have for the grapheme–phoneme relationship in the recipient language.

If, for example, French *pardõ* is transferred into German as *pardõ* and continues to be written ⟨pardon⟩, then the French G.P.C. rule ⟨on⟩ ↔ /õ/ has simultaneously been transferred into German. I call this *graphemic transference*. (A pronunciation which 'complies with the norm' thus presupposes knowledge of these G.P.C. rules, unless it is learnt for every word individually.) If the nasal vowel is phonemically integrated, then a new G.P.C. rule is created: ⟨on⟩ ↔ /oŋ/, a kind of interlanguage feature.

In a second step of a language-planning nature this G.P.C. rule can be replaced by adapting the foreign written form to the integrated pronunciation, as has happened extensively in Swedish ⟨betong⟩ and Norwegian ⟨føljetong⟩, Fr. ⟨on⟩ ↔ Swed., Norw. ⟨ong⟩. I call this change in the orthography of loan words *graphemic integration*.

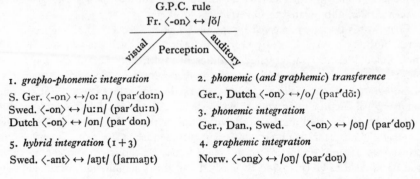

G.P.C. rule

Fr. ⟨-on⟩ ↔ /õ/

Perception

1. *grapho-phonemic integration*
S. Ger. ⟨-on⟩ ↔/oː n/ (par'doːn)
Swed. ⟨-on⟩ ↔ /uːn/ (par'duːn)
Dutch ⟨-on⟩ ↔ /on/ (par'don)

5. *hybrid integration* (1 + 3)
Swed. ⟨-ant⟩ ↔ /aŋt/ (ʃarmaŋt)

2. *phonemic (and graphemic) transference*
Ger., Dutch ⟨-on⟩ ↔/o/ (par'dõː)

3. *phonemic integration*
Ger., Dan., Swed.   ⟨-on⟩ ↔ /oŋ/ (par'doŋ)

4. *graphemic integration*
Norw. ⟨-ong⟩ ↔ /oŋ/ (par'doŋ)

Fig. 3. Types of graphemic and phonemic transference and integration

In addition in my examples there occasionally occurs a mixed form between grapho-phonemic and phonemic integration, which I call *hybrid integration*.

In French *ambulant, charmant,* etc. the nasal vowel in final position /ã/ is represented by the trigraph ⟨ant⟩. In grapho-phonemic integration the trigraph is interpreted monographically ⟨a⟩+⟨n⟩+⟨t⟩ in many Germanic languages (according to their G.P.C. rules) and the suffix is reproduced as /ant/. In phonemic integration biphonematic substitution by /aŋ/ occurs. Where these two types of integration compete with each other, as in Swedish and Norwegian, a blend /aŋt/ results. This blend can be explained as follows: the trigraph ⟨ant⟩ is interpreted as ⟨an⟩+ ⟨t⟩, whereby following a peripheral G.P.C. rule ⟨an⟩ is reproduced as ⟨aŋ⟩ corresponding to ⟨elan⟩ ↔ /elaŋ/ and ⟨ambulance⟩ ↔ /ambulaŋs/.

These five types of transference and integration are shown in Figure 3. (The double-ended arrows indicate the G.P.C. rules.)

1. *Grapho-phonemic integration* occurs where the written form of the source language is reproduced on the phonetic level by means of G.P.C. rules of the recipient language, when these rules are not identical with those of the source language. (Where the G.P.C. rules are identical interlingually no interference occurs, e.g. French, German ⟨p⟩ ↔ /p/ in *pardon*.)
Result: complete integration of the loan word as regards spoken form, written form and G.P.C. rules. The pronunciation in the source and recipient languages diverges in line with the contrast between the corresponding G.P.C. rules.

2. *Phonemic and graphemic transference:* transference of a phoneme from the source language and of the corresponding written form.
Result: transference of a peripheral phoneme and a peripheral G.P.C. rule into the recipient language.

3. *Phonemic integration:* substitution of a phoneme of the source language while retaining the written form of the source language.
Result: phonemically integrated pronunciation; the G.P.C. rule of the source language is modified accordingly.

4. *Graphemic integration:* substitution of a written form of the source language to conform to phonemic integration which has already taken place. As a result a

grapheme–phoneme correspondence in the recipient language is created which secures the integrated pronunciation.

Result: complete integration as regards spoken form, written form and G.P.C. rules.

5. *Hybrid integration:* a blend of grapho-phonemic 1, and phonemic integration 3.

Complete integration – i.e. the elimination of foreign phonemic and graphemic features (peripheral features) from the source language – can come about in two ways: (a) by grapho-phonemic integration and (b) in a longer way involving language planning – via phonemic and graphemic transference and integration (2, 3, 4).

In the first case (a) a short-cut is taken, as it were. As will be shown below, these four types of transference and integration compete with each other in different ways in my material. A rough comparison of the two final phases of complete integration, which appear above all in English (1) and in Swedish and Norwegian (4) gives the following largely familiar picture.

With grapho-phonemic integration the written form of the source language is retained, but on account of the application of specific G.P.C. rules of the recipient language in the source language, the pronunciation differs in the Germanic languages, in part to a considerable extent: cf. Fr. *bulletin* [byltɛ̃], Engl. [ˈbʊlɪtɪn], Dutch [bʌləˈtɛ̃], Ger. [bylˈtɛ̃] [byləˈtɛŋ], Dan., Norw. [byləˈtæŋ], Swed. [bʉləˈtiːn].

With phonemic and graphemic integration a pronunciation close to that of the source language is secured at the cost of in part considerable discrepancies in the written language: cf. Fr. ⟨feuilleton⟩ [fœj(ə)tɔ̃], Dan. ⟨føljeton⟩, Norw. ⟨føljetong⟩, Swed. ⟨följetong⟩ [följətɔŋ].

The debate about the integration of lexical borrowings has always swung between these two poles, according to whether priority is given to the 'international' written form or to securing a pronunciation close to that of the source language. Here arguments regarding language loyalty to the source language or to the mother tongue play a significant role. The latter appear as democratic concern for one's own language on behalf of speakers who have difficulty with the foreign G.P.C. rules or as an expression of purist concern for the mother tongue, which should be protected from hybridization.

So far this account has been limited to the phenomena of the transference and integration of the French nasal vowels, which are not present in the Germanic languages, and which are represented in French by the final grapheme sequences ⟨V+n(+t)⟩ (⟨on⟩, ⟨in⟩, ⟨ant⟩ . . .) or ⟨V+m⟩ (⟨om⟩, ⟨am⟩ . . .). Thus the investigation has been narrowed down to those contrasts which exist on both the phonological and the graphematical level. However, there are contrasts between the French and the Germanic languages which exist not on the phonological but exclusively on the graphematical level, and in order to complete the contrastive model and also to interpret particular cases in the material of this investigation we must deal with them here.

In this connection we may compare the final consonant in Fr. *alliance* [aljɑ̃ːs] with Ger. *Allianz* [aˈli̯ants] and Swed. *allians* [aliˈaŋs].[9] The final /s/ is represented graphically in French by ⟨ce⟩, in German by ⟨z⟩ and in Swedish by ⟨s⟩. In the loan words integration on the graphemic level has been carried out by applying the G.P.C. rules of the recipient language: Ger. /s/ ↔ /z/ (following a nasal, as in *ganz, Tanz*), Swed. /s/ ↔ ⟨s⟩. On the other hand, the nasal vowels are integrated in various ways, in German grapho-phonemically (Fr. /ã/ ↔ ⟨an⟩ → Ger. ⟨an⟩ ↔ /an/), in Swedish phonemically (Fr. ⟨an⟩ ↔ /ã/ → Swed. /aŋ/ ↔ ⟨an⟩).

One could likewise call this form of integration on the grapheme level graphemic integration, but in doing so would overlook the important difference that in this case integration has only taken place on the grapheme level, whereas in the cases discussed earlier the phoneme *and* the grapheme level have been affected. I therefore term the phenomenon just illustrated *graphetic integration*.

A glance at integration phenomena on the grapheme level shows that graphetic integrations occur relatively frequently, since they do not affect interlingual phonemic identity but rather consolidate it graphematically. From my corpus of examples I may cite the following:

/k/: Fr. ⟨c⟩ → Ger., Dutch, Dan., Swed., Norw. ⟨k⟩ (carton → karton, kartong)
/u/: Fr. ⟨ou⟩ → Norw., Swed. ⟨u⟩ (bouillon → buljong, coupon → kupong)
/š/: Fr. ⟨ch⟩ → Norw., Dutch ⟨sj⟩, Swed. ⟨sch⟩ (chance → Dutch sjans, Norw. sjanse, branche → Norw. bransje, Swed. bransch)
/ɛ/: Fr. ⟨ai⟩ → Ger. ⟨ä⟩, Dan. ⟨æ⟩, Norw., Swed. ⟨e⟩ (raison → Ger. Räson, Dan. ræson, Norw. resong, Swed. reson)

If graphetic integration does *not* occur in a loan word where the phonemes are interlingually identical but are represented graphematically in different ways, this implies that the G.P.C. rule of the source language is transferred. Accordingly I call this *graphetic transference*.

There are also numerous examples of this in my material. The following French graphemes and G.P.C. rules were transferred, for example:

Fr. /k/ ↔ ⟨c⟩ into Dan. *accent* (in contrast to Norw. *aksent*)
Fr. /u/ ↔ ⟨ou⟩ into Dutch *coulance*
Fr. /š/ ↔ ⟨ch⟩ into Dan. *chaiselong*, Swed. *chans*, Ger. *Chance*
Fr. /ɛ/ ↔ ⟨ai⟩ into Dan. *chaiselong*, Norw. *komplaisant*.

These examples also show that the ways in which graphetic integration was carried out in individual lexemes are very varied. The most common are the omission of the French accent sign and – on the morpho-graphemic level – the occurrence of the initial capital letter in the case of substantives in German.[10]

Using this classification system and this procedure it is possible to categorize all cases of transference and integration in the areas of phonology and graphematics.

In conclusion I will illustrate this using as an example the borrowings of the type *bassin, teint, terrain*. (Fig. 4, Ex. 137–55 in the Appendix.)

German has not changed the written form – except for the use of initial capital letters (graphetic integration). The loan words are partly phonemically transferred (/ɛ̃/), partly phonemically integrated (/ɛŋ/), whereby the pronunciation varies according to the frequency with which the lexemes occur (*Bassin, Terrain*) or to the speakers' level of education.

G.P.C. rule: ⟨in(t)⟩ ⟨ain⟩ ↔ /ɛ̃/, /ɛŋ/.

In all cases Danish integrates loan words phonemically as a rule (/ba'sɛŋ/) and retains the written form – except in *terræn* and *refræn*. Here the French trigraph ⟨ain⟩ is 'unwrapped' (⟨ai⟩ + ⟨n⟩) and following the pattern of Fr. *raison, saison* →

Fr. ⟨in⟩, ⟨int⟩, ⟨ain⟩ ↔ /ɛ̃/

1. *Grapho-phonemic integration*
   by 'unwrapping' the French
   diagraph or trigraph according to
   the G.P.C. rules of the recipient
   language e.g. ⟨int⟩ → ⟨i⟩+⟨n⟩+⟨t⟩
   (Engl., Dutch, Swed., Norw.)

   ⟨in⟩ ↔ /in/
   ⟨int⟩ ↔ /int/
   ⟨ain⟩ ↔ /ein/

2. *Phonemic and graphemic transference*
   (Ger.) Dutch)

   ⟨in⟩
   ⟨int⟩ ↔ /ɛ̃/
   ⟨ain⟩

3. *Phonemic integration*
   by 'unwrapping' the French phoneme
   and biphonematic substitution
   (Ger.) Dan., Norw., Swed.)

   ⟨in⟩
   ⟨int⟩ ↔ /ŋ/
   ⟨ain⟩

4. *Graphemic (and phonemic) integration*
   (Swed., Norw.)

   Swed. ⟨äng⟩
   Norw. ⟨eng⟩ ↔ /ɛŋ/

5. *Graphetic integration*
   (Dan.)

   ⟨æn⟩ ↔ /ɛŋ/

Fig. 4. Transference and integration of French /ɛ̃/

Dan. *ræson, sæson* only the vowel is graphetically integrated (/ɛ/: Fr. ⟨ai⟩ → Dan. ⟨æ⟩), while ⟨n⟩ is phonemically integrated according to the G.P.C. rule ⟨n⟩ ↔ /ŋ/.

G.P.C. rules: ⟨-in(t)⟩ ↔ /ɛŋ/
⟨-æn⟩ ↔ /ɛŋ/

Norwegian follows Danish in having a phonemically integrated pronunciation; however, in half of the examples it follows the example of Swedish in going further to graphemic integration (*basseng, refreng, . . .*).

G.P.C. rules: ⟨-in(t)⟩ ↔ /ɛŋ/
⟨-eng⟩ ↔ /ɛŋ/

With the exception of *teint, kusin, bulletin* and *embonpoint*, Swedish has integrated all the examples phonemically and graphemically (*mannekäng, poäng, . . .*). The consistent removal of foreign G.P.C. rules explains the fact that indigenous G.P.C. rules are also applied to *kusin, bulletin*.

G.P.C. rules: ⟨-äng⟩ ↔ /ɛŋ/
⟨-int⟩ ↔ /ɛŋ/
⟨-in⟩ ↔ /iːn/

Dutch mostly retains the French spelling and pronunciation. In some cases, with presumably underlying historic French written form ⟨-ein⟩, grapho-phonemic integration occurred (⟨ein⟩ ↔ /ei/ + /n/). (On ⟨ijn⟩ see below p. 244.)

G.P.C. rules: ⟨-in(t)⟩ → /ɛ̃/
⟨-ein⟩, ⟨-ijn⟩ ↔ /ein/

English retains the French spelling and integrates loan words solely grapho-phonemically.

G.P.C. rules: ⟨-in⟩ ↔ /in/ (/ˈmænɪkɪn/)
⟨-ain⟩ ↔ /ein/ (/teˈreɪn/)
⟨-int⟩ ↔ /int/ (/pɔɪnt/)

2   **Transference and integration of the nasal vowels in French loan words**

The following account is faced with the difficulty of making certain representative statements about the trends in and reasons for the transference and integration of French nasal vowels in the individual Germanic languages on the basis of a corpus which has been restricted for comparative purposes.

The following factors restrict the scope for the analysis of the individual languages:

(a) The number of borrowings common to the Germanic languages represents in some cases a high and in others a low percentage of the total number of borrowings in the individual languages (lower for English and Dutch, higher for German and the Scandinavian languages).

(b) The history of the contacts between the individual languages and French was only dealt with in general terms on the basis of reference books.

(c) The pronouncing dictionaries and the phonetic transcription given in the dictionaries of individual languages vary as regards quality and representativeness.

(d) The identification of French loan words from a synchronic viewpoint is far from simple. For frequently integration into an individual language following Latin models conceals the French origin (cf. e.g. p. 241). Sometimes it is not until after the integration into other Germanic languages has been compared that it is possible to decide whether the borrowing was from Latin or French. Thus all Gallicisms ending in ⟨-ion⟩ are quite regularly integrated according to the patterns of the corresponding Latinisms, and for this reason this group was completely disregarded here. The dictionaries of individual languages frequently do not distinguish between the source language from which a word was directly borrowed (French) and the Latin lexeme which historically underlies the word.

I have therefore essentially restricted myself to dealing with the more common suffixes and prefixes. Details can be seen in the corpus in the Appendix.

2.1   **German**

There are three pronouncing dictionaries for German: *Duden Aussprachewörterbuch* 1974, *Siebs Deutsche Aussprache* 1969 and *Wörterbuch der deutschen Aussprache* 1969 (*W.d.A.*). I have taken *W.d.A.* as my basis, because it is the only one which is based on recent empirical investigations (of news readers) and furthermore attaches great importance to the pronunciation of loan words in particular by giving variations (cf. Ungeheuer 1969: 210). The pronunciation of French loan words varies in German between the phonemic transference of the nasal vowels $\tilde{a}$, $\tilde{o}$, $\tilde{\varepsilon}$ and $\tilde{œ}$, and their phonemic integration and grapho-phonemic integration and presents a confusing, relatively unstable picture in this respect. Up to 60% of the nasal vowels of the source language are realized (by educated speakers), but in half of these cases phonemic integration is also possible. In a third of all cases grapho-phonemic integration occurs regularly, whereby this is more frequent in medial (e.g. no. 183: *dispensieren*) than in initial position (no. 164: *Emblem*). This rough overall picture can be explained in more detail.

The especially high regard for the French language and culture in Germany is reflected in the relatively frequent retention of the nasal vowels. This high regard originated in the French–German diglossia among the nobility and some of the upper-middle-classes in the 18th and 19th centuries. Thus in the present day the retention of the nasal vowel has a phonostylistic value: that a person is cultured is shown in his particular loyalty to the French language. However, in the individual case this pronunciation may be regarded as stilted and artificial, especially in everyday speech, which tends generally to phonemic integration. In other words, this variation in the pronunciation of French loan words is what Bühler calls 'symptomfunktional' in that it indicates the social position of the speaker ('diastratisch') and the communicative situation in which he finds himself ('diaphasisch') (cf. Bühler 1965: 28).

In addition by examining the material it is possible to identify the circumstances which are conducive to phonemic integration and those which hinder it. Phonemic integration occurs regularly with common lexemes, which refer to things of everyday life and for which there are no indigenous synonyms (e.g. *Karton, Ballon, Bronze, Waggon, Beton*). With lexemes which refer to supposedly specifically French characteristics of the culture and way of life (*Nonchalance, Chanson, Rendezvous*) or which contain several foreign features (foreign G.P.C. rules) (e.g. *Liaison, Mannequin, Impromptu*) the nasal vowels are realized as a rule.

Grapho-phonemic integration is encountered above all in the case of several common suffixes and prefixes. However, this integration is not primarily to be interpreted as a 'reading pronunciation', but as being connected with Latin models of integration, i.e. as morphological integration on the basis of interlingual identification on the morpheme level (cf. Kratz 1968: 455).

Almost all adjectives ending in ⟨-ant⟩ are integrated grapho-phonemically (/-ant/) by following the group of Latin lexemes in ⟨-ant⟩ such as *konstant, variant, signifikant*. In contrast the corresponding substantives (*Volant, Restaurant, Pendant*) do not follow such models (*Spekulant, Diamant*). With the adjectives there is apparently a further reason for grapho-phonemic integration: only in this pronunciation are they declinable. Thus *degoutant* can only be used predicatively in the source language pronunciation [degu'tã] ('Das ist degoutant'); grapho-phonemic integration [degu'tant] is the precondition for attributive use ('Ein degoutanter Anblick').

The majority of the French derivations ending in ⟨-ance⟩ and ⟨-ence⟩ are graphetically integrated (⟨-anz⟩, ⟨-enz⟩) and in pronunciation they are graphophonemically integrated (/ants/, /ents/). In this case, too, the group of Latin borrowings served as a model (*Substanz, Präsenz* etc.).

In individual cases it cannot definitely be established whether Latin models in ⟨-antia⟩, ⟨-entia⟩ are the direct underlying form. Many German speakers (and many dictionaries) consider them to be Latinisms. A more detailed explanation only emerges after comparison with the corresponding Scandinavian forms – cf. the Appendix nos. 89–132 – or after examining the history of the loan word (historical spelling).

Some lexemes ending in ⟨-ent⟩ (*Akzent, Moment, Präsent, Talent*) are also graphophonemically integrated following Latin models. (In the pronunciation of Swiss German this integration has taken place in all cases.)

Table 1. *Transference and integration of French nasal vowels in German*

Written form	1 grapho-phon. integration	2 phon. transference	3 phon. integration	2/3	1/3
⟨on⟩	/o: n/ (1)*	/õ/ (4)	/oŋ/ (3)	/õ/, /oŋ/ (16)	/o:n/, /oŋ/ (4)
⟨ant⟩ (Adj.)	/ant/ (17)	/ã/ (1)			
⟨(m)ent⟩	/ɛnt/ (6)	/ã/ (7)		/ã/, /aŋ/ (11)	
⟨ance⟩		/ãs/ (6)		/ãs/, /aŋs(e)/ (4)	
⟨anz⟩	/ans/ (17)				
⟨ence⟩				/ãs/, /aŋs/ (2)	
⟨enz⟩	/ens/ (13)				
⟨in(t)⟩, ⟨ain⟩		/ɛ̃/ (7)		/ɛ̃/, /ɛŋ/ (6)	/i:n/, /ɛŋ/ (1)
	54	25	3	39	5

* More frequent in South German pronunciation

Furthermore some prefixes (in-, im-, kon-) follow this pattern of integration.

Table 1 gives an overview of the transference and integration of common suffixes. It shows that phonemic integration certainly occurs frequently (44 times), but almost without exception as a variant (depending on social class and social context) alongside the retention of the nasal vowel (39 times).

2.2   English

The account of the integration of French loan words in English must begin with some historical background. English has an exceptional position in the Germanic languages on account of the intensive Germanic–Romance 'language-mixing' which took place following the Norman conquest and the English–Anglo-Norman diglossia which existed for several centuries in the Middle Ages. Between 1200 and 1450 50% of the Gallicisms which are still used in contemporary English were introduced, in the 18th century only 5.4%, in the 19th century, 7.2% (Scheler 1977: 56).[11]

The Gallicisms to be examined here also reflect the dominant position of Anglo-Norman as the written language until the 15th century and the fact that members of both language groups, English and French, learned the language of the other, which finally ended in a victory for the substratum, but with a structural change in the substratum caused by the superstratum. As early as the Middle English period numerous loan words of this kind were introduced (e.g. *variance, difference, agreement*, cf. Marchand 1969: 248ff., 331). After a long period of fluctuations in usage the word-stress of the Gallicisms underwent consistent prosodic integration as a rule (the stress was moved forward). The mixing of the grapheme systems, the incorporation of French graphemes in English words (e.g. ⟨ou⟩ for /u/ in *house*) and the denasalization of the French nasal vowels (Berndt 1960: 97, Mossé 1952: 31) are particularly interesting for the scope of our investigation. The writing system which was largely stabilized towards the end of the 14th century and which has on the whole been retained until now represents a relatively clear, if also very complex system of phoneme-grapheme correspondences (Venezky 1970), in which all

Gallicisms (and Latinisms) are included as indigenous lexemes. That is, the Early Modern English grapheme system contained *indigenous rules* for the reproduction of all Romanisms and Latinisms. Later borrowings from French (and Latin) could be fitted into this system without difficulty. They were grapho-phonemically integrated relatively easily following the model of the indigenous G.P.C. rules which already existed.

This explains the fact that in our corpus over 90% of the loan words are prosodically integrated and over 80% grapho-phonemically integrated.

As a result of prosodic integration (replacement of word-final stress by stress on a previous syllable) the numerous nasal vowels in final position or in suffixes (-on, -ant, -ment, -ance, -ence) become subject to secondary stress. Furthermore the process of shifting the stress seems to precede integration on the segmental level. This is indicated by the fact that – with the exception of some lexemes ending in ⟨-oon⟩, such as *balloon, cocoon, pontoon* – all prosodically integrated lexemes are also grapho-phonemically integrated, and a dozen more are already prosodically integrated, but not yet completely grapho-phonemically integrated (*nuance, entente, entree* etc.).

Where Jones 1977 gives nasal vowels, they are always followed by phonemically or grapho-phonemically integrated variants; for example, in *restaurant*, French [rɛstɔrɑ̃]: [ˈrestərɔ̃:(ŋ)], [-rɑ̃:(ŋ)], alongside (phonemically integrated) [-rɑ:ŋ] and (grapho-phonemically integrated) [-rɒnt, -rənt]. (As here, French /ɑ̃/ was repeatedly also rendered as /õ/ (*élan, mélange, avant-garde*).)

The nasal vowels are mostly interpreted as long. Phonemic integration takes place via the steps [ɑ̃:], [ɑ̃:ŋ], [a:ŋ], [aŋ]. In a series of our examples (10) we encounter 'denasalization', which is known to us from the history of the English language, as in *gendarme* [ʒɑ̃:(n)dɑːm, ʒɑːn-] and *nuance* [njuːˈɑ̃:(n)s, -ɑːns]. Obviously this is based on phonemic transference, but as a result of the assimilatory effect of the following dental, the alveolar and not the velar nasal is realized. (Similarly in German and Danish in the case of *gendarme*, no. 184.)

As the variants show, the few loan words which are still spoken with a nasal vowel are also frequently subject to grapho-phonemic integration in everyday speech. In this respect American English has already gone further, cf. inter alia, Engl. *bouillon* [buːjɔ̃:(ŋ)] and American English [ˈbuljan].

Many Gallicisms which have retained the nasal vowel must appear to a French observer to be strange hybrids, since all the other segments are grapho-phonemically integrated (cf. *en passant*, Fr. [ɑ̃ˈpasɑ̃], Engl. [ɑ̃:(m) ˈpæsɑ̃:(ŋ)], *nuance*, Fr. [nyɑ̃s], Engl. [njuːˈɑ̃:(n)s].

The loan words with the retained nasal vowel mainly belong to the more recent layer of loan words (17th to 19th century).

The numerous phonetical pronunciation variants serve a stylistic function and presumably also mark socio-linguistic differences. The retention of the nasal vowel seems to be a sort of 'foreign marker' for particular lexemes which are associated with French culture and the French way of life (*salon, liaison, demimonde*, cf. above p. 241).

If we disregard this small group of French loan words, it is characteristic of English in comparison with the other Germanic languages that there is no foreign word problem caused by French loan words. The mixed Germanic–Romance character of the English lexicon and grapheme system offered and still offers today the basis for an easy integration of French borrowings.

2.3   Dutch

After English Dutch is the Germanic language with by far the most French borrowings. They have been incorporated because of the very close political and cultural contacts between the French and the Dutch from the Middle Ages to the present-day and they were largely integrated as a result of early purist movements (cf. van der Meer 1927, Section 33; this thorough book in the Neogrammarian tradition offers in Sections 168–264 a detailed account of the integration of French 'sounds' with many examples). Our corpus contains only a small proportion of these loan words.

Almost all loan words have retained the word-stress of the source language (prosodic transference, cf. van Loey 1964, Section 90). A good 60% of all nasal vowels are grapho-phonemically integrated, a quarter were retained, and in the case of the remainder the pronunciation varies between these alternatives, whereby the retention of the nasal vowel is rated higher phonostylistically. In contrast to German and the Scandinavian languages there is no evidence of phonemic integration.

Almost all loan words with the suffixes ⟨on⟩, ⟨(m)ent⟩, ⟨ant⟩ (adjectives) and the prefixes ⟨kon⟩, ⟨in⟩ are grapho-phonemically integrated. What was probably decisive here was, on the one hand, the early date of the borrowing (as in English) and, on the other hand, the connection with Latin models (cf. van der Meer, Section 168). The suffixes ⟨ance⟩, ⟨ence⟩ have mainly been integrated morphologically as ⟨antie⟩, ⟨entie⟩ ([an(t)si], [en(t)si]) following the model of Latin loan words in ⟨antia⟩, ⟨entia⟩. Where this integration did not take place in the case of more recent borrowings (*coulance, elegance, nuance* etc.) the pronunciation varies between phonemic transference and grapho-phonemic integration (/ãːs(e)/, /anse/), (*balans, sjans* are older borrowings dating from as early as Middle Dutch; cf. van der Meer, Section 172).

A historical explanation also applies to the deviations from the rule in *pardoen, seizoen* [-ʹun] (graphetic integration of the older French pronunciation of *u*, van der Meer, Section 209), *chagrijn, satijn* etc. (Dutch diphthongization of older borrowings, van der Meer, Section 210), and *terrein, refrein* (Old French ⟨ei⟩, van der Meer, Section 213).

As in German, the variation in pronunciation reflects the conflict between loyalty either to French as the language of culture or to the mother tongue. Exotic words (*bon vivant, chanson, faience* etc.) in particular have retained the nasal vowel. The reason for the high overall degree of grapho-phonemic integration – here as in other areas Dutch lies 'tussen Duits en Engels' (between German and English) (van Haeringen 1955) – is presumably the historical depth and continuity of French–Dutch language contact; but a contributory reason may also be the relatively phonemically orientated orthography, which has been reformed several times, and which strongly suggests the consistent application of indigenous G.P.C. rules (cf. below on Swedish, p. 251). Table 2 illustrates the facts which have been presented.

Table 2. *Transference and integration of French nasal vowels in Dutch*

Written form	1 grapho-phon. integration	2 phon. transference	1/2
⟨on⟩	/on/ (20)	/õ/ (3)	/on/, /õ/ (4)
⟨ant⟩ (adj.)	/ant/ (19)		
⟨(m)ent⟩	/(m)ɛnt/ (24)		
⟨antie⟩*	/ansi/ (18)		
⟨ance⟩		/ãs(e)/ (6)	/anse/, /ãse/ (6)
⟨ans⟩	/ans/ (3)		
⟨entie⟩*	/ensi/ (11)		
⟨ence⟩		/ãse/ (4)	
⟨in⟩		/ɛ̃/ (6)	
⟨ein⟩	/ein/ (2)		
⟨ijn⟩	/ein/ (3)		

* Morphological integration: replacement of the French derivation morphemes ⟨ance⟩, ⟨ence⟩ by ⟨antie⟩, ⟨entie⟩ from Latin loan words.

2.4 Scandinavian languages

The French loan words which are present in the Scandinavian languages today were incorporated mainly between the 17th and 19th centuries (Bergmann 1970, Skautrup 1944–68: Vols 2, 3). As in German and Dutch they have in general retained the stress of the source language. Only in Danish was prosodic integration also carried out in few cases (*defensiv, intolerant, appartement,* inter alia, have initial stress).

Everywhere the nasal vowels are partly phonemically (and graphemically) and partly grapho-phonemically integrated. (However, the *O.D.S.* differs from the *Nudansk Ordbog* in also noting in some cases an alternative 'French pronunciation', i.e. phonemic transference, inter alia, in the case of *demi-monde, embonpoint, enthousiasme, ensemble, tantieme.*)

Furthermore the loan words differ, in part to a considerable extent, in written form and pronunciation. The following examples may be quoted: Norw. *agrement,* Swed. *agremang;* Dan. *bouillon,* Norw., Swed. *buljong;* Dan. *dekadence,* Norw. *dekadanse,* Swed. *dekadans;* Dan. *ræson,* Norw. *resong,* Swed. *reson.*

The main reasons for this are the various attempts to reform the orthographic system and the effects these have had on how the correspondence between graphemes and phonemes is perceived. Historical reasons (borrowing via German) have only rarely been decisive. The fact that the pronunciation of loan words in Danish differs greatly from that in Norwegian and Swedish is due to rapid language change in recent years and to phonemic and phonetic integration (lenition, vowel lowering, *Stød* etc.).

While Danish has retained the written form of French loan words almost without exception, there have been conspicuous alterations in Swedish and Norwegian. The fact that today French loan words are to a large extent graphetically and graphemically integrated in Swedish is however not the fruit of democratic progressiveness in this century, as an uninformed observer might think, but goes back

Table 3. *Integration of the French suffixes* ⟨on⟩, ⟨ent⟩, ⟨in(t)⟩ *in the Scandinavian languages*

Fr.		1. grapho-phon. integration	3. phon. integration	4. graphem. integration	1/3
⟨on⟩	Dan.	/on/ (1)	/oŋ/ (25)	—	—
↕	Norw.	⟨on⟩←/on/ (1)	⟨on⟩←/oŋ/ (6)	⟨ong⟩↘/oŋ/ (23)	—
/õ/	Swed.	/uːn/ (1)	/oŋ/ (5)	/oŋ/ (21)	—
⟨ent⟩	Dan.	/ent/ (1)	/aŋ/ (22)		⟨ent⟩-/aŋ/, /ent/ (3)
↕	Norw.	⟨ent⟩←/ent/ (3)	⟨ent⟩←/aŋ/ (20)	⟨ang⟩ /aŋ/ (1)	
/ã/	Swed.	/ent/ (10)	—	/aŋ/ (14)	
⟨in(t)⟩,	Dan.	—	⟨in(t)⟩↘/ɛŋ/ (10)		⟨int⟩-/ɛŋ/, /eint/ (1)
⟨ain⟩	Norw.	—	⟨æn⟩		
↕			⟨in(t)⟩-/ɛŋ/ (6)	⟨eng⟩-/ɛŋ/ (5)	
/ɛ̃/	Swed.	⟨in⟩-/iːn/ (3)	⟨in(t)⟩-/ɛŋ/ (2)	⟨äng⟩-/ɛŋ/ (10)	

to the reform of Swedish orthography by the 'Svenska Akademien' in 1801, which adopted the radical proposals of Carl Gustav Leopold (*Afhandling om svenska stafsättet*). The reasons given for this drastic reform sound modern all the same – to prevent speakers of the language being misled into using an incorrect pronunciation and to prevent the hybridization of the mother tongue 'ett brok-verk av inhemska ock främmande ord' (Leopold 1801: 215, cf. Lindstam 1946: 3f., 89ff.) Since the middle of the 19th century Norwegian orthography has been even more extensively reformed (especially as regards graphetic integration) in a move to free the language from its Danish heritage and in part following the example of the Swedish reform. In 1917 in the course of this reform all loan words in particular were radically integrated (Lindstam 1946: 16ff., further information in Karker 1976).

As regards the French graphemes which represent nasal vowels, the situation is as follows: graphemic integration is limited to the suffixes with final syllable stress: French ⟨(m)ent⟩, ⟨on⟩ and ⟨in(t)⟩ (to Norw. ⟨ang⟩, ⟨ong⟩, ⟨eng⟩, Swed. ⟨ang⟩ or ⟨mang⟩, ⟨ong⟩, ⟨eng⟩, cf. also Table 3), while in all initial and medial positions the French written form is retained. This is also the case with the common suffixes ⟨once⟩, ⟨ance⟩, ⟨ence⟩, ⟨anche⟩, where in Norwegian and Swedish – in different ways – only the final spirant was graphetically integrated (/s/: Fr. ⟨ce⟩ → ⟨s⟩, ⟨se⟩; /ʃ/: Fr. ⟨che⟩ → ⟨sje⟩, ⟨sch⟩; cf. Table 4).

The retention of the final ⟨e⟩ in Norw. ⟨ance⟩, ⟨anse⟩, ⟨onse⟩, ⟨ansje⟩ takes account of the already usual 'reading pronunciation' in Danish [aŋsə], [oŋse] etc., which was probably also usual in Norwegian even before the orthographic reforms.

Tables 3 and 4 give an overview of the three types of integration – graphophonemic, phonemic and graphemic – in the case of the most important suffixes in Danish, Norwegian and Swedish. The numbers in brackets refer to the number of examples and thus give us an indication of the distribution of the various patterns of integration. The rough picture given by the summary in Table 5 of the numbers in Tables 3 and 4 is altered to a certain degree when the nasal vowels in all suffixes

Table 4. *Integration of the French suffixes* ⟨ance⟩, ⟨ence⟩, ⟨once⟩, ⟨anche⟩ *in the Scandinavian languages*

Fr.	1. grapho-phon. integration	3. phon. integration	1/3
⟨ance⟩ ↕ /ãs/	Dan. /ans/ (6) ⟨ans⟩ Norw. /ans/ (3) Swed.	⟨ance⟩—/aŋse/ (23) ⟨ance⟩ (22) ⟨anse⟩ /aŋse/ (1) ⟨ans⟩—/aŋs/ (4) ⟨ans⟩—/aŋs/ (8)	⟨ans⟩—/ans/, /aŋs/ (1) — ⟨ans⟩-/ans/, /aŋs/ (23)
⟨ence⟩ ↕ /ãs/	Dan. ⟨ens(e)⟩ /ens(e)/ (7) Norw. /ens(e)/ (3) Swed. ⟨ens⟩—/ens/ (5)	⟨ence⟩ (9) ⟨anse⟩ /aŋse/ (10) ⟨ens⟩—/aŋs/ (2)	— — ⟨ens⟩-/ens/, /aŋs/ (5)
⟨once⟩ ↕ /õs/	— —	Dan. ⟨once⟩ /oŋse/ (2) ⟨onze⟩ (1) Norw. ⟨onse⟩—/oŋse/ (2) ⟨ons⟩—/oŋs/ (1) Swed. ⟨ons⟩—/oŋs/ (3)	— — —
⟨anche⟩ ↕ /ãʃ/	— — Swed. ⟨ansch⟩/anʃ/ (1)	Dan. ⟨anche⟩ /anʃe/ (3) Norw. ⟨ansje⟩ (3)	⟨ansch⟩-/anʃ/, /anʃ/ (2)

Table 5. *Integration of French suffixes in the Scandinavian languages (frequency)*

	1. grapho-phon. integration	3. phon. integration	4. graphemic (+phon.) integr.	5. hybrid integr.	1/3	1/5
Dan.	15 (29)	93 (31)	— (—)	(—)	5 (4)	(—)
Norw.	10 (22)	75 (29)	29 (—)	(3)	— (4)	(5)
Swed.	20 (6)	20 (18)	45 (—)	(3)	30 (15)	(20)

Table 5 shows a quantitative evaluation of Tables 3 and 4.

and particularly in initial and medial positions are also taken into account (numbers in brackets in Table 5). The large number of pronunciation doublets in Swedish (65 compared to 9 and 12 in Danish and Norwegian respectively) and the many cases of hybrid integration are particularly striking. This is obviously connected with the largely completed graphemic integration of the suffixes (cf. Table 3) by which phonemic integration (/õ/ → oŋ/) is consolidated graphemically (indigenous G.P.C. rule: /oŋ/ ↔ ⟨ong⟩). In all the cases where this graphemic consolidation did not take place, uncertainty could then arise as to whether, for example, in the case of the written form ⟨ant⟩ indigenous rules were also to be applied (⟨ant⟩ ↔ /ant/) or whether a modified French rule should be applied (⟨ant⟩ ↔ /aŋ/). This leads to

the two forms /ant/ and /aŋ/ existing alongside each other (column 1/3) and also to hybrid integration /aŋt/ (column 1/5). The fact that pronunciation doublets are relatively rare in Danish shows that conservative adherence to the French written forms has resulted in a relatively definite G.P.C. rule ⟨Vowel+Nasal+(t)⟩ ↔ /Vowel+ŋ/.
This will be presented in more detail in the next section.

2.5   Danish

In the absence of an up-to-date pronunciation dictionary, I have used the practically identical notations in the *O.D.S.* 1918–56 and the *Nudansk Ordbog* 1969. The questions to be examined are: What are the effects of the retention of the French written form in loan words on the pronunciation? Which pronunciation has become generally accepted?

As a rule phonemic integration takes place. This is the case with all noun suffixes (⟨on⟩ ↔ /oŋ/, ⟨(m)ent⟩ ↔ /(m)aŋ/, ⟨ant⟩ ↔ /aŋ/, ⟨once⟩ ↔ /oŋsə/, ⟨ance⟩, ⟨ence⟩ ↔ /aŋsə/, ⟨anche⟩ ↔ /aŋʃə/, ⟨in(t)⟩, ⟨æn⟩ ↔ /ɛŋ/) and in the majority of cases with the French diagraphs ⟨on⟩, ⟨an⟩, ⟨en⟩ in initial and medial position (/oŋ/, /aŋ/). Hansen 1956: 81f. points out that in the case of some pronunciation doublets /ŋ/ is partly regarded as vulgar (*centimeter* /saŋ-/) and partly as 'refined' (*enthousiasme* /aŋ-/).

Furthermore the adjective suffix ⟨ant⟩ and the prefixes ⟨kon⟩ and ⟨in⟩ are grapho-phonemically integrated, as are the diagraphs ⟨om⟩, ⟨em⟩, ⟨am⟩ in the majority of cases. The 'spelling pronunciation' of *frappant*, *pikant*, etc. follows either the German model – until the 19th century German was the language of the court, the administration and the military in Denmark (Skautrup III and IV) – or the example of corresponding Latin formations, as in German. This is certainly the case with the prefixes mentioned and also with single lexemes, such as *dispensere*, *defensiv*, which are phonemically integrated in Norwegian and Swedish.

In a similar fashion a series of lexemes of the French type ⟨ance⟩ are treated as Latinisms in Danish (*ordonnans, finans . . .*) or have been borrowed from German where they had already been integrated in this way (*prægnans, resonans*). The conflict between the pronunciation following the French or Latin models (phonemic or grapho-phonemic integration) is also apparent in several (partly also graphemic) doublets: *korrespondance*, -ens, *(in)kompetence*, -ens, *konference*, -ens [-ɐŋsə], [-æns] with a difference in meaning in the case of *differance*, *differens* (math.), *accent* [ag'sæn'd], [ag'saŋ] and *talent* [ta'laŋ, ta'læn'd]. On the whole the principle of phonemic integration is only violated in the case of borrowings from German and where a connection with a morphological model in Latin is possible.

2.6   Norwegian

Norwegian and Danish only differ slightly in the pronunciation of nasal vowels in French loan words. The obvious explanation is the dominant position of Danish in the history of the Norwegian language. (The pronunciations cited are taken from Berulfsen's excellent dictionary of 1969.) Phonemic integration is the rule (with the exceptions mentioned), whereby this is consolidated by the graphemic integration of the suffixes ⟨on⟩ → ⟨ong⟩ and ⟨in⟩ → ⟨eng⟩. (In only one case ⟨ent⟩ → ⟨ang⟩ in *presang*.) On account of identical pronunciations the French suffixes ⟨ance⟩ and ⟨ence⟩ are regarded as one and graphetically integrated (⟨anse⟩), whereby the mute French ⟨-e⟩, which is also reproduced grapho-phonemically in the Danish pronunciation, is retained.

Norwegian follows Danish in the graphetic integration as well, e.g. *finans, instans, ordonnans, pregnans, resonans*; however, phonemic integration (/aŋs/) takes place in the pronunciation on account of the similarity with ⟨anse⟩. (However, Danish makes a clear distinction between the classification of lexemes as French or Latin in origin: ⟨ance, ence⟩ ↔ /aŋsə/, ⟨ans⟩ ↔ /ans/). The probable Latin borrowings *assonans, dominans, dissonans, impedans* and others are also in part subject to this rule of pronunciation (/aŋs/ alongside /ans/.) There is a similar tendency in the case of the written form ⟨en⟩ in medial position, which, unlike in Danish, is also phonemically integrated (*dementi, defensiv, dispensere*: ⟨en⟩ ↔ /en/ or /aŋ/). This classification is also valid in the case of *parentes* (/paren'teːs/ or /paraŋ'teːs/).

There is considerable uncertainty in dealing with the adjective suffix ⟨-ant⟩. Here the pronunciation varies between phonemic, grapho-phonemic and hybrid integration.[12]

1.	grapho-phon. integration:	/ant/ (7)	Doublets (4)
5.	hybrid integration:	/aŋt/ (3)	Doublets (2)
3.	phonemic integration:	/aŋ/ (4)	

This uncertainty between conventional phonemic integration corresponding to Danish on the one hand, and grapho-phonemic integration on the other, can be explained by the circumstance that the extensive graphic and graphemic integrations in the system of written Norwegian strongly suggest the consistent application of indigenous G.P.C. rules. Corresponding written forms (⟨ans⟩, ⟨ens⟩) in lexemes which are not borrowed from French, are also affected by this uncertainty. Where, as an exception to the rule, graphematic integration did not take place, as in the case of ⟨teint⟩, the 'spelling pronunciation' has recently also become usual /teint/. The example of Norwegian, seen against the common linguistic background of Denmark and Norway, illustrates some unforeseen consequences of orthographic reforms.

2.7   Swedish

In Swedish the pronunciation and spelling of the loan words in question differ considerably from those in Danish and Norwegian. The frequent occurrence of doublets between phonemic and grapho-phonemic integration is particularly striking.

The works of reference used in this account were: *Svenska Akademiens Ordbok* 1893ff. (*S.A.O.B.*), *Svenska Akademiens Ordlista* 1976 (*S.A.O.L.*) and the 'studentenkät' by Widmark 1972. The information on pronunciation given in those works differs considerably and a clear trend in the development of integration can also be seen. Before I outline how the integration took place, on the basis of *S.A.O.L.* and with reference to Widmark 1972, I shall briefly compare the three works.

Because of the historical material it contains, *S.A.O.B.* gives numerous indications of the graphematic development in the course of the 18th and 19th centuries. Roughly speaking these entries reflect the conflict between retention of the French written forms (as in Danish) and graphemic integration. This was largely completed towards the end of the 19th century. Only in few examples did further integration not take place until a later date (⟨moment⟩ → ⟨momang⟩) or was an earlier graphemic integration reversed (⟨deplacemang⟩ → ⟨deplacement⟩, ⟨detachemang⟩ → ⟨detachement⟩, ⟨departemang⟩ → ⟨departement⟩, ⟨bonvivang⟩ → ⟨bonvivant⟩).

The discrepancies as regards the pronunciation given are more interesting. The comparison of *S.A.O.B.* and *S.A.O.L.* alone shows the tendency to greater graphophonemic integration:

> The frequency of the occurrence of phonemic and grapho-phonemic integration is exactly reversed (/aŋs, ans/ → /ans, aŋs/) in the case of *extravagans, instans, intolerans, revansch* and also of some adjectives ending in ⟨ant⟩;
>
> grapho-phonemic integration appears as a pronunciation variant (alongside phonemic integration) in some substantives ending in ⟨ans⟩ such as *ambulans, balans, nyans*;
>
> phonemic integration is replaced by grapho-phonemic integration (*bransch, expektans*);
>
> the same development can be observed with nasal vowels in medial position: grapho-phonemic integration replaces previous variation e.g. in *karambolage* (/aŋ, am/ → /am/), similarly in the case of *kontenance, dementi*; grapho-phonemic integration occurs as a variant alongside phonemic in *emballage, emblem, empir* (/aŋ, am/ → /aŋ, am, em/),[13] and in a corresponding fashion in *dispens(era), enkät, pension*.

In the case of some loan words ending in ⟨ment⟩, in which the otherwise usual graphematic integration (⟨ment⟩ → ⟨mang⟩) did not take place or (see above) was reversed, the original phonemic integration /aŋ/ was replaced by grapho-phonemic integration (*aksent, departement, ressentiment, sentiment*).

Counter evidence to this unmistakable trend is provided by a few examples where in exactly the opposite way phonemic integration supersedes an older graphophonemic integration (/ans/, /aŋs/ → /aŋs/: *allians, chans, kondoleans, seans, dispens, prononcera*).

The percentages given in Widmark's empirical investigation confirm the general trend to the 'spelling pronunciation', but they also confirm the counter tendency just mentioned in the case of some lexemes such as *korrespondens, dispens(era), pension* (Widmark 1972: 44, 70ff.).

This seems to confirm that the conflict between the two patterns of integration is not yet resolved. (Incidentally it must be noted with Widmark's data that only one social group and age group is covered because he restricted himself to student informants.)

In some cases the classification as 'salong-miljö' – salon milieu (Widmark 1972: 78) may be decisive for phonemic integration ('franskt uttal' – French pronunciation) as has already been observed several times in our discussion of English, German and Dutch; in addition in the case of a few lexemes such as *cendré* /saŋ′dre:/, *pensé* / paŋ′se:/ the effect of foreign graphemic features (⟨é⟩) may be decisive for phonemic integration.

From *S.A.O.L.* the following picture emerges: As regards graphemic integration Swedish goes still further than Norwegian. In addition to the suffixes ⟨on⟩ and ⟨in(t)⟩ (⟨ong⟩, ⟨äng⟩), ⟨ment⟩ was graphemically integrated as ⟨mang⟩; moreover ⟨once⟩ was integrated graphetically as ⟨ons⟩ (*brons*), ⟨ance⟩ as ⟨ans⟩ (*allians*), ⟨ence⟩ as ⟨ens⟩ (*patiens*) and ⟨anche⟩ as ⟨ansch⟩ (*bransch*). As a result almost all loan words have acquired a 'native' appearance from a graphemic point of view. As in the most common suffixes the velar nasal /ŋ/ is graphemically represented by ⟨ng⟩, it is obviously assumed that wherever such a marking does not occur pronunciation according to indigenous G.P.C. rules is correct. In some cases where the suffixes were not graphemically integrated (in contrast to Danish and Norwegian), this led to grapho-phonemic integration, i.e. that indigenous rules are also applied here: ⟨on⟩ ↔ /uːn/ in *champignon, compagnon, ponton, raison, pardon*;[14] ⟨in⟩ ↔ /iːn/ in *bulletin*; ⟨ment⟩ ↔ /ment/ in *departement, detachement, gouvernement, ressentiment, sentiment, temperament.* Pronunciation doublets between phonemic and grapho-phonemic integration are also the rule with the written forms ⟨in⟩, ⟨on⟩ and ⟨an⟩ in medial position (/V+n/ or /V+ŋ/) as well as in the suffixes ⟨ons⟩, ⟨ans⟩, ⟨ens⟩ (/V+n+s/ or /V+ŋ+s/), cf. above Table 4.

Only ⟨om⟩ and ⟨am⟩ and ⟨in⟩ in initial position are for the most part graphophonemically integrated, as in Danish and Norwegian.

With the adjectives ending in ⟨ant⟩ the pronunciation varies mostly between grapho-phonemic and hybrid integration (/ant/ or /aŋt/); here the development is further advanced than in Norwegian (see above p. 249).

The graphetic integration of the French loan words in ⟨ance⟩ and ⟨ence⟩ as ⟨ans⟩ and ⟨ens⟩ leads even more frequently than in Norwegian to a direct correspondence with the Latin loan words in ⟨ans⟩. As a result even Latinisms like *konkordans, konsonans, dominans, relevans, varians* and others were drawn into the uncertainty of pronunciation (/ans/ or /aŋs/).

The uncertainty as regards pronunciation which is characteristic of Swedish is apparently the result of the conflict between a traditional phonemic integration of the nasal vowels, as is still predominantly the case in Danish and Norwegian (and in part also in the older entries in *S.A.O.B.*), and the impression, which extensive graphetic and graphematic integration conveys, that only indigenous G.P.C. rules are still valid in Swedish. As, however, phonemic integration is only consolidated graphematically in the suffixes ⟨ong⟩, ⟨eng⟩ and ⟨mang⟩ and not in the case of other suffixes and in initial and medial position, in these latter cases the uncertainty remains as to whether indigenous G.P.C. rules are to be applied (⟨en⟩ interpreted as ⟨e⟩+⟨n⟩ ↔ /e/+/n/) or a modified transferred G.P.C. rule (⟨en⟩ ↔ /aŋ/).

If the trend to the 'spelling pronunciation', which Widmark observed, becomes stabilized, the pronunciation of French loan words in Swedish will have reached a state which largely fails to fulfil the aim of Leopold's orthographic reform (avoidance of a faulty pronunciation with respect to the norm of the source language). This development in Swedish also clearly runs counter to the aims of recent inter-Scandinavian language planning to reconcile diverging features of the Scandinavian languages or at least to prevent a further divergence.

In carrying out the Swedish reforms the consequences of graphetic and graphemic integrations, particularly when – as in this case – they were not consistently carried through, have obviously been greatly underestimated. While the orthographic reformers restricted themselves to isolated changes, the speakers of the language have obviously understood better the regular nature of the overall graphemic system and the competing rules contained in it. The fact that, compared with Danish and Norwegian, the drastic reform in Swedish has at the same time resulted in greater uncertainty in the pronunciation, leads one to doubt not just the quality of this orthographic reform but also whether it has any point whatsoever. The example of Danish shows that the speakers of the language can certainly be expected to cope with some foreign written forms and G.P.C. rules – if the latter are a self-contained system – apparently without a regular pronunciation being endangered; that is, the implicit assumption of all orthographic reformers that foreign written forms and foreign G.P.C. rules are *eo ipso* a burden to a language seems to be based less on empirical evidence but rather to be the product of a purist attitude to language.

In conclusion I will briefly compare the different ways in which French loan words are integrated in German and in the Scandinavian languages.

Whereas in German the retention of the nasal vowels is regarded as the sign of loyalty to French and phonemic integration as 'Germanizing', and as a feature of everyday speech, in the Scandinavian languages this phonemic integration is regarded as 'franskt präglat uttal' (French-influenced pronunciation) and only the 'spelling pronunciation' is regarded as 'anpassat till svenska uttalsvanor' (adapted to Swedish pronunciation practice) (Widmark 1972: 42 and passim.) Thus the same facts are evaluated differently on the basis of different paradigms of possibilities of transference and integration.

3   Summary

Before I sum up the results of this comparative study, I shall outline again its premises and principles. The starting point is the observation that nowadays the speaker of a language has a representation of his language on two levels, as spoken and written language, which are connected by grapheme–phoneme correspondence rules. Consequently the basis of the analysis is a systematic comparison of the written form and pronunciation of the loan words with the corresponding models in the source language. The fact that the correct point of reference ought to be the representation of the loan word in the source language at the historical point in time when it was borrowed is disregarded here. I have by and large ignored this point because the majority of French loan words entered the Germanic languages between the 17th and 19th centuries and correspond almost entirely phonologically and graphemically to present-day language use. Furthermore this is also a point of reference for dealing with older loan words today – in view of the widespread knowledge of French.

The scope of the investigation has been further limited as follows: (1) The phenomena of phonetic transference and integration are not dealt with, (2) on the phonological and graphemic level only the paradigmatic units are investigated, not the conditions of their syntagmatic distribution, since this is not relevant in the case of the nasal vowels.

The paradigmatic contrastive analysis which has been undertaken gives an idea of the regularities underlying the processes of transference and integration as well as of their realizations in the individual languages.

The fact that a loan word is incorporated simultaneously as a grapho-lexeme (grapheme sequence) *and* as a phono-lexeme (phoneme sequence) has the result that, whenever differences exist between the source language and the recipient language on the graphemic and/or phonological level, foreign G.P.C. rules are by implication transferred at the same time, e.g. in German *Chanson* /ʃãsõ/ the G.P.C. rule ⟨-on⟩ ↔ /õ/, which is contrary to the indigenous German G.P.C. rule ⟨-on⟩ ↔ /oːn/ in ⟨Demonstration⟩ /demonstratsjoːn/.

Integration into the recipient language takes place on both levels of representation and can lead in three ways to complete integration, i.e. to the creation of an indigenous phoneme and grapheme sequence and to the establishment of indigenous G.P.C. rules between them.

(a) In the case of source language phonemes which also occur in the recipient language, but which are represented by different written forms in the two languages, the written form of the recipient language replaces that of the source language by *graphetic integration*, e.g. Fr. ⟨-c-⟩ ↔ /-s-/ to ⟨-s-⟩ ↔ /-s-/ in Fr. *ambulance* → Norw. *ambulanse*. Thus the source-language G.P.C. rule is replaced by one from the recipient language.

(b) In the case of source-language phonemes which do not occur in the recipient language, there are two ways in which they can be integrated:

(i)   *grapho-phonemic integration:* a source-language written form is phonically interpreted according to the G.P.C. rules of the recipient language and not those of the source language, e.g. Fr. ⟨ment⟩ ↔ /mã/ to Swed. ⟨ment⟩ → /ment/ (*departement*).

(ii)   *phonemic and graphemic integration:* after phonemic substitution (/õ/ to /o/ + /ŋ/), which leads to modification of the source language G.P.C. rule (⟨on⟩ ↔ /oŋ/), a second step follows in which the written form is adjusted to the phonemic form after phonemic integration (/oŋ/ to ⟨ong⟩) with the same result as mentioned above: the phoneme and grapheme sequence and the G.P.C. rule connecting them correspond to indigenous patterns (e.g. Swed., Norw. *balkong*).

The distinction between -etic and -emic integration takes up a terminological proposal of Althaus (1980), to distinguish between an integration which only effects the level of the written form (graphetic integration) and one (graphemic integration) which at the same time includes phonemic integration, i.e. in which the grapheme represents a different phoneme than in the source language.

The transference and integration of the French nasal vowels in the Germanic languages reveal three language areas in which the procedures are similar: (1) English, (2) Dutch and German, (3) the Scandinavian languages. However, English and Dutch on the one hand, and German and the Scandinavian languages on the other, exhibit related phenomena.

On account of regular prosodic integration and consistent grapho-phonemic integration English has a special status which is based on the contacts with French in the Middle Ages. These contacts were a major factor in English being separated from the historical Germanic language group, and in the way in which it integrated French loan words English has displayed greater independence and a greater capacity to impose indigenous language rules than the other Germanic languages. In German and Dutch the nasal vowels have been retained to a large extent, which can be explained by the strong loyalty to the French language and French culture among France's immediate neighbours and the widespread knowledge of French. Extensive phonemic transference is particularly common in the case of exotic words and those lexemes which contain several non-native phonological and graphemic features from French (*impromptu, embonpoint, entrée* etc.). (The same is also partly true of English.)

By contrast the Scandinavian languages have nowhere retained the nasal vowels but have regularly integrated them phonemically. A comparable integration is lacking in Dutch and by and large also in English.

In all Germanic languages the nasal vowels are grapho-phonemically integrated, but with varying frequency. In this respect it is possible to establish a clear scale ranging from English (the rule) to Dutch (common) to German and the Scandinavian languages (rare).

Grapho-phonemic integration frequently takes place in accordance with the morphologically similar patterns of Latin loan words which are integrated according to indigenous G.P.C. rules in each individual language. Here the well-known terms 'Leseaussprache', 'skriftspråksuttal', 'spelling pronunciation' suggest an explanation which is misleading. The numerous examples show that every integration can be seen as an attempt to find a connection to a model in the recipient language (interlingual identification) and not only on the phonological and graphemic but also on the morphological level. In particular the morphologically related Latinisms are models in the recipient language for French loan words.

Regular pronunciation doublets, which serve in part a stylistic function (varieties indicating social class and social context) occur frequently in Dutch, German, Swedish and Norwegian. However, the different types of integration and transference that occur vary in every language: in Dutch phonemic transference and grapho-phonemic integration (e.g. /õ/ and /on/), in German phonemic transference, phonemic integration and grapho-phonemic integration (e.g. /õ/, /oŋ/, /oːn/), in Swedish and Norwegian phonemic and grapho-phonemic integration (e.g. /aŋ/, /ant/).

Different factors are decisive for the occurrence of doublets; in German and Dutch the conflict in loyalty between a desire to respect the French source-language phonemes and graphemes and a desire to integrate into the recipient language, in Swedish and Norwegian the inconsistent implementation of graphetic or graphemic integration, which in the case of identical grapheme sequences leaves it open as to whether they should be interpreted according to source language or recipient language G.P.C. rules. Danish remained unaffected in this respect, because of all the Germanic languages it retained the source language written form in the most conservative way; as a result these forms stand out clearly from the indigenous graphemes and signal the application of source language G.P.C. rules.

For the purposes of orthographic language planning one of the conclusions that can be drawn from these observations is that such alterations may not be carried out in isolated cases, but that every alteration in the system of orthography must be carried out systematically, that is, e.g. that a graphemic substitution of ⟨V+n+g⟩

for ⟨V+n⟩ is to be carried out in all lexemes in which the written form ⟨V+n⟩ corresponds to the spoken form ⟨V+ŋ⟩. A complete integration and certainty regarding pronunciation will not be achieved until the foreign G.P.C. rule has been replaced in all lexemes.

As indicated, changes in the grapheme system can be of two kinds: graphetic or graphemic integration. The difference lies in the fact that in the first case with interlingually identical phonemes, only the spelling system and the G.P.C. rules are different, but in the second case there is also a phonological contrast, which was removed beforehand by phonemic integration. The distinction is relevant for language planning in relation to orthography in that graphetic integrations do not result in any pronunciation doublets. They are therefore the less problematic part of any reform.

My observations have changed me from being originally a supporter of orthographic reforms in the area of so-called foreign words to a sceptic in these matters. Today I wonder whether a language community cannot after all cope with a series of foreign G.P.C. rules perfectly well. The comparison of Danish and Swedish in particular is revealing here. During all orthographic reforms – and this is the problematic point – pressure is created to continue such alterations, just as in the case of a woman, who dyes her hair when she notices her first grey hairs and from then on has to have it dyed again every three weeks if she wants to avoid looking more piebald than before.

The independence and systematic nature of written systems require that once changes have been made they must be applied to every new case. For reformed orthographies which are based on indigenous G.P.C. rules exclusively, lead the speakers of the language to apply these rules to all grapho-lexemes, also to those which the necessary reform has not yet affected. Thus a situation is created where different types of integration exist alongside each other, as is exemplified by Swedish and Norwegian.[15]

Appendix: Corpus of French loan words in the Germanic languages

The following corpus (see Introduction above on how the material was selected) is intended to give the reader a comparative survey of the similarities and differences in the ways in which the French loan words with nasal vowels are integrated in the Germanic languages, independently of the evaluation in this article. For this reason alphabetical order was not used but a functional order according to the occurrence of the nasal vowe's and their distribution:

Nasal vowel in final position or in a final suffix: /õ/ 1–37, /ã/ 38–136, /ɛ̃/ 137–51, /œ̃/ 152;
Nasal vowel in initial position: /ã/ 153–65, /ɛ̃/ 166;
Nasal vowel in medial position: /õ/ 167–71, /ã/ 172–89, /ɛ̃/ 190.

In the case of examples which have already been given in other groups the number of the example is indicated.

The system of phonetic transcription follows the relevant lexicographical works of reference: Warnant (Fr.), Jones (Eng.), Conninck (Dutch), O.D.S. and Nudansk Ordbog (Dan.), Berulfsen (Norw.), S.A.O. and S.A.O.L. (Swed.) and WdA (Ger.).

The rather varied degrees of representativeness and exactness of these sources presented a certain problem. While Jones, WdA, Conninck and Berulfsen give relatively exact information (in the last case almost without variants, however), for Danish there is only the older information in the *O.D.S.*, whereas for Swedish indications of pronunciation with phonetic transcriptions are mostly lacking. Here a relatively broad transcription on the basis of *S.A.O.* and *S.A.O.L.* has been attempted. In order nevertheless to make it possible to read the phonetic transcriptions in the corpus in parallel, the following alterations were made in the mode of transcription of individual sources:

Danish: The symbols [*w*] and [ļ] in the *O.D.S.* are reproduced as [ɔ] and [l].

Norwegian: Syllable stress is indicated by ['] *before* the stressed syllable. [å] in Berulfsen is reproduced as [ɔ], extremely open [ä] in Berulfsen as [æ]. Otherwise open or closed vowel quality remains unmarked in line with the practice in the source.

Swedish: Syllable stress is marked as in Norwegian. The non-technical pronunciation entries are altered as follows: sj → [ʃ], ng → [ŋ], å → [ɔ], tj → [tɕ], ä → [æ], o' → [uː], unstressed e → [ə], [*ɪn*] (*SAO*) → [ʉ]. No further distinction in the vowel quality is made.

In accordance with the dictionaries, the assimilation of apical [r] with the following dental or /l/ to retroflex ţ, ḑ, ṇ, l in Swedish and Norwegian (e.g. [paˈdɔŋ]) has also been disregarded here.

The varying degrees of exactness of the transcriptions are certainly inconvenient, but irrelevant for the main purposes of this investigation.

Appendix

Corpus of French loan words with nasal vowels in the Germanic languages

(On the order of entries and the transcription see p. 255f above; a sign of repetition (∼) instead of an entry means: the same orthography as in French (e.g. Eng., Dutch, Norw., Swed., abandon), but with the omission of all accents where relevant (e.g. Fr. compétence, Eng., competence). Dash (—)means: no example of a corresponding loan word in the standard dictionaries.)

Fr. /õ/ in final position or in a suffix ⟨-on⟩

	French	German	English	Dutch	Danish	Norwegian	Swedish
1	abandon abɑ̃dɔ̃	Abandon abã'dɔ̃·	∼ ə'bændən	∼ aban'dɔn	—	∼ abaŋ'dɔŋ aban ∼	∼ abaŋ'dɔŋ
2	balcon (Ital. balcone) balkɔ̃	Balkon bal'kɔŋ, ∼'koːn	balcony 'bælkənɪ	balkon bal'kɔn	balkon bal'kɔŋ	balkong bal'kɔŋŋ	balkong bal'kɔŋ
3	ballon (Ital. ballone) balɔ̃	Ballon ba'lɔŋ, ∼'loːn	balloon bə'luːn	∼ ba'lɔn	∼ ba'lɔŋ	ballong ba'lɔŋŋ	ballong ba'lɔŋ
4	béton betɔ̃	Beton be'tɔŋ, ∼'toːn	—	∼ bə'tɔn	∼ be'tɔŋ	betong be'tɔŋ	betong be'tɔŋ
5	bon bɔ̃	Bon bɔŋ	∼ bɔn	∼ bɔn	∼ bɔŋ	∼/bong bɔŋŋ	bong bɔŋ
6	bonbon bɔ̃bɔ̃	Bonbon bɔŋ'bɔŋ bɔ̃·'bɔ̃·	bon-bon 'bɔnbɔn, 'bɔm∼,'∼bɔŋ, 'bɔ̃:(m)bɔ̃:(ŋ)	bɔ̃'bɔ̃:, bɔm'bɔ̃:, bɔm'bɔn, bɔn'bɔn	∼ bɔŋ'bɔŋ	∼ bɔŋ'bɔŋŋ	—
7	bouillon bujɔ̃	Bouillon buI'jɔŋ	'buːjɔ̃:(ŋ)	∼ bu'(j)ɔn, buI'jɔn	∼ bul'jɔŋ	buljong bul'jɔŋ	buljong bul'jɔŋ

Appendix (*cont.*)

	French	German	English	Dutch	Danish	Norwegian	Swedish
8	carton (Ital. cartone) kartɔ̃	Karton kar'tɔŋ, ~'toːn	'kɑːtən, ~tn	karton kar'tɔn	karton kɐr'tɔŋ	kartong kar'tɔŋ	kartong kar'tɔŋ
9	champignon ʃɑ̃piɲɔ̃	Champignon 'ʃampinjɔŋ, ʃɑ̃pi'njɔ̃·	tʃæm'pinjən	ʃampi'nɔn, ʃɑ̃ ~, ~'ɲɔ̃	ʃampin'jɔŋ, 'ʃam ~	sjampinjong ʃampin'jɔŋ	champinjon ʃampin'juːn
10	chanson ʃɑ̃sɔ̃	Chanson ʃɑ̃'sɔ̃·	—	ʃɑ̃'sɔ̃ː	—	—	—
11	cocon kɔkɔ̃	Kokon ko'kɔŋ, ~'kɔ̃·	cocoon kə'kuːn, kɔ' ~	ko'kɔn	kokon ko'kɔŋ	kokong ko'kɔŋ	kokong ko'kɔŋ
12	compagnon kɔ̃paɲɔ̃	Compagnon/Kom- 'kɔmpanjɔŋ, ~'jɔ̃·	companion kəm'pænjən	kompa'ɲɔn	kompagnon kɔmpan'jɔŋ	kompanjong kɔmpan'jɔŋ, ~'jɔ̃·	kompanjon kɔmpan'juːn
13	cotillon kɔtijɔ̃	Kotillon 'kɔtiljɔ̃	—	koti'jɔn, ~til' ~	kotillon 'kɔtiljɔŋ, ~til'jɔŋ	kotiljong kɔtil'jɔŋ	kotiljong kɔtil'jɔŋ
14	coupon kupɔ̃	Coupon/Ku- ku'pɔŋ, ~'pɔ̃·	'kuːpɔn, ~pɔːŋ, ~ pɔːŋ	ku'pɔn	kupon ku'pɔŋ	kupong ku'pɔŋ	kupong ku'pɔŋ
15	feuilleton fœj(ə)tɔ̃	Feuilleton fœjə'tɔ̃·, fœjə'tɔŋ	'fɜːtɔ̃ː(ŋ), ~tɔŋ, fɜːlt ~	fœːi(j)ə'tɔn, fœːiljə ~	føljeton følje'tɔŋ	føljetong følje'tɔŋ	följetong følje'tɔŋ
16	flacon flakɔ̃	Flacon/-kon flɑ'kɔ̃, flɑ'kɔŋ	—	flɑ'kɔn	flakon flɑ'kɔŋ	flakong flɑ'kɔŋ	flakong flɑ'kɔŋ

17 jargon ʒargɔ̃	Jargon ʒarˈgɔŋ, ~gɔ̃	ˈdʒɑːgən	ʒarˈgɔ̃; ~ˌgɔn	ʒarˈgɔ̃	sjargong ʃarˈgɔŋ	jargong ʃarˈgɔŋ
18 jeton ʒ(ə)tɔ̃	Jeton ʒəˈtɔ̃	—	—	ʃeˈtɔŋ	sjetong ʃeˈtɔŋ	jetong ʃeˈtɔŋ
19 liaison ljɛzɔ̃	Liaison liɛˈzɔ̃, ~ˈzɔ̃	liːˈɛɪzɔ̃ː(ŋ), liːˈɛɪ~, ~ˈzɔn, zɛn	li(j)ɛˈzɔ̃	liˈeˈzɔŋ	lieˈsɔŋ	—
20 pardon pardɔ̃	Pardon parˈdɔŋ, ~ˈdɔ̃	ˈpaːdn	~/-doen parˈdɔ̃; ~ˈdɔn parˈdun ~/pensioen	parˈdɔŋ	pardong parˈdɔŋ	parˈduːn, parˈdɔŋ
21 pension (Ital. pensione) pãsjɔ̃	Pension pãʃˈzɔ̃ːn	ˈpãː(ŋ)stɔ̃ː(ŋ) ˈpɔː(ŋ)~, ˈpɑːns~, pɑːŋstɔːŋ, ˈpɔns~, -sjɔ(ŋ)/ ˈpɛnʃn (monetary allowance)	pãnˈsjɔn, pãˈsjɔn, pɛnˈsjɔn, pɛnˈʃ(j)ɔn/ pɛnˈsjun	pãnˈʃoːn	pension	pãnˈʃuːn, pɛnˈ~, pan~
22 perron pɛrɔ̃	Perron pɛˈrɔŋ, ~ˈrɔ̃	—	~ pɛˈrɔn, pə~	pɛˈrɔŋ	perrong pɛˈrɔŋ	perrong pɛˈrɔŋ
23 pompon pɔ̃pɔ̃	Pompon pɔ̃ˈpɔ̃, pɔmˈpɔ̃	ˈpɔ̃ː(m)pɔ̃ː(ŋ), ˈpɔːmpɔːŋ, pɔmpɔn	pompom/-pon pɔmˈpɔm/ pɔmˈpɔn	pɔmˈpɔŋ	pompong pɔmˈpɔŋ	pompong pɔmˈpɔŋ
24 ponton (Ital. pontone) pɔ̃tɔ̃	Ponton ˈpɔntɔŋ, pɔ̃ˈtɔ̃	ˈpɔntoon pɔntoon	~	pɔnˈtɔŋ	pongtong	~
25 raison rɛzɔ̃	Raison/Rä- rɛˈzɔ̃, ~ˈzɔ̃	raison (d'être) rɛɪzɔ̃ː(n)' (dɛtrə), ~ˈzɔn'(~)	(~)/ræson ræˈsɔŋ, ræˈsoˈːn	rɛˈzɔ̃ː	resong rɛˈsɔŋ	reson rɛˈsuːn

Appendix (*cont.*)

	French	German	English	Dutch	Danish	Norwegian	Swedish
26	saison sɛzɔ̃	Saison zɛˈzɔŋ, sɛˈzɔ̃.	season ˈsiːzn	seizoen sɛiˈzun	sæson sæˈsɔŋ	sesong seˈsɔŋ	säsong sæˈsɔŋ
27	salon (Ital. salone) salɔ̃·	Salon zaˈlɔŋ, saˈlɔ̃·	~/saloon səˈluːn	~ saˈlɔn	~ saˈlɔŋ	salong saˈlɔŋ	salong saˈlɔŋ
28	talon talɔ̃	Talon taˈlɔŋ, ~lɔ̃	~ ˈtælan	~ taˈlɔn	~ taˈlɔŋ	talong taˈlɔŋŋ	talong taˈlɔŋ
29	wagon vagɔ̃	Waggon vaˈgɔŋ	waggon ˈwægən	wagon wɑˈgɔn	vaggon vaˈgɔŋ	~ ˈvaggon, vaˈgɔŋ	vagong vaˈgɔŋ
30 ⟨-ond⟩	blond blɔ̃	blond blɔnt	blond(e) blɔnd	~ blɔnt	~ blɔnˀd	~ blɔnn	(blɔnd) blond
31	fond fɔ̃	Fond fɔŋ, fɔ̃	~ fɔnd	~ fɔː	~ fɔŋˀd	~ fɔŋd, fond	~ fɔŋd, fond
32 ⟨-ont⟩	front frɔ̃	Front frɔnt	~ frɔnt	~ frɔnt	~ frɔnˀd	front, frɔnt	(frɔnt) frɔnt
33 ⟨-omb⟩	aplomb aplɔ̃	Aplomb aˈplɔ̃	~ əˈplɔm, ˈæplɔ̃ː(ŋ), ~plɔ̃ːm	~ ɑˈplɔː	~ aˈplɔŋ	~ aˈplɔmb	~ aˈplɔmb
34 ⟨-once⟩	annonce anɔ̃ːs(ə)	Annonce aˈnɔŋsə, ~ˈnɔ̃ːs(ə)	announce əˈnauns	~ ɑˈnɔ̃ːsə, ɑˈnɔnsə	~ aˈnɔ̃ːsə	annonse aˈnɔnsə	annons aˈnɔns, aˈnɔŋs

⟨-onze⟩

35 renonce
r(ə)nɔ̃s(ə)

36 bronze
(Ital. bronzo)
brɔ̃z(ə)

⟨-onge⟩

37 allonge
alɔ̃ʒ(ə)

Fr. /ã/ in final position or suffix

⟨-ant⟩
(adj.)

38 ambulant
(ambulans)
ɑ̃bylɑ̃

39 arrogant
arɔgɑ̃

40 brillant
brijɑ̃

41 brisant
brizɑ̃

42 charmant
ʃarmɑ̃

43 complaisant
kɔ̃plezɑ̃

44 coulant
kulɑ̃

45 élégant
(Lat. elegans)
elegɑ̃

	Renonce rə'nɔ̃s	renounce rɪ'nauns, rə'n~		re'nɔ̃s	renons re'nɔ̃s	renons re'nɔ̃s, re'nɔ̃s
35	~	rɪ'nauns, rə'n~	rə'nɔ̃sə, ~'nɔ̃nsə brons	re'nɔ̃s	renons re'nɔ̃s	renons re'nɔ̃s, re'nɔ̃s brons
36	Bronze	bronz	brons	'brɔ̃sə	bronse	(brɔ̃s) brons
37	Allonge a'lɔ̃ʒə, -'lɔ̃ʒ(ə)	—	a'lɔ̃ːʒə	a'lɔ̃ʒə	a'lɔ̃ʒə	a'lɔ̃ʃ
38	ambu'lɑ̃	'æmbjʊlənt	ɑmbu'lant	ambu'lanɕd	—	ambʉ'laŋt
39	aro'gɑ̃	'ærogənt, ~rʊ'g~	aro'gant	aro'ganɕd	aro'gɑ̃t	aro'gɑ̃t, aro'gɑ̃t
40	bril'jɑ̃t	brilliant 'brɪljənt	briljɑ̃t bril'jɑ̃t	bril'jɑ̃ɕd	briljɑ̃t bril'jɑ̃t, bril'jɑ̃t	briljɑ̃t bril'jɑ̃t, ~'jɑ̃t
41	bri'zɑ̃t	—	bri'zɑ̃t	—	bri'sɑ̃t, bri'sɑ̃t	(bri'sɑ̃t) ~'sɑ̃t
42	ʃar'mɑ̃t	(charming) (tʃɑːmɪŋ)	ʃar'mɑ̃t	ʃar'manɕd	~, sʃarmant ʃar'mɑ̃t	ʃar'mɑ̃t, ~'mɑ̃t
43	—	kəm'pleɪz(ə)nt	complaizant kɔmple'zɑ̃t	—	komplaisant kɔmple'sɑ̃ŋ	—
44	kulant ku'lɑ̃t	—	ku'lɑ̃t	kulant ku'lɑ̃ɕd	kulant ku'lant	—
45	ele'gɑ̃t	'elɪgɑ̃t	elə'gɑ̃t	ele'gɑ̃ɕd	elə'gɑ̃t	elə'gɑ̃t, ~'gɑ̃t

Appendix (*cont.*)

	French	German	English	Dutch	Danish	Norwegian	Swedish
46	en passant ɑ̃pasɑ̃	~ ɑ̃pa'sɑ̃·	~ ɑ:(m)'pæsɑ̃:(ŋ), ɔ:(m)'pæsɔ̃:(ŋ), ɑ:m'pæsɑ:ŋ, ɒm'pæsɒŋ	~ ɑ̃pa'sɑ̃:; am ~	~ ɑŋpa'saŋ	~ aŋpa'saŋŋ	~ aŋpa'saŋ
47	extravagant ɛkstravagɑ̃	~ 'ɛkstravaɡant, ~ ~' ~	~ ik'strævagənt, ek's~, ~vɪɡ~	~ 'ɛkstrava'ɡant	ekstravagant, ægsdræva'ɡan'd	ekstravagant ekstrava'gant	~ ekstrava'gant, ~'gant
48	flamboyant flɑ̃bwajɑ̃	Flamboyant(stil) flɑ̃bŏa'jɑ̃·	flæm'bɔɪant	flambwa'jant	—	flamboa'jaŋŋ	—
49	frappant frapɑ̃	~ fra'pant	(frapping) (fræpɪŋ)	~ fra'pant	~ fre'pan'd	fra'pant, fra'paŋt	~ fra'pant, (~paŋt)
50	imposant ɛ̃pozɑ̃	~ impo'zant	~	~ impo'zant	~ empo'san'd	impo'saŋt, impo'sant	impo'sant, ~'saŋt
51	intéressant ɛ̃teresɑ̃	~ Intərə'sant	(interesting) ('ɪntrɪstɪŋ)	intərə'sant, ~tərɛ ~	~ ent(e)rə'san'd	intere'saŋŋ	intressant, intre'sant ~'saŋt
52	intolerant (Lat. intolerans) ɛ̃tɔlerɑ̃	~ 'Intolarant	~ In'tɔlər(ə)nt	intɔlə'rant, ~le'~	'entɔlərɛn'd, ~ ~	'Intɔlərɑŋ(t), intɔlə'raŋ(t)	intɔlə'rant, ~'raŋt
53	marquant markɑ̃	markant mar'kant	—	markant mar'kant	markant mɐr'kan'd	markant mar'kant	markant mar'kant, ~'kaŋt
54	nonchalant nɔ̃ʃalɑ̃	~ nɔ̃ʃa'lɑ̃	~ 'nɔn(ʃ)(ə)lant	nɔ̃:ʃa'lant non~	nɔŋʃa'lɑŋ, ~'lɑŋ'd	~ nɔŋʃa'laŋŋ, ~'laŋt	nɔŋʃa'laŋt, non~, ~'lant
55	piquant pikɑ̃	pikant pi'kant	~ 'pi:kant, ~kɑ:nt	pikant pi'kant	pikant pi'kan'd	pikant pi'kant	pikant pi'kant, ~'kaŋt

	Headword						
56	suffisant / syfizã	süffisant / syfi'zant	~	sʌfi'zant, sy~	sufi'san'd,	sufi'saŋt	~, syffisant / sʉfi'saŋt
57	tolérant (Lat. tolerans, -tis) / tolerã	tolerant / tole'rant	~	tolə'rant	tolə'rɛn'd	tolə'raŋt	tolə'raŋt, ~'rant
58	vacant / vakã	vakant / va'kant	~	—	vakant / va'kan'd	vakant / va'kant	vakant / va'kant, ~'kaŋt
59 ⟨-ant⟩ (noun)	bon vivant / bõvivã	Bonvivant / bõvi'vã·	—	bon-vivant / bõvi'vã·	bonvivant / bɔɳvi'vaŋ	bonvivant / bɔɳvi'vaŋŋ	bonvivant / bɔɳvi'vaŋ
60	pendant / pãdã	Pendant / pã'dã·, paŋ'daŋ	~ 'pendant	pendant / pã'dã·; pan'dant, pɛn'dant	~ paŋ'daŋ	~ paŋ'daŋ	pendang / paŋ'daŋ
61	restaurant / restɔrã	Restaurant / resto'raŋ, ~'rã·	'rest(e)rɔ̃ː(ŋ), ~rɑ̃ː(ŋ), ~rɒŋ, 'rest(e)rɒnt, ~rant	resto'rɑ̃ː / ~'rant	resdo'rɛŋ	~ restaeu'raŋŋ, restu'raŋŋ	restaurang / resto'raŋ,
62	suppléant / sypleã	Suppleant / zyple'ant	suppliant / 'sʌpliant, ~pljənt	suppliant / sʌpli'(j)ant	suple'an'd	suple'ant	suple'ant, ~'an, (~'aŋt)
63	volant / vɔlã	Volant / vɔ'laŋ, ~'lã·	~ / 'vɑʊlant	vɔ'lɑ̃ː, ~, cɑ	vo'laŋ	volang / vɔ'laŋŋ	volang / vɔ'laŋ
64 ⟨-(m)ent⟩	abonnement / abɔn(ə)mã	Abonnement / abɔnə'maŋ, ~'mã·	—	abɔnə'ment	abɔnə'maŋ	abɔnə'maŋŋ, abɔn~	abonnemang / abɔnə'maŋ
65	accent (Lat. accentus) / aksã	Akzent / ak'tsent	~	ak'sent	ag'sɛn'd, ag'saŋ	aksent / ak'sent, ak'saŋŋ	aksent / ak'sent, ak'saŋ

Appendix (*cont.*)

	French	German	English	Dutch	Danish	Norwegian	Swedish
66	accompagnement akɔ̃paɲ(ə)mɑ̃	Akkompagnement akɔmpanjə'mɑ̈·	accompaniment ə'kʌmpənimənt	~ akompaɲə'mɛnt	akkompagnement akɔmpanjə'maŋ	akkompagnement akompanjə'maŋŋ, akɔm~	ackompanjemang akɔmpanjə'maŋ
67	agrément agremɑ̃	Agrément agre'mɑ̈·	agreement ə'gri:mənt	~ agre'mɛnt	—	~ agre'maŋŋ	agremang agre'maŋ (amendemang)
68	amendement amɑ̈d(ə)mɑ̃	Amendement amɑ̈də'mɑ̈·	amendment ə'men(d)mənt	~ amɛndə'mɛnt	~ amanjə'maŋ	~ amandə'maŋŋ	(amendemang) amandə'maŋ
69	appartement apartəmɑ̃	Appartement apartə'mɑ̈·, ~'maŋ	apartment ə'pɑ:tmənt	~ apartə'mɛnt	~ 'apɛrdəmaŋ	~ apartə'maŋŋ	—
70	arrangement arɑ̈ʒ(ə)mɑ̃	Arrangement arɑ̈ʒə'maŋ, arɑ̈ʒə'mɑ̈·	ə'rein(d)ʒmənt	arɑ̈ʒə'mɛ̈nt, ~rɑn~	~ arɑ̈ʃə'maŋ	~ arɑnʃə'maŋŋ	arrangemang arɑnʃə'maŋ, arɑnʃ~
71	bombardement bɔ̃bardəmɑ̃	Bombardement bombardə'mɑ̈·, ~'maŋ	bombardment bɔm'bɑ:dmənt, bɔm~	~ bombardə'mɛnt	~ bombɑrdə'maŋ	~ bombardə'maŋŋ	bombardemang bombardə'maŋ
72	compliment (Ital. complimento) kɔ̃plimɑ̃	Kompliment kompli'mɛnt	'komplimənt	~ kompli'mɛnt	kompliment kompli'maŋ, ~'mæn'd	kompliment kompli'maŋŋ	komplimang kompli'maŋ
73	département departəmɑ̃	Departement depart'mɑ̈·, ~'maŋ	department di'pɑ:tmənt	~ departə'mɛnt	~ depɛrdə'maŋ	~ departə'maŋŋ	departement departə'mɛnt
74	détachement detaʃ(ə)mɑ̃	Detachement detaʃə'mɑ̈·	detachment di'tætʃmənt	~ detaʃə'mɛnt	~ detaʃ(ə)'maŋ	detasjement detaʃə'maŋŋ	detaʃə'mɛnt
75	engagement ɑ̈gaʒ(ə)mɑ̃	Engagement ɑ̈gaʒə'maŋ, ɑ̈gaʒə'mɑ̈·	in'geidʒmənt, ɑ̈~, en~	~ ɑ̈ngaʒə'mɛnt, ɑ̈ya~	~ ɑ̈ngaʃ(ə)'maŋ	engasjement ɑ̈ngaʃə'maŋŋ	engagemang ɑ̈ngaʃə'maŋ
76	enjambement ɑ̈ʒɑ̈b(ə)mɑ̃	Enjambement ɑ̈ʒɑ̈b(ə)mɑ̈·	enjambment in'dʒæmmənt, en~	~ ɑ̈ʒɑ̈mbə'mɛnt, ɑ̈nʒɑm~, ɛnjɑm~	~ ɑ̈nʃɑ̈bə'maŋ	~ ɑ̈nʃɑ̈mbə'maŋŋ	enjambemang ɑ̈nʃɑ̈mbə'maŋ

No.	French	German	English				
77	établissement / etablis(ə)mɑ̃	Etablissement / e'tablɪsə'mɑ̃·, ~'mɑŋ	establishment / ɪ'stæblɪʃmənt, e˞s~	~ etablisə'ment	~ etablisə'mɑŋ	~ etablisə'mɑŋŋ	etablissemang/-ment, etablisə'mɑŋ, ~'ment
78	gouvernement / guvernəmɑ̃	Gouvernement / guvernə'mɑŋ, ~'mɑ̃·	government / 'gʌvnmənt, ~və(n)mənt	guvernə'ment, ~vɛr~	~ guvernə'mɑŋ	guvernement / guvernə'mɑŋŋ	guvernement / guvernə'ment
79	moment (Lat. momentum) / momɑ̃	Moment / mo'ment	moment / 'moumənt	mo'ment	~ mo'mæn'd, mo'mɑŋ	~ mo'ment	~/momang; mɔ'ment/ mɔ'mɑŋ
80	présent / prezɑ̃	Präsent / prɛ'zɛnt	present / 'preznt, ~zənt	~ prɛ'sɛnt, pre'~	~ prɛ'sɑŋ	presang / prɛ'sɑŋ	~ pre'sent
81	raffinement / rafin(ə)mɑ̃	Raffinement / rafinə'mɑŋ, ~'mɑ̃·	—	~ rafinə'ment	~ rəfinə'mɑŋ	~ rafinə'mɑŋŋ	raffinemang / rafinə'mɑŋ
82	raisonnement / rɛzɔn(ə)mɑ̃	Räsonnement / rɛzɔnə'mɑ̃·	—	~ rɛzɔnə'ment	rɑsɔnə'mɑŋ	resonnement / rɛzɔnə'mɑŋŋ	resonemang / resɔnə'mɑŋ
83	règlement / regləmɑ̃	Reglement / reglə'mɑŋ, ~'mɑ̃·	—	~ reglə'ment	~ reglə'mɑŋ	~ reglə'mɑŋŋ	(reglemente) / reglə'mente
84	ressentiment / r(ə)sɑ̃timɑ̃	Ressentiment / resɑ̃ti'mɑ̃·, resɑŋti'mɑŋ	—	~ resenti'ment	—	—	(~) / resenti'ment, ~'mɑŋ
85	sentiment / sɑ̃timɑ̃	Sentiment / sɑ̃ti'mɑ̃·	sentiment / 'sentimənt	senti'ment	~ sɑŋti'mɑŋ	~ sɑŋti'mɑŋŋ	~ senti'ment
86	talent (Lat. talentum) / talɑ̃	Talent / ta'lent	talent / 'tælənt	ta'lent	ta'læn'd, ta'lɑŋ	ta'lent	talang / ta'lɑŋ
87	tempérament (Lat. temperamentum) / tɑ̃peramɑ̃	Temperament / tɑ̃perə'ment	temperament / 'temp(ə)rəmənt	tempərə'ment, ~pe~	tæmb(ə)rə'mɑŋ	tempərə'mɑŋŋ	~ tempəra'ment

Appendix (*cont.*)

		French	German	English	Dutch	Danish	Norwegian	Swedish
⟨-an⟩	88	élan elɑ̃	Elan e'lɑ:n, e'lɑ:	∼ eɪ'lɑ:(ŋ), ∼lɔ:(ŋ)	∼ e'lɑ:	—	∼ e'lɑŋ	—
⟨-ance⟩	89	alliance aljɑ̃:s(ə)	Alliance/-anz a'liɑ̃ts	alliance ə'laɪəns	alliantie ali'(j)ɑnsi, ∼tsi	∼ ali'ɑŋsə	allianse ali'ɑŋsə	allians ali'aŋs
	90	ambulance ɑ̃bylɑ̃:s(ə)	Ambulanz ambu'lants	'æmbjuləns	amby'lɑnsə, ∼'lɑ:sə	∼ ambu'lɑŋsə	ambulanse ambu'lɑŋsə	ambulans ambʉ'lɑŋs, ∼'lans
	91	arrogance arɔgɑ̃:s(ə)	Arroganz aro'gants	∼ 'ærəgəns ∼rʊg∼	arrogantie aro'gɑnsi, ∼tsi	∼ aro'gɑŋsə	arrogancse aro'gɑŋsə	arrogans arɔ'gaŋs, ∼'gans
	92	assistance asistɑ̃:s(ə)	Assistenz asis'tents	ə'sist(ə)ns	assistentie asis'tensi, ∼tsi, asi'∼	∼ asi'stɑŋsə	assistanse asi'stɑŋsə	assistans asi'staŋs, ∼'stans
	93	assonance asonɑ̃:s(ə)	Assonanz aso'nants	'æsə(ʊ)nəns	assonantie aso'nɑnsi, ∼tsi	assonans aso'nɑŋs	assonans aso'nɑŋs	assonans asɔ'naŋs
	94	avance avɑ̃:s(ə)	Avance a'vɑ:s, ∼'vɑŋsə	—	avances (Pl.) avɑ̃:sees	∼ a'vɑŋsə	∼/avanse a'vɑŋs/ a'vɑŋsə	avans a'vaŋs
	95	balance balɑ̃:s(ə)	Balance ba'lɑŋsə, ∼'lɑ:s	'bæləns	balans ba'lɑns	∼ ba'lɑŋsə	balanse ba'lɑŋsə	balans (ba'laŋs), ∼'lans
	96	brisance brizɑ̃:s(ə)	Brisanz bri'zants	—	brisantie bri'zɑnsi, ∼tsi	—	brisans bri'sɑŋs	brisans bri'saŋs, ∼sans
	97	chance ʃɑ̃:s(ə)	Chance 'ʃɑŋsə, ʃɑ̃:sə	∼ tʃɑ:ns	sjans ʃɑns	∼ 'ʃɑŋsə	sjanse 'ʃɑŋsə	chans ʃaŋs, tʃans

#							
98	condoléance kɔ̃dɔleɑ̃ːs(ə)	Kondolenz kɔndoˈlɛnts	condolence kənˈdəʊləns	~/condoleantie kɔndoleˈ(j)ɑ̃ːs(ə)/ kɔndoleˈ(j)ɑ̃ːsə, ~tsi	kondolence kɔndoˈlɑ̃ːsə	kondolanse kɔndoˈlɑ̃ːsə, kɔn~	kondoleans kɔndoleˈɑŋs
99	contenance kɔ̃t(ə)nɑ̃ːs(ə)	~/Kontenance kɔ̃təˈnɑ̃ːs	countenance ˈkaʊntənəns, ~ti~	~/contenantie kɔ̃təˈnɑ̃ːs(ə)/ kɔ̃təˈnɑ̃ːsi, ~tsi correspondentie	kontenance kɔntəˈnɑŋsə	kontenanse kɔntəˈnɑŋsə	(kontenans) kɔntəˈnɑŋs, ~ˈnɑns korrespondens
100	correspondance kɔrɛspɔ̃dɑ̃ːs(ə)	Korrespondenz kɔrɛspɔnˈdɛnts	correspondence ˌkɔrɪˈspɒndəns, ~rə's~ —	correspondentie	korrespondance/ -ens kɔrɛsbɔnˈdɑ̃ːsə/ ~ˈdɑ̃ːns	korrespondanse kɔr~	korrespondens kɔrɛspɔnˈdɛns, ~spɔŋˈdɑŋs
101	(coulance) kulɑ̃ːs(ə)	Kulanz kuˈlants	—	kuˈlɑ̃ːs(ə), ~lɑ̃ːsə	kulance kuˈlɑ̃ːsə	kulans kuˈlɑns	—
102	distance (Lat. distantia) distɑ̃ːs(ə)	Distanz disˈtants	ˌdist(e)ns	distantie disˈtɑ̃ːs, ~tsi	distanse	distanse disˈtɑŋsə	distans disˈtɑŋs, ~tɑns
103	élégance (Lat. elegantia) elegɑ̃ːs(ə)	Eleganz eleˈgants	ˈelɪgəns	~/elegantie	elaˈgɑ̃ːsə	eleganse elaˈgɑŋsə	elegans elaˈgɑŋs, ~gɑns eleganse
104	extravagance ɛkstravagɑ̃ːs(ə)	Extravaganz ɛkstravaˈgants	ˌikˈstrævəgəns, ek's~, ~vɪg~	extravagantie ˈɛkstravɑ gɑ̃ːsi, ~tsi	extravagance æɡsdræva ˈgɑŋsə	ekstravaganse ɛkstravaˈgɑŋsə	extravagans ɛkstravaˈgɑns, ~ˈgɑŋs
105	finance finɑ̃ːs(ə)	Finanz finants	faɪˈnæns, fiˈ~, ˈfaɪnæns	financie fiˈnɑnsi	finans fiˈnɑns	finans fiˈnɑns	finans fiˈnɑns, (~ˈnɑŋs)
106	instance (Lat. instantia) ɛ̃stɑ̃ːs(ə)	Instanz inˈstants	ˈInstens	instantie	instans	instans	instans inˈstɑns
107	intolerance (Lat. intolerantia) ɛ̃tɔlerɑ̃ːs(ə)	Intoleranz inˈtolərants	inˈtɒlər(ə)ns	intoleˈransi, ~le ~, ~tsi	intolerance ˈintoleraŋsə, intolara ˈɳsə	intoleranse	intolerans ɛ̃tɔleˈrans ~rɑŋs

Appendix (*cont.*)

	French	German	English	Dutch	Danish	Norwegian	Swedish
108	nonchalance nɔ̃ʃalɑ̃ːs(ə)	Nonchalance nɔ̃ʃaˈlɑ̃ːs	~ ˈnɔnʃ(ə)ləns	nɔ̃ʃɑˈlɑ̃ːsə, nɔn~	~ nɔnʃɑˈlaŋsə	nonchalanse nɔnʃaˈlaŋsə	nonchalans nɔnʃaˈlaŋs, nɔn~, ~lans
109	nuance nyɑ̃ːs(ə)	Nuance nyˈaŋsə, ~ɑ̃ːsə	~ njuːˈɑ̃ː(n)s, njũ~, ~ɔ̃ː(n)s, ~ˈɑːns	nyˈ(w)ɑ̃ːsə, ~ˈ(w)ɑnsə	~ nyˈaŋsə	nyance nyˈaŋsə	nyans nyˈaŋs, ~ans
110	ordonnance ɔrdɔnɑ̃ːs(ə)	Ordonnanz ɔrdɔˈnants	ordnance ˈɔːdnəns	ordonnans ɔrdɔˈnans	ordonnans ɔrdoˈnans	ordonnans ɔrdoˈnans, ɔrdoˈnans	ordonans ɔrdoˈnans, ~ˈnans
111	prégnance preɲɑ̃ːs(ə), pregnɑ̃ːs(ə)	Prägnanz prɛgˈnants	pregnancy ˈpregnənsi	pregnantie preɲˈnɑnsi, ~tsi	prægnans prɛɡˈnanʔs	pregnans pregˈnans	pregnans preɲˈnans, preg~, (~ˈnaŋs)
112	renaissance r(ə)nesɑ̃ːs(ə)	Renaissance rəneˈsɑ̃ːs	~/renascence rəneɪs(ə)ns, rɪˈn~ ˈrene~, ~sɑ̃ː(n)s, ~sɔ̃ː(n)s, ~sɑːns/ rɪˈnæsns, rəˈn~	~ rənɛˈsɑ̃ːsə	renaissance renæˈsaŋsə	renessanse renəˈsaŋsə	renässans renæˈsaŋs
113	résonance rezɔnɑ̃ːs(ə)	Resonanz rezoˈnants	~ ˈrezənəns	resonantie rezoˈnɑnsi, ~tsi	resonans resoˈnanʔs	resonans resoˈnanʔs, resɔˈ~	resonans resɔˈnaŋs, resuˈ~
114	romance (Span. romance) rɔmɑ̃ːs(ə)	Romanze roˈmantsə	~ rəʊˈmɑːns, rʊˈm	~ roˈmɑ̃ːsə, ~ˈmɑnsə	roˈmaŋsə	romanse roˈmaŋsə	romans rɔˈmans, ~ˈmaŋs
115	séance seɑ̃ːs(ə)	~ seˈɑ̃ːs	ˈseɪɑ̃ː(n)s, ~ɔ̃ː(n)s, ~ɑːns	~ seˈ(j)ɑ̃ːs(ə)	~ seˈaŋsə	seanse seˈaŋsə	seans seˈaŋs
116	suffisance syfizɑ̃ːs(ə)	Süffisance syfiˈzɑ̃ːs	—	suffisantie safiˈzɑnsi, ~tsi	~ sufiˈsaŋsə	suffisanse sufiˈsaŋsə	suffisans/syffisans sufiˈsaŋs,

	French	German	English	Dutch			
117	tolérance tɔlerɑ:s(ə)	Toleranz tole'rants	~ 'tɒlər(ə)ns	tolerantie tolə'rɑnsi, ~tsi	~ tolə'rɛŋsə	toleranse tɔlə'raŋsə tol ~	tolerans tɔlə'raŋs, ~'rans
118	transe (trance) trɑ:s(ə)	Trance trɑ:s	trance trɑ:ns	trance 'trɑ:s(ə), 'trɑnsə	trance 'trɛŋsə	trance traŋs, 'traŋsə	trance/trans trans, trans
⟨-ence⟩							
119	vacance vakɑ:s(ə)	Vakanz va'kants	vacancy 'veɪk(ə)nsɪ	vakantie va'kɑnsi, ~tsi	~ va'kɑŋsə	vakanse va'kaŋsə	vakans va'kans, ~'kaŋs
120	compétence kɔ̃petɑ:s(ə)	Kompetenz kɔmpe'tɛnts	~ 'kɔmpɪt(ə)ns, ~pət ~	competentie kɔmpə'tɛnsi, ~pe ~, ~tsi	kompetence/-ens kɔmbə'taŋsə/ ~'tɛns	kompetanse kɔmpə'taŋsə, kom ~	kompetens kɔmpe'tɛns
121	concurrence (M. Lat. concurrentia) kɔ̃kyrɑ:s(ə)	Konkurrenz kɔnku'rɛnts	kən'kʌr(ə)ns, kəŋ'k ~	concurrentie kɔŋky'rɛnsi, ~kʌ ~, ~tsi	konkurrence kɔŋku'raŋsə kɔŋ ~	konkurranse kɔŋ ~ konkurranse	konkurrens kɔn ~, ~raŋs
122	conférence (M. Lat. conferentia) kɔ̃ferɑ:s(ə)	~, Konferenz kɔnfe'rɛnts	~ 'kɔnf(ə)r(ə)ns	kəfe'rɑ:sə, kɔn ~ / kɔnfə'rɛnsi, ~fe ~, ~tsi /conferentie	konfə'raŋsə ~'tɛn's	konference/-ens kɔn ~ konferanse	konferens kɔnfə'rɛns, ~'raŋs
123	décadence (Lat. decadentia) dekadɑ:s(ə)	Dekadenz deka'dɛnts	~	decadentie deka'dɛnsi, ~tsi	dekadence	dekadanse deka'daŋsə	dekadans
124	différence (Lat. differentia) diferɑ:s(ə)	Differenz difə'rɛnts	~ 'dɪfr(ə)ns, ~fər(ə)ns	differentie difə'rɛnsi, ~tsi	differance/-ens difə'rɛns	differanse difə'raŋsə/ difə'rɛns	differens
125	essence (Lat. essentia) esɑ:s(ə)	Essenz ɛ'sɛnts	'esns	~	essens	dekadanse deka'daŋs, ~'dans	difə'rɛns, difə'raŋs essens

Appendix (*cont.*)

	French	German	English	Dutch	Danish	Norwegian	Swedish
126	excellence (Lat. excellentia) ɛksɛlɑ̃ːs(ə)	Exzellenz ɛkstsɛ'lɛnts	~ 'eks(ə)ləns	excellentie ɛksə'lɛnsi, ~ sɛ' ~, ~ tsi	~ ægsə'lænsə	eksellense eksə'lɛnsə	excellens eksə'lens
127	faïence fajɑ̃ːs(ə)	Fayence fa'jɑ̃ːs, ~'jaŋs	faience far'ɑ:(n)s, fe' ~ ~'ɔ̃(n)s, ~'ɑɪns	fa'jɑ̃ːsə	fajance fa'jaŋsə	fajanse fa'jaŋsə	fajans fa'jaŋs, ~'jans
128	incompétence ɛ̃kɔ̃petɑ̃ːs(ə)	Inkompetenz inkɔmpe'tɛnts	in'kɔmpɪt(ə)ns, ŋ'k ~	incompetentie iŋkɔmpə'tɛnsi, in ~, ~ pe' ~, ~ tsi	inkompetence/-ens enkɔmbə'taŋsə/ ~ 'tɛns	inkompetanse inkɔmpə'taŋsə, 'inkɔmpətaŋsə	inkompetens inkɔmpə'tens
129	patience (Lat. patientia) pasjɑ̃ːs(ə)	Patience pɑ'sjɑ̃ːs, ~'sjaŋs	~ 'peɪʃns	pɑ'sjɑ̃ːs(ə)	~ pɑ'ʃaŋs(ə)	pasi'aŋs	patiens pasi'aŋs
130	préférence preferɑ̃ːs(ə)	Präferenz prefe'rɛnts	~ 'pref(ə)r(ə)ns	preferentie prefə'rɛnsi, ~ fe' ~, ~ tsi	~ præfə'raŋsə	preferanse prefə'raŋsə	preferens prefə'raŋs, ~'rens
131	référence referɑ̃ːs(ə)	Referenz refe'rɛnts	~ 'refr(ə)ns	referentie refə'rɛnsi, ~ tsi, refə' ~, refe' ~	~ refə'raŋsə	referanse refə'raŋsə	referens refə'rens
〈-ense〉 132	dispense (Lat. dispensatio) dispɑ̃ːs(ə)	Dispens dis'pens	dispense di'spens	dispensatie dispɛn'sa:(t)si, ~ pən' ~	—	dispens dis'pɑŋs	dispens dis'paŋs
〈-ange〉 133	mélange melɑ̃ːʒ(ə)	Melange me'lɑ̃ːʒ(ə)	~ mer'lɑ̃ː(n)ʒ, ~'lɔ̃ː(n)ʒ	me'lɑ̃ːʒə	~ me'laŋʃə	me'laŋʃ	me'laŋʃ
〈-anche〉 134	branche brɑ̃ːʃ(ə)	Branche brɑ̃ːʃə	branch brɑ:n(t)ʃ	'brɑ̃ːʃə	~ 'braŋʃə	bransje 'branʃə	bransch branʃ

		Planche 'plɑ̃ːʃə	planch plɑ̃ːʃ	—	'plɑ̃ʃə	plansje 'plɑ̃ʃə	plansch plɑ̃ʃ, plɑ̃ʃ
135	planche plɑ̃ːʃ(ə)			—	‚plɑ̃ʃə		
136	revanche r(ə)vɑ̃ːʃ(ə)	Revanche re'vɑ̃ːʃ, ~ 'vɑ̃ʃə	revenge rɪ'ven(d)ʒ, rə'v ~	rə'vɑ̃ːʃ(ə) ~ ~ 'vɑ̃n ~	~ re'vɑ̃ʃ(ə)	revansj(e) re'vɑ̃ʃ(ə)	revansch re'vanʃ, ~ 'vanʃ

Fr. /ɛ̃/ and /œ̃/ in final position

⟨-in⟩

137	bassin basɛ̃	Bassin ba'sɛŋ, ~ 'sɛ̃ː	basin 'beisn	bɑ̃'sɛ̃ː	ba'sɛŋ	basseng ba'seŋŋ	bassäng ba'sæŋ
138	bulletin (Ital. bulletino) byl(ə)tɛ̃	Bulletin	~	~	~	~	bʉlə'tiːn
139	chagrin ʃagrɛ̃	byl'tɛ̃, bylə'teŋ Chagrin ʃa'grɛ̃	'bʊlɪtɪn, ~ lət ~ 'ʃægrɪn, ʃa'griːn	byl(ə)'tɛ̃, bɑlə ~ chagrijn ʃa'grɛ.in	bylə'teŋ ʃa'grɛŋ	bulə'teŋŋ, bylə'~ sjagreng, ʃa'grɛŋŋ	~, chagräng ʃa'græŋ
140	cousin kuzɛ̃	Cousin ku'zɛŋ, ~ 'zɛ̃ː	'kazn	—	—	—	kusin ku'siːn
141	crétin kretɛ̃	Kretin kre'tɛ̃ː	'kretɪn, 'kriːt ~	kre'tɛ̃ː	~	(kretiner) kre'tiːnər	(kretin) kre'tiːn
142	dessin desɛ̃, dɛ ~	Dessin de'sɛ̃, dɛ ~	—	dɛ'sɛ̃ː	~ /dessein de'sɛŋ	dessein de'seŋŋ	(dessäng) de'sæŋ
143	gobelin gɔb(ə)lɛ̃	Gobelin gɔbə'lɛ̃ː, ~ 'liːn	'gəʊbəlɪn, gɔb(ə) ~	gobə'lɛ̃ː, yɔ ~, yo ~	gobə'lɛŋ	gɔbə'leŋŋ	gobeläng gɔbə'læŋ
144	mannequin man(ə)kɛ̃	Mannequin manə'kɛ̃, ~ ~	'mænɪkɪn	manə'kɛ̃ː	man(ə)'kɛŋ	manə'keŋŋ	mannekäng manə'kæŋ

Appendix (*cont.*)

	French	German	English	Dutch	Danish	Norwegian	Swedish
⟨-ain⟩ 145	satin satɛ̃	Satin zɑˈtɛŋ, sɑˈtɛ̃·	~ ˈsætin	satijn sɑˑteˑin	~ sɑˈtɛŋ	sateng sɑˈtɛŋ	satäng sɑˈtɛŋ
146	marocain marokɛ̃	Marocain marɔˈkɛ̃·	~ ˈmærəkin	marokijn marɔˈkeˑin, ~rɔˈ~	maroquin marɔˈkɛŋ	marokin marɔˈkeŋ	marokäng marɔˈkæŋ
147	refrain r(ə)frɛ̃	Refrain rəˈfrɛ̃·, reˈfrɛŋ	~ riˈfretn, rəˈf ~	refrein rəˈfrɛˑin	refræn rəˈfrɛŋ	refreng reˈfreŋ	refräng reˈfræŋ
148	terrain terɛ̃	Terrain teˈrɛ̃·, ~ˈrɛ̃·	~ teˈrein, ~	terrein tɑˈreˑin	terræn tɛ̞(r)ˈrɛ̞ŋ	terreng teˈreŋ, tæˈreŋ	terräng teˈræŋ
⟨-int⟩ 149	embonpoint ɑ̃bɔ̃pwɛ̃	Embonpoint ɑ̃bɔ̃ˈpõɛ̃·	ɔː(m)bɔ̃ː(m)- ˈpwæː(ŋ), ɒmbɒmˈpwɑːŋ, ~ˈpwɒŋ, ~ˈpwæŋ	ɑ̃bɔ̃ˈpwɑ̃ː; ~ˈpwɑ̃m	ɑ̃bɔ̃poˈæŋ	ɑŋbɔɔpoˈeŋŋ	aŋbɔŋpuˈæŋ, am ~ ~
150	point pwɛ̃	Point poˈɛ̃·	point	ˈpwɑ̃ː; ~	~ poˈæŋ	poeng poˈeŋ	poäng puˈæŋ
151	teint tɛ̃	Teint tɛŋ, tɛ̃·	~	tɛ̃ː; ~	tæŋ	teint, teŋ	(~), tæŋ
⟨-um⟩ 152	parfum parfɔ̃	Parfum/-füm parˈfym	perfume pəˈfjuːm, pɜːˈf~, pɛːf~	parˈfœ; ~ˈfʌm	parfume pɛrˈfyːmə	parfyme parˈfyːmə	parfym parˈfyːm
⟨an-⟩ 153	ancienneté ɑ̃sjen(ə)te	Anciennität ɑ̃sjeniˈtɛːt	—	anciënniteit ɑnsjeniˈteˑit	anciennitet ɑŋsjeniˈteˑd	ansiennitet ɑnsienniˈteˑt	anciennitet ansieniˈteˑt, aŋ~ ~

Fr. /ɑ̃/ *in initial position*

	encyclopédie ɑ̃siklopedi	Enzyklopädie entsyklopeˈdiː	encyclopaedia ɛnsaɪklə(u)ˈpiːdjə, ɪnsaɪk~, ~klɒp~, ~dɪə —	encyclopædi ɛnsiklopeˈdiˑ, ɑ̃~, an~, ~	encyclopædi ɑ̃nsyˈklopɑˈdiˑ, ɑ̃nsy~, ɑnky~	encyclopedi ɑ̃syklopeˈdiː	encyclopedi ɛnsyklopeˈdiː, ɑ̃n~ ~
⟨en-⟩							
154 encyclopédie ɑ̃siklopedi		~	encyclopaedia ɛnsaɪklə(u)ˈpiːdjə, ɪnsaɪk~, ~klɒp~, ~dɪə	~ ɑ̃ˈfɑs	encyclopædi ɑ̃nsyˈklopɑˈdiˑ, ɑ̃nsy~, ɑnky~	encyclopedi ɑ̃syklopeˈdiː	encyclopedi ɛnsyklopeˈdiː, ɑ̃n~ ~
155 en face ɑ̃fas(ə)		~ ɑ̃ˈfas	—	ɑ̃ˈfas ~	~ ɑ̃ˈfɑs	~ ɑ̃ˈfɑːs	~ ɑ̃ˈfas
156 engager ɑ̃gaʒe		engagieren ɑ̃gaˈʒiːrən, ɑ̃gaˈʒiːrən	engage ɪnˈgeɪdʒ ɪŋ~, en'~	engageren ɑ̃ngaʒeːrən, ɑ̃ya~	engagere ɑ̃ngaˈʃeˑrə	engagiere ɑ̃ngaˈʃeːrə	engagera ɑ̃ngaˈʃeːra
157 enquête ɑ̃kɛt(ə)		Enquete ɑ̃ˈkɛːt	~	ɑ̃nˈkɛːta, ɑ̃ˈ~	ɑ̃nˈkæ·d(ə)	ɑ̃nˈkeːt	~ ɑ̃nˈkæːt, en'~
158 ensemble ɑ̃sɑ̃ːbl(ə)		Ensemble ɑ̃ˈsɑ̃ːbəl, ɑ̃nˈsɑːmbal	ɑ̃ː(n)ˈsɑ̃ː(m)bl, ɔ̃ː(n)ˈsɔ̃ː(m)bl, ɑːnˈsɑːmbl, ɒnˈsɒmbl	ɑ̃ˈsɑ̃ːbla, ~bal	ɑ̃ˈsɑ̃ŋbl(ə)	ɑ̃ˈsɑ̃mbal, ɑ̃ˈsɑ̃mbla	~ ɑ̃nˈsɑ̃mbal
159 entente ɑ̃tɑ̃ːt(ə)		Entente ɑ̃ˈtɑ̃ːt	ɑ̃ː(n)ˈtɑ̃ː(n)t, ɔ̃ː(n)ˈtɔ̃ː(n)t, ɑːnˈtɑːnt, ɒnˈtɒnt	ɑ̃ˈtɑ̃ːta, ɑ̃n'~	ɑ̃ˈtɑ̃ŋd(ə)	ɑ̃ˈtɑ̃nt(ə)	entent/ ~ ɑ̃ˈtɑ̃nt
160 enthousiasme ɑ̃tuzjasm(ə)		Enthusiasmus entuˈziasmʊs	enthusiasm ɪnˈθjuːzɪæz(ə)m, en'~, ~θu~, ~zjæ~	ɑ̃ntuziˈ(j)ɑsmə, ɛn~	entusiasme æntusiˈɑsmə, ɑ̃n~	entusiasme entusiˈɑsmə:	entusiasm ɑ̃ntʉsiˈasm, en~
161 entrée ɑ̃tre		Entree ɑ̃ˈtreː	ˈɒntreɪ, ɔ̃ː(n)t~, ɑ̃ː(n)t~, ɑːnt~	entré ɑ̃nˈtre	entré ɑ̃nˈtreː	entré ɑ̃nˈtreː	entré ɑ̃nˈtreː
(Cf. 46, 75f)							
162 emballage ɑ̃balaːʒ(ə)		Emballage ɑ̃baˈlaːʒə	—	amballaːʒə ɑmbaˈlaːʒə	ɑ̃ŋbaˈlaːʃə	emballasje emballaːʃə emballaˈʃə	embaˈlaːʃ, am~
⟨em-⟩							

Appendix (*cont.*)

	French	German	English	Dutch	Danish	Norwegian	Swedish
163	embarquer ãbarke	—	embark im'bɑːk, em' ~	embarkeren ɑmbɑr'keːrən, ɛm ~	—	embarkere embar'keːrə	embarkera embar'keːra, am ~
164	emblème (Lat. emblema) ãblem(ə)	Emblem ɛm'bleːm, ã' ~	'ɛmbləm, ~ləm, ~lɪm	embleen ɛm'bleːm	emblem æm'bleˑm	emblem em'bleːm	emblem em'bleːm, aŋ' ~
165	empire ãpiːr(ə)	Empire ã'piːr	~ 'ɛmpaɪə	'ɛmpaɪə (Engl.), ã'piːr (Fr.)	aŋ'pir	~ aŋ'piːr	empir/ ~ aŋ'piːr, em' ~

(Cf. 149)
(No. 38, 90)

⟨am-⟩   *Fr. /ɛ̃/ in initial position*

	French	German	English	Dutch	Danish	Norwegian	Swedish
166	impromptu ɛ̃prɔ̃(p)ty	Impromptu ɛ̃prɔ̃ty:	~ im'prɔm(p)tju:	impromp'ty	~ ɛprɔm'ty	impromtu im'prɔmtu	in'prɔmptʉ

(Cf. 50)
(No. 51, 52, 106, 107, 128)

⟨im-⟩

Fr. /ɔ̃/ in medial position

⟨in-⟩

	French	German	English	Dutch	Danish	Norwegian	Swedish
167	bon mot bɔ̃mo	Bonmot bɔŋ'moː, bɔ̃'mo:	—	bon-mot bɔ̃'mo:	bɔŋ'mo	~ bɔŋ'mo:	bonmot bɔŋ'mo:
168	chaise longue ʃɛːz (ə)lɔ̃ːg(ə)	Chaiselongue ʃɛzə'lɔ̃ŋ, ʃɛzə'lɔ̃ːg(ə)	—	chaise-longue ʃɛːz 'lɔ̃ː:yə, ʃɛzə' ~	chaiselong ʃɛsə'lɔŋ	sjeselong ʃesə'lɔŋ	(hist. schäslong)
169	demi-monde d(ə)mimɔ̃d(ə)	Demimonde dəmi'mɔ̃ːd(ə)	demi'mɔ̃ː(n)d, ~'mɔːnd, ~'mɔnd	də'mi'mɔ̃ːdə	demimonde demi'mɔndə	demimonde demi'mɔnd	demimond demi'mɔnd

⟨-on-⟩

	prononcieren pronɔ̃ˈsiːrən	pronounce prəˈnauns, prʊˈn~, prn̩ˈaʊns	prononceren pronɔnˈseːrən	prononcere pronɔŋˈseˑrə ~nɔn~	prononsere pronɔŋˈseːrə	prononcera pronɔŋˈseːra, ~nɔnˈs~
170 prononcer pronɔ̃se						
171 rondelle rɔ̃del(ə)	Rondell rɔnˈdɛl, rɔ̃ˈ~	rondel ˈrɔndl̩	rondeel rɔnˈdeːl	rondel ˈrɔndeˑl	rondell rɔnˈdell, rɔnˈdell	rondell rɔnˈdel, (rɔŋˈ~)

(Cf. 5, 24, 25, 54, 59, 98f., 108, 121f., 149)
(No. 12, 43, 66, 71f., 120, 128, 166)

⟨-om-⟩

Fr. /ã/ and /ɛ̃/ in medial position

⟨-an-⟩

	prononcieren	pronounce	prononceren	prononcere	prononsere	prononcera
172 avancer avɑ̃se	avancieren avɑ̃ˈseːrən	—	avanceren avɑ̃ˈseːrən, avan~	avancere avɑŋˈseˑrə	avansere avɑŋˈseːrə	avancera avɑŋˈseːra, avanˈ~
173 brillantine brijɑ̃tin(ə)	Brillantine briljɑ̃ˈtiːnə	brilliantine briljanˈtin, ~~	briljanˈtiːnə, brilˈ~, brl̩~	briljanˈtiːnə	briljantin(e) briljaŋˈtiːn, briljaŋˈtiːn	briljantin briljaŋˈtiin, ~jan~
174 distancer distɑ̃se	distanzieren distanˈtsiːrən	distance ˈdɪst(ə)ns	distantiëren distanˈsjeːrən, ~tant~	distancere disdɑŋˈseˑrə	distansere distaŋˈseːrə	distansera distaŋˈseːra, ~an~
175 tantième tɑ̃tjɛm(ə)	Tantieme tɑ̃ˈtieːma	—	tanˈtjɛm, tɑ̃~	taŋˈtiɛm(ə)	taŋˈtieːma, taŋˈtieːm	tantiem taŋˈtieːm, tan~, ~æːm
176 trancher trɑ̃je	tranchieren trɑ̃ˈjiːrən, trɑ̃ˈ~	—	trancheren tranˈjeːrən	tranchere traŋˈjeˑrə	tranchere traŋˈjeːrə	tranchera traŋˈjeːra

(Cf. 1, 10, 70)

⟨-am-⟩

	prononcieren	pronounce	prononceren	prononcere	prononsere	prononcera
177 campagne (Ital. campagna) kɑ̃paɲ(ə)	Kampagne kamˈpaɲə	campaign kæmˈpeɪn	kamˈpaɲə	kampagne kamˈpaɲə	kampanje kamˈpanjə	—
178 carambolage karɑ̃bɔlaːʒ(ə)	Karambolage karɑ̃boˈlaːʒə	—	karɑmboˈlaːʒə, karɑ̃~	karambolage karɑmboˈlaːʃə	karambolasj(e) karɑmboˈlaːʃ(ə)	karambolage karɑmboˈlaːʃ

(Cf. 9, 48, 76)

Appendix (*cont.*)

276

		French	German	English	Dutch	Danish	Norwegian	Swedish
⟨-ant⟩	179	avant-garde avɑ̃gard(ə)	Avantgarde, aˈvantgardə, aˈvɑ̃ːgardə	ˈ~ ævɑ̃ː(ŋ)ˈgɑːd, ~vɒ̃ː(ŋ)~, ~ːˈcɑ~, ~ː(ŋ)cʌ~, ~vɒŋ~, ~vɑː(ŋ)~, ~veɑ~	ˈ~ avɑ̃ˈɣardə	avantgarde avɑŋˈgɛrdə	avantgarde aˈvaŋgardə	avantgarde aˈvaŋgardə aˈvant~, (aˈvaŋt~)
⟨-en-⟩	180	centime sɑ̃tim(ə)	Centime sɑ̃ˈtiːm	ˈsɒntiːm, sɑ̃ː(n)~, sɔ̃ː(n)ɛ~, ˈsɑːnt, sɔːntˈ~	centiem/ ~ sɛnˈtiːm	saŋtiˈm	saŋˈtiːm	—
	181	défensif defɑ̃sif	defensiv defɛnˈziːf	defensive diˈfɛnsɪv	defensief defɛnˈsiːf ~ziːf	defensiv ˈdef(ə)nsiˈv, ~	defensiv ˈdefɑnsiˈv, ˈdeːfɑŋsiˈv	defensiv defɛnˈsiːv, (defɑŋ siv)
	182	démenti demɑ̃ti	Dementi deˈmɛntiˈ	—	demɑ̃ˈti	demɑnˈtiˈ	demɛnˈtiː, demɑŋˈtiː	demɛnˈtiː, (demɑŋˈtiː)
	183	dispenser dispɑ̃se	dispensieren dispɛnˈziːrən	dispense diˈspɛns	dispenseren dispɛnˈseːrən, ~ˈzeːrən	dispensere dispɛnˈseˈrə	dispensere dispɑŋˈseːrə	dispensera dispɑŋˈseːrə, ~pɛn~
	184	gendarme ʒɑ̃darm(ə)	Gendarm ʒanˈdarm	ˈʒɑ̃ː(n)dɑːm, ʒɔ̃ː(n)d~, ʒɑːnd~, ʒɒnd~	zɑ̃ˈdarm, ʒɑ̃n~, ʒɛn~	gendarm ʃɑŋˈdɛrm, ʃɑn~	gendarm ʃɑŋˈdarm	gendarm ʃaŋˈdarm
	185	genre ʒɑ̃ːr(ə)	Genre ˈʒɑ̃ːər	genteel/gentile dʒɛnˈtiːl, dʒən~ / dʒɛnˈtaɪl	ˈʒɑ̃ːrə	ʃɑŋrə	ˈʃɑŋŋər	ˈʃaŋər
	186	gentil ʒɑ̃ti	ʒɛnˈtiːl, ʒɑ̃ˈ~	—	—	ʃɑŋˈtiˈl	ʃɑŋˈtiːl	ʃaŋˈtiːl
	187	rendez-vous rɑ̃devu	Rendezvous rɑ̃dəˈvuː, ˈrɑŋdəvuː	rendezvous ˈrɒndɪˈvu, ˈrɑː(n)d~, ˈrɔ̃ː(n)d~, ˈraɪnd~, ~deɪv~	rɑ̃deˈvu, rɑ̃n~	rendezvous rɛŋdəˈvu	rendezvous raŋdəˈvuː	rendezvous raŋdəˈvuː

188	sensible sãsibl(ə)	sensibel zen'ziːbəl	'sensəbl, ~sɪbl	sensibel sen'si.bəl, ~'zi~	sensibel sɑŋ'si·'b(ə)l, sæn si·'b(ə)l	sensibel sɑŋ'siːbəl, sen'~	sensibel sen'siːbəl, (sɑŋ'~)
	(Cf. 21, 60, 84f., 159)						
189	camembert kamãbeːr	Camembert 'kamɑmbeːr, kamã'beːr	'kæmɑmbeə	kamã'beːr	kamɑŋ'bæːr	kamɑm'bæːr	—
	(Cf. 87, 158)						
⟨-em-⟩							
190	timbre tɛ̃ːbr(ə)	Timbre tɛ̃ːbr(ə)	'tæ(m)br(ə), 'tæm~, ~bə, 'tɪmbə	tɛːbrə, ~bər	'tæŋbrə	'tæŋbər	'tæŋbər
⟨-im-⟩							

Notes

1 In fact the number of corresponding French transferences in the individual languages is significantly greater in part (English and Dutch). However, on account of the intended comparison and in order to keep the corpus a reasonable size, only those lexemes were included which occur in at least three of the four language groups English, German, Dutch and the Scandinavian languages. Although this selection reduces the statistical representativeness of the results, the examples are sufficient in number for our purpose here – to show the types and trends of integration.

2 My Swedish friends in particular (the editor *et al.*) found fault with many of the phonetic transcriptions given in the *S.A.O.* What they considered to be out-dated I have put in brackets in my corpus. In general it can be said that the modern Swedish standard pronunciation tends towards the elimination of doublets, whereby grapho-phonemic integration is preferred.

3 Cf. Weinreich 1963: 44; Munske 1980: 661ff; Munske 1982, 1983.

4 The distinction between phonemic or phonetic transference and integration is in itself an interpretation of interferences which occur interlingually from the point of view of the recipient language. This must be emphasized, for the interferences themselves occur on the phonic, not the phonemic or the subphonemic level, as Ternes 1976 has correctly pointed out. An interpretatory classification is however to be preferred for investigations which deal with the effect of borrowings on the recipient language and with the changes of elements and rules of the source language.

5 In recent bilingual dictionaries (e.g. Langenscheidt 1979) word stress is no longer marked to take account of the dominant French sentence stress to which French lexemes are subject. Yet all speakers of Germanic languages apparently perceive French lexemes as 'mots phonetiques' with corresponding final stress. The question remains open as to how far this already represents an integration into the pattern of fixed word-stress (in the sense of a syntagmatic prosodic integration). This way of perceiving stress in French lexemes is perhaps made possible by the fact that the Germanic languages as a rule do not have a general fixed word-stress, but only one fixed stress for each individual word which follows morphological rules ('answer, be'hind, under'stand; cf. Gimson 1980: 221). The phenomena of prosodic transference or integration are more complex than this dichotomy makes them appear. However for this investigation the dichotomy is adequate to indicate where the final stress has been retained and where the stress has been moved forward.

6 The character of a quotation – a phenomenon which is otherwise difficult to define – is here regarded as an undeclinable syntactic sequence of two lexemes.

7 Cf. Weinreich 1957: 8. In addition Ternes 1976: 30: 'the sound in the target language, which is in reality homogeneous, is divided into two auditory components and realized according to these components'. Ternes calls the components 'Oral vowel' and 'Nasality'. This auditory model of interference does not take sufficient account of the fact that the auditory perception and in particular the imitative realization already is an interpretation on the basis of the bundle of distinctive features in the language of the hearer.

8 E.g. Haugen 1956: 46; Clyne 1975: 27.

9 Here we consider [ts] after [n] as an allophone of /s/.

10 In order to avoid making the classificatory model still more complicated, I have decided not to follow one of the well-known complicated grapheme theories (e.g. that of McLaughlin, cf. Althaus 1980). I have not gone into graphemic and

graphetic integration which is caused syntagmatically (not paradigmatically) in more detail either, although the grapheme systems also have autonomous rules here.

11 I do not know of comparable investigations of other Germanic languages. Nevertheless it can be assumed in the case of German and the Scandinavian languages that the great majority of French loan words were introduced between the 17th and 19th century.

12 It is interesting that one case of hybrid integration which is mentioned in *O.D.S.* 4: 337 (charmant /ʃarˈmaŋt/) is regarded in Danish as stilted or vulgar.

13 /ŋ/ is replaced by the homorganic nasal /m/ before /p/ (assimilation), similarly in pension /panˈʃuːn/; cf. Widmark 1970: 42, Ternes 1976: 30 and above p. 243.

14 The interjection is (in contrast to the substantive) phonemically integrated: ⟨pardon⟩ /parˈdoŋ/.

15 I would like to thank my staff, Birgit Sahlmann, Brigitte Volland, Hildegard König and Manfrid Brückner, for their valuable assistance for producing and correcting the complicated manuscript; above all, however, I am indebted to Iain Clarkson for carrying out the difficult task of translating the original version into English.

Bibliography

Althaus, H.-P. 1980: Graphetik, Graphematik. In H. P. Althaus, H. Henne and H. E. Wiegand (eds.), *Lexikon der Germanistischen Linguistik*. 2nd edn. Tübingen, pp. 138–51.

Bergmann, C. 1970: *Kortfattad Svensk språkhistoria*. 2nd edn. Stockholm.

Berndt, R. 1969: *Einführung in das Studium des Mittelenglischen*. Halle (Saale). 1960.

Berulfsen, B. 1969: *Norsk Uttaleordbok. Utgitt av bymålslaget*. Oslo.

Bierwisch, M. 1973: *Lautstruktur und Schriftstruktur*. Studia grammatica 11. Berlin.

Bühler, K. 1965: *Sprachtheorie. Die Darstellungsfunktion der Sprache*. Stuttgart.

Clyne, M. 1975: *Forschungsbericht Sprachkontakt*. Kronberg/Ts.

Conninck, R. H. B. 1970: Groot Uitspraakwoordenboek van de Nederlandse Taal. Antwerpen.

Duden Aussprachewörterbuch. Vol. 2., ed. Max Mangold. Mannheim 1974.

Gimson, A. C. 1980: *An Introduction to the Pronunciation of English*. 3rd edn. London.

Hansen, A. 1956: *Udtalen i moderne Dansk*. Copenhagen.

Haugen, E. 1956: *Bilingualism in the Americas. A Bibliography and Research Guide*. Alabama.

Jones, D. 1977: *Everyman's English Pronouncing Dictionary*. Vol. 14, ed. A. C. Gimson. London.

Karker, A. 1976: Nordisk retskrivning. *Språk i Norden*. Lund, pp. 39–84.

Kratz, B. 1968: Deutsch-französischer Lehnwortaustrausch. W. Mitzka (ed.), *Wortgeographie und Gesellschaft*. Berlin, pp. 445–87.

Langenscheidts Großwörterbuch. 1979: Französisch–Deutsch. Begründet von K. Sachs and C. Vilatte, ed. von E. Weis. Berlin.

Leopold, C. G. 1801: *Afhandling om svenska stafsättet*. Stockholm.

Lindstam, C. S. 1946: *Nordisk rättstavning*. Stockholm.

Marchand, H. 1969: *The Categories and Types of Present-Day English Word-Formation*. 2nd edn. Munich.

Morciniec, N. 1976: Interferenzerscheinungen als Ergebnis distributioneller Kontraste distinktiver phonologischer Merkmale. *Jahrbuch Deutsch als Fremdsprache* 2: 95–101.

Mossé, F. 1952: *A Handbook of Middle English*. Baltimore.

Munske, H. H. 1980: Germanische Sprachen und deutsche Gesamtsprache. In H. P.

Althaus, H. Henne and H. E. Wiegand (eds.), *Lexikon der Germanistischen Linguistik*. 2nd edn. Tübingen, pp. 661–72.

1982: Die Rolle des Lateins als Superstratum im Deutschen und in anderen germanischen Sprachen. In: P. Sture Ureland (ed.), *Die Leistung der Strataforschung und der Kreolistik*. Tübingen, pp. 237–63.

1983: Zur Fremdheit und Vertrautheit der 'Fremdwörter' im Deutschen. Eine interferenzlinguistiche Skizze. In: Dietmar Peschel (ed.), *Germanistik in Erlangen. Hundert Jahre nach der Gründung des Deutschen Seminars*. Erlanger Forschungen, Reihe A, Bd 31, pp. 559–95.

Nudansk Ordbog. Vol. 6. revid. og forøgede udgave ved Erik Oxenvad. København 1969.

O.D.S. = *Ordbog over Det Danske Sprog*. Grundlagt af Werner Dahlerup, utgivet av Det Danske Sprog-og Litteratursellskap. 28 Vols. København 1919–56.

S.A.O. = *Ordbok över Svenska Språket*, Utgiven av Svenska Akademien. Stockholm 1893ff.

S.A.O.L. = *Svenska Akademiens Ordlista över Svenska Språket*. 10. uppl. Stockholm 1976.

Scheler, M. 1977: *Der englische Wortschatz*. Berlin.

Siebs = H. de Boor, H. Moser and Chr. Winkler (eds.): *Siebs. Deutsche Aussprache. Reine und gemäßigte Hochlautung mit Aussprachewörterbuch*. 19th edn. Berlin 1969.

Skautrup, P. 1944–68: *Det Danske Sprogs Historie*. Vols. 1–4. København.

Szulc, A. 1973: Die Haupttypen der phonischen Interferenz. *Zeitschrift für Phonetik, Sprachwissenschaft und Kommunikationsforschung* 26, 111–19.

Ternes, E. 1976: *Probleme der kontrastiven Phonetik*. Hamburg.

Tesch, G. 1978: *Linguale Interferenz. Theoretische, terminologische und methodische Grundfragen zu ihrer Erforschung*. Tübingen.

Ungeheuer, C. 1969: Duden, Siebs und WDA: drei Wörterbücher der deutschen Hochlautung. In *Festschrift für Hugo Moser zum 60. Geburtstag*, eds. U. Engel, P. Grebe and H. Rupp. Düsseldorf, pp. 202–17.

van der Meer, M. J. 1927: *Historische Grammatik der niederländischen Sprache*. Vol. I, *Einleitung und Lautlehre*. Heidelberg.

van Haeringen, C. B. ca. 1955: *Nederlands tussen Duits en Engels*. Den Haag o.J.

van Loey, A. 1964: *Schönfelds historische Grammatica van het Nederlands*. 7th edn. Zutphen o.J.

Venezky, R. L. 1970: *The Structure of English Orthography*. The Hague/Paris.

Warnant, L. 1964: *Dictionnaire de la prononciation française*. 2nd edn. Gembloux.

Weinreich, U. 1957: On the Description of Phonic Interference. *Word* 13: 1–11.

1963: *Language in Contact*. 2nd edn. The Hague.

Widmark, G. 1972: *Om Uttal och uttalsnormering*. Ord och Stil. Språkvårdssamfundets skrifter 4. Lund.

Wörterbuch der deutschen Aussprache, collectively edited by Hans Krech *et al.* 2nd edn. München 1969.

11 The influence of American English on American Swedish – a case study on the nature of interference

P. STURE URELAND

'Utvandrarna själva bör främst få vittna om sitt språk' (V. Moberg in *Svenska Dagbladet* 23 Dec. 1960)
(Let the emigrants themselves first bear witness to their language)

Introduction

The present article is a contribution to intense and extended polemics between the Swedish writer Vilhelm Moberg and two critics of his American Swedish:[1] the Swedish literary critic Jöran Mjöberg and the American scandinavianist Einar Haugen. Although more than two decades have elapsed since 1960, when the series of articles with these polemics appeared in the Swedish newspaper *Svenska Dagbladet*, the central problem of the debate is still of vital interest: Is the American Swedish as reconstructed by Vilhelm Moberg in his immigrant novels plausible or is it, as one of his critics claimed, 'a hotch-potch of absurdities'?

Through the extensive research on the Swedish language in America which has been carried out during the past 20 years after the debate by linguists such as Hasselmo, Hedblom, and Ureland, we are today in a more favourable position to answer this question than in 1960, when Moberg had to defend his reconstructed specimens of American Swedish on his own.

Furthermore, as no Swedish philologist, dialectologist or linguist so far has explicitly tried to answer the provocative question of realism or fiction raised by Moberg's critics,[2] it will be done here by comparing Moberg's reconstructed americanisms in the immigration novels with authentic American–Swedish examples recorded in a number of American–Swedish settlements in Texas, Kansas, and Illinois.

Such a direct comparison with authentic examples of americanisms aids us in fulfilling one of Moberg's wishes quoted above: to allow the American Swedes to bear witness to their own language. Rather than allowing the American Swedes to speak for themselves, Moberg's critics seem to have imposed their own aesthetic and/or theoretical views on the nature and degree of American–English interference in immigrant Swedish.

In a still unpublished manuscript, *Utvandrarnas språk* 'The Language of the

Emigrants', Moberg has tried to describe the linguistic background of the Swedish immigrants.[3] He gives a number of authentic americanisms excerpted from American–Swedish letters and his own notes made during field work in America between 1948 and 1956. However, as a linguistic lay-man Moberg did not know of the various hypotheses concerning mixing in bilingual speech. Knowledge of theory formation in bilingual research could have given him support in the defence of his reconstructed americanisms. Moberg had to rely on his intuition as a writer without the help of modern linguistics. Furthermore, due to inadequate research on American Swedish, he did not, in the late forties and early fifties, have access to such extensive sources of American Swedish as we possess today (cf. Source III in Fig. 1). The present article will therefore first discuss the 'Hypothesis of ordered selection of lexical and grammatical items' (cf. Section 2); second, a historical-comparative model will be elaborated for arriving at the authenticity of Moberg's reconstructions of 19th century Swedish spoken in the Territory of Minnesota (cf. Section 3); and third, comparisons between Moberg's americanisms and authentic americanisms will be made so that the reader himself can judge what is plausible (cf. Sections 5–9).

1   Critical attacks on Moberg's americanisms

Mjöberg initiated the polemics as a literary critic by objecting to Moberg's 'country-hick obscenities', but at the same time admiring 'the portrayal of local color' in Moberg's American epic. Moberg is known for the realistic use of the Swedish language in his earlier novels and is generally considered to be an accurate observer of dialectal speech habits and everyday expressions. The tendency to mix English with Swedish exemplified by Moberg's immigrants and settlers is, according to Mjöberg, most developed in those Swedes who had the least education, as for instance Ulrika from Wästergöhl, the prostitute.

Mjöberg deplores the fact that a considerable knowledge of English is required to understand Moberg's American novel: *Invandrarna* 'The Immigrants' 1952, *Nybyggarna* 'The Settlers' 1956, and *Det sista brevet till Sverige* 'The Last Letter to Sweden' 1959. Mjöberg admits that the extensive mixing which occurs in Moberg's dialogues is a common linguistic phenomenon among American Swedes. Moberg tries to reconstruct this mixing sensitively, but Mjöberg adds that Moberg allows himself to become seduced by his material and thereby to lose objectivity. Furthermore, according to Mjöberg, Moberg is led astray by his imagination and his language is his Achilles' heel.

Mjöberg also asks if Moberg has mastered the American–Swedish language which he sets out to portray. Mjöberg thinks not as far as the language of Ulrika from Wästergöhl and other Swedish settlers in America is concerned.

Mjöberg's only criterion for launching his last attack is his own subjective and aesthetic introspection which is not based on any empirical facts. Lack of objectivity on Moberg's part was the very criticism raised by Mjöberg himself. On the contrary, Moberg spent several years of research in American–Swedish communities, making notes of contemporaneous language usage, studying more than 1,000 letters from America to Sweden, and also American–Swedish diaries (cf. Moberg's own statements in his first article 22 May, 1960 and Eidevall's 1974 summary of Moberg's research in America, pp. 333–4).

2   Interference hypotheses

2.1   The hypothesis of ordered selection of lexical and grammatical items

The basic argument against Moberg and his reconstructed americanisms is based on the hypothesis that there exists 'an ordered selection of items' in the process of borrowing in bilingual speech. There is, according to some linguists, 'a scale of adoptability' which directs the borrowing of foreign elements from the source language into the recipient language. This group of linguists have therefore claimed that only 'superficial morphological interfluencings' occur between two languages and that there are 'but superficial additions on the morphological kernel of the language' (cf. Sapir 1949: 203–6), or that 'function words which normally occur only as part of utterances are seldom borrowed' (cf. Haugen 1956: 67), or even that 'one hardly borrows truly grammatical forms' (cf. Meillet 1958: 87).

2.2   The less restricted hypothesis of interference

However, another group of linguists have claimed the opposite, i.e. that there is in principle 'no limit to the influence which one morphological system may have upon another' (cf. Bazell 1949: 303).[4]

A third group has taken the position between these two extremes in their treatment of the nature of mutual interferences in the Indo-European languages by claiming that larger lexical items are freely borrowed (nouns, adjectives, verbs etc.), but that 'morphemes with complex grammatical functions seem to be less likely to be transferred by the bilingual than those with simpler functions' (cf. for instance, Weinreich 1967: 34 and Rosetti 1945: 73).

In his excellent survey of the state of the art in bilingual studies, Weinreich 1967: 35 warns of the 'hypothetical nature of the scale of adoptability' suggested by Haugen 1950:224. Instead Weinreich recommends 'painstaking observation and analysis' to test the adequacy of a strict order of selection of items in bilingual speech. 'Flowing speech of bilinguals' has, according to Weinreich, been neglected in earlier studies because of its transitoriness.

2.3   Present-day methods of studying interference

Through the invention of the tape-recorder we are now in a better position than in the fifties to study the flow of spontaneous speech and the true nature of bilingual speech, especially as far as its morphosyntactic and syntactic aspects are concerned.[5] (An extensive corpus of spoken sentences has proved to be necessary in order to observe empirically violations of syntactic and morphosyntactic structures. Such a corpus now exists as far as contemporary American Swedish is concerned (cf. Source III in Fig. 1).)

Bilingual research carried out in other bilingual areas apart from the United States yields results which do not support unanimously the rigid hypothesis of an ordered selection of lexical or grammatical items or the scale of adoptability (cf.

for instance the studies of Schuchardt 1928: 195, Bazell 1949: 303, Sandfeld 1930 and 1938, etc. who have treated interferences between the Indo-European languages in Europe).[6]

Even in the United States itself, i.e. in bilingual Swedish America, the present writer has not found evidence which supports the hypothesis of ordered selection of lexical or morphological items.

As the Swedish language in America has ceased to function as a means of everyday communication, how could such a principle of ordered selection of items exist? We are witnessing the suicide of the Swedish language in America.[7] The American Swedes have, to a very large extent, ceased to use their language. Under such circumstances it is implausible that there should exist a given principle for how they use Swedish or English words on the few occasions when American Swedish is spoken.

The situation was of course different 50 or 100 years ago when immigration from Sweden to America still brought thousands of new speakers from the 'old country' and when the Swedish immigrants lived in fairly homogeneous Swedish-speaking areas with their own churches and schools. But the complete break-down of the Swedish language proficiency among contemporary American Swedes indicates that 100 years of mixing has caused such a bewildering language situation that later American–Swedish generations dispense voluntarily with the use of their forefathers' language. If a norm had existed in the use of specific American–Swedish rules and elements, then they would not have experienced the frustrations in speaking Swedish with each other or with visitors from Sweden.

The ultimate reason for the suicide of a given language is of course the decreasing social role which it plays in society. Since there no longer exist cultural or political centres in the United States from which the specific characteristics of American Swedish could obtain sociolinguistic support for development and maintenance through language cultivation or language planning, the historical changes in the lexicon, the morphology, and syntax described in Sections 5–9 are to be seen as the signs of an ongoing process of linguistic dissolution.[8] By studying the process of linguistic dissolution we gain insights into the great problems of linguistic change and linguistic suicide which have occurred throughout man's history.

In the light of the contradictory hypotheses on the nature of borrowing in bilingual speech referred to above, and on the strength of the present results of comparisons between authentic and reconstructed americanisms, Moberg's inconsistent use of americanisms in his American epic can be defended.

3   Historiographical perspectives of interference research

Thus there is complete disagreement on the nature of (morphological) interference within the three camps of linguistic interference theory mentioned in Section 2. From a historiographical point of view the inadequate normative statements made by some structuralists that there are practically no morphological interferences in language contact can today be seen as the result of a biased type of structuralism which did not allow for the possibility that suffixes or function words could be borrowed. The more realistic approach to interference, as found among the comparative indo-europeanists (e.g. Bazell, Pisani, Sandfeld etc.), was based on a wider data-coverage of modern and ancient European languages and this broader data-base allowed them to describe the whole range of interference processes – morphological, syntactic or lexical – in a more unbiased way (see Note 4).

In addition language contact studies in the 1960s and 1970s have confirmed the claims of the Indo-Europeanists of radical morphological and syntactic restructurings in the European languages which are due to the interaction of two or more languages. We only need to refer to the interesting results arrived at in Black-English studies (e.g. Labov 1969 and Dillard 1972), creole and pidgin studies (e.g. Hall 1966, Bickerton 1972 and 1975, the articles in Hymes (ed.) 1971, Schumann 1978, etc.), synchronic language contact studies in Europe (e.g. Meisel (ed.) 1977, Ureland (ed.) 1978, 1979, and 1981, Caudmont (ed.) 1981, Nelde (ed.) 1980, etc.), and studies on the languages of the migratory workers of Europe (e.g. Clyne 1968, the Heidelberger Pidgin–Deutsch Project 1973–1976, Klein and Dittmar 1979, Orlović-Schwarzwald 1978, Keim-Zingelmann 1981, etc.) In view of this overwhelming evidence of the great impact which one dominating language might exert upon *all* the grammatical and lexical components of another language, the criticism of Moberg's reconstructions of American Swedish in the early sixties seems not very convincing today and – what is worse – misleading to those who have not worked in the field of bilingual studies. However, since such groundless criticism continues to be repeated, it is the task of the present article to counteract some of the most misleading arguments and to present pertinent data from present-day American Swedish so that the reader may form an independent opinion of the nature of the interferences involved in Moberg's reconstructions.

In two articles Haugen has modified his earlier narrow view of the effects of language contact in the bilingual individual, but remnants of the former normative view also linger on in these articles (cf. Haugen 1972 and 1977). Confronted with all the evidence of morphological and syntactic interference found in field work on American Swedish (cf. Hasselmo 1972 and 1974 and the articles of this writer 1970, 1971, 1974 and 1975), he now accepts that function words and syntactic patterns are also transferred between two languages in contact with each other. However, as an echo of the former 'scale of adoptability' a new term 'communicative norm' is introduced, which is some kind of bilingual norm in the Norwegian and Swedish settlements and which directs the choice of lexical and inflectional elements (cf. Haugen 1977: 93). This norm is also used in order to reject Moberg's reconstructed americanisms in the dialogue of his immigration novels. According to Haugen, Moberg violated this communicative norm, i.e., certain principles or rules of selecting word-formation elements, phrases, syntactic patterns and even normal words. Haugen refers to a number of unnamed doctoral dissertations on immigrant communities in America (ibid.) and quotes Hasselmo 1974, who, using a different concept – ordered selection – within a completely different theoretical framework, tries to describe the bilingual behaviour of switching between English and Swedish among the Minnesota Swedes. Haugen is consequently trying to patch up his earlier deficient approach to the nature of interference in the Scandinavian settlements in America, not by drawing conclusions from modern interference research and from variational studies as a whole, but by reformulating inadequate structuralist concepts of the early fifties. This writer has expressed serious doubts about and arguments against the existence of such a norm in bilingual communities which are in the process of being dissolved (cf. especially Ureland 1975). Similar criticism has also been raised by Kjær and Baumann-Larsen 1974.

What is involved here is not only the question whether Moberg was realistic in his reconstructions of American Swedish or whether – as his critic Haugen claims – he completely distorted it, but also the important general question of the nature of linguistic interference. The present investigation is to be seen as a contribution to solving the great problem of the effects of two languages in contact in America: American Swedish and American English.

4   The historical approach to present-day americanisms

Instead of claiming from an introspective point of view that certain americanisms in Moberg's dialogues must be contrived, authentic americanisms occurring in speech situations are the point of departure for the present discussions. In interviews with American Swedes, where spontaneous Swedish speech is used, we obtain empirical material for an evaluation of Moberg's americanisms. Compare for instance the unsupported criticism of Moberg's usage of the verbs *jusa* and *maka* for *använda* and *göra* respectively, and the criticism of *den vägen* instead of *på det sättet* 'in that way'. These verbs and the verb phrase adverbial are frequent interferences in American–Swedish speech recorded both by Hasselmo 1974 and Ureland 1971. It is rather useless to discuss fiction or reality until linguistic reality is known, only then can we make significant comparisons between the language of the novels and that of reality.

We are involved here with the difficult task of comparing americanisms reconstructed by Moberg in the 1950s with those of 19th-century Swedish immigrants in North America. How did Moberg approach the problem of reality and how should a linguist today tackle this problem? Does the linguistic lay-man's approach differ fundamentally from that of the linguistic expert? Judging from the methods which were used by Moberg we think not. It is a comparative approach to the americanisms in Moberg's novels which will help us to arrive at more reliable answers to these questions. Since Moberg applied a comparative method in his field studies of American Swedish, his results are more closely in agreement with our own results than with those arrived at by the approach of one of his critics in which the hypothesis of an ordering in the lexical selection of items has been over-emphasized.

4.1   Moberg's counter attack

Moberg's reply in *Svenska Dagbladet* 22 May, 1960 was a strong counter-attack on the subjective criticism of his two opponents and a defence of his own historical empiricism. Whereas his critics' judgements were primarily based on their own present-day intuition, Moberg assured them that he had consulted and studied the 'very sources' of 19th-century American Swedish by reading a large number of letters from America to Sweden,[9] a great number of diaries written by American Swedes, among which *Andrew Peterson's Diary* between 1854–98 had been his primary source of information: 'I draw upon this document in all its essential details in reconstructing the language of the settlers' – 'Why should I,' Moberg asks after being criticized because of his lack of linguistic consultation, 'take the detour through linguistics and be contented with what had been [previously] written about American Swedish?' Moberg gives in the same article a description of Andrew Peterson's Diary and how he found this important document of Early American Swedish in the Historical Library in St Paul, Minnesota.[10] This diary was written in some kind of American Swedish by the unschooled Swedish farmer Andrew Peterson 100 years ago.[11]

The historical perspective in dealing with Peterson's diary is stressed by Moberg. He considers this diary to be historical material which is far closer to the linguistic reality of 19th-century American Swedish than his critics' theoretical judgements made 100 years later within a different socio-historical framework.[12] Moreover, there is, as Moberg says, a time-span of more than one generation between Andrew Peterson and his own generation.

Moberg then points out the transitoriness of spoken language: 'The first emigrants have been dead for a long time. We cannot hear their voices anymore; but in their diaries they have left us evidence of their everyday speech, their speech habits, and their characteristic expressions.' Since his critics have not studied the diary which constituted the main basis for reconstructing 19th-century American Swedish, they do not fulfil the requirement of being versatile judges. (The existence of this document was unknown to both Haugen and Mjöberg at the beginning of the polemics.)[13]

4.2   Moberg's sources for reconstructing early American Swedish

The criticism of Moberg for not having considered sufficiently the American–Swedish environment, its language and customs, is also unfounded. The facts which we now have concerning Moberg's preparatory work for writing his American epic support Moberg's own defence.[14]

A Swedish literary historian, Gunnar Eidevall, has published evidence of Moberg's working methods. This evidence is based partly on personal interviews with the writer himself before he died in the summer of 1973, and partly on both manuscripts and other written material donated by Moberg to 'The House of Emigrants' located in Växjö, Småland.

According to Eidevall 1974, Moberg visited American–Swedish settlements four times for extensive field work. The first visit took place in 1948–9; the second in 1950; the third in 1952, and finally the fourth in 1954. (Cf. ibid. 334.) Furthermore, Eidevall presents a long list of historical sources used by Moberg for his preparatory work in America itself as well as in Sweden, such as Andrew Peterson's Diary, collections of letters from Moberg's relatives in America to his parents, and of other letters to Sweden from America during the past century etc.[15]

Thus, the amount of historical documentation used by Moberg for reconstructing 19th-century American Swedish can be said to have been large not only in regard to the socio-cultural setting but also in regard to the language.[16] (For ethnic, social, and demographic aspects of the Swedes in America, see Beijbom 1971 and Lindmark 1971.)

4.3   A comparative method for testing the plausibility of Moberg's americanisms

Of course Moberg was not concerned with the theoretical aspects of his reconstructed americanisms, but rather relied more upon his judgements as a poet. By basing his creativity on empirical observations, however, his genius guided him to reasonably correct reconstructions. Eidevall 1974: 201–2 reports Moberg's numerous self-corrections in the manuscripts of the immigration novels, as for instance from *möteshuset* to *mitinghuset*, from *barnen* to *kidsen*, but also from *Har du trajat blodförnyaren* to *Har du försökt blodförnyaren* 'Have you tried the blood cleaner?'

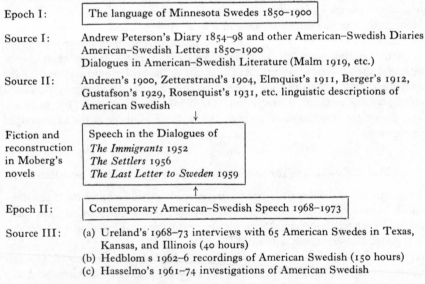

Epoch I: | The language of Minnesota Swedes 1850–1900 |

Source I: Andrew Peterson's Diary 1854–98 and other American–Swedish Diaries
American–Swedish Letters 1850–1900
Dialogues in American–Swedish Literature (Malm 1919, etc.)

Source II: Andreen's 1900, Zetterstrand's 1904, Elmquist's 1911, Berger's 1912, Gustafson's 1929, Rosenquist's 1931, etc. linguistic descriptions of American Swedish

Fiction and | Speech in the Dialogues of
reconstruction | *The Immigrants* 1952
in Moberg's | *The Settlers* 1956
novels | *The Last Letter to Sweden* 1959

Epoch II: | Contemporary American–Swedish Speech 1968–1973 |

Source III: (a) Ureland's 1968–73 interviews with 65 American Swedes in Texas, Kansas, and Illinois (40 hours)
(b) Hedblom s 1962–6 recordings of American Swedish (150 hours)
(c) Hasselmo's 1961–74 investigations of American Swedish

Fig. 1 Moberg's novels in relation to historical sources of American Swedish

There is no doubt that Moberg is a careful observer and recorder of language and that the creative process of reconstruction must have been an agonizing one.[17]

A theoretical model is suggested below which will enable us to test whether Moberg's americanisms are plausible or not. We will compare the evidence of authentic interferences from three different sources of American Swedish with the evidence of interference in Moberg's dialogues. Such comparative testing of Moberg's americanisms yields insights into what interferences are likely to occur in American Swedish. Figure 1 summarizes the comparative-historical method used in evaluating Moberg's americanisms.

The richest source of present-day American Swedish is described in Source III, where the investigations and recordings carried out by Hedblom, Hasselmo, and

Ureland constitute a considerable body of published and unpublished data. However, this article will draw mainly upon the recordings and observations made by the present writer between 1968 and 1973. Additional data from Hasselmo and Hedblom will also be included to support the adequacy of americanisms observed in American–Swedish regions other than Texas, Kansas and Illinois.

The second source of American Swedish (Source II) is found in Andreen 1900, Berger 1912, etc. who report their observations of early occurrences of americanisms in the speech of the Swedes in America.

The third source to be discussed here (Source I) is the diary written by Andrew Peterson between 1854 and 1898, diaries written by other American Swedes, written documents such as American–Swedish letters to Sweden, and finally dialogues in American–Swedish literature (e.g. Malm 1919).

In addition to this representation of three sources of spoken and written American Swedish we have represented in two boxes of Fig. 1 two epochs of the Swedish language in America with which we are involved. It is clear that the Minnesota Swedish of Epoch I and the American Swedish of Epoch II are two abstractions which we can only describe on the basis of the historical sources, that is Source I plus II and III respectively. The arrows in the figure denote the paths of reconstructions of Early American Swedish which have been used in this article.

Moberg did not have Source III in the form of recordings or data presented by the linguists mentioned here, but had to rely upon his own intuition and impressionistic notes of contemporary American Swedish (cf. Eidevall 1974: 337). As a lay-man he had to use the direct method of making notes on hearing certain characteristic americanisms in the present-day speech of American Swedes. (This is also a common procedure among contemporary linguists doing field work in areas of bilingualism.)

Moberg dispensed voluntarily with Source II, i.e. Andreen 1900, Berger 1912, etc. and, to Haugen's dissatisfaction, descriptions of the Scandinavian languages in North America.[18] Such descriptions constituted a 'detour through linguistics' to Moberg. He wanted to study Source I directly instead, which, according to him, was the only reliable source of American Swedish. However, from a scientific point of view Source II must be considered to be equally as valid as Source I. The direct observations by reliable observers of linguistic change are extremely valuable sources of information and can also be used as linguistic evidence of previous stages of a given language (cp. for instance, Panini's descriptions of Sanskrit and The First Grammatical Treatise on Old Icelandic (ed. by Benediktsson 1972)).

The large box in the centre of Fig. 1 represents Moberg's reconstructed speech dialogues in his immigrant novels. The two arrows pointing to this box symbolize Moberg's data approach to arrive at the Early American–Swedish language of Epoch I.

Haugen's argument against Moberg is that the latter did not include Source II and the linguistic investigations of American Norwegian available in the fifties after the publication of Haugen 1950 and 1953, which would constitute the corresponding linguistic works listed in Source III. (Notice that Moberg had finished the second volume of his American epic, The Immigrants, in September 1952 and in September 1956, the third volume was completed, i.e. *The Settlers*.) Moberg replied, however, that Source I and his own experience in American–Swedish settlements was a sufficient data-base for reconstructing Early American Swedish of Epoch I.

In this investigation we will test the adequacy of some of Moberg's americanisms by including the two linguistic sources which Moberg did not consider or which were not at his disposal, that is Source II and Source III.

4.4   Recordings of American Swedish as a means of reconstruction

The adaptation to American–English phonology, morphology, and syntax which is exemplified by Moberg's reconstructed americanisms in his dialogues between Swedish immigrants (Karl Oskar, Kristina, Ulrika, etc.) has been found to occur in authentic American Swedish spoken by present-day American Swedes. In numerous recordings in Texas, Kansas, and Illinois where immigrants or descendants of immigrants from Småland, Värmland, and Hälsingland are interviewed in the Swedish language, authentic examples of interference from American English have been registered (cf. for instance, Ureland 1970, 1971, 1972, and 1974, Hasselmo 1974, and Hedblom 1969).

It is not accidental that we can demonstrate in Sections 5–9 below such close correspondences between the americanisms in Moberg's dialogues and those in the interviews recorded by this writer or other linguists working on the Swedish language in America.

In each of the 65 interviews made by the author of this article, further types of adaptation to American English besides those mentioned above have been registered; for instance semantic and lexical structures such as loan translations from American English, transfer of American–English phrases and idioms into American–Swedish phrases and idioms are often heard. Many of these syntactic and lexical adaptations are americanisms which have not been reported in earlier studies of the Scandinavian languages in America, but which have been treated recently as occurring in the Swedish language in America due to syntactic and lexical interference (cf. Ureland 1971, 1974, 1975 and Hasselmo 1974).

Moberg was not always able to reconstruct the whole range of violations against semantic selectional and syntactic subcategorization rules. Although many of his reconstructions of syntactic violations seemed implausible to his critics, their authenticity has been confirmed in recordings, as for instance the violation of the Standard Swedish inversion rule. The following sentence was excerpted from Moberg's (M.) *The Settlers*: (M. 55) *Ett äpplaträ du säger?* (1968a: 31) 'Do you say an appletree?'

Moberg, like his critics, did not have access to tape-recorded conversations. Conversations on tape allow repeated listening. By playing a recorded sentence over and over again, the linguist of today can study and register larger speech units such as complicated syntactic and phraseological patterns than earlier linguists could.

In spontaneous conversation the listener is inclined to disregard violations of large speech units in an effort to arrive at the semantic intention of the speaker, that is to decode the message by means of phonological, syntactic, and semantic listening strategies.

5 American–English interference in the American–Swedish verb phrase

In the following treatment Moberg's reconstructed americanisms occupy the left column, whereas the right column is reserved for the corresponding americanisms excerpted from recorded interviews with Smålänningar, Värmlänningar, Hälsingar and their children who now live in Texas, Kansas, and Illinois.[19] The difference between the geographical location of the latter American Swedes from that of the Minnesota Swedes can be disregarded here, as a similar Middle West American–English dialect is spoken in the entire area and no greater syntactic or morphological difference exists between its northern and southern parts.[20]

Examples of authentic American–Swedish speech can provide comparative evidence for how plausible Moberg's americanisms in fact are. By using excerpts from recordings we will first demonstrate the influence of American English on the American–Swedish verb phrase.

5.1 Main verbs

5.1.1. *Morphosyntactic adaptation.* Main verbs constitute a syntactic class which is often subject to interference from American English. Some verb types in Moberg's novels will be presented here, the use of which has been questioned by critics.

The first point of criticism involves the graphemic representation of for instance *maka* [meika] for *göra* 'make'. It has been asserted that the phonological form is always /meka/, not /maka/. Therefore Moberg should have spelled the verb with an ⟨e⟩ not with an ⟨a⟩. This may be correct as far as the pronunciation is concerned, but the problem is how to transliterate American–Swedish speech forms into graphemic representation.

However, like Moberg in (M. 2) below, the present writer has also found it more adequate to use the grapheme ⟨a⟩ than ⟨e⟩ in the spelling of *maka* 'make' in the Texas–Swedish example (AS 2). The use of ⟨a⟩ instead of ⟨e⟩ or even ⟨ei⟩ maintains the American–English origin of the word. The American–English spelling marks the loan words as borrowings and makes them easier to identify. (Cp. also Hasselmo 1974: 117 who transcribes the English *make* as AS *make-ar* in *ja make-ar pä'ngar på däj'* 'I make money on you'.)

The second point of criticism raised involves the alternating use of English and Swedish verbs within the same sentence or within the same dialogue text, e.g. Moberg's inconsistent use of *jusa* 'use' and *bruka* 'use' in the dialogue between the farmer from Hälsingland, Petrus Olausson and Karl Oskar (cp. *Bara svenska people brukar woodenshoes* (Moberg 1968a: 13) and (M. 1) *Vilken träsort jusar du..*). However, such criticism is unsupported by authentic examples, since in one and the same sentence a switching from an American–English to an American–Swedish verb can often be heard (cp. *makar han* with *gör han* 'he makes' in (AS 2) and *understand* with *förstå* 'understand' in (AS 3)).

Main verbs in Moberg's reconstructed dialogues	Main verbs in authentic American–Swedish dialogues
JUSA 'use' and MAKA 'make'	JUSA 'use' and MAKA 'make'
(M. 1) Vilken träsort *jusar* du, när du	(AS 1) /vi *jusar* mest engelska/ (Tex. 9:
(M. 2) *makar* träskor, Nelson?	10) 'we use mostly English'
(Moberg 1968a: 13) 'What	(AS 2) /ju mer pengar *makar* han/ . . .
kind of wood do you use, when	gör han/ (Tex. 15: 4) 'the
you make wooden shoes,	more money he makes'
Nelson?'	
UNDERSTAND 'understand'	UNDERSTAND 'understand'
(M. 3) Du måste *understand* oss!	(AS 3) /vi kan tacka Gud att vi har ett
(Moberg 1968a: 149) 'You must	språk som vi *understand*/ som vi
understand us'	förstår (Tex. 14: 4) 'we can
	thank God that we have a
	language which we understand'

It has been claimed that the English verb *understand* cannot cooccur in a sentence with a Swedish subject, which Moberg has exemplified in (M. 3). Such a claim can easily be rejected by pointing out such cooccurrence in authentic recordings, for instance of a first generation Texas Swede from Gränna, Småland, made in 1968 (cf. (AS 3)).

In (AS 3) both the English verb *understand* and the Swedish verb *förstå* are selected. The latter verb occurs as a self-correction. Such self-correction may be a sign that the cooccurrence of a Swedish subject and an English verb was felt to be awkward by the speaker. However, such cooccurrences do occur and are an indication that there is vacillation in the lexical selection of English or Swedish verbs, although the subject of the sentence is a Swedish noun phrase. Many examples like (AS 3) give us reason to question the hypothesis of an ordered selection of lexical and grammatical elements suggested by some linguists. The principle of ordered selection is too normative and rigid. Are these linguists trying to describe the language of an idealized bilingual speaker? (Cf. e.g. Haugen 1950: 224, 1972: 321, and 1977: 97 or Hasselmo 1972: 264 and 1974: 135–65.)

In authentic recordings of American Swedes it is often very time-consuming to find the americanisms which correspond exactly to Moberg's americanisms. A systematic excerptation of Moberg's americanisms and of those found in authentic recordings would be necessary to give us an overall picture of the nature and degree of correlation between fiction and reality. It is often purely accidental that the same usage of americanisms have been observed in the two different corpora. Sometimes one observes the borrowing of an American–English verb in Moberg's novels but not in the tape-recorded material; sometimes it is the other way round.

The verb *visita* 'visit' is for instance a verb which has been retrieved in both the corpora.

VISITA 'visit'	VISITA 'visit'
(M. 4) And jag hittade på att *visita*	(AS 4) å *visitat* en annan liten stad
dej! (Moberg 1968a: 123)	(Tex. 3: 78) 'and has visited
. 'And I happened to visit you'	another small town'

This verb could safely be used as a verb in a fictitious AS dialogue, as it has been retrieved both in Peterson's diary and in present-day Texas–Swedish speech.

Although Moberg did not have recordings at his disposal, he compared the use of American–English verbs in diaries, letters, etc. with the occurrence of these verbs in present-day American–Swedish speech to be able to reconstruct American Swedish in his novels.

5.1.2. Phonological and morphological adaptation. The following American–Swedish verbs *organajsa* 'organize' and *expekta* 'expect' used by Moberg have not been found in recorded American–Swedish interviews. They must nevertheless be considered as fully plausible American–Swedish verbs. Another verb like *graduejta* 'graduate' which has been retrieved from recordings shows us that American–English verbs containing the diphthong *ei* are subjected to a phonological conversion rule /ei/^{AE} > /ej/^{AS}, where the superscript AE here stands for the American–English pronunciation and AS for the American–Swedish pronunciation. Thus Moberg's reconstruction of the pronunciation [aj] in *organajsade* in (M. 5) is a phonological form which also can be expected from American Swedes. It is a result of the conversion /ai/^{AE} > /aj/^{AS}, where *j* implies more friction than *i*.

ORGANAJSA 'organize'

(M. 5) I Andover *organajsade* vi en
svensk församling (Moberg
1968a: 26) 'In Andover we
organized a Swedish
congregation'

GRADUEJTA 'graduate'

(AS 5) /di köm från Bethany/ Ni ser
/College/ di *graduejta* (Kans. Li.
6: 43) 'they came from Bethany
College, you see, they
graduated'

If such a phonologically complicated verb as *changa* [tʃeindʒa] 'change' is adopted in American Swedish as exemplified in (AS 6), then the phonologically less complicated *ekspekta* 'expect' is also a plausible reconstruction by Moberg (cf. Berger's 1912 mentioning of *ekspekta* as an American–Swedish verb in footnote 18).

EKSPEKTA 'expect'

(M. 6) Gud *ekspektar* dä int så titt och
tätt! (Moberg 1968a: 127) 'God
does not expect it so often'

CHANGA 'change'

(AS 6) så den *changa* hans namn
(Kans. Li. 1: 4) 'so he changed
his name'

VOTA 'vote'

(M. 7) Wi *votade* då för Grant till
President (A. Peterson, 3 Nov.
1868) 'We voted for Grant'[21]

VOTA 'vote'

(AS 7) /jag har aldrig *votat* för
Johnson/ (Tex. 19: 7) 'I have
never voted for Johnson'

The four last authentic cases of American–English loan words under phonological adaptation are examples of English verbs that do not have any phonological similarity with the verbs which the Swedish emigrants used when they left Sweden for America. However, due to the continuous contact with American social and political institutions, the American–English verbs were adapted to a pseudo-Swedish phonological form.

Not only phonologically *dissimilar* verbs are borrowed with adaptation as discussed above, but also phonologically *similar* verbs such as English *organize* can replace Swedish *organisera*.

The French suffix /-era/ is substituted by the American–English verb suffix /-ize/

(cf. also Hasselmo's 1974: 242 treatment of the same verb suffix). The change of a verb suffix has taken place despite the fact that the acquisition of the American–English suffix results in a considerable violation of the Swedish morphological and phonological systems. In Swedish, diphthongs occur only rarely in loan words and not in regular verb suffixes.

The borrowing of *graduejta* exemplified in (AS 5) from American–English *graduate* 'pass an exam' is another example of lexical and phonological adaptation which differs from Standard Swedish usage (cp. Swedish *graduera* 'give a doctor's degree').

5.1.3. *The problem of ragged mixing in the verb phrase.* One critic doubts the authenticity of such ragged mixing as occurs in the question to Karl Oskar by the Hälsingland farmer Petrus Olausson in *The Settlers* (cp. (M. 8)) or in Ulrika's admonition to Kristina (cp. (M. 9)). Examples of this type of mixing can be found in authentic recordings of American Swedish, however. In a recording of 11 December, 1968 a Texas–Swedish informant used an American–English verb phrase (*to go*) after an American–Swedish subject (*jag*) and the American–Swedish verb (*hoppas*).

(TO) GO	TO (GO)
(M. 8) Hur far *to go* (Moberg 1968a: 15) 'How far to go'	(AS 8) /jag hoppas *to go*/ Tyskland /England/ å France /
(M. 9) Och nu vi *go*! (Moberg 1968a: 42) 'And now we go!'	(AS 9) /vi gick till Belgium/ (Tex. 8) 'I hope to go to Germany, England, and France; we went to Belgium'

Ragged mixing is characteristic of American Swedish and the norm which is referred to in discrediting Moberg's inconsistent mixture of Swedish and English verbs does not exist. Nobody can for instance tell us why the Texas–Swedish informant uses *to go* in the authentic excerpt in (AS 8) under adoption of American–English phraseology which corresponds to the verb phrase *hope to go*. Mixing occurs here despite the fact that the informant has chosen a Swedish main verb *hoppas* 'hope'. It is evident that the informant's American–Swedish verb *hoppas* has acquired a new syntactic characteristic, a so-called subcategorization feature, from American–English *hope*, in that *hoppas* like *hope* can take an infinitive complex as a verb complement, whereas in Standard Swedish a full *att*-clause with a tensed verb must occur: *Jag hoppas (att) jag kan fara* 'I hope that I can go'. The infinitival complement as in **Jag hoppas att fara* is ungrammatical in Standard Swedish.

Nor does the same informant's use of *go* and *gick* in the same sentence lend support to the hypothesis of an ordered selection of lexical items in bilingual speech. This hypothesis is not only Haugen's but also Hasselmo's 1974: 136–7 basic tenet. In spite of the American–English pronunciation of Belgium, the informant in (AS 9) selects AS *gick* 'went' with American–English meaning 'travelled' but American–Swedish pronunciation. To assert here that there is an ordered principle in the choice of an English or a Swedish verb is to describe the speech habits of bilinguals from an idealized or normative point of view. Haugen 1977 has divided his norm concept into *rhetorical norm* and *communicative norm* If the latter means a great range of variation in bilingual communities, the term norm has lost its fundamental meaning and is thus to be regarded as an empty denotation, since we are involved with variable competence, the consistency of which is not to be defined in such unstable linguistic communities as the American–Swedish settlements, where the process of language suicide is going on. Therefore it is doubtful that the principle of an ordered selection of lexical items can function in an area of bilingualism which is so socially heterogeneous as contemporary Swedish America, where the Swedish language has ceased to function as an everyday means of communication. If a norm did exist 100 years ago in the choice of lexical items, it is today impossible to recover it.

In the light of these theoretical and practical deficiencies no model or principle can be elaborated which adequately explains and describes the degree and nature of interferences in the speech of bilinguals. Moberg's use of *to go* and *go* in (M. 8) and (M. 9) is therefore plausible.

5.2   Auxiliaries

The question of interference of function words such as auxiliaries, prepositions, conjunctions etc. has been touched upon above. It has been claimed in the sense of Sapir 1949: 203 that only 'superficial morphological interfluencings' are possible between two given languages, or in the sense of Meillet 1958: 87 that the grammatical systems of two languages are fairly impenetrable to each other: 'on n'emprunte guère de vraies formes grammaticales'.

As the following disclosure of American–Swedish function and structure words borrowed from American English indicates, the claim that American–English function words do not occur in American Swedish is also to a large extent exaggerated.

Hasselmo 1974: 121 gives numerous examples of the occurrence of the conjunctions *and, but* in American Swedish sentences, which, besides *of course* and *you know*, perform the function of being 'sequence signals' in his terminology.

Furthermore, both Hasselmo 1974 and this writer have registered the direct borrowing of American–English auxiliaries in spoken American Swedish. As example (AS 10) demonstrates, such a frequent verb as *bliva* 'become' can be replaced by *become*. The verb form *bekam* occurred in a recording of a Texas–Swedish informant originating from Forserum, Småland, in Austin, Texas, on 11 December, 1968:

BEKOMMA 'become' and VILL 'will'	BEKOMMA 'become'
(M. 10) Jag *vill* be tillbaka när jag *bekommit* en Rik man (Moberg 1968a: 27) 'I will be back when I have become a rich man'	(AS 10) /efter en tid så *bekam* han en pastor/ (Tex. 7: 2) 'after some time he became a pastor'

However, the replacement of Swedish *skall* or *komma att* by *vill* from American–English *will* is more rare (cp. (M. 10) and (M. 11)). Hasselmo 1974: 222 reports no examples of future tense use of American–Swedish *vill* from spoken language, nor has this writer heard any such examples. Hasselmo quotes an example from American–Swedish literature as given in (AS 11) which corresponds well to Moberg's (M. 11):

WILL and VILL	VILL 'will'
(M. 11) när jag är back igen, *will* jag tell Dig and Kristina (Moberg 1968a: 27) 'when I am back again, I'll tell you and Kristina'	(AS 11) hon *vill* ha kalf till julen (Hasselmo 1974: 222) 'she will have veal for Christmas'

A clearer example of the substitution of an American–English auxiliary for an American–Swedish auxiliary is *used to*, which occurs frequently in recordings. The first example in (AS 12) is taken from an interview with a second/third generation Kansas Swede born in Lindsborg, Kansas, and recorded on 13 October, 1973; the second example was spoken by a Texas–Swedish informant of the second generation, whose parents came from Hjo, Västergötland, and who was recorded in December 1968:

> USED TO
> (AS 12) /hans namn *used to* be Karl Johnsson/ (Kans. Li. 1 : 4) 'his name used to be Karl Johnsson'
> (AS 13) /min far/ han *used to* tala. . ./ (Tex. 12 : 10) 'my father, he used to speak . . .'

No example of the use of *used to* has been found in Moberg's dialogues. The examples in (AS 10)–(AS 13), however, are of importance for rejecting the claim that function words are not borrowed from one language into another. Although the subjects are Swedish noun phrases (*han* 'he', *hon* 'she', *hans namn* 'his name') in all the four sentences borrowing has taken place. In (AS 12) one could claim that it is the entire verb phrase *used to be Karl Johnsson* which has been borrowed. The informant seems to lack *brukade* as a Swedish auxiliary in his active vocabulary and the choice of *used to* triggers a switching into English to complete the sentence.

In order to measure the degree of the acceptability of *vill* and *kommer att* as future tense auxiliaries in American–Swedish speech, Hasselmo 1974: 222 has conducted a test of acceptability. He measures the acceptability of a given form with an index among his informants. If the value *above* 0.5 is obtained between the choice of a Swedish or an English form, the Swedish form is preferred. If the Swedish form obtains a value *below* 0.5, the English form is preferred (cf. pp. 215 and 218). In the test he obtains the values 0.70 for *vill* and 0.98 for *kommer att*. If his results are valid, we can assume that *vill* may occur as a future-tense auxiliary in the speech of American Swedes, although no authentic examples of its use have been registered. Moberg's use of *will* in (M. 10) and (M. 11) can thus be said to be plausible.

5.3   Temporal adverbs

Moberg has also been criticized for using temporal adverbs such as *often, seldom* etc. in ragged mixing as exemplified in (M. 14)–(M. 18). Both in Ureland's Texas- and Kansas–Swedish material as well as in the Minnesota- and Massachusetts– Swedish material presented by Hasselmo 1974: 225 frequent occurrences of English temporal adverbs has been observed in American–Swedish speech.

OFTEN

(M. 14) Dä ä omåttlit att hålla
gudstjänst så *often* (Moberg
1968a: 127) 'It is unreasonable
to hold church services so
often'

SELDOM

(AS 14) /det är *seldom* att vi gör det/
(Tex. 19: 8) 'We seldom
do so'

STILL

(AS 15) /han är *still* här/ (Tex. 18: 19)
'he is still here'
(AS 16) /oh/ jag visste inte /att de
sti . . . /hade den ännu/
(Kans, Sca. 2: 16) 'Oh! I didn't
know that they still had it'

The inclination to use *still* in (AS 16), but the sudden interruption of the pronunciation of this temporal adverb (cf. *sti*..) and the immediate switch to *ännu* within the same sentence in a recording of a first generation American Swede who emigrated to Kansas from Norrköping in 1918, is convincing evidence that there exists an optional lexical selection of temporal adverbs in American Swedish. There seems to be a principle of polarity in the choice of Swedish or English temporal adverbs. Examples (AS 14)–(AS 16) thus support Moberg's use of *often* in (M. 14) and other temporal adverbs elsewhere and rejects the claim of an ordered selection of temporal adverbs. (Cf. Hasselmo's 1974: 224 results from acceptability tests, in which the use of *still* in American–Swedish sentences obtains the value between 0.53 and 0.65.)

5.4   Modal adverbs

There are numerous examples of the use of American–English modal adverbs in American–Swedish speech in Texas and Kansas which correspond well to Moberg's examples of direct borrowings of this word class such as *of course, all right* etc. as well as adapted modal phrases of the type *mesta parten* 'for the most part' and *den (ena) vägen* 'that way' or 'the only way'. Mjöberg criticized the use of especially the latter modal phrase in his article of 27 April, 1960. He contended that this use of *den (ena) vägen* instead of *det enda sättet* makes the understanding of the text more difficult for the Swedes in Sweden who have not mastered English so well that they can associate this phrase with the English phrases *that way* or *the only way*. He is furthermore of the opinion that such americanisms are a hindrance to the acceptance of Moberg's American novels among the broad masses in Sweden.

Even if this may be true to some extent, such criticism is of less significance, as Moberg's interest and foremost intention was to reconstruct the speech habits of 19th-century American Swedes.

The following excerpts from Moberg's novels and the tapes made in Texas, Kansas, and Illinois demonstrate how precisely Moberg treated American Swedish with respect to modal adverbs.

OF COURSE

(M. 17) ett little tempel av logg, ett Guds hus av simpelt timmerträ, *offkås* (Moberg 1968a: 26) 'a little temple of logs, a God's house of simple timber, of course'

OF COURSE

(AS 17) /ja/jag har alltid varit där/ *course* jag var ute å arbetade på olika platser/ (Tex. 14: 21) 'yes, I have always been there (of) course I was out working in different places'

ALL RIGHT

(M. 18) I guess att din make är *all right* den vägen (Moberg 1968b: 70) 'I guess that your husband is all right that way'

ALL RIGHT

(AS 18) /no/ du talar *all right*/ (Kans. Li. 4: 10) 'no you talk all right'

MESTA PARTEN 'for the most part'

(M. 19) Jag är *mesta parten* svensk (Moberg 1968a: 18) 'I am for the most part Swedish'

FÖR MIN PART 'as far as I am concerned'

(AS 19) /well/ de' kan jag inte säja *för min part*/ (Tex. 3: 24) 'well, I can't say so for my part'

DEN (ENA) VÄGEN 'in one way'

(M. 20) Men en kvenna kan va häppi *den ena vägen*, men olöckli den annra (Moberg 1968b: 47) 'But a woman can be happy in one way, but unhappy in another'

DEN (ENDE) VÄGEN 'the only way'

(AS 20) /den ende vägen jag kunde veta att min klass kom opp/ (Tex. 19: 6) 'the only way I could tell that my class was next'

Also in Haugen's 1953 phonograph recordings of spoken American Norwegian *å'l ra't* (p. 535), *åv kårs'* (p. 530), and *dæn vei'en* (p. 544) occur as direct or adapted americanisms.

Although *right* and *rätt* resemble each other phonetically, the former is used nevertheless in the modal adverb *all right*. It seems as if borrowing operates on whole syntactic chunks and phrases, not on specific words. The same can of course be said about *course* and *kås* in *of course*. Such modal adverbs as exemplified in (AS 17)–(AS 18) constitute a whole phrase and are borrowed into American Swedish irrespective of whether they are phonologically similar or not to American English.

5.5   Local adverbs

Only in Robert's letter from California to Karl Oskar and Kristina have clear examples of direct loans of local adverbs been retrieved, for instance, *home till* and *back igen* (cp. (M. 21) and (M. 22) respectively). In American–Swedish recordings direct loans and adaptation of American–English local adverbs and adverbial phrases are very frequent, perhaps more frequent than Moberg reconstructs interferences of this word-class in his dialogues. This difference in the frequency of occurrence between Moberg's America novels on the one hand, and the recordings of American–Swedish on the other, may be due to our insufficient excerptation from Moberg's novels.

HOME

(M. 21) Den vägen är long as Du
förstår, den är nästan lika
long som vägen tillbaka *home
till* Sverige (Moberg 1968a: 27)
'That road is long as you
understand, it is almost as long
as the road back home to Sweden'

BACK

(M. 22) Wi har mött många Äfentyr,
när jag är *back* igen will
jag tell Dig och Kristina
allting (Moberg 1968a: 27)

RÄTT HÄR 'right here'

(AS 21) /hon bodde *rätt här*/ (Kans.
Li. 11: 9) 'she lived right
here'

ALLT ÖVER 'all over'

(AS 22) /*allt över* är det svenskar/
(Tex. 14: 8) 'there are
Swedes all over'

ACROSS

(AS 23) /men han gick aldrig *across*/
(Tex. 8: 5) 'but he never
went across'

A clear phonological interference has caused a homonymy of the Swedish stative and directional adverbs *här* and *hit* to become *här* in American Swedish, because the distinction is lacking in American English. No such examples have been found in Moberg's novels, however.

HÄR 'here'

(AS 24) /han kommer *här* ofta/ (Kans.
Li 7: 86) 'he comes here
often'

Also in Haugen's material of 1953 *all' å'ver* for *all over* (p. 547) occurs as a direct loan and *run't hær* 'around here' (p. 547) and *oppe dæ'r* 'up there' (p. 511) occur as adapted local phrases in American Norwegian. Such evidence of direct borrowing or adaptation from our American–Swedish material as well as from Haugen's own recordings support Moberg's use of American–English local adverbs or adaptations of them.

6 American–English interference in the noun phrase

6.1 Personal pronouns

Personal pronouns must be considered to be function words above all, as they can be bearers of the subject or object functions in a sentence. Two American–English personal pronouns have been found to occur in American–Swedish interviews as [jʉ] 'you' and [əs] 'us' as opposed to Swedish [dʉ]'du' and [ɔs] 'oss' respectively.[22] In (AS 30) the American–English personal pronoun *us* has been selected from the informant's American–English lexicon and has been inserted after the American–Swedish preposition *till* 'to'. The latter lexical selection is further evidence for the inconsistency in the lexical selection of items.

JU 'you'

(AS 29) /de meste av dom är dö ikring
här/*ju* vet/ (Kans. Li. 1: 3)
'most of them are dead
around here, you know'

US 'us'

(AS 30) /hon bruka skriva svenska till
us [əs]/ (Tex. 8: 3) 'she used
to write Swedish to us'

So far such daring examples of pronominal interference in Moberg have not been found, even though such borrowings would have been quite acceptable judging from the experience gained in field work and recording among Texas and Kansas Swedes. Again it seems impossible to posit a norm for the lexical borrowing of American–English pronouns and the phonological adaptation of American–English pronouns because of the numerous psycholinguistic and social variables in bilingual areas. It seems as if the American–Swedish speakers have developed such integrated English articulatory commands in habitually speaking American English, that these commands also dominate the phonological realization of American–Swedish lexical items.

6.2   Indefinite pronouns

Only one example of borrowing of an indefinite pronoun in Moberg has been retrieved so far, that is *all* meaning 'the whole'. From a Kansas–Swedish interview the indefinite pronoun *certain* has been observed. Indefinite pronouns do not seem to be borrowed into American Swedish with a high frequency.

ALL

(M. 31) over *all* de land (Moberg
1968a: 186) 'over all the
land'

CERTAIN

(AS 31) /vid en *certain* tid/ (Kans.
Sca. 3: 5) 'at a certain time'

In the 40 hours of American–Swedish speech recorded by this writer between 1968 and 1973 the borrowing of personal and indefinite pronouns is rare. The sentences in which such borrowings were found were spoken by second- and third-generation American Swedes. Compare also Hasselmo 1974: 217 who discusses only American–English interference with the American–Swedish possessive and demonstrative pronouns but not the occurrence of American–English personal pronouns in American Swedish. If a personal pronoun does occur, it appears, according to Hasselmo, in so-called expressive routines: *you know*, *you bet*, etc. (pp. 119–20), but not as isolated items. However, authentic examples (AS 29) and (AS 30) give evidence of use of an isolated American–English subject pronoun in an expressive routine phrase as well: *ju vet* 'you know' or after an American–Swedish preposition: *till us* 'to us'. Not only do we have a morphosyntactic interference here, but also a syntactic ordering interference from American English in that the subject pronoun *ju* occurs before the tensed verb *vet*, although a Swedish ordering should have been *vet ju*. The expressive routine in American English forced the speaker to violate the verb-second constraint of Swedish. (Cf. also 7.2.3.)

6.3   Prepositions

If by function word we also mean prepositions, the criticism of Moberg's mixing of American–English prepositions with American–Swedish nouns is inadequate. The following examples of direct loans from English (*from, to, about, since*, etc.) and the examples of phraseological adaptation of prepositional phrases (e.g. *för flera år* 'for many years' instead of *i flera år, flera år sedan* 'many years ago' instead of *för flera år sedan*) support Moberg's use of such americanisms in his dialogues.

6.3.1. *Adaptation to American–English prepositional phraseology*

TILL 'to'

(M. 32) Du är snäll å helpsam *till* mig
(Moberg 1968b: 36) 'you are
kind and helpful to me'
(Swedish: hjälpsam *mot*)

TILL 'for'

(AS 32) /det var en improvement *till*
mig/ (Tex. 19: 13) 'it was an
improvement for me'
(Swedish: en förbättring för)

FÖR 'for'

(AS 33) /Question: /Skriver Ni nån
gång?/
Answer: /inte *för* flera år/
(Kans. Li. 8: 19) 'not for
several years'
(Swedish: inte *på* flera år)

SEDAN 'ago'

(AS 34) /men flera år *sedan*/ (Kans. Li.
8: 19) 'but several years ago'
(Swedish: för flera år sedan)

Hasselmo's 1974 data also verify the correctness of our observation of adaptation from American–English prepositional phraseology to American–Swedish phraseology, e.g. American–Swedish *van till* 'used to' instead of *van vid*, American–Swedish *tacksamhet till* 'gratitude to' instead of *tacksamhet mot*, etc. (p. 227). Also the adaptation from American–English temporal expressions such as American–Swedish *för fem år* instead of *i fem år* 'for five years', American–Swedish *i nitton-sextiosju* for *nittonhundrasextiosju* 'in nineteen sixty seven', etc. are mentioned by Hasselmo (ibid.).

6.3.2. *Direct borrowing of English prepositions.* Both in Hasselmo's and this writer's recorded material abundant examples of direct borrowing of American–English prepositions are found.

TO

(M. 35) Du måste gå *to* en medical
man! (Moberg 1968b: 7) 'you
have to go to a medical man'

FROM–TO

(AS 35) /sen flyttade de *from* Stockholm
to Texas/ (Tex. 19: 1) 'then
they moved from Stockholm
to Texas'

ABOUT

(AS 36) /allting var svenska härute till
about 1940/ (Tex. 19: 11)
'everything was Swedish out
here till about 1940'

SINCE

(AS 37) /vatt på trucken *since* nästan
'43/ (Tex. 15: 9) 'been on
the truck since almost 1943'

The reason we do not find so many American–English prepositions in Moberg's dialogues may be that too many incorrectly used prepositions or prepositional phrases would have caused too ridiculous an effect. Consequently Moberg intuitively dispensed with too many prepositional americanisms. One could even assert that Moberg was actually more careful with the use of American–English prepositions than he would have had cause to be, judging from the evidence of authentic American Swedish.

6.4   Quantifiers

If by function words or structural words we also mean quantifiers such as *plenty*, *a couple of* etc., Moberg's use of such americanisms in the American–Swedish noun phrases is a correct reconstruction of American–Swedish speech. The selection of an American–English quantifier can occur despite its cooccurrence with a following American–Swedish noun (cp. *a couple of månader* in (AS 42)). The most common type of interference affects the entire prepositional phrase, however, so that only American–English lexical items are selected (cp. *part of it* in (AS 41)). In the latter case the American–English quantifier is said to have a 'triggering effect' (cf. Clyne 1967).

EVERY

(M. 38) *Every moment of* vårt lif
måste vi vakta på . . .
(Moberg 1968a: 149) 'every
moment of our lives we must
watch . . .'

PLENTY

(M. 40) å sjön har *plenty av* fesk
(Moberg 1968a: 21) 'and the
lake has plenty of fish'

PLENTY

(AS 40) /det var *plenty med* sovel/
(Hasselmo 1974: 215) 'there
was plenty of food'

PART OF

(AS 41) /det var ju *part of it*/ (Tex.
8: 5) 'well it was part of it'

A COUPLE OF

(AS 42) /det var inte mer än en
månad . . . *a couple of*
månader/ (Kans. Li. 2: 5)
'it was no more than a month
. . . a couple of months'

In Hasselmo 1974: 215 acceptability tests give the very high value of 0.80 for *plenty* together with a Swedish noun (*fisk*), e.g. *plenty fisk* and the same high value for an English noun, e.g. *plenty deer*. These results, together with the numerous examples of actual English quantifiers cooccurring with Swedish nouns as in (AS 40) and

(AS 42), indicate that Moberg's use of English quantifiers in (M. 38) and (M. 40) is a correct reconstruction of American Swedish.

6.5   The definite article

6.5.1. *Ragged mixing of articles.* There is an interesting morphosyntactic difference between the pre-positive article *the* in English: $[_{NP}$ Art # N$]_{NP}$ and the post-positive articles /-n/, /-t/, /-na/ etc. in Swedish: $[_{NP}$ N+Art #$]_{NP}$. Interference is consequently to be expected with respect to the placement of the definite article in American Swedish. Moberg gives some indication of such morphosyntactic interference in American–Swedish dialogues. Both direct loans of American–English nouns and American–English nouns adapted to American–Swedish phonological forms attract the prepositive article (AE *the* or AS *de*). The latter phonological form can also be heard in the American–English dialects themselves.

For instance Robert answers Kristina in his description of where gold is to be found with the prepositional phrase *over all de land* (Moberg 1968a: 186). Judging from the spelling *land*, Moberg does not indicate whether Robert uses an English or a Swedish pronunciation, as the spelling is the same in both languages. In his letter to Karl Oskar and Kristina Robert writes from California *de children* 'the children'. The adopted definite article *de* is a well chosen form here to reflect the pronunciation difficulties of [ðə] among first-generation American Swedes.

AE Definite article and AE noun	(AE Definite article) AS noun and AS article
(M. 43) over all *de land* (Moberg 1968a: 186) 'over all the land'	(AS 43) /många av di där som är ... leader of *the landet*/ (Kans. Li. 6: 43) 'many of those who are the leaders of the country'
(M. 44) Jag helsar gott till Kristina and *de children* (Moberg 1968a: 28) 'I greet cordially to Kristina and the children'	(AS 44) /efter *second kriget*/ (Kans. Li. 1: 10) 'after the second war'

(In American–English dialects of the Mid West *dem* for *them* and *dat* for *that* are also frequently heard.)

In the Texas- and Kansas–Swedish recorded material some examples of American–English definite article plus American–English nouns have been found, in which also the Swedish post-positive definite article redundantly occurs (cf. (AS 43)). If Moberg had used such definite noun phrases as exemplified in (AS 43) and (AS 44), he would have certainly been reproached for having distorted the American–Swedish language. These two examples of morphosyntactic mixing are spoken by two American–Swedish informants born in Kansas; the former is a second-generation Kansas Swede from Lindsborg, and the latter is of the second/third generation from the same city. To be sure, it cannot be claimed that this type of mixing is frequent in American–Swedish speech. However, its existence must be mentioned here. The fact that such an inconsistent usage of the English pre-positive and Swedish post-positive articles, or even a combination of these two types of articles, occurs in American Swedish, is further evidence that the principle of lexical or grammatical selectional ordering does not always hold.

The informant of (AS 43) has access to two morphosyntactic systems in his linguistic competence, i.e. he speaks both Swedish and English. First he selects an English form of the head noun phrase in the compound, *the leader*, then he selects an English determining genitival prepositional phrase, *of the landet*, whereby the choice of the English preposition *of* also triggers the choice of the English pre-positive article *the*. However, it is inexplicable why the speaker chooses to select a Swedish noun [land]. Due to a second triggering effect, he chooses a Swedish definite article /-et/ to produce *landet* [landet] 'the country'.

It is clear that we cannot describe interference structures such as the one exemplified in (AS 43) only in terms of mechanically operating categorical rules. A complicated set of triggering and feed-back effects must be considered. We need much more sophisticated models of perceptual and productive strategies to be able to describe the psycholinguistic variables involved in morphosyntactic interference between two or more languages in contact.

In his approach to the American–English or American–Swedish definite articles in American Swedish, Hasselmo 1974: 148 claims that the combination *the tough-ø guy-en* for 'the tough guy' is ungrammatical, because 'articles and adjective endings are either English or Swedish'. Example (AS 43) demonstrates that both an English and a Swedish definite article can occur contemporaneously in the same noun phrase.

To posit a principle of an ordered selection of articles in American–Swedish speech as Hasselmo 1974 does, is not adequate in order to describe what actually happens in language contact. The psycholinguistic variables are too complex to describe the choice of morphosyntactic structures in terms of a rigid normative principle.[23]

The triggering effect discussed above does not always operate. In (AS 44) the ordinal *second* has not triggered a choice of an English definite article, nor has it triggered the selection of an English noun, i.e. *war*, although the two words constitute a semantic unit, *the second war*. Instead a Swedish noun and a Swedish post-positive article are selected.

Considering these additional facts of mixing in American Swedish, no ordered selection can be assumed. Furthermore, we must also reject Hasselmo's 1974 claim that 'if the noun is Swedish, then only a choice of a Swedish adjective can be made' (p. 148). The noun phrase *tough-ø gubbar* 'tough guys' is therefore considered ungrammatical by Hasselmo. According to him, *second kriget* in our example (AS 44) would also be marked as deviant American Swedish. Such normative descriptions of American Swedish cannot be the purpose of investigating American immigrant languages. Instead authentic americanisms should be described.

6.5.2. *Consistent use of the Swedish definite post-positive articles.* The ragged mixing of English and Swedish definite articles is relatively rare. The most common morphosyntactic phenomenon in American Swedish is, however, the adaptation of American–English nouns together with American–Swedish post-positive definite articles.

AE Noun plus AS Definite Article
CRADELN 'the cradle'
(M. 45) han visade med stolthet
   cradeln (Moberg 1968a: 29)
   'he showed the cradle
   proudly'

CLAIMEN 'the claim'
(M. 46) förkovran på *claimen*
   (Moberg 1968a: 29)
   'improvement on the claim'[24]

AE Noun plus AS Definite Article
COLLEGEN 'the college'
(AS 45) /men den står på *collegens* land
   eller property/ (Kans. Li. 7:
   60) 'but it is situated on the
   land or property of the college'

COUNTRYT 'the country'
(AS 46) /det var ut i *countryt*/ (Tex. 7:
   5) 'it was out there in the
   country'

6.6 Adoption of American–English nouns

Adoption of American–English nouns takes place in American Swedish partly through phonological adaptation (cp. *doktare* 'doctor' in (AS 47b)) and *ting* 'thing' in (AS 48)), partly through semantic adaptation (cp. (AS 49)) to the American–English noun. Haugen 1952: 80 calls words which maintain the American–English phonological form 'direct or pure borrowings' (cp. *collegens* in (AS 45) and *countryt* in (AS 46) above), words which retain some part of the American–English phonological form he calls 'loan blends' (cp. *tings* 'things' in (M. 48), where an American–English plural form is preserved), and finally American–Swedish words which undergo semantic adaptation to American English so that they lose their original meaning or obtain partly a new meaning, Haugen calls 'loan shifts' (cp. *lotter* 'plots of land' in (AS 49)). These terms are well-chosen for describing the different processes of change. Phonological and semantic adaptation and adoption are involved in the changes to which the American–Swedish lexicon is subject in contact with American English.

Such adaptation and adoption were observed at an early stage by American Swedes themselves such as Berger 1912 and Andreen 1900 who collected an excellent corpus of americanisms, in which most of the different types of interferences described in this article are exemplified.

Moberg has also been criticized for creating a number of compounds and phrases which are said to be products of his own imagination. His *svenska people* in (M. 47a) has been mentioned as an example of such a strange phrase. However, in American–Swedish speech one does find authentic examples of such wildly mixed noun phrase structure, that is an American–Swedish adjective denoting nationality together with an American–English mass noun, e.g. *amerikanska folks* 'American folks' (cf. (AS 47a)).

AS Adjective plus AE Noun
(M. 47a) Bara *svenska people* brukar
   woodenshoes (Moberg 1968a:
   13) 'only Swedish people
   use woodenshoes'

AS Adjective plus AE Noun
(AS 47a) /jag hade varit omkring
   amerikanska folks så länge/
   (Tex. 19: 12) 'I had been
   around American people so
   long'

The word for *doctor* in Moberg's novels occurs as *doktare*. It is a perfect reconstruction, as the same form can be heard in authentic American Swedish (cp. (AS 47b)). According to information provided by Prof. Hedblom, Uppsala, the form *doktare* also occurs in Swedish dialects (cf. Rietz 1962: 92). One may therefore treat the form either as a dialect form or as an English loan under phonological adaptation.

DOKTARE 'doctor'

(M. 47b) en *doktare* skulle äxaminera mej (Moberg 1968b: 26) 'a doctor was going to examine me'

DOKTARE 'doctor'

(AS 47b) /det är väldigt dyrt att kalla *doktare* till hemmet/ (Tex. 14: 10) 'it is very expensive to call for doctors to come'

Borrowing and adaptation of American–English nouns such as is exemplified by *tings*, 'things' and *lotter* 'plots of land' illustrate three kinds of adaptation: (1) the phonological conversion $[\text{þ}]^{AE} > [\text{t}]^{AS}$; (2) the morphological adoption of /-s/ as a plural marker $\left[\begin{smallmatrix} -s \\ +Pl \end{smallmatrix}\right]^{AE} > \left[\begin{smallmatrix} -s \\ +Pl \end{smallmatrix}\right]^{AS}$; and (3) the semantic transfer of the American–English meaning 'plot of land' to the Swedish noun *lott* 'a lottery lot' according to the following transfer rule $[+\text{Plot of land}]^{AE} > AS \textit{ lott}$ 'plot of land'.[25]

TINGS 'things'

(M. 48) Di gör alla *tings* simplare (Moberg 1968a: 13) 'They make all things simpler'

TING 'thing'

(AS 48) /jag skulle säga en *ting*/ (Tex. 3: 65) 'I was going to say one thing'

LOTT 'plot of land'

(AS 49) /son betalning fick de *lotter* här/ (Kans. Li. 7: 1) 'as payment they received lots here'

Another interesting example of semantic extension of an American–Swedish noun due to its contact with American English is the word *text* 'text'. The phonological form *taxt* or *taxter* is used in American Swedish for denoting 'tax' or 'taxes'. The two forms are probably a contamination of American–English *tax* and the Swedish word *text* 'text'. Although the form *tax(t)* or *täxt* has not yet been found in Moberg's novels, these two forms occur in authentic American–Swedish sources.

In Peterson's Diary for instance, the latter form occurs as in the diary notes of 2 July, 1858, *min täxkt war 3 daler och 37 c* 'my tax was $3.37'. Andrew Peterson does not give a hypercorrect spelling here, but probably attempts to reflect the pronunciation of the word as used in 1858 in Minnesota. Both Hasselmo 1974: 250 and the present writer have found phonetic evidence of the *t*-spelling for American–Swedish *tax*: (Ureland 1974: 94) *men så klagade de att de' är så höga taxter* (Tex. 14: 14) 'but then they complained that the taxes were so high', which was recorded in December 1968 from a first-generation Texas–Swedish informant born in Gränna, Småland, not far away from Bellö, Andrew Peterson's own place of birth in Småland, near the city of Eksjö.

7   American–English influence on American–Swedish syntax

The modifications which have been described above as occurring in the Swedish language in America involve mainly phonological, morphological, and lexical changes. A number of different lexical insertion rules have been shown to exist in the American–Swedish verb and noun phrases which are different from the

Standard Swedish insertion rules. Both major American–Swedish syntactic categories such as nouns (N) and verbs (V) and minor syntactic categories such as auxiliaries (Aux), different kinds of adverbs (Adv$_M$, Adv$_L$, Adv$_T$ etc.), conjunctions (Conj.), personal pronouns (Pers. Pron.), indefinite pronouns (Indef. Pron.), and quantifiers (Quant.) are subject to interference from American English. This interference has been treated here from a lexical point of view, but it is clear that adaptations and borrowings from one language into another also imply syntactic and semantic consequences, that is a change or modification of the syntactic and semantic rules. The vacillation which has been shown to exist between the selection of American–Swedish or American–English definite articles in (AS 43) is of course due to morphosyntactic influence from American English.

The borrowings accompanied by phonological and semantic adaptation observed in American Swedish are unavoidable and are of course a natural consequence of the intense language contact between American Swedish and American English. In this respect the Swedish language is subjected to the same forces of change as other Scandinavian languages in America (cf. for instance, Haugen's 1953 description of American Norwegian) or other Germanic languages in America or Australia (cf. Gilbert 1964, Gilbert (ed.) 1971, Seifert 1947, etc. on German in America and Clyne 1967 and 1972 on German in Australia).

In the last sections on American–English interference in American Swedish the changes in American–Swedish syntax will be treated.

7.1   **Semantic adaptation of American–Swedish verbs to American–English verbs**

In Peterson's diary the verb *planta* 'plant' is used with corn, potatoes and plum trees as object noun phrases, e.g. *hackade och Plantade jag Potater på mitt kläm* (Peterson 19 June, 1855). Accordingly, in Moberg's novels the use of American–Swedish *planta potatis* 'plant potatoes' for *sätta potatis* and *planta corn* 'plant corn' for *så majs* reflects correctly American–Swedish phraseology. Moberg reconstructs in a realistic way the semantic/syntactic interference which the American–Swedish verb *planta* or *plantera* undergoes in American Swedish due to its phonological similarity to American–English *plant* according to the following transfer rule: AS *planta* (majs, potatis, träd) < AE *plant* (corn, potatoes, trees).

In Ureland 1971 the semantic restrictions on the use of *plantera* in Standard Swedish have been discussed. Only objects with roots can be planted in Standard Swedish, whereas this semantic cooccurrence constraint does not exist in American English (cp. *plant grass or trees*). The American–English semantic field of *plant* is consequently much more extensive and, through exposure to this wider use of the phonologically similar American–English *plant*, the American–Swedish *planta* has lost the semantic selectional restriction of being limited to take objects denoting roots, so that *planta gräs och korn* is also fully acceptable in American Swedish.

Such semantic adaptation between two phonologically similar verbs has syntactic consequences which are characteristic of immigration languages like American Swedish. (The French word formation suffix /-era/ is also lost in the transfer as discussed above in 5.1.2 in connection with *organajsa* 'organize'.)

PLANTA

(M. 50) I fjol *plantade* han fyra
bushels *potatis* (Moberg
1968a: 21) 'last year he
planted four bushels of
potatoes'

(M. 51) *cornet* skall du *planta* upp på
filen (Moberg 1968a: 30)
'you must plant the corn in
the field'

PLANTA

(AS 50) hackade och *Plantade* jag
Potater på mitt kläm
(Peterson 19 June, 1855) 'I
hoed and planted potatoes on
my claim'

(AS 51) /yeah/ de' är *plantat gräs*/
(Tex. 1: 27) 'yes, grass has
been planted'

RESA 'collect'

(AS 52) /den som är president/ han är
mycket bra te *resa* pengar/
(Kans. Li. 6: 46) 'the one
who is president, he is very
good in raising money'

RESA 'rear, raise'

(AS 53) /han va *rest* te gå te kyrkan/
uppfostrad/ (Tex. 5: 8) 'he
was raised to go to church'

The American–Swedish verb *resa* also undergoes a semantic change and adopts some semantic components from the American–English corresponding verb *raise* due to its phonological similarity. The following transfer rules recapitulate these changes in progress: AS *resa* (pengar) 'collect (money)' < AE *raise* (money); AS *resa* (barn) '*educate* (children)' < AE *raise* (children). So far this use of American–Swedish *resa* has not been retrieved in Moberg's novels.

7.2   Syntactic adaptation

7.2.1. *Bekomma* 'become'. In 5.2 above the English auxiliary 'become' was exemplified as a possible point of interference of American–English function words and American–Swedish function words. Such borrowing implies that the American–English phonological form is adapted to an American–Swedish phonological form: *bekomma*. The original Standard Swedish *bekomma* which is a transitive verb meaning 'obtain' or 'do somebody good or bad', 'make an impression on somebody', i.e. [+V, +Transitive . . .], is changed into a completely new syntactic category, that is into an inchoative auxiliary [+Aux, +Inchoative . . .]. Since Standard Swedish *bekomma* is primarily used in literary contexts, it is uncertain whether this verb existed as an entry in the lexicon of the Texas–Swedish informant as [+V, +Transitive . . .] associated with all the three meanings just mentioned. A recategorization of one of the three transitive usages of American–Swedish *bekomma* was therefore possible according to the following rule: *bekomma* [+Aux, +Inchoative . . .]^{AS} < *become* [+Aux, +Inchoative . . .]^{AE}.

BEKOMMA 'become'

(AS 54) /efter en tid så *bekam* han en
pastor/ (Tex. 7: 2) 'after some
time he became a pastor'

7.2.2. *Säga hur att* 'tell how to'. No exact parallel to Moberg's interrogative phrase *Hur far to go?* 'How far to go?' (cf. (M. 54)) has been found in recordings. However, the use of *hur* 'how' under different circumstances from the usage in Standard Swedish will be discussed here.

In a Kansas-Swedish recording the *verbum dicendi säga* 'say' cooccurs with an infinitival construction as a verb complement. This type of verb complement is of course a result of the transfer of an American–English syntactic characteristic: *säga*: [+ V, *hur att* + Infinitive]^{AS} < *tell*: [+ V, *how to* + Infinitive]^{AE}:

Interrogative *hur* + *Adj* + *to* + *V*	Conj *hur* + *te(att)* + *V*
(M. 54) *Hur* far to go? (Moberg 1968a: 15) 'How far is it to go?'	(AS 54) /di kunde ju inte säja/ tell mej *hur te tala* engelska (Kans. Li. 6: 18) 'they could not tell me how to speak English'

The informant of (AS 54) gives us evidence of the polarized nature of the choice of syntactic constructions. In the recording of 15 October, 1973 he produced first *säga*, but then, because of the feed-back mechanism, he added *tell* as a repetitious element, since the verb complement *how to* seems to have dominated his productive strategy. Having probably forgotten that Swedish *säga* only takes a finite verb construction with an overt subject marker, i.e. *hur jag skulle tala engelska* 'how I was to speak English', he switched over to the English verb *tell*. Thereby he projected the subcategorization feature of *tell* onto the complement structure to be produced in Swedish: *hur te tala engelska* < *how to speak English*.[26]

Example (AS 54) demonstrates exactly the mechanism of transfer through which new syntactic cooccurrence characteristics are created from the verb of one language onto the corresponding verb of another language. The next step in the development towards a new subcategorization feature is the selection of only one verb without the superfluous repetition of the other verb.

By studying the violations of verb complement structure as exemplified in (AS 54) we are witnessing syntactic change in progress. The rigid principle of an ordered selection of lexical items would not allow for the introduction of new cooccurrence features as for instance [+ *hur* + *te* + Inf] in the lexical entry of *säga* of this Kansas–Swedish informant and other American Swedes.

It is clear that in spoken American Swedish we are confronted with a period of syntactic instability as far as the selection of lexical and morphological items is concerned. This instability is the very source of lexical and syntactic innovation.

7.2.3. *Violation of the Swedish inversion rule.* Moberg has been criticized for letting his imagined American Swedes violate the Standard Swedish inversion rule. There exists in declarative clauses a well-known surface structure constraint on the ordering of the verb, that is the verb-second-constraint. This constraint which requires the verb to occur in the second position is found not only in Swedish, but in other Germanic languages as well (German, Dutch, etc.). However, due to contact with Romance languages (French), English has lost a syntactic constraint which was common in Germanic. This difference in the ordering of elements is of course the source of syntactic deviations in American Swedish as compared to the ordering in Standard Swedish.

Moberg's intuition has correctly guided him when he violates the Standard Swedish verb-second-constraint in (M. 55). By doing so he correctly reconstructs American–Swedish syntax. Authentic evidence for the loss of the verb-second-constraint in American Swedish is presented in (AS 55) and (AS 56) which were recorded in Texas from second/third generation Texas Swedes in November and December 1968.

Violation of the verb-second-constraint	*Violation of the verb-second-constraint*
(M. 55) Ett äpplaträ *du säger?* (Moberg 1968a: 31) 'Did you say an apple tree?'	(AS 55) /han har inte varit i skolan mer än/ *jag tänkte* första graden/ (Tex. 8: 5) 'he has not been in school more than I think the first grade'
	(AS 56) /di har inte levat under Hitler/ därför *di förstår* inte/ (Tex. 3: 57) 'they have not lived during the reign of Hitler, that is why they do not understand'

Hasselmo 1974 gives further examples of the violation of the Standard Swedish verb-second-constraint in American Swedish: *på armén vi sjunger ju svenska* 'at the (Salvation) Army we sing Swedish' and *när jag vill skriva hem, jag vet inte vad jag skulle säga* 'when I want to write home, I do not know what to say' (p. 230).

In his acceptability tests, however, Hasselmo obtained low values for the violation of the verb-second-constraint: 0.28 for *igår han plantade* 'yesterday he planted' versus 0.95 for *igår plantade han* (p. 231).

Hasselmo's test results and our own observations indicate that a syntactic change is in progress. If American Swedish should be allowed to develop freely without the normative influence from Standard Swedish it would probably lose its verb-second-constraint, which happened to English long ago.

In the light of the evidence from authentic American Swedish, Moberg's violation of the Standard Swedish inversion rule in (M. 55) seems more than plausible.

7.2.4. *Violation of the reflexive possessive structures in Swedish.* Moberg has so far not been found to violate the rules for the use of reflexive possessive pronouns in his American–Swedish dialogues, i.e. *sin, sitt, sina* 'his, its, their'. Such violations are to be expected in American Swedish, as the differences in the use of Swedish and English possessive pronouns are considerable. A whole set of conditions determine the use of the Standard Swedish *sin, sitt, sina* (cf. Anward 1974 and Braunmüller 1978). We cannot go into details here, but can only observe that Moberg must have hesitated to take such a radical step as letting Karl Oskar or Kristina use American–Swedish possessive pronouns (*hans, hennes, deras*) instead of the Standard Swedish reflexive possessive pronouns (*sin, sitt, sina*).

As (AS 57) and (AS 58) indicate, non-reflexive possessives do occur in authentic American Swedish:

Loss of reflexive possessive pronouns
(AS 57) /hon_i vandrade till Amerika
med hennes_i mor/ (Tex. 8: 2)
'she_i emigrated to America
with her_i mother'
(AS 58) /min var 12 år gammel/ när
hon_i kom /hon_i komma med
hennes_i föräldrar/ (Kans. Li.
6: 7) 'mine was 12 years old/
when she_i came with her_i
parents'

Because of the phonological similarity between the American–English *his, her*, and *their* on the one hand, and American–Swedish *hans, hennes* and *deras* on the other, the use of the reflexive possessive pronouns *sin, sitt, sina* is diminishing in American Swedish. One could also put it another way and say that the insertion rules of possessive pronouns in American Swedish operate under different conditions so that two coreferential noun phrases cause the insertion only of *h*-forms, whereas the *s*-forms may have disappeared.

The following transfer rule must have operated before (AS 57) and (AS 58) were produced (the rule can be seen as a historical rule):

$$[hon_i \ldots \ldots \ldots \ldots hennes_i]^{AS} < [she_i \ldots \ldots \ldots \ldots her_i]^{AE}$$

The lack of a distinct surface form for the reflexive possessive in American English must have acted as a blocking factor for the insertion of *sin* in the two American–Swedish examples given above.

We are again involved with a morphosyntactic process of change which is taking place in present-day American Swedish. Hasselmo 1974 has tried to measure the extent of this change and has performed acceptability tests among American Swedes. He obtained fairly high values for both types of possessive structures, the reflexive and non-reflexive, that is between 0.87 (for *hans pengar* 'his money') and 0.93 (for *deras egen son* 'their own son'), whereas somewhat higher values were obtained for *sina pengar* and *sin egen son*, that is 0.92 and 0.97 respectively (p. 218). According to Hasselmo the *sin, sitt, sina* forms are preferred by his informants, however. His results may refer to the specific test situations; what is more pertinent is the behaviour of American Swedes in spontaneous speech.

7.2.5. *Violation of the sentence pronominalization rule.* Moberg gives an example of another type of syntactic violation seen from the Standard Swedish point of view when he leaves out the sentence pronoun *det* 'it' as exemplified in (M. 59):

Omission of sentence pronoun
(M. 59) Kristina's question: Doppade han honom så stor han va i strömmen? 'Did he dip him as big as he was into the stream?'

Answer: Offkås, *han gjorde*! (Moberg 1968a: 101) 'Of course he did!'

Omission of sentence pronoun
(AS 59) Assertion: /Texas-Posten/ den heter så/ 'Texas-Posten, that is what it is called'

Answer: /oh/ *gör den*/ ja/ (Kans. Sca. 3: 1) 'Oh, is it?'

Omission of sentence pronoun

(AS 60) Assertion: /du talar ju ingen
skånska/ 'you don't speak any
Skåne dialect'
Answer: /gör jag inte/ (Kans.
Li. 6: 10) 'don't I?'

(AS 61) Question: /skriver ni nånsin
till Sverige?/ 'do you ever
write to Sweden?'
Answer: /många år sedan
gjorde jag/ (Tex. 19: 15)
'many years ago I did'

It is a riddle how Moberg could register the occurrence of violations against the sentence pronominalization rule exemplified in (M. 59), as his primary sources of American Swedish consisted of written letters and diaries and not of American–Swedish speech. It is above all in spoken dialogues that this type of anaphoric pronoun occurs and not in written texts. In the authentic evidence presented in (AS 59) and (AS 60) a first generation and a second generation American Swede respectively violate the Swedish sentence pronominalization rule by being influenced either by another American–English construction (*be called*) in (AS 59) or, in the case of (AS 60), the obligatory deletion of *it* (*don't I*); as far as the example (AS 61) is concerned *det* is obligatory (*gjorde jag det*), whereas the corresponding dummy *so* may optionally be deleted in English (*I did(so)*). The following transfer rules recapitulate the syntactic changes just discussed:

for (AS 59): [gör den Ø]^{AS} < [is it (called)]^{AE}
for (AS 60): [gör jag inte Ø]^{AS} < [don't I Ø]^{AE}
for (AS 61): [gjorde jag Ø]^{AS} < [I did (so)]^{AE}

It is clear that the obligatory or optional omission of an overt sentence pronoun in English has been the primary cause of the loss of the American–Swedish pronoun *det* in (AS 59)–(AS 61). (Notice that in colloquial Swedish the omission of *det* is also heard in examples such as (AS 59) and (AS 60), but *not* in (AS 61)!: *för många sedan gjorde jag det* 'many years ago I did'.) Hasselmo 1974 confirms the existence of violation of the sentence pronominalization rule in American–Swedish speech (cf. his examples *Talar de svenska* 'Do they speak Swedish?' – *Norma gör* 'Norma does' (p. 222)).

Both Hasselmo's and this writer's examples constitute exact parallels to (M. 59) and thus support the correctness of Moberg's reconstruction.

7.2.6. *The passive auxiliary*. In connection with the description of interference in the American–Swedish lexicon from American English, we stressed the importance of phonological similarity between the Swedish and English lexical items. Not only major lexical items are dependent on phonological similarity, but also minor morphosyntactic or syntactic items seem to be phonologically sensitive for undergoing or not undergoing borrowing or adaptation.

The American–Swedish passive auxiliary *vara* 'be' obtains somewhat different conditions for insertion into passive constructions through its contact with the American–English past tense auxiliaries *was/were*. It is the aspectual distinction between stative and non-stative *Aktionsart* which is lost in American Swedish through the aspectual recategorization of *var* < AE *was/were*. In Standard Swedish *var* plus perfect participle of the main verb obtains a stative interpretation, as discussed in Ureland 1971: 48.

Change of passive auxiliary
var betraktade 'were regarded'

(M. 62) Indianerna var för nybyggarna ett vilt och främmande folkslag och de *var betraktade* som listiga, lömska, opålitliga och grymma (Moberg 1968b: 133) 'The Indians were a wild and strange race to the settlers and they were regarded as cunning, treacherous, unreliable and cruel'

Change of passive auxiliary
var konfirmerad 'was confirmed'

(AS 62) Question: /har du konfirmerats på svenska?/ 'have you been confirmed in Swedish?' Answer: /yes/ jag *var konfirmerad* på svenska/ (Kans. Li. 2) 'yes, I was confirmed in Swedish'

var flyttat 'was moved'

(AS 63) Question: /står det (tornet) i vattnet där?/ 'is it (the steeple) still standing in the water?' Answer: /no/ det *var flyttat* upp på . . . på berget/ (Kans. Sca. 3: 4) 'no, it was moved up on the mountain'

Moberg himself seems to have been subconsciously influenced by the passive *was/were* construction in writing (M. 62). The normal Standard Swedish passive expression should have been *betraktades* instead of *var betraktade* 'were regarded' (Mjöberg points out this violation in his article of 27 April, 1960).

7.2.7. *Copying of the American–English progressive rule.* Moberg gives some examples of American–Swedish progressive constructions in his AS dialogues:

vara hunting 'be hunting'[27]

(M. 64) Jag *är hunting* for guld (Moberg 1968a: 27) 'I am hunting for gold'
vara tänkande 'be thinking'
(M. 65) Just va jag *är tänkande* (Moberg 1968b: 70) 'Exactly what I am thinking'

vara liggandes 'be lying'

(AS 64) jag *är Liggandes* af Ryggwärk (A. Peterson 31 March, 1881) 'I am lying in bed with a back ache'
vara sending 'be sending'
(AS 65) Ruth *är sending* eder kaffe . . . 'Ruth is sending you coffee . . .' (in an American–Swedish letter to Moberg's parents acc. to Eidevall 1974: 198)

The existence of productive American–Swedish progressive forms in American–Swedish speech has been doubted by Hasselmo 1974: 229. Only lexicalized phrases like *going on, coming out,* etc. or nominalized verbs like *husking* are considered by him to occur in American–Swedish speech. This claim seems correct to the present writer, as no clear evidence has been found that the progressive rule might be productive also in American Swedish. However, other American–Swedish sources than those of Hasselmo and Ureland do contain evidence of the use of the progressive construction, either as direct loan as in (AS 65) or as morphosyntactic adaptation as in (AS 64): cf. *är sending* 'is sending' and *är Liggandes* 'am lying' respectively.

The question is how to treat these authentic examples of borrowing and adaptation of the progressive construction. It may be the case that Andrew Peterson's example (AS 64) of V+*andes* is a genuinely older syntactic construction which occurs also in the dialects of Småland. (Compare also Haugen 1953 *att han itte notisa træne, som kom runnandes me full spid* (Chap. 19) 'that he did not notice the train, which came running at full speed'.)

In the case of *är sending* in (AS 65) genuine borrowing must be assumed, as the verb is still American English. If Moberg had evidence like (AS 65) he was justified in creating examples like (M. 64) and (M. 65), although we cannot retrieve such forms from contemporary American–Swedish speech. Perhaps the morphosyntactic situation was different in the 19th century from that of today. Examples like (AS 64) and (AS 65) seem to indicate that.[28]

8   American–English influence on Swedish conjunctions

One of the strongest arguments against the plausibility of Moberg's americanisms was the latter's use of American–English conjunctions such as *but, as, and,* etc. in American–Swedish dialogues. Both Hasselmo 1974 and this writer have found examples of the use of not only these conjunctions, but a number of other conjunctions as well. Compare the following excerpts from Moberg's novels and authentic excerpts from American–Swedish recordings:

AND

(M. 66) *And* dä ä grömmast att vakna opp (Moberg 1968b: 39) 'And it is cruel to wake up'

(M. 67) *änd* wi säljer wårt wete (Moberg 1968b: 228) 'and we sell our wheat'

AND

(AS 66) *And* när vi ha a'rrbeta enn ti' (Ma 1: Hasselmo 1974: 121) 'and when we have worked for a time ...'

(AS 67) *And* ja kunna ju innte så vidare ä'ngelska dänn tiden (Ma 1: Hasselmo 1974: 121) 'and I did not know English so well at that time'

BUT

(AS 68) |*but* ... de mesta åv dom kom från Sverjet/you know| (Kans. Li. 1: 6) 'but most of them came from Sweden, you know'

(AS 69) |*But*- dåmm frå'ga mäj åm ja hörde te U'nion (Ma 1: Hasselmo 1974: 121) 'but they asked me if I belonged to the Union'

The empirical evidence for the correctness of Moberg's use of the American–English conjunctions *and, but,* etc. is abundant. Criticism of Moberg can thus be rejected also on this point.

Furthermore, Hasselmo 1974 claims incorrectly that such interference of American–Swedish conjunctions is limited to first generation American Swedes

(p. 232). This claim is contradicted by the American–Swedish examples in (AS 68), (AS 70)–(AS 72), recorded from second and third generation Kansas and Texas Swedes by this writer. Since Hasselmo makes such a claim, his material must be too limited or his test results incorrect. Considering the signal function of *and*, *but*, etc. it is most likely that all generations of American Swedes will borrow these conjunctions; not only the first generation. Spontaneous speech examples indicate that all American–Swedish generations use American–English conjunctions when speaking American Swedish.

EXCEPT

(AS 70) /det var svenska alltihop *except* när hon läste mina verser/ (Tex. 6: 6) 'everything was Swedish except when she read my verses'

SINCE

(AS 71) /de' var så många år *since* vi läste svenska (Tex. 12: 22) 'it has been so many years since we studied Swedish'

THAN

(AS 72) /Han trodde/ han kunde göra mycket bättre här i Amerika *than* han kunde göra/ (Tex. 8: 2) 'He thought he could do much better here in America than he (actually) did'

The difference between Hasselmo's and this writer's observations of the occurrence of American–English conjunctions in American–Swedish speakers may be explained by the two different approaches to American Swedish: the observation of informants in test situations versus the direct observation of informants in spontaneous speech acts. Labov 1970: 39 has pointed out the unreliability of using native-speakers' judgements about their own language as the last criterion: 'If we are to make good use of speakers' statements about language, we must interpret them in the light of unconscious, unreflecting productions.' By doing as Labov suggests, we are confident that Moberg's use of American–English conjunctions in American–Swedish dialogues is a correct reconstruction of American Swedish.

9   Violation of Swedish phraseology

With respect to the influence of American English on American–Swedish phraseology Moberg often gives correct reconstructions. He has been criticized for using American-English *so long* after the American–Swedish main verb *dröja* 'last' in (M. 73). However, (AS 73) shows that such a transfer of an adverbial phrase is not so implausible, since the entire American–English phrase *take long* can be adapted into American–Swedish *ta länge*. A gradual adaptation of an American–English phrase is absolutely plausible. The close correspondences between the adapted phrases in (M. 73)–(M. 75) on the one hand, and (AS 73)–(AS 75) on the other, lends support to Moberg's reconstructions.

dröja long 'take long'

(M. 73) Dä har *dröjt så long* (Moberg (1968a: 43) 'It has taken so long'

göra skillnad 'make any difference'

(M. 74) men kunde det *göra* så stor *skillnad* (Moberg 1968b: 95) 'but could it make such a great difference'

vara misstagen 'be mistaken'

(M. 75) Du ä *misstagen*, Nelson. (Moberg 1968a: 20) 'You are mistaken, Nelson'

ta länge 'take long'

(AS 73) /det *tar* inte *länge* te lära sej så mycke engelska/ (Tex. 18: 26) 'it does not take so long to learn so much English'

göra vänner 'make friends'

(AS 74) /vi *gjorde vänner*/ när vi var där/ (Kans. Li. 11: 7) 'we made friends when we were there'

vara misstagen 'be mistaken'

(AS 75) /en annan kunde ju *vara misstagen*/ (Tex. 18: 9) 'one could of course be mistaken'

Summary

The degree and nature of borrowing between American Swedish and American English has been in the focus of the present investigation. The reconstructed americanisms of Vilhelm Moberg have been used as a starting point for the pertinent question: What kind of borrowings or interferences does the Swedish language undergo in its contact with English in North America?

Since Moberg's reconstructed americanisms in the dialogues of his American epic have been questioned by some critics, authentic americanisms from contemporary American–Swedish speech have been presented and compared in order to test the plausibility of Moberg's reconstructions of 19th-century American Swedish. Evidence from Hasselmo's 1974 and this writer's recordings has been presented; sometimes the historical source of Andrew Peterson's diary between 1854 and 1898 has been used.

Furthermore, Eidevall's 1974 research on Moberg's preparatory work for writing the American epic has also been drawn upon. Information material published in Beijbom (ed.) 1972 has also supported the conclusion drawn here concerning Moberg's reconstruction of 19th century American–Swedish culture and language. As far as Moberg's americanisms have been treated and compared in this study they must be said to be plausible reconstructions of 19th-century American Swedish.

Notes

1 This article is a revised and enlarged version of Ureland 1974. The work on it was supported by the Alexander von Humboldt Stiftung, Bonn–Bad Godesberg. I want to thank Prof. F. Hedblom, Uppsala, Prof. T. Markey, Ann Arbor, Michigan, and Prof. E. Haugen, Cambridge, for helpful criticism. To the 'House of Emigrants' in Växjö and especially to Mrs A. Ozolins I also extend my thanks for letting me borrow a micro-film copy of Andrew Peterson's Diary and other valuable material on Vilhelm Moberg.

2 The literary historian, G. Eidevall, has tried to counter some of the criticism against Moberg's americanisms in his book *Vilhelm Mobergs emigrantepos*, Stockholm 1974, pp. 188–200. However, no systematic linguistic comparisons between authentic and reconstructed americanisms are carried out by Eidevall.

3 The manuscript consists of seven pages of type-written, double-spaced, text with a number of corrections. Moberg describes the educational background of the 19th century Swedish emigrants (p. 1); he gives examples of mixing in authentic American–Swedish speech which he has heard himself in America (p. 2); he reproduces a letter from America to Sweden without naming the author or the date (p. 3); then he gives a description of Peterson's Diary (p. 4); he concludes by pointing out the moribund character of American Swedish.

4 At the 6th International Congress of Linguists held in 1947 in Paris an entire section was devoted to the question: 'Dans quelles conditions et dans quelles limites peut s'exercer sur le système morphologique d'une langue l'action du système d'une autre langue?' The following quotations from the Proceedings of this Congress illustrate that indo-europeanists in Europe were well aware of the fact that non-native morphological elements occur in various European languages as a result of language contact. It was mainly the spread of the definite article and the rise of periphrastic tenses (the perfect and the future) which were mentioned as examples of morphosyntactic interference between European languages. Similar statements had already been made before the Second World War by Sandfeld as the first quotation demonstrates:

> On a surtout contesté la possibilité d'emprunts morphologiques, mais ils existent aussi bien que ceux d'ordre phonétique ou syntaxique (Sandfeld 1938: 59).

> il n'existe absolument pas de limites à la pénétration du système morphologique d'une langue par celui d'une autre (Bonfante 1949: 304).

> Quant aux conséquences que l'action du système morphologique des langues de cultures ... peut avoir pour les langues moins évoluées, elles peuvent être énormes (Pisani 1949: 333).

The opinions of these European scholars contrast sharply with those of Meillet 1958: 87, Sapir 1949: 203–6, and Haugen 1956: 67 quoted in Section 2.1.

5 Hedblom is one of the field workers who has pointed out the necessity of working with recordings to arrive at reliable observations of authentic speech (cf. Hedblom 1967). By applying some of his methods in field work the present writer has gained results which present another picture of bilingualism than that found in current literature.

6 It is especially the writings of Sandfeld 1930 and 1938 and those of Weinreich 1967 which have convinced this writer that the Indo-European languages in Europe offer more reliable data for elaborating an interference theory than do the Indo-European languages in North America. The sociolinguistic situation in the New World is historically so different from that of normal language contact in the Old World that results of observations of bilingualism in America are not always applicable to the languages in Europe. American linguists have tended to over-emphasize the results gained in America in formulating theories of bilingualism.

7 The term 'suicide of a language' is more appropriate than 'death of a language'. The former term has been suggested by Denison 1977.

8 The role of language cultivation and language planning for the development of a given language has been emphasized by Haugen 1966, Rubin 1973, Neustupný 1975, etc. Both types of language policy probably play a greater role in the history of a language than one has assumed earlier. This refers especially to minority languages. As long as the schools and churches in Swedish America carried on

their functions as centres of indirect language cultivation, American Swedish seems to have survived. The year the American–Swedish churches ceased to use Swedish in their service, informants felt that they lost important support for their Swedish proficiency.

9 Moberg describes his empirical approach to American Swedish in the following way: 'Redan under min första amerikavistelse 1948 sökte jag mig alltså till utvandrarnas egna, efterlämnade dokument, deras egna ord, uttryck och talesätt-till källan själv' ('From the very beginning of my first stay in America I looked for the documents which the emigrants themselves had left behind, their own words, expressions and locutions – for the very source [of American Swedish].' *Svenska Dagbladet* 22 May, 1960.)

10 Peterson's Diary is registered as two micro-films in Växjö, Sweden under the following title: *The Andrew Peterson Diaries* 1854–1898. From the originals in the possession of the Minnesota Historical Society, St Paul, Minnesota. Collation of the originals; 7 volumes. Manuscript Department, November 1960.

11 According to information given in Beijbom (ed.) 1972, Andrew Peterson's original name was Anders Petersson. He was born in Bellö, near Eksjö, Småland 20 October, 1818 and died 31 March, 1898 in Waconia, Chisago Lake County, Minnesota.

12 Space does not allow an extensive description of the language in this diary. As Haugen correctly points out in his article of 2 December, 1960, the hand-written diary is a monotonous enumeration of Peterson's daily work on his farm in Chisago Lake County during 44 years. However, to a patient linguist interested in the development aspects of mixing between two languages, Peterson's diary provides reliable data. A special study of his diary should be carried out in detail to be able to measure the rate at which interferences occur in a bilingual person's language. It is thanks to Moberg that we have this diary at our disposal for a historical treatment of the rise of bilingualism in one person during a period of almost 50 years. Here only a few examples of interferences in Peterson's vocabulary and syntax can be given: *tog jag ut mitt forsta nattjomal Papper* (30 April, 1853) 'I got my first national paper', *Sittisens Papper* (30 April, 1853) 'citizen's paper', *alians mitingen* (20 January 1890) 'alliance meeting', *jag är i bedden altgemt* 19 February 1890) 'I am still in bed', *pojkarna endast sysslade om kreaturen* (26 February, 1890) 'the boys only took care of the cattle', etc.

13 After having read Peterson's diary Haugen could point out a great number of mistakes, in an article of 2 December, 1960 in *Svenska Dagbladet*, which Moberg had made in copying some parts of the diary, published in Moberg's *Den okända släkten*, Stockholm, 1950. These mistakes arose in the process of copying from various manuscripts and they are of an orthographic character. (Moberg admitted his insufficient philological accuracy in his reply of 23 December, 1960.) However, these copying mistakes do not disqualify Moberg from reconstructing americanisms for his American epic. Moberg's inadequate copying of Peterson's diary was, at the end of the debate of 1960, used as over-all compromising evidence against *all* his americanisms.

14 Hulenvik writes in Beijbom (ed.) 1972: 15 that Moberg bases his observations on empirical facts in his reconstruction of environments: 'Det är intressant att se hur Moberg hela tiden står på dokumentär grund och samtidigt utnyttjar bestämmelsernas formuleringar till reflektioner av och kring Karl-Oskar och hans familj.' ('It is interesting to see how Moberg stands on an empirical base throughout his American novels by using such formulations which reflect the circumstances around Karl-Oskar and his family.')

15 In *Berättelser ur min levnad*, Moberg has himself described Peterson's diary in the following way: 'Andrew Pettersons dagbok är skriven på ett blandspråk, som

består av svenska, engelska och västgötadialekt, och den är mycket svårtolkad. En del uttryck däri kvarstår ännu för mig som gåtor. Den s.k. svensk-amerikanskan framträder fullt utbildad i denna handskrift, som är det mest upplysande dokument jag känner till när det gäller den första bosättningen i Nordamerika' ('Andrew Peterson's diary is written in a mixed language which consists of Swedish, English, and Västgötland dialect. It is therefore very difficult to interpret. Some of its expressions remain riddles to me. The so-called American–Swedish appears fully developed in this hand-written document, which is the most informative document I know dealing with the first Swedish settlement in North America' p. 309.)

However, Hedblom has examined the language used in Peterson's diary and came to the conclusion that the dialect used in this diary was reminiscent of the dialects spoken in southern Östergötland and northern Småland (oral communication). Moberg falsely claims that Peterson wrote his diary in a dialect which is spoken in Västergötland. He was born in Bellö, near Eksjö, in Småland and continued to speak his parents' dialect in Minnesota.

16 Eidevall 1974 enumerates the following sources of American Swedish which Moberg used for his reconstructions: (1) books on emigration by Helge Nelson, Blegen, Semmingsen etc.; (2) contemporary descriptions of travels to and life in the Middle West by Norelius, Unonius, Grönberger; (3) manuscripts and settlers' diaries by Andrew Peterson, Mina Anderson, Otilla Magnet etc.; (4) collections of letters from emigrants; (5) children's books, textbooks of science, a cookery book; (6) correspondence with contemporary American Swedes; (7) visits to museums and conversations with experts and farmers on nature, distances, farm implements, etc. (pp. 336–7). Thus, the historical documentation can be said to have been enormously large, not only in regard to the language, but also in regard to the socio-historical setting in which the American Swedes lived and died.

17 In the archives of 'The House of Emigrants' in Växjö six of Moberg's notebooks are preserved which indicate that Moberg spent a considerable amount of time on studying not only Peterson's diary, but other diaries written by American Swedes of the past century as well.

18 Both Berger 1912 and Andreen 1900 give examples of americanisms which correspond almost exactly to the americanisms recorded in Texas, Kansas and Illinois, although more than 70 years have elapsed between the linguistic observations made of American–Swedish speech. The two writers present lists of lexical borrowing: AS nouns in Berger: lott 'plot of land', väg 'manner', lägg 'leg'; AS verbs pulla 'pull', mova 'move', expekta 'expect', gå 'travel', leva 'live' instead of bo; AS non-reflexive possessive pronouns hans, hennes, deras instead of sin, sitt, sina; AS prepositional phrases adapted to AE phrases: e.g. sjuk för tre veckor 'sick for three weeks' instead of sjuk i tre veckor, tio veckor sedan 'ten weeks ago' instead of för tio veckor sedan etc. Such exact parallels to the present-day americanisms support the methods of the historical-comparative approach outlined in Section 4.3.

19 A complete list of the Texas–Swedish communities is found in Ureland 1971, which contains detailed information about 45 Texas Swedes interviewed in the period 1968–9. There were 20 additional American Swedes interviewed and recorded in the fall of 1973 in Bishop Hill, Galesburg, Rock Island, and Moline, Illinois; further recordings were made in Kansas: Lindsborg, Scandia, Hays, and Chanute. In all, recordings have been made in 24 different American–Swedish communities in the two periods of field work. The total time of recordings is about 40 hours. One and the same questionnaire has been used for the recordings, which contains 30 questions concerning biographical data on parents, origin,

emigration year and sociolinguistic observations on language attitudes. The use of the same standard format of questions in all interviews gave a constant frame of reference.

A list of explanations for the indices used for the examples in the present article is given here:

> AS = American Swedish
> Kans. Li. = Recording made in Lindsborg, Kansas, 1973
> Kans. Sca. = Scandia, Kansas, 1973
> Tex. 1 = Elgin, Bastrop County, Texas, 1968
> Tex. 3 = Lund, Travis County, Texas, 1968
> Tex. 5 = New Sweden, Travis County, Texas, 1968
> Tex. 6 = Lund, Travis County, Texas, 1968
> Tex. 7 = Elgin, Bastrop County, Texas, 1968
> Tex. 8 = Austin, Travis County, Texas, 1968
> Tex. 9 = McDade, Bastrop County, Texas, 1968
> Tex. 12 = Elgin, Bastrop County, Texas, 1968
> Tex. 14 = Austin, Travis County, Texas, 1968
> Tex. 15 = Elgin, Bastrop County, Texas, 1969
> Tex. 17 = Elgin, Bastrop County, Texas, 1969
> Tex. 18 = Melvin, McCulloch County, Texas, 1969
> Tex. 19 = Ericsdale, Jones County, Texas, 1969

(See Ureland 1971:70, Table F for further details on the geographical origin of the informants from Sweden who were interviewed in Texas in the period 1968–1969.)

20 To be sure, some lexical and phonological differences are to be found between the American–English dialects of the Middle West, but they are of less significance for the purpose of this investigation.

21 The examples from Peterson's diary have been excerpted from a photocopy of the entire manuscript kindly put at my disposal by the 'House of Emigrants' in Växjö, Sweden. (Cf. Peterson 1898.)

22 It is possible that the form [əs] 'us' in AS 30 not only derives from American English but that the Småland dialect pronunciation of the personal pronoun has also played a role. In Forserum, Småland, from where the parents of the informant Tex. 8 originate, the Swedish pronoun *oss* is pronounced as [øs] *öss*.

23 Cf. also Hasselmo's 1972 'sequential hypothesis'.

24 In A. Peterson's Diary *kläm* for 'claim' is used: 'hackade och Plantade jag Potater på mitt kläm' 'I hoed and planted potatoes on my claim' (A. Peterson, 19 June, 1855).

25 Berger 1912 has the same example of the use of AS *lott* in the sense of 'plot of land' in his list of AE lexical borrowings in AS (cf. also Note 18).

26 The Småland dialect form *te* (from *till*) for the infinitive marker *att* is of course phonologically very similar to AE *to*. The transfer of AE *how to* > AS *hur te* has been facilitated by this similarity.

27 Cf. Hasselmo's 1974 acceptability test result for the *ing*-construction in *Han var husking* 0.60, although the native Swedish *höll på att*-construction was rated higher: *han höll på och huskade*: 0.92 (p. 179).

28 The translation process in a bilingual individual seems to be an innate linguistic capacity, which operates independently within each bilingual generation. Bilingual English–Swedish children may produce americanisms which are not derived historically from their parents. Compare the examples of spontaneous interferences which were caused by the translation process in the speech of my 46-month-old

daughter in 1975 (cf. Ureland 1975: 96–7, Fn. 1). Examples of direct copying of the conjunction *than* (*dänn*), the *do*-construction (*Gör inte äta mig* 'Don't eat me!', and the emphatic reflexive *self*-construction (*Jag skall ta ut godis min själv* 'I will get out the goodies myself' have been presented. Since Ylva up till then had never heard American Swedish spoken in her environment, the interferences mentioned here must be regarded as spontaneous, that is created by herself in a translation process.

Bibliography

Andreen, G. 1900: Det svenska språket i Amerika. *Verdandis Småskrifter* 87. Stockholm.

Anward, J. 1974: Swedish Reflexivization. In Ö. Dahl (ed.), *Papers from the First Scandinavian Conference on Linguistics*, 30–31 March, 1974, Göteborg, pp. 17–35.

Bazell, C. E. 1949: Reply to Question IV at the 6th International Conference of Linguists in Paris: Dans quelles conditions et dans quelles limites peut s'exercer sur le système morphologique d'une langue l'action du système d'une autre langue? *Actes du Sixième Congrès International des Linguistes*, p. 303. Paris.

Beijbom, U. 1971: *Swedes in Chicago. A Demographic and Social Study of the 1846–1880 Immigration*. Växjö.

(ed.) 1972: *Utvandrarromanens källor. Förteckning över Vilhelm Mobergs samling av källmaterial*. Emigrantinstitutets skriftserie 1. Växjö.

Benediktsson, H. (ed.) 1972: *The First Grammatical Treatise. Introduction. Text. Notes. Translation. Vocabulary. Facsimiles*. Reykjavík.

Berger, V. 1912: *Vårt språk. Ett bidrag till kännedomen om engelska språkets inflytande på svenska språket i Amerika*. Rock Island, Illinois.

Bickerton, D. 1972: The Nature of a Creole Continuum. *Language* 49: 640–69.

1975: *Dynamics of a Creole System*. Cambridge.

Bonfante, G. 1949: Reply to Question IV at the International Congress of Linguists in Paris. *Actes du Sixième Congrès International des Linguistes*, p. 333. Paris.

Braunmüller, K. 1978: On Possessive Pronouns in Germanic Languages. In J. Weinstock (ed.) 1978, pp. 303–12.

Caudmont, J. (ed.) 1981: *Sprachen in Kontakt – Langues en Contact*. Tübingen.

Clyne, M. G. 1967: *Transference and Triggering*. The Hague.

1968: Zum Pidgin–Deutsch der Gastarbeiter. *Zeitschrift für Mundartforschung* 35: 130–9.

1972: *Perspectives on Language Contact. Based on a Study of German in Australia*. Melbourne.

Denison, N. 1977: Language Death or Language Suicide. In W. Dressler and R. Wodak-Leodolter (eds.), *Language Death*. International Journal of the Sociology of Language 12, pp. 13–27.

Dillard, J. L. 1972: *Black English*. New York.

Eidevall, G. 1974: *Vilhelm Mobergs emigrantepos*. Stockholm.

Elmquist, A. L. 1911: Ett och annat rörande svenskan i Amerika. *Språk och stil* 11: 17–28.

Gilbert, G. 1964: The German Dialect of Kendall and Gillespie Counties. *International Journal of Applied Linguistics* 30: 139–72.

Gilbert, Glenn (ed.) 1971: *The German Language in America*. Austin.

Gustafson, W. 1929: Swedish in America. Unpublished Ph.D. Dissertation.

Hall, R. A. Jr. 1966: *Pidgin and Creole Languages*. Ithaca/London.

Hasselmo, N. 1961: American Swedish: A Study in Bilingualism. Unpublished Ph.D. dissertation. Harvard University.
1963: Language in Exile. In J. I. Dowie and E. M. Espelie (eds.) *The Swedish Immigrant Community in Transition*. Rock Island, Illinois.
1969: How Can we Measure the Effects which One Language May Have on the Other in the Speech of Bilinguals? In L. G. Kelly (ed.), *Description and Measurement of Bilingualism: an International Seminar*. pp. 91–117. Toronto.
1972: Code-Switching as Ordered Selection. In E. Firchow, K. Grimstad, N. Hasselmo and W. A. O'Neil (eds.), *Studies for Einar Haugen*. The Hague.
1974: *Amerika–Svenska. En bok om språkutvecklingen i Svensk–Amerika*. Skrifter utgivna av Svenska språknämnden 51. Lund.
Haugen, E. 1950: The Analysis of Linguistic Borrowing. *Language* 26: 210–31.
1952: The Impact of English on American–Norwegian Letter Writing. Studies in Honor of Albert Morey Sturtevant. *Humanistic Studies* 29: 76–102.
1953: *The Norwegian Language in America*. 1–2. Philadelphia/Oslo.
1956: *Bilingualism in the Americas. A Bibliography and Research Guide*. American Dialect Society. November 1956. Univ. of Alabama.
1960a: Vilhelm Mobergs amerikasvenska – sammelsurium av orimligheter *Svenska Dagbladet*. 11 May, 1960.
1960b: Mobergs amerikasvenska – en replik. *Svenska Dagbladet*. 3 June, 1960.
1960c: Andrew Petersons språk. *Svenska Dagbladet*. 2 December, 1960.
1966: *Language Conflict and Language Planning: the Case of Modern Norwegian*. Cambridge, Mass.
1972: The Stigmata of Bilingualism. In A. S. Dil (ed.) 1977: *The Ecology of Language*, pp. 307–24. Stanford.
1977: Norm and Deviation in Bilingual Communities. In P. A. Hornby (ed.), *Bilingualism*, pp. 91–102. New York.
Hedblom, F. 1962: On svenska folkmål i Amerika. Från Landsmåls- och Folkminnesarkivets bandinspelningsexpedition 1962. *Svenska Landsmål och Svenskt Folkliv*, pp. 115–57.
1965: Bandinspelningsexpeditionen till Svensk–Amerika 1964. *Svenska Landsmål*, pp. 1–34.
1966: Den tredje inspelningsexpeditionen till Svensk–Amerika. En rapport från resan 1966. *Svenska Landsmål*, pp. 97–117.
1967: Om avlyssning och utskrivning av dialekttexter i fonogram Några erfarenheter och problem. *Nysvenska studier. Årg.* 47: 201–34.
1968: Svenska folkmål i Nya Världen. Från 1960-talets fältundersökningar i Amerika. *Saga och sed*, pp. 38–49.
1969: Amerikasvenska texter i fonogram. Hälsingland. Bergsjömål. *Svenska Landsmål*, pp. 1–52.
1972: Bishop Hill after a Century. In E. Firchow, K. Grimstad, N. Hasselmo and W. A. O'Neil (eds.), *Studies for Einar Haugen*, pp. 281–95. The Hague.
1974: Review of N. Hasselmo 1974 *Amerikasvenska*. *Språkvård* 4: 13–5.
1978: Swedish Dialects on American Soil. Some Experiences of a Field Researcher. In J. Weinstock (ed.), 1978: 182–8.
Heidelberger Forschungsprojekt Pidgin–Deutsch 1973–6: *Untersuchung zur Erlernung des Deutschen durch ausländische Arbeiter*. Heidelberg.
Hymes, D. (ed.) 1971: *Pidginization and Creolization of Languages*. Cambridge.
International Congress of Linguists 6th: *Actes du Sixième Congrès International des Linguistes*. Paris.
Keim-Zingelmann, I. 1981: *Das Deutsch türkischer Gastarbeiter*. University of Mannheim. Dissertation.

Kjær, I. and M. Baumann-Larsen 1974: De messy ting. In P. Anderson (ed.), *Festskrift til Kristian Hald*, pp. 421–30. Copenhagen.

Klein, W. and N. Dittmar, 1979: *Developing Grammars*. Berlin/Heidelberg/New York.

Labov, W. 1969: The Logic of Non-Standard English. In J. Alatis (ed.), *Georgetown Monograph Series on Languages and Linguistics*. 22: 1–43. Washington D.C.

1970: The Study of Language in its Social Context. *Studium Generale* 23: 30–87.

Lindmark, S. 1971: *Swedish America. Studies in Ethnicity with Emphasis on Illinois and Minnesota*. Uppsala.

Malm, G. N. 1919: *Härute, Verklighetsbild ur svensk-amerikanskt hvardagslif i fyra akter*. Lindsborg, Kansas.

Meillet, A. 1958 (1921): *Linguistique historique et linguistique générale*. Paris.

Meisel, J. (ed.) 1977: *Langues en Contact. Pidgins–Creoles. Languages in Contact*. Tübingen.

Mjöberg, J. 1960: Nybyggarnas språk. *Svenska Dagbladet*, 27 April, 1960.

Moberg, V. 1948: Den försvunna släkten. *Svenska Dagbladet*. 2 February, 1948.

1952: *Invandrarna*. Stockholm.

1960a: Utvandrarnas språk. *Svenska Dagbladet*. 22 May, 1960.

1960b: Utvandrarna vittnar om sitt språk. *Svenska Dagbladet*, 23 December, 1960.

1968a (1956): *Nybyggarna*. Stockholm.

1968b (1959): *Sista brevet till Sverige*. Stockholm.

1968c (1950): *Den okända släkten*. Stockholm.

1968d: *Berättelser ur min levnad*. Stockholm.

(ms.) Utvandrarnas språk. Unpublished type-written manuscript donated to 'The House of Emigrants in Växjö' (7 pp.).

Nelde, Peter (ed.) 1980: *Sprachkontakt und Sprachkonflikt*. Wiesbaden.

Neustupný, J. V. 1975: Review of A. S. Dil (ed.) 1972 Essays by Einar Haugen. *Language* 51: 236–42.

Orlović-Schwarzwald, M. 1978: *Zum Gastarbeiterdeutsch jugoslavischer Arbeiter im Rhein-Main Gebiet*. Mainzer Studien zur Sprach- und Volksforschung 2. Wiesbaden.

Peterson, Andrew, 1898: *The Andrew Peterson Diaries* 1854–1898. From the Originals in the Possession of the Minnesota Historical Society. St Paul, Minnesota. Collation of the originals 7 Volumes. Manuscript Dept., November 1960.

Pisani, V. 1949: Reply to Question IV at the 6th International Congress of Linguists in Paris. *Actes du Sixième Congrès International des Linguistes*, p. 304. Paris.

Rietz, J. E. 1962 (1862–1867): *Svenskt dialektlexikon*. (Photolithographic Reproduction of the 1862–1867 Edition.) Lund.

Rosenquist, C. M. 1931: Linguistic Changes in the Acculturation of the Swedes of Texas. *Sociology and Social Research*. 1931–2, pp. 221–31.

Rosetti, A. 1945: Langue mixte et mélange des langues. *Acta Linguistica* 5 (1945–9): 73–9.

Rubin, J. 1973: Language Planning: Discussion of Some Current Issues. In J. Rubin and R. Shuy (eds.), *Language Planning: Current Issues and Research*. 1–10. Washington D.C.

Sandfeld, K. 1930: *Linguistique balkanique. Problèmes et resultats*. Paris.

1938: Problèmes d'interfèrences linguistiques. *Actes du Quatrième Congrès International de linguistes*. Copenhagen 1936. 59–61.

Sapir, E. 1949: *Language*. New York.

Schuchardt, H. 1928: *Hugo Schuchardt-Brevier*, ed. L. Spitzer. Halle.

Schumann, J. 1978: *The Pidginization Process*. Rowley, Mass.

Seifert, L. W. 1947: The Problem of Speech Mixture in the German Spoken in Northwestern Dane County, Wisconsin. *Transactions of the Wisconsin Academy of Sciences, Arts and Letters*. 1947–1949, pp. 127–39.

Ureland, P. S. 1970: Preliminary Report on Texas–Swedish Research 1968–1969. In H. Benediktsson (ed.), *The Nordic Languages and Modern Linguistics*, pp. 540–50. Reykjavík.

1971: Report on Texas–Swedish Research. *Svenska Landsmål och Svenskt Folkliv*, pp. 27–74.

1972: Observations on Texas–Swedish Phonology. *Studia Linguistica* 25 (11): 69–110.

1974: Verkliga eller diktade amerikanismer i Vilhelm Mobergs amerikaromaner. In *Svenska, Hyllningsskrift för Sigurd Fries*. 22 April, 1974. 85–97. Umeå.

1975: The Swedish Language in America. Review of Hasselmo 1974 *Amerikasvenska*. In *Svenska Landsmål och Svenskt Folkliv*, pp. 83–105.

(ed.) 1978: *Sprachkontakte im Nordseegebiet*. Tübingen.

(ed.) 1979: *Standardsprache und Dialekte in mehrsprachigen Gebieten Europas*. Tübingen.

(ed.) 1981: *Kulturelle und sprachliche Minderheiten in Europa*. Tübingen.

Weinreich, W. 1967 (1953): *Languages in Contact*. 5th edn. The Hague.

Weinstock, J. (ed.) 1978: *The Nordic Languages and Modern Linguistics*, Vol. 3. Austin, Texas.

Zetterstrand, E. A. 1904: Engelskans inflytande på det svenska språket i Amerika. In *Ungdomsvännen*. Rock Island, Illinois.

Topic index

Abbreviations

American	Am		High German	HG
American English	AE		Italian	It
American Swedish	AS		Jutlandish	Jutl
Danish	Da		Lappish	Lap
Dutch	Du		Latin	Lat
East	E		Low German	LG
English	Eng		North	N
Faroese	Fa		Norwegian	Nw
Finnish	Fi		Russenorsk	RN
Finno-Ugric	Fi-Ug		Russian	Russ
French	Fr		Scandinavian	Sc
Frisian	Fris		Slavic	Sl
German	Ger		South	S
Germanic	Gmc		Swedish	Sw
Gothic	Go		West	W
Greek	Gk			

-*a* suffix: adjective and adverb marker in RN, 35; general noun marker in RN, 33–4, 53; in RN pronouns, 35; in RN word formation, 37

acceptability test (Hasselmo), 296, 297, 302, 310, 311, 320

accusative construction: in possessive perfect in Russian, 122

active periphrastic perfect: with 'have' in German, French and Italian, 115; in N Russ dialects, 113

adaptation of the lexicon: in language death, 196

adaptivity theory: as explanation of similarities between RN and other pidgins, 29

adjective: in RN noun phrase, 43, 44

adoption: of AE adverbs in AS, 298; of AE nouns in AS lexicon, 305, 306

AE pronunciation, 293, 294

affixation process (Lappish): and -*a* noun marker in RN, 34

agent instrumental: in Russ perfect, 119

Aktionsart: loss of distinction stative/non-stative, in AS, 313

Alans (Blond Alans), 105

Alfred, King of England, 91

Al-madjūs (Northmen), 151

Americanisms: in AS speech, 289, 297, 305, 319; authentic, 282, 284, 286, 290, 304, 316, 317, 319; Moberg's, *see* reconstructions

analogical levelling: in Scottish Gaelic morphology, 218

analytic perfect: Romance type of, in Macedonian, 118

Andrew Peterson's Diary, 287, 288, 289, 306, 307, 316, 317, 318. 319

Anglo Saxon Chronicle, 10

Anna, Yaroslav the Wise's daughter, 100

Annales Bertiniani, 100, 103, 135, 144, 145, 146, 148, 149, 151, 156

Anti-Normanists, 97, 100, 102, 105, 108, 127, 136–7

approaches to analysing AS, 315, 318

archaeological excavations: in Gnezdovo, 102; in Smolensk, 102

article: in RN noun phrase, 44

AS diaries, 288, 319

AS letters, 288

AS literature, 288, 319

AS pronunciation, 293, 294

AS sources, 288–90, 319

AS speech, 286–319 *passim*

transfer/transference, 3, 12; of AE adverbial phrase to AS, 315; of AE 'how to' construction to AS, 309; of Fr nasal vowels in the Gmc languages, 11, 231–56 *passim*; of function words and syntactic patterns from AE to AS, 285

transference structures: in bilingual speech, 3

translation process: in a bilingual Eng–Sw child, 320–1

Treaty of Novgorod, 112

Treaty of Smolensk, 112

'triggering effect' in AS: by AE article, 304; by AE auxiliary, 296; by AE quantifier, 302

u+genetive construction (N Russ), 119, 120, 121, 125, 126; used to express the agent, 120; used to express the possessive relationship, 118, 121

-*um* suffix (RN), *see* -*om* suffix

unity of the glottogonic process (Marr's hypothesis), 127

Vandals, 105

Varangian Calling-in Legend, 98, 100, 104, 107, 135, 153

Varangian Guard, *see* Imperial Guard of Byzantium

Varangian Rus', 108

Varangians, 1, 8, 10, 13, 75, 100, 101, 102, 111

variable competence: in AS, 295

Varðin (Fa periodical), 186

verb phrase: order of items in RN, 43

verb-second-constraint: in Gmc languages, 309; in Nw, 41; violation of Sw, in AS, 300, 309–10

verbal participles: use of, as main predicates in N Russ dialects, 117

Vikings, 4, 8, 10, 67, 75, 144, 151, 152, 154

violation: of Sw phraseology in AS, 315–16; of Sw verb complement structure in AS, 309

Vita Constantini, 105

Vladimir the Holy, 98, 102

vocabulary deficiencies: in Ger–Da bilingualism, 221

Vogul people, 88

Votyak people, 88

vowel lowering in Da, 245

Wiedingharde–Frisian dialect: linguistic descriptions of, 192–3

word formation suffix /-era/ (Sw): replaced in AS, 293, 307

Yaroslav the Wise, 100, 111

Zyryan people, 88

Index of personal names

Index of languages

(Including whole families and groups)

Albanian, 113, 115
Anglo-Norman, 242
American English, 12, 281–321; Middle West American-English dialects, 291
American Norwegian, 289, 298, 299, 307
American Swedish, 12, 281–321
Arabic, 13, 100, 106, 107, 134, 139, 149, 151, 152, 156, 157, 166; Classical, 134, 138
Archangel dialect, 48

Balkan–Romance, 118
Baltic dialects, 13
Baltic–Finnic languages, 113
Baltic–Finnish languages, 137, 147, 148
Basque, 13
Breton, 13
Bulgarian, 111, 113, 114
Byzantine, 111, 112, 136, 139, 146
Byzantine–Greek, 111

Celtic, 13; Insular, 13; Island, 10
Czech, 156

Danish, 2, 10, 11, 12, 157, 161, 177–88, 192, 211, 221–7, 231–79; Low, 217; Standard, 11, 191, 199, 206, 207, 221, 223, 224, 226
Dutch, 7, 8, 12, 32, 47, 115, 231–79, 309; Middle, 244

East Yakut, 128
English, 1, 8, 12, 13, 32, 37, 47, 115, 179, 231–79, 285, 304, 309, 310, 316, 319; Old, 84, 116, 122, 140
Estonian, 8, 9, 67, 74, 86, 87, 88, 134, 137, 147, 148, 161, 219

Faroese, 10, 13, 177–88; dialects, 171, 173; language, 177–88
Finnish, 4, 8, 9, 13, 47, 67, 73, 74, 78, 82, 83, 84, 86, 87, 88, 91, 92, 93, 118, 128, 134, 136, 137, 138, 142, 143, 145, 147, 148, 149, 158, 161, 166, 219; dialects, 13, 71, 83, 84, 85
Finnish, East, 142

Finno–Ugric, 114, 118; languages, 128, 134, 138, 147, 148
French, 1, 8, 13, 36, 47, 115, 179, 213–79, 309
Frisian, 204; East, 217; North, 11, 191, 192, 199–206, 208–10, 211, 213–16, 217, 221–7; dialects, 193
Gaelic, 13; Scottish, 11, 196, 218
German, 1, 11, 12, 115, 122, 124, 139, 179, 221–7, 231–79, 309; in America, 307; Low, 7, 8, 11, 35, 47, 191, 192, 199–206, 208, 209, 211, 213–16, 217, 218, 221–7; Middle High, 139, 157; Middle Low, 1, 7; New High (Standard), 1, 11, 125, 191, 192, 194, 199, 203, 204, 205, 206, 211, 213, 214, 215, 216, 217, 218, 221, 222, 223; Old High, 122, 134, 136, 157; Swiss, 241
Germanic, 2, 9, 13, 114, 115, 116, 117, 121, 122, 127, 147, 158, 221, 309; East, 143; North, 4, 9, 84, 88, 93, 94, 111–30, 137, 140, 148; North Germanic dialects, 3; West, 124; West Germanic languages, 9, 12
Gothic, 105, 106, 122, 134, 148, 156, 157, 158, 161, 167
Gøtudanskt, 180, 184, 186
Greek, 89, 100, 104, 111, 112, 124, 125, 134, 139, 146, 148, 149, 156, 157, 161, 166; Middle, 8, 134, 139, 141, 156, 157, 167; Modern, 115

Hungarian, 114, 139

Icelandic, 2, 90, 114, 134, 161; Old, 84, 86, 89, 101, 107, 134, 158, 168, 289
Indian, Old, 105
Indo–European, 117, 283, 284, 317; Proto-, 156
Ingrian, 195
Iranian, 105
Irish, 13
Italian, 13, 115

Jutlandish, *see* South Jutlandish

Karaim, 195

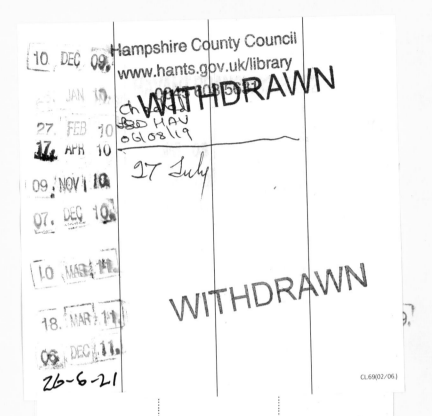